Contents

Introduction

Searchlights is as much about God's search for us as our search for God. God seeks to meet us through his creation, through each other, through our experiences, as well as through Scripture and tradition. *Searchlights* seeks to share in the exciting discovery that God actually looks for us and wants contact with us. God, like the shepherd in the parable, seeks after that which is lost until he finds it (Luke 15:3-7). It is wonderful to discover that if we turn towards God – what the Bible calls repentance – we find he runs almost with an indecent haste to meet us in love and forgiveness (see Luke 15:11-32). In using *Searchlights* we must let this seeking God find us and give himself to us.

Searchlights is also about our probing the darkness and uncertainty of our lives to discover the light and the sureness of God. We are to seek God through the regular reading of the Scriptures, through worship in church, through meeting together and through our day-to-day experiences of life. We may be mature in years and yet a child in our faith. Sometimes a new awareness will come as fresh to us as it would to an infant. Sometimes the lesson for the children may speak stronger than thoughts set out for the adults. If so, let us use that and let it speak to us. The light we search for is the Light of God.

Each Sunday is based on Common Worship and the readings set for the day. Year A will mainly use St Matthew's Gospel, Year B will use St Mark, and Year C will use St Luke. St John's Gospel is used throughout the three years to enrich the season or the passages being used. I have focused mainly on the Gospel readings, trying to draw out various aspects to meet the needs of different stages of life. My overall aim is to show that God seeks each of us and desires to speak to us and through us. The difficult task for all who lead worship is to keep a freshness and a liveliness that can be so easily lost; along with this is a need for the Gospel to relate to our present situation. Remember, God is never boring – by his very nature God cannot be boring; we should not present or preach dullness in his name! Though my overall aim is to come before God and to bring others into the awareness of his presence and love, I have tried to keep these other aims within my sights.

Different age groups need a different approach and things that relate to their experience and ability. Yet I have, as far as possible, kept all groups within the setting of the lectionary readings and season. There are separate lessons for children and young people of each age group to help them grow in the faith. The age-related teaching and worship aim to bring the three groups gradually into the fuller worship of the whole church. On major festivals it is good that the whole church worships together and shares with each other. The aim is not just to give children or adults facts about what we believe but rather to introduce them to the living and loving Lord.

Let all the material be seen as flexible. If you are inspired by a children's lesson or the thought for the week, use that. Let the heart be touched by God; use all your senses in proclaiming his presence and his power.

Draw near to God, and he will draw near to you.
James 4:8

David Adam

How to use this book

What you are to use on the Sunday should be prayed over and pondered from the Monday to the Saturday. Use the set readings for your Bible study and meditation time throughout the week leading to the Sunday. All who are called to teach, preach or lead study groups need to know that their aim is to introduce people to the God whom they know and not to provide a Sunday lecture or lesson. We need to take time to discern what God wants us to say and how we are to do it. Pray, prepare, ponder the words before you seek to present them to others.

Each week is set out as follows:

Aim

It is important to make sure that you focus on what is to be taught. Above all, be sure that your focus is on the Presence and love. You may like to print the aim of the week in any handout or magazine that your church has. If you carry the aim around with you during the week, it often draws other events into focus which you can then relate to others.

Preparation

This is over and above your personal preparation and relates to what the aim is seeking to convey. It also involves seeing that you have the necessary material before the Sunday arrives.

Opening activity

This is an opportunity to show that worship is not just within formal settings and services. It also seeks to attract attention to the issues of the week. The more people who are involved in the activities, the better. Sometimes, if the whole church cannot do the activity, it can be transferred to one of the groups of young people.

Opening prayer

Though this is to focus the mind on the issues of the Sunday, it obviously also helps us to turn our hearts and minds to the ever-present God.

Opening song

This ought to relate to the theme of the day. Sometimes it is good for it to be sung by an individual and for the congregation to sit quietly. If it is a new song, let the musicians play it over two or three times before worship begins.

Readings

It is good to have these printed in the monthly magazine or pew leaflet saying what is to come next week. On the day, if you have a handout, try and include the readings in full. It is important that all who read are audible; if necessary, rehearse the readers. Encourage everyone to read the Scriptures and think about them at home and before coming to church, as this enriches the whole church. Where possible, it is good to use more than one voice for the readings and to include a dramatic presentation. Let there be silences after each reading.

I have used the New Revised Standard Version of the Bible.

As far as the children are concerned, separate and illustrated Bible stories, such as those published by Lion, are a good starting point. Once children can read, the International Children's Bible (New Century Version) is suitable for young readers. There is a helpful dictionary, pictures and maps to go with this version. New Century also produce The Youth Bible for the older ones.

Thought for the day

This is meant to touch the heart and the will as well as the mind. If you are using the thought for the day, do spend a good deal of time with it the week before. This can also be used as preparation for those who are teaching the young people. The thought is meant to lead to some sort of action or reaction.

Question time

The questions are useful for a study group or those who are seeking to teach and preach. Beware of over-analysis and much talk. Make sure you speak to God more than you talk about him.

Illustration

The illustration is meant to go with the thought for the day but can often be used in one of the groups. Find illustrations from your locality that relate to what is going on and which throw a light on the Scripture passages or are enlightened by these passages. Remember, visual aids often speak more directly than words, as does your own way of life.

Intercessions

It is good to start by telling the congregation the response for the prayers and then keep a short silence before the prayers begin. After each section keep a short silence. I have started the intercessions with an act of praise or thanksgiving to God rather than plunging straight in. It helps to give people time to focus their thoughts and their attention on the ever-present God. Sometimes a piece of music playing gently in the background during the intercessions or someone playing a single instrument can create the right feeling. A variety of voices, people, and places around the church for the intercessions are good. Again, make sure they are audible.

Memory verse

For many people learning verses is out of fashion. I find that learning by heart (not just the mind) helps us to store up a treasure we can use in times of dryness or doubt. The verse is used to strengthen our faith and often it is an affirmation of what we believe.

Suggested music

Do not be afraid to use recorded music. Have a variety of instruments and allow children to take part in simple playing. The organ is not always the ideal instrument for setting the scene or leading the people. Remember music is important to people and often helps to set the atmosphere and get into the right frame of mind. Music can be used to set a feeling of calm and to give people a space to express themselves. Involve as many people in the musical presentation as is possible or practical. Remember, young children love making and playing instruments.

The main sources of music I have used are:

Hymns Old and New: One Church, One Faith, One Lord (Kevin Mayhew, 2004)

New Hymns and Worship Songs (Kevin Mayhew, 2000)

The Children's Hymn Book (Kevin Mayhew, 1997)

Kidsource (Kevin Mayhew, 2002)

Celtic Hymn Book (Kevin Mayhew, 2005)

Candles, Lamps and Torches each have their own aims, teaching, activities and songs. The names for these groups imply the receiving of light and the giving out and handing on of light.

CANDLES – 3-5 year olds

This group especially needs to be made to feel at home in church, to be welcomed and accepted. There is need for much play and song and a lot of adult attention. It is good to involve young parents with this group as helpers; they often learn as much as the children. It is important that the feeling given to the children is that they are loved and cared for by God who is ever with them. Parents should be encouraged to see what their child is doing and to pray with them each week.

LAMPS – 6-10 year olds

This is an age range of greatly varying abilities, so it may be necessary to split the group into two and use the teaching and activities according to their ability. This age group is very ready to adventure and stretch themselves. Let what they do help to extend their awareness and vision of each other, of what is around them and of their God. Some at least will enjoy reading out aloud and many will like a little drama; seek to use this potential as much as possible.

TORCHES – 11 plus

This is the group that the church finds hardest to keep. There is a feeling they have heard it all and know it all! Help them to discover that church can be fun and yet at the same time bring before them the depths of life and faith that are to be discovered, adventured and enjoyed. These young people are journeying towards adult life and cannot be treated just as children. Respect their growing pains and their problems: if possible, allow any of them to talk freely to you. It is important to have more than one adult present in our dealings with these young people. An additional helper is always useful. Encourage this group to become part of the church congregation as often as possible. It is best if they have specific tasks that are theirs to do within the main body of the church. Readers, intercessors, musicians and singers, future teachers and priests can come from this group. Remember you are dealing with the Church of today and tomorrow in these young people. Strengthen their faith and support them in their searching.

ADVENT
First Sunday of Advent

Aim

To encourage each other to be aware of Christ's coming to us today.

Preparation

Prepare an Advent wreath with four candles for the Sundays of Advent and a central candle for Christ to be lit on Christmas day.

Opening activity

Have a lighted taper pass down the church. As it is handed over, the one holding it says, 'Christ comes to you', and the recipient says, 'His light shines upon you'. The last person to receive it lights one Advent candle and says in a loud voice:

Christ comes to us.

All reply: His light shines upon us.

Opening prayer

Lord God, awaken us
to the beauty of the world,
to the wonders of creation.
Awaken us to your love
and to your presence this day.
As you came to patriarchs and adventurers of old,
you come to us;
help us to be aware of your coming.
Amen.

Opening song

Christ is the world's true light

Readings

Isaiah 2:1-5
Psalm 122
Romans 13:11-14
Matthew 24:36-44

Thought for the day

(Produce an alarm clock and let it ring, then switch it off.) 'I'll just doze for a few more minutes.' (Let the alarm ring again.) 'I'll hit the snooze button. That's better. I like a good sleep – then the rush was on: no time to have proper breakfast, no time to tidy up. I bumped into someone because I did not notice her. I knocked over a bin because I did not even see it. Then when I got there the train had just gone. "You're just too late," said the man on the station. Now I'll be late for school – it would not matter so much if I were not the headmaster!'

Jesus warns us about being too sleepy and not noticing what is going on around us. We must also prepare our-selves for the coming of the Son of Man. We are to be prepared not only for Christmas but also for the coming of Christ to us.

Advent celebrates the coming of Jesus. Jesus has come through being born of the Virgin Mary. Jesus is come – and comes to each of us now today. Jesus will come again in glory. Will he find us ready in his coming to us?

Are we awake to the fact – are we aware – that Jesus comes to us? Hear him say:

I searched for you and I love you.
I knocked at your door.
I called in your dreams.
I spoke in your life.
I kept coming to you.
But you were unaware.
You did not come to me.
You did not open your door.
You were too engaged to hear my call.
You were too busy to respond to me.
I came but you had no room for me.
Yet I will keep coming.
I will call to you,
until you have time to find me.

Question time

In all our preparations for Christmas, do we make certain that we are preparing to welcome our Lord into our lives and homes?

How can we make the season of Advent more meaningful for the people of today: how do you celebrate Christ's promised coming?

Illustration

When the devil wanted to ruin the lives of many people he called a meeting of his fallen angels and sought suggestions. 'I will tell them there is no God,' said the first. The devil replied, 'Any sensitive and thinking person knows there is a God and this will not lead them astray.' A second said, 'I will tell them there is no hell.' 'What is the use of that?' asked the evil one. 'Everyone will experience a taste of hell and know that it is a reality.' A third then spoke up and said, 'I will tell them there is no hurry. Put it off until tomorrow – for I know tomorrow never comes.' With this the devil was delighted and this is how most people fail to turn to God.

Pablo Picasso said, 'Never put off today anything that you do not want to leave undone for ever.'

Intercessions

Blessed are you, Lord our God,
for you have created us out of your love
and for your love.
You have given us eyes to see, minds to understand and hearts to love you.

Help us to be aware of your presence
and your coming to us
this day and always.

We ask your blessing
upon all preachers and ministers of the word,
that they may proclaim your presence
and the coming of your kingdom.
We remember before you
all who seek to witness to your abiding love
and your dwelling among us.
We pray for your faithful people
as they prepare to celebrate Christmas
and to rejoice in your love for them.

Silence

Come, Lord God,
make yourself known among us.

We pray for all who watch during the darkness of night
and seek our safety.
We remember the police, coastguards, fire crews,
the ambulance service and all doctors and nurses.
We ask your blessing
upon all who work through the night
to provide us with our daily needs.

Silence

Come, Lord God,
make yourself known among us.

We give you thanks for our homes and our loved ones.
At this time of preparation for Christmas
help us to make sure we have time
for each other and for you.
We remember all who will be lonely and troubled
at this time.

Silence

Come, Lord God,
make yourself known among us.

We give thanks for our health and well-being.
We remember in your presence
all who have suddenly become ill
or been injured in accidents,
and those whose lives have been darkened
by the loss of a loved one.
We ask your blessing
upon all who are homeless or hungry
and all who fear the future.
May they know your presence
and so have courage and hope in their troubles.

Silence

Come, Lord God,
make yourself known among us.

We rejoice that you come to us
and offer us life that is eternal.
We remember in your presence
our loved ones departed and all your saints.
May we all rejoice for ever in your love.

Silence

Merciful Father,
**accept these prayers
for the sake of your Son,
our Saviour Jesus Christ.
Amen.**

Memory verse

Come, let us walk in the light of the Lord!
Isaiah 2:5

Suggested music

Awaken me, Lord
Awake, awake: fling off the night
We are marching in the light of God

CANDLES

Aim

To begin to prepare for Christmas.

Teaching

Today is called Advent Sunday and it tells us that someone is coming soon. Who does the church tell us is coming? Jesus is coming. Who can tell me the day we remember when Jesus is born? Yes, it is Christmas Day. Counting from today, do you know how many Sundays are left before Christmas? There are four including today. Next week, how many will there be? So Christmas will soon be here. Advent time tells us to watch, look, for the coming of Jesus.

While we sleep some people have to stay awake and care for others. Tell me some of the people who watch and work at night. Police, doctors, nurses, rescue workers, ambulance crews and fire crews all have people who work at night. We also have people who make and bring our food to the shops and those who drive trains, fly aeroplanes or sail on the sea. Does anyone have a father or mother who works at night? Many people work at night and have to watch and be ready for action.

Long ago most people did not work at night but a few had to. Shepherds worked at night out on the hill-sides. Why did they work in the dark? They had to be on watch. This meant being very brave because they had to watch in case there were robbers who came to steal the sheep. They had to watch in case there was a wolf or a lion after the sheep. They had to watch in case a sheep got into trouble and needed help. They could not sleep but had to keep awake and watch in the night. Sometimes when they looked at the stars they thought of God and his love.

One night on the hills above the town of Bethlehem shepherds were watching. Suddenly the sky seemed to get brighter and they heard singing. 'Look, look,' shouted one of the shepherds. It made the rest jump with surprise. They thought a wolf might be coming. But when they looked they saw an angel of God in the sky and it made the brave shepherds afraid. At first they wanted to cover their eyes and not look at the angel. The angel said, 'Do not be afraid, I bring you good news.' The angel then told them how Jesus was coming and that he would be born in Bethlehem. After this all the angels sang a wonderful song: 'Glory be to God in the highest and peace on earth.' Then suddenly they were gone. The shepherds were amazed at what they had seen. Because they had been watching in the night, they had seen angels; if they had been sleeping, they would have missed this wonderful sight. The shepherds knew what they had to do: they had to go to Bethlehem and see the baby Jesus.

Activity

This week we will make shepherds. Next week we will make an angel, then Mary and Joseph and the fourth week we will make the baby Jesus and the crib. It is necessary for young children to be prepared in advance for the great events of Christmas.

Prayer

Lord God, we thank you
for all who watch and work
while we are asleep.
As the shepherds came to Jesus,
may we come to him
and give him our love.
Amen.

Song

Christ is coming. Christ is coming.
Do you know, do you know?
Are you ready for him?
Are you ready for him?
Yes, I am. Yes I am.
Are you ready for him?
Are you ready for him?
Yes, I am. Yes I am.

(Tune: 'I hear thunder')

LAMPS

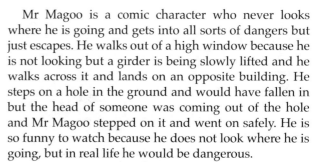

Aim

To show the importance of looking and watching.

Teaching

(Start with the Activity.) Whenever we go anywhere we need to know the direction, so we have a map or a compass. Ask how these help with a journey. If we have been there before, we might not need these. But even when we go somewhere we know we have to watch where we are going and look out for traffic and anything dangerous.

The key is for the car. If you drive, you have to be very watchful. You cannot close your eyes or look away when you are driving. What sort of things do you have to look out for?

The watch is so that we know the time. There are some things that depend on us being on time and if we are too late, we will miss out. See if the children can give examples.

Mr Magoo is a comic character who never looks where he is going and gets into all sorts of dangers but just escapes. He walks out of a high window because he is not looking but a girder is being slowly lifted and he walks across it and lands on an opposite building. He steps on a hole in the ground and would have fallen in but the head of someone was coming out of the hole and Mr Magoo stepped on it and went on safely. He is so funny to watch because he does not look where he is going, but in real life he would be dangerous.

We all need to look where we are going. Some time someone will say to us ,'Look out' or 'Watch where you are going'. We need to use our eyes and be aware of what is around us.

Today is Advent Sunday. Who knows how many Sundays there are in Advent? It is the same every year. Advent is the beginning of the Church year and it is also the four Sundays before Christmas. Let us count them backwards together and then say. 'Christmas': '4, 3, 2, 1, Christmas.' Advent reminds us that it is soon time to celebrate that Jesus came to earth. Who was his mother? Who was her husband? Where was Jesus born (the name of the town and the place in that town)?

Advent means 'coming'. It reminds us that Christmas is coming but it also tells us God comes to us, Jesus comes to us and wants to be our friend. Too often we fail to meet Jesus because we do not look for him; we do not fix a time to be with him in prayer. We need to give more attention to the fact that God comes to us and that he loves us. Here is a special prayer for you to say each day, so that you can invite Jesus into your life and home:

Come to my heart, Lord Jesus,
there is room in my heart for you.

Activity

Tell the children that we are to pretend we are going on a journey but we cannot begin until we find certain things. Tell them of the things you have hidden and ask them to find them: a watch, a map, a compass and a key. Ask them to look for them but not to touch them or to tell anyone else. Let each come to you when they know where the four things are. The last ones can be helped a little. Once all have seen the objects, get four people to bring the different things.

Prayer

Lord God, open our eyes to your presence,
open our ears to your call,
open our hearts to your love,
that we may be aware of you
and your coming to us.
Amen.

Song

Let him find us watching when he comes.
Let him find us watching when he comes.
Let him find us ready,
With a heart that's steady
Let him find us watching when he comes.

(Tune: 'She'll be coming round the mountain')

TORCHES

Aim

To show how we are called to be watchful and attentive.

Teaching

Happy New Year! Well, it is the Church New Year because the Church year begins with Advent. How many Sundays are there in Advent? This is a count-down time to Christmas and it is about being ready and prepared. Are you ready for Christmas, have you got your presents and cards sorted out? Have you made arrangements for a guest coming to stay, or for going out to parties? Christmas is a great time to celebrate, and as Christians we must remember its main purpose is to celebrate the coming of Jesus.

The four Advent Sundays are to help us prepare not only for the coming of Jesus in the past at Bethlehem but his coming to us and to our lives. The message of this first week is 'watch'. This is the commonest command of the New Testament: we are asked to be watchful, attentive.

St Paul says, 'Now is the moment for you to awake out of sleep' (Romans 13:11). We are not to go around with our eyes closed or in a doze. We are to be awake and alert.

Jesus says, 'Keep awake, therefore, for you do not know on what day your Lord is coming' (Matthew 24:42). Commenting on this verse St Augustine of Hippo said, 'The last day is secret, so that every day may be watched.' It is easy to be distracted from the fact that Jesus comes to us and seeks to be our friend. Some of St Paul's last words to the people of Ephesus were 'Keep watch'(Acts 20:28).

In the book of Revelation the church at Sardis is asked to 'Wake up' (3:1-6). The city of Sardis was built on a steep rock and it was almost impossible to capture. It stood like a watchtower over the valley. But the people who lived there had become careless and were not watchful. Even when the Persian army attacked their town they were not watchful. For 14 days Cyrus, the king of the Persians, besieged the city and he offered a reward to anyone who could find a way in. One of his soldiers watching saw a soldier from Sardis drop his helmet over the battlements and then clamber down a secret path to retrieve it. Cyrus was informed and that night a group of crack troops climbed up and gained entry into the city. When they got over the battlements they found it unguarded and so it fell to the Persians because no one was watchful.

Today's Gospel asks us to be watchful for we do not know when our Lord comes. We need to be ready for his coming to us each day. It is easy to put off and think the Lord delays, yet he comes to us each day seeking our friendship and our attention. We need to seek to be aware of his coming through prayer and giving our attention to him.

(If there is time, you could explore the theme of watchfulness. See Matthew 26:41; Mark 13:35-37; 1 Corinthians 16:13; 1 Thessalonians 5:6; 1 Peter 5:8.)

Activity

There is a wordsearch about vision on the worksheet.

Prayer

Lord, awaken me to your love.
Make me aware that you come to me
today and every day.
Help me to rejoice in your coming
and in your abiding presence.
Amen.

Song

Awaken me, Lord

Second Sunday of Advent

Aim
To prepare for the coming of the Lord.

Preparation
Have an Advent wreath with four candles for the Sundays of Advent and a central candle for Christ to be lit on Christmas Day.

Opening activity
Have a lighted taper passed down the church. As it is handed over, the one holding it says, 'The Lord is my light', and the recipient says, 'He is my salvation'.

The last person to receive it lights two Advent candles and says in a loud voice:

The Lord is our light.

All reply: He is our salvation.

Opening prayer
Blessed are you, Lord our God,
for you send your messengers and prophets
to tell of your coming.
As John the Baptist was a burning and shining light
in the darkness,
help us to show your presence in our daily life.
Amen.

Opening song
Hark! a herald voice is calling

Readings
Isaiah 11:1-10
Psalm 72:1-7, 18, 19
Romans 15:4-13
Matthew 3:1-12

Thought for the day
For a long time there had been no one to whom the Jews would have given the name of 'prophet'. They said that prophecy had been dead for four hundred years. Then suddenly out of the desert of Judea came John. He was dressed in clothing of camel hair and had a leather belt about his waist. This was how Elijah was described in 2 Kings 1:8. As the Jews had a belief that Elijah would return before the Messiah came (Malachi 4:5), John is to be seen as the herald of the Christ. Matthew links John with the prophecy from Isaiah 40:3 and describes him as 'the voice of one crying out in the wilderness, "Prepare the way of the Lord, make his path straight"' (Matthew 3:3). Like the man who went ahead of the visiting king to make sure the road was good and the people were prepared, John came to get people ready for the coming of Jesus.

John sought to bring people not to himself but to God and to make them aware that Christ was coming. John told the people he was not even worthy to carry the sandals of the One who was to come. (Such a task was usually the work of a slave.) John was sure that the Christ was much greater than him.

John challenges us. In this time of busyness and activity when you are preparing for Christmas, are you truly preparing to let the Christ into your life? Are you ready for his coming? John calls the people to 'Repent for the kingdom of heaven has come near' (Matthew 3:2). This is the same as the message we get from Jesus in Mark 1:15. We would do well to hear the call. The word 'repent' means 'turn around': you are looking the wrong way, you are going the wrong way. 'Turn around': you are going in the wrong direction; that is not the way to meet the King. Can we relate this call to much of what we are doing at Christmas and how we are living our lives? Are we truly prepared or preparing to welcome the King? Like going the wrong way down a road, the further you go, the longer the journey back. Have you got your directions right? Today turn to God, turn to Christ. As a preparation for Christmas, turn each day in prayer to the One who comes, and comes to you.

Question time
How can we prepare in a better way to celebrate the coming of Christ?

In the baptism service, the question is asked of the God-parents: 'Do you turn to Christ?' How can you put the reply, 'I turn to Christ', into a daily action?

Illustration
Making a journey was not easy in biblical times. An eastern proverb states, 'There are three states of misery: illness, fasting and travel.' Before anyone went on a journey they were advised to 'pay all debts, provide for dependants, provide parting gifts, return all articles under trust, take money and a good temper, then bid farewell to all'. Roads were often in poor condition, full of holes and bumps that made travel difficult if not dangerous. Journeying was never done for pleasure. There were few cared-for roads. Josephus tells us that King Solomon laid a causeway of black basalt stone along the roads that led to Jerusalem 'to manifest the grandeur of his riches and government'. All surfaces and built-up roads were originally built for the king and for his use. Before the king was due to visit an area, the inhabitants were visited and warned to be ready. They had to make sure the road didn't have any obstacles to make the king's journey difficult. They also had to be prepared to welcome him. John the Baptist is to be seen as one who tells us of the need to prepare the way for the coming of the King, of the Christ.

Intercessions
Blessed are you, Lord our God,
for you sent the prophets and John the Baptist
to prepare your way.

You have told us of your coming
and you reveal yourself to us in Jesus.
You come to each of us in power and in love.
Blessed are you, Father, Son and Holy Spirit.

Father, we give thanks
for all who tell of your love
and who proclaim your coming.
We ask your blessing upon all priests and preachers,
upon all who teach the Scriptures
and tell of your coming.
Bless all who are baptised into your presence and power.
Lord, we ask forgiveness
when your Church misuses
the resources you have given it
and when we fail to live up to your teaching and love.

Silence

Lord, come to us:
forgive us and guide us.

We remember in your presence
the troubles and sorrows of our world.
We pray for all who are caught up in war or violence,
all who suffer from the greed and insensitivity of others.
May we not misuse or squander the earth's resources
but use them with care and for the benefit of all.
We ask your blessing upon all leaders and politicians.

Silence

Lord, come to us:
forgive us and guide us.

We ask your blessing
upon all who do not look forward to Christmas.
We remember all who will be homeless or lonely
and all who are poor or deeply in debt.
We pray that our homes
may be places of love and peace
where you are welcome.
May we know that in the coming of others to us
you also come and seek our love.

Silence

Lord, come to us:
forgive us and guide us.

We remember all who are ill and suffering at this time,
all who are distressed
and those who are overburdened.
May they know your peace and your presence.
May all who walk in darkness
come to know your light and your love.
We pray for all who are in hospital
or in care at this time.

Silence

Lord, come to us:
forgive us and guide us.

We remember all our loved ones departed,
and we pray for any who have died recently.
May they rejoice in the fullness of life
and be with you in glory.

Silence

Merciful Father,
accept these prayers
for the sake of your Son,
our Saviour Jesus Christ.
Amen.

Memory verse

Repent, for the kingdom of heaven has come near.
Matthew 3:2

Suggested music

On Jordan's bank the Baptist's cry
Wait for the Lord
Hark, the glad sound

CANDLES

Aim

To continue to prepare for Christmas.

Teaching

Who can remember where the shepherds were last week? They heard a message from God and special singing. Who brought the message and sang for the shepherds to hear?

Today we will hear about one special angel and about Mary before Jesus was born. Let us say her name together: 'Mary'.

Mary was a young woman who loved God and spoke to him often in her prayers. She tried to do what God wanted her to do. At home she looked after the house with her mother, she helped to cook and to clean. She would carry water from the well and gather sticks for the fire. She was often on her own and it was quiet.

Mary often thought of Joseph because she was going to marry him and they would have a house of their own. Then she would cook for him and look after him. Thinking of this made Mary happy.

Mary lived at a place called Nazareth. Let us say it together: 'Nazareth'. One day Mary had a very special visitor sent to her from God. The visitor came with a special message. Because it was a messenger from God, we know this visitor was an angel. Let us say together: 'Angel'. We know the angel's name for the angel was called Gabriel. Let us say together: 'the angel Gabriel'.

The angel Gabriel said to Mary, 'Greetings, favoured one! The Lord is with you.' Mary was puzzled; she did not understand the angel Gabriel. Why was she favoured, chosen by God? She thought it was wonderful to know that God was with her. (God is with us too.) But Mary was a little afraid of the angel Gabriel and of his message. She wanted to hide her eyes and not look at him. But the angel Gabriel was a kind angel and said, 'Do not be afraid, Mary, God loves you and is very pleased with you. God has something very special he wants you to do. God wants you to have a baby, a special baby, and to call him Jesus. Let us all say quietly: 'Jesus'.

Mary did not really understand how this would happen but the angel Gabriel told her that God could make it happen if she said she would do what God wants. If she said 'Yes' then she would become the mother of Jesus.

Mary was still not sure she understood it all but she wanted to do what God wanted her to do, so she said 'Yes'. The angel Gabriel was very happy and would be able to tell God he had delivered his message and Mary had said 'Yes'.

Activity

We will make an angel this week and then put the angel with the shepherds. Next week we will make Mary and Joseph.

How many candles are there to colour in?

Play 'Simon says'. Make sure they only do what 'Simon says' and nothing else. Tell them this is to help them to listen carefully and to do what they are asked.

Prayer

God, we thank you for the angel Gabriel
and the message brought to Mary.
We would like to work for you
and do what you want us to do.
We are happy that you love us.
Amen.

Song

Father God, I know you love me so

LAMPS

Aim

To learn about John the Baptist and the need to prepare.

Teaching

Who knows the motto of the Scouts? 'Be prepared'. Throughout our lives we need to prepare for various things. Every day meals need to be prepared – and there's special preparation for parties. We have to prepare for school and for any sport we will take part in. If we are going on a journey, we need to prepare – the car will need petrol, we may need tickets and passports, and we also need to know where we are going. What other preparations can you think of?

In the times of Jesus and John the Baptist, if a king was going on a journey, one of his main preparations was to send someone down the road before him. Because the roads were often just dirt tracks, this man had to make sure there were no dangerous holes in the road or big bumps. He had to ensure that the road was as level as possible for the coming of the king. Then he had to visit the places where the king was going and warn the people in advance. Then they could not say they did not know he was coming, and at the same time they could prepare for the coming of the king.

Before Jesus began his work John the Baptist tried to prepare the people for the coming of Jesus. He told them they were going in the wrong direction to meet the king and they should turn around. The word he used was 'repent'. That meant they should be sorry for the wrong

things they were doing and seek to do what is right. John told them to be ready because Jesus was coming soon and Jesus was more powerful than John. A lot of people came to John and were baptised by him in the river Jordan. They were plunged into the river to show that their sins were washed away. He wanted people to be ready, to be prepared, for the coming of Jesus.

Which Sunday in Advent is this? It is the second Sunday. How many more Sundays are there until Christmas? Christmas is when we celebrate the coming of Jesus into the world and his coming into our lives. When Jesus came people were not ready for him; there was no room. So, where was he born?

You might have got all your cards written out, you may have bought your presents – who has? – but are you ready also to let Jesus into your life and your home? Are you prepared for Jesus coming and for him wanting to be friends with you? John the Baptist said, 'Prepare the way of the Lord.' Will we remember those words and get ready for Jesus?

Activity

Play 'In the river, on the bank'. Let the children stand in a circle and when you say, 'In the river', they have to jump forward. You can repeat it. If you say, 'On the bank', they have to jump backwards. If you say, 'On the river' or 'In the bank', they are not to move at all. Anyone who does the wrong thing is out.

Prayer

Jesus, we are getting ready
to celebrate your birthday.
Let us make sure we make room for you that day.
As you come to us in love,
may we come to you
and give you our love.
Amen.

Song

Jesus, come among us
with your glorious light.
Jesus, come among us;
help us do what's right.

Jesus, come among us,
come now and every day.
Jesus, come among us;
hear us as we pray.

(Tune: Caswall, 'Glory be to Jesus')

TORCHES

Aim

To prepare for the coming of Jesus and to understand the need for repentance.

Teaching

Have you ever gone down a wrong road on a journey? The further you go down it, the longer it takes to get back. Sometimes you are on a road that does not let you turn around. Do you know what the sign says? 'No U-turns.' On some roads you then have to travel miles before you are able to turn. Without guidance it is easy to get lost on the journey we make through this world.

John the Baptist lived in the wilderness, a land of burning heat and emptiness. He was like one of the prophets from the old days. He wore the simplest of clothes made from camel hair and had a leather belt around his waist. For those who knew their Scriptures he was like Elijah who was described as a hairy man with a leather belt about his waist (2 Kings 1:8). Malachi (the last book in the Old Testament and written 400 years before the coming of John) promised that Elijah would come again before the Anointed One – the Christ – came (Malachi 4:5). Now John came to prepare the way of the Lord. He came to tell people to get ready, to be prepared. We should ask ourselves if we are ready for the coming of Christ into our lives. It is not much use celebrating Christmas if we do not welcome Christ into our lives and our homes. In the seventeenth century Angelus Silesius wrote:

> Though Christ a thousand times
> in Bethlehem be born,
> if he is not born in you,
> you are still forlorn.

Discuss what this means for us.

John the Baptist called people to repent. This was like saying, 'Turn around, you are going the wrong way. You are going in the wrong direction. You are missing the target because you have set your sights wrongly.' He invited people to confess their sins, their failing to live up to what God asked of them, and to be baptised, immersed in water, as a symbol of their cleansing.

John says clearly, 'Christ is coming. Get ready.'

Activity

Discuss how we can prepare for the coming of Christ through turning to him, giving him our attention and love, through prayer and worship.

Prayer

Lord, inspire us by the life of John the Baptist
that we may live simply
so that others may simply live.
Let us turn to you and your love each day
and seek forgiveness of our sins,
so that we may walk in newness of life.
Amen.

Song

O come, O come, Emmanuel

Third Sunday of Advent

Aim
To rejoice in the Christ who comes.

Preparation
Have an Advent wreath with four candles for the Sundays of Advent and a central candle for Christ to be lit on Christmas Day.

Opening activity
Have a lighted taper passed down the church. As it is handed over, the one holding it says, 'Christ comes to lighten our darkness', and the recipient says, 'Come, Lord, and save us'.

The last person to receive it lights three Advent candles and says in a loud voice:

The Lord sets prisoners free. *(lights candle 1)*
Response: **Come, Lord, and save us.**

The Lord opens the eyes of the blind. *(lights candle 2)*
Response: **Come, Lord, and save us.**

The Lord lifts up those who are bowed down.
(lights candle 3)
Response: **Come, Lord, and save us.**

Opening prayer
Lord God, we rejoice in your coming to us
and in the strength and joy given to us
through the coming of Jesus Christ.
We give you thanks
for all who have revealed your salvation
in the way they have lived
and witnessed to your love.
Amen.

Opening song
We have a Gospel to proclaim

Readings
Isaiah 35:1-10
Psalm 146:5-10 or Canticle: Magnificat
James 5:7-10
Matthew 11:2-11

Thought for the day
The Scriptures never promise and easy life for those who seek to do good. Here is John the Baptist in prison for speaking out against evil. John had dared to speak out against Herod Antipas of Galilee. Herod had dismissed his wife and married his brother's wife, after seducing her. Because John spoke against this he was held prisoner in the fortress of Machaerus up in the mountains near the Dead Sea. John had proclaimed Jesus as the Christ, but there in prison either he or his disciples seem to be having doubts. Perhaps John wanted to point his disciples in the direction of Jesus. John's disciples came to Jesus and asked, 'Are you the one who is to come, or are we to wait for another?'

Jesus does not answer, 'Yes', or explain in words. He does not argue his case but rather asks them to tell what they hear and see. 'Do not tell John what I am saying but what I am doing, what is happening. The blind receive their sight, the lame walk, lepers are cleansed, the deaf hear, the dead are raised, and the poor have the good news brought to them.' Not only are the powers of darkness being defeated but the Scriptures are being fulfilled. (See today's Old Testament Reading, Isaiah 35:1-10.) This is Good News!

Look again at last week's Gospel and the demands of John the Baptist (Mathew 3:1-12). Perhaps the disciples of John were worried about this 'friend of publicans and sinners'. Jesus is not as hard or as judgemental as they would like him to be. This was not a message of destruction for the wicked but one of the love of God. Perhaps John's disciples would have liked a little more severity. Jesus says to the disciples of John, 'Blessed is anyone who takes no offence in me.' We have to accept him as he is and not change him into who we want him to be. In accepting him he will transform our lives as he transformed those of the people he met.

Question time
How do we meet any doubts we have? Do we seek to let Jesus speak for himself?

How can we invite Jesus and his transforming power into our lives?

Illustration
When Bede writes about St Aidan he says, 'The highest recommendation of his teaching to all was that he and his followers lived as they taught. He never sought or cared for any worldly possession, and loved to give away to the poor who chanced to meet him whatever he received from kings or wealthy folk. Whether in town or country, he always travelled on foot unless compelled by necessity to ride; and whoever the people he met on his walks, whether high or low, he stopped and spoke to them. If they were heathen, he urged them to be baptised; and if they were Christians, he strengthened their faith and inspired them by word and deed to live a good life and to be generous to others.'

It was the example of a life lived for God that spoke out louder than the words he spoke and backed up what he preached.

Intercessions
Blessed are you, Lord our God,
who has promised us your salvation
through the prophets,
and that in you we will find healing and peace.
We come to you,
for in our coming we turn away from the darkness
and enter into the light of your presence and your love.

Mighty God and Saviour,
we pray for your Church throughout the world,
that it may witness to you
not only in word but also in deed.
May the Church reflect your love for the world
and show your acceptance and forgiveness
for all peoples.
We remember at this time
all who are persecuted for their faith
and all who are prisoners of conscience.

Silence

Come, Lord,
for our hope is in you.

We remember in your presence
all who are oppressed by tyranny or evil.
We pray for those
who have been driven out of their homes
and who have been separated from loved ones.
We ask your blessing
on all who suffer from poverty or hunger
and all who are caught up in war
or live in fear of terrorism.

Silence

Come, Lord,
for our hope is in you.

We give thanks for those who have taught us the faith
by the example of the way they live.
May we be a good example to others.
Lord, bless our homes and our loved ones
with the light of your presence.
We remember all who are struggling in their relationships
and those whose minds are full of doubt.

Silence

Come, Lord,
for our hope is in you.

Lord, we come to you for renewal and healing,
for strength and for light.
We ask your blessing
upon all who suffer from a disability
or who are ill at this time.
We remember those who are blind, lame or deaf
and those who suffer from leprosy.
We pray for all who have lost loved ones this week
and for those who are caring for the terminally ill.

Silence

Come, Lord,
for our hope is in you.

We give thanks for your renewing powers
and that you give us life and life eternal.
We remember friends and loved ones
who are departed from us.
May they rejoice in fullness of life
and in the glory of your presence.

Silence

Merciful Father,
**accept these prayers
for the sake of your Son,
our Saviour Jesus Christ.
Amen.**

Memory verse

My soul magnifies the Lord, and my Spirit rejoices in
God my Saviour.
Luke 1:46b, 47

Suggested music

O for a thousand tongues to sing
Hark, the glad sound
It is a thing most wonderful

CANDLES

Aim
To continue to build up the Christmas story.

Teaching
Can anyone tell me how many Sundays after today
there are until Christmas? Today we have used up three
of our Advent Sundays and that means there is only
one left.

Who can remember what we made last week? An
angel. Can you tell me who the angel came to? The
angel came to Mary, and what did he tell her? That God
wanted her to have a baby and the baby's name was to
be Jesus.

When Mary told all this to Joseph he could not
understand it. How had an angel spoken to Mary, and
was she sure about this baby? Then one night when
Joseph went to bed he had a dream. In his dream an
angel came to him and had a message for him. The
angel said, 'Joseph, son of David, I want you to look
after and to love Mary and the baby she is going to
have. You are to call the baby Jesus, because he is coming
to save people.' When Joseph woke up he could not forget
the dream. He knew an angel had spoken to him. He
took Mary to be his wife and he loved her. He promised
her he would look after the baby Jesus when he was
born. They lived in a house in a place called Nazareth.
(Let us say the name together: 'Nazareth'.)

After a while Joseph had to go on a long journey. He
had to leave Nazareth and go about 76 miles. There were
no cars or trains in those days so he had to walk or ride
on a donkey or camel. In a car we could go that far in
about two hours, but it would take Joseph a whole week
to get there. He would have to walk all day every day
for nearly a week. He did not mind that but he did
worry about Mary. Mary's baby would be born soon and
it was a long journey for her to make. Because the baby
was soon to be born they would not be able to travel
quickly and Joseph would have to look after Mary.
Mary could walk but often she would have to ride on
their donkey and Joseph would walk along beside her.

What would they need to take for the journey? They
would need food and they would need something to

drink. At night they would camp out in the countryside with other travellers and share a campfire. There were a lot of people travelling to Jerusalem and beyond, like Joseph and Mary going to Bethlehem. It seemed a very long way to Mary. She was glad the donkey could carry all they needed and sometimes it would also carry her. By the end of the week she was very tired and she knew the baby was soon to be born.

Activity

We will make Joseph and Mary this week. How many candles are there to colour in?

If you want a game you could play 'Pin the tail on the donkey'.

You could also cover two children with a brown blanket to make a donkey. You could add donkey ears. Then during the singing let 'Joseph' and 'Mary' lead the donkey around the room.

Prayer

God, we thank you that Joseph loved Mary
and looked after her.
We thank you for our parents
and ask you to look after them always.
Amen.

Song

Play verse 1 (on CD if possible) of 'Little Donkey' and then get the children to sing the first verse.

LAMPS

Aim

To show Jesus as the One who is to come.

Teaching

Who remembers last week's story? It was about John the Baptist. Can you tell me what he said to people and what he did? He wanted people to do what God wanted, to do what was right and not wrong. He told people when they were going the wrong way and asked them to turn around. He also took them to the river and dipped them in the water to show how God made them clean.

This week we hear that John the Baptist is a prisoner in a castle. He had done nothing wrong but he had spoken against King Herod. John said the king had done wrong and wicked things. The king was angry with John for saying this about him and he locked him up in a castle. While John was there he wondered what was happening to Jesus and if Jesus was the special person God had promised. He sent some of his disciples to ask Jesus, 'Are you the One who is to come or do we look for another?' (What do you think he meant by this?)

Jesus sent a message back. He told John's disciples, 'Tell John what I am doing. He will understand that I am doing what is expected from the Promised One. Tell him that the blind receive their sight, the lame walk, lepers are cleansed, the deaf hear, the dead are raised up and the poor have the good news brought to them.'

Not everyone could do the things that Jesus was doing. The wonderful things Jesus did pointed to the fact that he was God's Chosen One: the One who people were waiting for. John would know that these are the things that the Christ would do. Can you tell me any of the other wonderful things that Jesus did?

We do not know what John said when his disciples told him of all that was happening but he must have felt pleased to know that God's work was being done and that Jesus was God's Promised One.

Activity

The worksheet asks the question John asked and then gets the children to act like detectives and look at the evidence.

Prayer

Jesus, help us to know you as our friend
and as our Saviour and our God.
We thank you for all the wonderful things you do.
Help us to know your power and your love.
Amen.

Song

What a wonderful Saviour is Jesus

TORCHES

Aim

To look at what Jesus was doing and to see that it fulfilled what was promised.

Teaching

When John the Baptist saw people doing wrong things he spoke out and told them. He told people when they were going the wrong way and said, 'Turn around.' Can you remember the word John used when he told people to turn around? It was 'repent'. It meant to be sorry for the wrong done and to try and do better.

There are some people who find it hard to say sorry and there are people who will not stop doing wrong things. King Herod had done wrong: he had taken his brother's wife away from him, got rid of his own wife and married his brother's wife. (See if they can work this out.) John the Baptist spoke out against Herod and said Herod had done wrong. For this Herod took John prisoner and locked him up in the castle of Machaerus, high in the mountains near the Dead Sea. It was while he was in prison that John wondered about what Jesus was doing and if Jesus really was the Promised One of God. John managed to send some of his disciples to meet Jesus and to ask, 'Are you the One who is to come or do we look for another?'

Jesus said they should go back and tell John what he was doing – he was doing things that Isaiah said the Promised One would do. Get the group to look at Isaiah 35:1-10 and to read out aloud verses 3-6. Now read the response of Jesus to John in Matthew 11:4-6. Jesus did not say, 'Listen to what I tell you', but rather, 'Look at what I am doing and seek to understand.'

Activity

Get the group to gather evidence that Jesus is the Messiah. Encourage them to look at the miracles and the life of Jesus. It is a good opportunity to revise and to check on their understanding of the Gospel story.

Prayer

Lord God, we thank you
for the bravery and the message
of John the Baptist.
May we see Jesus as our Saviour and our God.
Amen.

Song

Thou didst leave thy throne

Fourth Sunday of Advent

Aim

To show, through the example of Joseph, that God waits upon our obedience to accomplish his work.

Preparation

Have an Advent wreath with four candles for the Sundays of Advent and a central candle for Christ to be lit on Christmas Day.

Opening activity

Have a lighted taper passed down the church. As it is handed over, the one holding it says, 'The light has come into the world', and the recipient says, 'Emmanuel, God is with us'.

The last person to receive it lights four Advent candles and says in a loud voice:

Jesus Christ our Saviour is the Light of the World.
(lights candle 1)
Response: **God is with us. Alleluia.**

In Jesus our Saviour darkness is defeated.
(lights candle 2)
Response: **God is with us. Alleluia.**

Jesus our Saviour comes to us. *(lights candle 3)*
Response: **God is with us. Alleluia.**

Jesus our Saviour is with us always. *(lights candle 4)*
Response: **God is with us. Alleluia.**

Opening prayer

Lord God, we give you thanks for Joseph
and for his courage to do your will.
Help us to bring in your kingdom
by our obedience to you this day and always.
May we show that we dwell in you and you in us.
Amen.

Opening song

O come, o come, Emmanuel

Readings

Isaiah 7:10-16
Psalm 80:1-7, 16-18
Romans 1:1-7
Matthew 1:18-25

Thought for the day

There are times when it is as if the whole world waits on the reaction of one person. Today's Gospel is such a moment. Mary is betrothed to Joseph. They may have been promised to each other since Mary was a child. Betrothal is usually for a year and it is when the couple agree to the promises that were made for them. At this stage they are known as man and wife and the relationship is binding. It can now only be terminated by divorce.

Mary has told Joseph she is pregnant and he knows it is not his child. How could he begin to understand when Mary told him of her encounter with the angel?

Joseph's reaction is a natural one. He cares for Mary; he does not want her to face public disgrace, but he feels he must dismiss her. These thoughts obviously disturbed him day and night. But he made up his mind: he knew what he would do. Then he had a dream that changed the course of the world. An angel came and spoke to him: 'Joseph, son of David, do not be afraid to take Mary as your wife, for the child conceived in her is from the Holy Spirit.'

Joseph would never understand this but he could obey God's messenger. Without Joseph's willingness, the whole plan of the birth of Jesus could come to nothing. Often God depends on us for achieving what he wants done in the world. Without our cooperation the kingdom of God cannot come on earth. When we do what God wants us to do, wonderful things happen.

Joseph is told how Mary will bear a son and 'You are to name him Jesus, for he will save his people from their sins.' By naming him, Joseph is accepting Jesus as his own son. By calling him Jesus, which is Greek for the Hebrew name Joshua and means 'Jehovah is Salvation' or 'God is Saviour', Joseph is to acknowledge what is promised through Jesus.

Matthew is keen to show that the coming of Jesus into the world is God's work, and sets out his credentials from Isaiah: 'Look, a virgin shall conceive and bear a son, and they shall name him Emmanuel', which means 'God is with us'.

God *is* with us but this reality cannot be achieved without our obedience and cooperation. It is when we say, 'Your will be done' that the possibility of the kingdom of God takes shape in our lives. When Joseph awoke from sleep he did as he was commanded. Through Joseph, as well as Mary, obedience brought the possibility of Emmanuel, God in our midst.

Question time

Do we realise how God waits upon us and our obedience to his will?

How can we, as part of the Church, show that 'God is with us'?

Illustration

Ivan lived under an oppressive regime. If those in power wanted anything, they took it. If they wanted you to do something, you had to do it or your life was at risk. The state police did not knock on doors; they forced their way into people's homes, and if they wanted anything, they took it. Everyone lived in fear and was oppressed. It was during this time that Ivan learnt the Good News of the Gospel. God did not force himself on people. He waited for Mary and Joseph to agree to his plans. In Jesus he did not oppress people but liberated them. Jesus did not burst into lives but said, 'I stand at the door and knock.' Ivan was amazed that so many ignored this loving, saving God. From the moment Ivan heard of such a God he sought to serve in that service which is 'perfect freedom'.

Intercessions

Blessed are you, Lord our God,
for in your love you wait on us.
You trust us with your plans
and allow us to share
in the bringing in of your kingdom.
Help us at all times to trust in you
and to seek to do your will.
Blessed are you, Father, Son and Holy Spirit.

Lord, ever with us, help your Church
to proclaim your presence and your saving power.
May we seek to do your will
and help to bring in your kingdom.
As we give thanks for Joseph,
we give thanks for all men and women of vision
and all who have dedicated their lives in your service.
We ask your blessing upon all preachers
and ministers of the sacraments.
Guide all who serve you quietly in their daily lives.
We remember especially
all who struggle to serve you
while surrounded by difficult circumstances
and opposition.

Silence

God, come among us:
make your home with us.

God of freedom,
we pray for all who are oppressed.
We ask your blessing upon all who suffer
through tyranny or terrorism.
We remember all whose freedom has been diminished
through war or violence.
We pray for the poor, the hungry and the homeless.

Silence

God, come among us:
make your home with us.

We give thanks for our homes
and for all who love us.
May we show your presence in our daily living.
We pray for homes where there is neglect or lack of love,
where there is cruelty or deep selfishness.
We remember all who live alone
and those who are lonely.

Silence

God, come among us:
make your home with us.

Lord, you are with us even when it is dark.
We ask your blessing upon all who are in pain or in fear.
We pray for those who are ill at home or in hospital
and all who have been injured this week.
We remember those who feel life has little meaning
and those who have lost their way
or who are anxious about their future.

Silence

God, come among us:
make your home with us.

We give thanks that in you life is eternal
and we ask your blessing upon our friends and loved ones
who are departed from us.

Silence

Merciful Father,
**accept these prayers
for the sake of your Son,
our Saviour Jesus Christ.
Amen.**

Memory verse

'Look, the virgin shall conceive and bear a son, and they shall name him Emmanuel,' which means 'God is with us.'
Matthew 1:23

Suggested music

The advent of our King
Jesus, Name above all names
Lord Jesus Christ *(Living Lord)*

CANDLES

Aim

To share in the joy of the birth of Jesus.

Teaching

Play verse 1 (on CD if possible) of 'Little donkey' and then get them to sing the first verse. Play the rest of the song and get them to re-enact Joseph and Mary travelling to Bethlehem. While it is being played remind the children how Joseph and Mary travelled for a whole week. They would not travel on the Sabbath day (like our Sunday). What do you think they would do instead? They would go to church and pray to God.

After travelling all day for many days Mary was very tired and she began to walk more slowly. She wished she could go faster but she knew that she must go slowly because the baby Jesus was soon to be born. Even when sitting on the donkey she asked Joseph to make it walk slowly. Joseph wished they could go faster because it would be dark before they got to Bethlehem but he knew he could not hurry Mary. By the time they got near to Bethlehem the stars were beginning to shine in the sky and there was hardly anyone else travelling. Everyone had got to where they had wanted to be. Because Bethlehem had a lot of people visiting, it was very full. All the inns were full and Joseph and Mary could not find a place to stay. Mary was getting very worried because she knew she needed to lie down for soon Jesus was to be born.

One kind innkeeper looked at Mary and saw she needed somewhere to rest. He had no spare room but he did have a stable behind the inn. If they did not mind sharing with his donkey and hens, they could be quite comfortable among the straw. Because Jesus was soon to be born Mary thought this was better than a crowded inn. Soon they settled down. Mary made sure that Joseph got water to wash the baby when it was born and that he had the things to wrap it up in.

Suddenly there in the stable the baby Jesus came into the world. Mary hugged him, fed him and loved him. Joseph helped to make Jesus and Mary comfortable and he loved them both. Mary and Joseph were very happy that what God had promised had come true. They both said 'thank you' to God for the birth of Jesus.

Activity

There is a picture of Jesus lying among the straw to colour in. Glue the ends to make the crib. This can be taken home to join the rest of the crib figures and placed where they can all be seen.

Prayer

Thank you for Jesus.
We welcome you, Jesus,
into our hearts and our homes.
Jesus we love you,
we are glad that you have come into our world.
Amen.

Song

Away in a manger

LAMPS

Aim

To look at the coming of Jesus through the eyes of Joseph.

Teaching

Who can tell me how Mary discovered she could be the mother of Jesus? The angel Gabriel came from God and told her that if she was willing she would become the mother of Jesus.

At this time Mary was preparing to marry Joseph. In fact, everyone was already calling them man and wife. Joseph was looking forward to marrying Mary. But when he heard she was going to have a baby he was not so happy. It was not his baby, so why should he look after it? He was upset and decided to send Mary back home to her parents. Joseph thought they could have the job of looking after her and her baby. Though he planned to do this it made Joseph very sad. He did love Mary.

One night, after he had finished working in his carpenter's shop and gone to bed, Joseph had a dream. He remembered this dream for always. In his dream an angel came to him, just as an angel had come to Mary. The angel spoke to him and said, 'Joseph, son of David, do not be afraid to take Mary as your wife, for the child conceived in her is from the Holy Spirit.' So Joseph now knew what Mary had told him was true. The angel then said, 'She will bear a son and you are to name him Jesus, for he will save his people from their sins.' Joseph was

not sure he understood all this but he did know he was to give the baby his name and so call him his own son. He knew that the baby was to be called Jesus and that is the same as Joshua and it means 'God saves'.

Joseph knew he would do what the angel had said. He would not send Mary away but he would love her and the baby Jesus.

Activity

On the worksheet there is a picture to make showing the angel appearing to Joseph. Using finger paints, the group could make a big banner that says 'GOD SAVES' and show the Christ child in a manger.

Prayer

God, we thank you for Joseph
and that he cared for Mary.
We are glad he did what you asked him to do.
Help us to do what you want us to do.
Amen.

Song

The world was in darkness

TORCHES

Aim

To show that our God wants us to share in his work.

Teaching

John told his mother he was praying to God for a better world. His mother said to him, 'You could help by tidying up your room.'

Dawn said to her teacher that she had asked God that she might do well in her exams. The teacher said he was sure God would help but only if she did her homework and paid more attention in the classroom.

God is ready to help us but he asks us to do what we can. Sometimes God depends on us for getting things done. God seeks our help and our cooperation. God seeks to make a better world through us and what we do. God's kingdom will not come on earth unless we work for the King. This is why we pray, 'Your kingdom come: your will be done.'

If Mary had said to God, 'Go away and find someone else', Jesus could not have been born when God planned. God would not force Mary to be the mother of Jesus. It was only possible if Mary said, 'Yes'. Mary said, 'Here am I the servant of the Lord; let it be with me according to your word' (Luke 1:38).

But even now it would be difficult for Mary if Joseph decided he did not want this baby to be born. Unless Joseph cooperated no one knows what would have happened. At first Joseph thought he would send Mary away. He would divorce her, let someone else look after this baby. But then he had a dream and he saw an angel come to him and say, 'Joseph, son of David, do not be afraid to take Mary as your wife, for the child conceived in her is from the Holy Spirit. She will bear a son, and you are to name him Jesus, for he will save his people from their sins.' When Joseph awoke he was sure that he had a message from God. He could have ignored it. He could have said, 'Not me.' But we are told that 'he did as the angel of the Lord commanded him'. By cooperating with God, Joseph also helped to make it possible for Jesus to come into the world.

Because Joseph and Mary did what God asked, the world was changed for ever. Are there any ways in which we can work for God and help to bring in his kingdom?

Activity

Spend some time letting the group answer the question above. On the activity sheet there is a wordsearch of various names and titles given to Jesus. They could also explore the meaning of each: Jesus, Christ, Saviour, Son of God, Son of Man, Emmanuel, Word, Lord, Teacher, Rabbi.

They could also create banners with the names of Jesus to put around the church for Christmas Day.

Prayer

Lord God, as Mary and Joseph said 'Yes' to you
and did your will,
help us to work for the coming of your kingdom
and to serve you.
Amen.

Song

Jesus, good above all other

CHRISTMAS
Christmas Day

Aim

To celebrate the birth of Jesus and to give thanks for the presence of God with us.

Preparation

Have some of the titles of Jesus around the church, together with crib figures that the children have made. If possible, there should be a central crib with figures. Invite the children to come to church dressed as shepherds or angels. Choose someone to come as Mary and someone as Joseph. A mother may like to bring her baby as the baby Jesus.

Opening activity

Have four people with lighted tapers in different corners of the church. Let a fifth person with a lighted taper stand in the centre of the church. (This is more effective if the lights are left off until the advent candles are lit.) Let the fifth person begin by saying, 'Emmanuel', and asking the congregation to say, 'Alleluia. Amen,' each time he/she says it and to say it loudly. The people with tapers come down the church in turn and light a single candle. After each one lights a candle, the fifth person says, 'Emmanuel', and the congregation respond.

1   The Christ is come into the world. *(lights candle)*
5   Emmanuel.
All **Alleluia. Amen.**

2   Jesus is born among us. *(lights candle)*
5   Emmanuel.
All **Alleluia. Amen.**

3   Our God has taken upon him our flesh.
    (lights candle)
5   Emmanuel.
All **Alleluia. Amen.**

4   This is the light that defeats the darkness.
    (lights candle)
5   Emmanuel.
All **Alleluia. Amen.**

    (Number 5 now lights the central candle.)
5   God is with us. Emmanuel.
All **Alleluia. Amen.**

Opening prayer

Blessed are you, Lord our God,
for in your deep love for us
you have shared in our humanity
that we might share in your glory.
Help us to make room in our lives
to be aware of you
and of your coming to us through Jesus Christ,
the Word made flesh.
Amen.

Opening song

O come, all ye faithful

Readings

Set I
Isaiah 9:2-7
Psalm 96
Titus 2:11-14
Luke 2:1-14 (15-20)

Set II
Isaiah 62:6-12
Psalm 97
Titus 3:4-7
Luke 2:(1-7) 8-20

Set III
Isaiah 52:7-10
Psalm 98
Hebrews 1:1-4 (5-12)
John 1:1-14

(For a service with children the Luke readings are easier.)

Thought for the day

It is not hard to imagine the crowded inn. Friends and relatives have got together and seek to celebrate; the place is packed. Some who are weary are trying to sleep. The place is full to capacity. There is much conversation, perhaps some singing and dancing. There is no room here for Mary who is about to bring forth her son. There was no room at the inn.

How common these words are, though they may be said in different ways: 'Do not disturb me, I am busy'; 'I would like to help but I do not have the time'; 'I like a routine and I don't want anything to interfere with it'; 'I cannot come and see you, I have business to attend to.' And every time we excuse ourselves, we exclude ourselves from certain experiences. Being pre-occupied is a great defence against anything new happening. 'I would have said my prayers but there is too much happening to me.' In such ways we miss the coming of God.

Yet the innkeeper, busy, hard-pressed, found room. He offered a space to Joseph and Mary. Simple accommodation and into it came the Christ child. The innkeeper made room and the Christ was able to come into his place.

Amid all the busyness of Christmas, the activity that threatens to overwhelm us, you have made room. You are here to rejoice that God comes, he comes into the world and he comes to you. We can rejoice in the mystery of the God who seeks to share in our daily life. We celebrate the greatest of miracles that the Word is made flesh and dwells among us. Let us quietly think over these words of St John: 'to all who received him, who believed in his name, he gave power to become children of God' (John 1:12). We will keep a short silence and in it let us give thanks for the coming of Christ into the world and for his coming to us. Let us open our hearts to him and say, 'Come to my heart, Lord Jesus, there is room in my heart for you.'

Question time

Do we make sure we have room in our hearts and lives each day for the Christ who comes?

How can we witness to the fact that our God comes to us?

Illustration

Nan-in was a great Japanese teacher of the art of Zen. One day a university professor came to seek some teaching. Nan-in served the traditional tea to his guest. He poured until his visitor's bowl was full and then kept pouring and the tea overflowed, as there was no room for it in the bowl. The professor watched until he could no longer restrain himself and said, 'It is overfull and no more will go in.' Nan-in said, 'You are like this cup. You are full of ideas and speculations. How can I pour more in unless you empty your cup? You need to make space to learn.'

In the same way we need to make a space in our lives each day for our God who comes to us.

Think upon these words by Angelus Silesius:

Though Christ a thousand times
in Bethlehem be born,
if he is not born in you,
you are still forlorn.

Intercessions

Blessed are you, Lord our God,
for in Jesus Christ, the Word made flesh,
you share in our humanity.
You come among us to be one with us
and that we may come to you.
Blessed are you, Father, Son and Holy Spirit.

Lord God, we welcome you
into our hearts, our homes our lives.
We ask your blessing upon the Church
as it worships you throughout the world.
May it ever witness to your presence and your love.
Guide all preachers of the word
and ministers of the sacraments,
that they may lead us to you
and help us to know you and to love you.

Silence

Lord, come to us.
Save us and help us, O Lord.

We rejoice with the shepherds
and pray for peace on earth and goodwill
among all peoples.
We ask your blessing upon all areas
where there is war, conflict and oppression.
We remember those who are not at peace
with themselves or with others.
We pray for all who are disturbed or distressed.

Silence

Lord, come to us.
Save us and help us, O Lord.

Lord, born into an ordinary home,
come to our homes,
that they may reflect your peace and your glory.
We ask your blessing upon all our loved ones,
those with whom we share this Christmas
and those who are not able to be with us.

Silence

Lord, come to us.
Save us and help us, O Lord.

We remember all who find this a stressful time.
We pray for the world poor
and those who are deeply in debt.
We remember before you the homeless
and we pray for the work of Shelter
and other relief organisations.
We seek your blessing upon all who are lonely
and those who feel neglected or forgotten at this time.
We remember also all who are ill and in hospital.

Silence

Lord, come to us.
Save us and help us, O Lord.

Lord, we rejoice that you came down to earth
as a human,
that we might share in the joys of the kingdom of heaven.
We remember before you friends and loved ones departed,
especially those who have died this year.
We rejoice in the fellowship of Mary and Joseph
and all your saints.
May we share with them in your glory.

Silence

Merciful Father,
**accept these prayers
for the sake of your Son,
our Saviour Jesus Christ.
Amen.**

Memory verse

To all who received him, who believed in his name, he gave power to become children of God.
John 1:12

Suggested music

Child in the manger
A great and mighty wonder
It came upon the midnight clear
See him lying on a bed of straw
Once in royal David's city
While shepherds watched
Of the Father's love begotten
Good Christians all, rejoice
Silent night
In the bleak midwinter
Unto us a boy is born
Ding dong, merrily on high

CANDLES, LAMPS and TORCHES

There are times when it is important for the whole congregation to worship together and Christmas is one of them. There are no worksheets for Christmas Day as there is plenty of activity within the service. Let the children be as involved as possible. Let them sing a carol on their own: 'Away in a manger' is possibly the simplest but they may like to attempt something like 'The Virgin Mary had a baby boy' or 'Christmas greetings, Christmas joy'.

The children could carry the crib figures in procession and add them to the crib during the singing of the hymn before the Gospel.

If an activity is needed let the children make a 'welcome card' for Jesus.

First Sunday of Christmas

Aim

To show that Jesus knows our joys and our sorrows.

Preparation

Have posters of refugees around the church, especially homeless families. The Advent candles are still lit every week until Candlemas.

Opening activity

Have four people with lighted tapers in different corners of the church. Let a fifth person with a lighted taper stand in the centre of the church. (This is more effective if the lights are left off until the candles are lit.) Let the fifth person begin by saying, 'In his love and in his pity', and asking the congregation to say, 'he has redeemed us' each time he/she says it, and to say it loudly. The people with tapers come down the church in turn and light a single candle. After each one lights a candle the fifth person says, 'In his love and in his pity', and the congregation respond, 'he has redeemed us'.

1   The Jesus is born in a stable. (*lights candle*)
5   In his love and in his pity
All **he has redeemed us.**

2   Our God has taken upon him our flesh. (*lights candle*)
5   In his love and in his pity
All **he has redeemed us.**

3   He is taken as a refugee into Egypt. (*lights candle*)
5   In his love and in his pity
All **he has redeemed us.**

4   By his bruises we are healed. (*lights candle*)
5   In his love and in his pity
All **he has redeemed us.**

(*Number 5 lights the central candle*)
5   In his love and in his pity
All **he has redeemed us.**

Opening prayer

Loving God,
you seek to rescue us from our troubles
and are with us in our dangers.
Be our strength and guide at all times
and help us to know you are with us always.
Amen.

Opening song

A great and mighty wonder

Readings

Isaiah 63:7-9
Psalm 148
Hebrews 2:10-18
Matthew 2:13-23

Thought for the day

I like all the glitter of Christmas but we must remember Jesus did not live in tinsel town. Jesus was born into a turbulent world where there was oppression and rebellion, cruelty and evil. King Herod (king from 37-4 BC) typifies the times. Herod was appointed 'king of the Jews' by the Roman Senate and was quite paranoid about anyone who challenged his position or power. Friends, courtiers, priests, nobles were often killed on the suspicion that they might oppose him. That the wise men went to him and enquired about the 'king of the Jews' was unfortunate. This brought about the massacre of the children at Bethlehem. As Bethlehem was not all that large, it would probably amount to 20 to 30 children.

Fortunately, Joseph had another dream of an angel who said, 'Get up, take the child and his mother and flee into Egypt.' The baby Jesus escaped the tyrant as the baby Moses had escaped Pharaoh. Joseph made the journey into Egypt where long ago another Joseph cared for his family in time of trouble.

When Herod died, the kingdom was divided between his three sons: Archelaus ruled in Judea, Herod Antipas ruled Galilee and Perea, Philip ruled Iturea, Trachonitis and the territory in the north-east.

Joseph had another dream while in Egypt and this time the angel told him to return to Israel because Herod was dead. Joseph once again obeyed but decided that Archelaus was still a danger, so he took Jesus to Galilee and to Nazareth. This was only slightly safer. Herod Antipas was the one who had John the Baptist beheaded. This Herod would meet Jesus briefly at Jesus' trial.

We do not know how long the Holy Family was in Egypt but it would not have been very long. It must have been a great relief to the parents of Mary when they saw her again and found not only was she safe but so was the baby Jesus. From the very beginning Jesus shares in our sorrows as well as our joys. His family are homeless and refugees. It would take a while for Joseph to build up his work in Egypt and again in Nazareth, and without work they would not eat. The shadow of the cross often touched the carpenter's workplace. Let us give thanks that Jesus shares in our humanity and understands our troubles. Our God is not a God who is far-off but a God who loves us and comes among us.

Question time

Do we invite Jesus to be with us in our joys and in our sorrows? We can bear much more when we are not alone.

How can we show a greater love for homeless people and refugees?

Illustration

There are many stories of how people have been protected by angels; this one is from Vanuatu (the New Hebrides). The Reverend John Paton went as a missionary to the Hebridean Islands. One night a group of hostile natives surrounded his mission and home. Paton prayed for God to protect him. When morning came Paton was amazed to see his attackers leaving. About a year later the chief accepted Christianity and became a believer. The Reverend John asked him why they had not attacked his house and burned it down. The chief in turn asked him, 'Who were those men you had with you there?'

John replied, 'There were no men, only my wife and I.' The chief argued that he saw many men, big men in shining white garments with drawn swords standing guard.

Intercessions

Blessed are you, Lord our God,
for you are always ready to help and protect us.
You are a present help in all our needs and troubles.
Blessed are you, Father, Son and Holy Spirit.

God our Redeemer, we thank you
for the Church throughout the whole world.
We remember especially today
the Coptic Church of Egypt.
We ask your blessing upon all Christians
who are being persecuted or penalised for their faith.
We pray for Christians who are exiled
or imprisoned for their beliefs.
We remember all who are struggling with doubt
and those who lack any teaching in the faith.

Silence

God our Redeemer,
hear us and help us.

We give thanks for our land and its freedom.
We remember in your presence
all who are refugees or homeless at this time.
We ask your blessing upon the world poor
and all who are unable to use their abilities and talents.
Bless the work of Fair Trade organisations
and all who strive to relieve injustice and poverty.

Silence

God our Redeemer,
hear us and help us.

We give thanks for the love and protection of our parents.
We ask your blessing upon our homes
and all our loved ones,
that they may live in peace and be free from poverty.
We remember all children who have been taken into care
and all families who find it difficult to cope.
We pray for any parents who have lost a child
over this last year.

Silence

God our Redeemer,
hear us and help us.

We give thanks for the medical profession
and for all who care for our well-being.
We ask your blessing upon all who are ill
at home or in hospital.
We remember any who have been injured
in accidents or through acts of violence.

We pray especially for families
where there is a child who is ill or suffering.

Silence

God our Redeemer,
hear us and help us.

We give thanks that you are our Redeemer;
that you seek that we should not perish
but have everlasting life.
We remember friends and loved ones
who are departed from us.
We rejoice in the fellowship of all your saints
and ask that we may share with them in your glory.

Silence

Merciful Father,
**accept these prayers
for the sake of your Son,
our Saviour Jesus Christ.
Amen.**

Memory verse

It was no messenger or angel that saved them; in his love and in his pity he redeemed them.
Isaiah 63:9

Suggested music

Angels from the realms of glory
Lord Jesus Christ *(Living Lord)*
It came upon the midnight clear

CANDLES

Aim

To tell how Joseph was warned in a dream to escape from Herod.

Teaching

Who can remember the name of the mother of Jesus? Let us say her name together: 'Mary.' What was her husband called? Now let us say his name: 'Joseph.' Now, who can tell me how Joseph was told to marry Mary? He was told by an angel in a dream.

Where was Jesus born? He was born in a stable in Bethlehem. Let us say together: 'Bethlehem.' Tell me who came to see the baby Jesus. The shepherds and the wise men came to see him. There was someone else who wanted to see him: the wicked King Herod, and he wanted to kill Jesus. He did not like to think that Jesus was to be a king.

When Joseph went to sleep he had another dream. An angel came to Joseph and said, 'Get up, take the child and his mother and flee to Egypt, and remain there until I tell you: for Herod is about to search for the child to destroy him.' When Joseph woke up it was still night and it was dark but what do you think he did? He woke Mary and told her to get all their things ready and leave Bethlehem. Mary hurried to get ready after Joseph told her of his dream. If they did not get away quickly, the wicked Herod would kill Jesus. The three of them travelled as quickly as they could out of Bethlehem and towards Egypt. It took them a good few days to get there and then they had to find somewhere to live.

After a while the wicked king died and when Joseph heard this he decided it was time to take Mary and Jesus back to their own land. They did not go back to Bethlehem or to Jerusalem because Joseph thought it was too dangerous. They went to live in a place called Nazareth. Let us say together: 'Jesus lived in Nazareth.' Joseph was a carpenter in Nazareth and made things for people and mended things. He spent a lot of time making and mending. Can you tell me some of the things he might make or mend?

Jesus lived in Nazareth with Joseph and Mary and he stayed in Nazareth until he had grown up and set out to work for God his Father.

Activity

Play hide and seek. Let the seeker be called Herod. When there are still two to be found let them be called Joseph and Mary. Joseph and Mary can walk to Egypt while the rest pretend to be asleep.

They can colour in the Holy Family on the worksheet and add their own family.

Prayer

God, we thank you
that Jesus escaped the wicked Herod.
We ask you to care for all children
who are in danger.
Amen.

Song

He's got the whole world in his hands

LAMPS

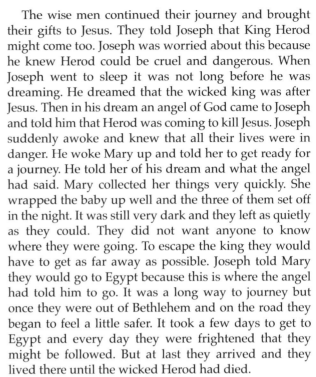

Aim

To show how Jesus had to escape from Herod

Teaching

Many people work for the rescue services. Can you tell me any of them? Firemen, ambulance crews, doctors, nurses, paramedics, lifeboat crews and police are some of them. Does anyone have a parent who is part of a rescue team?

When Jesus was born in Bethlehem wise men came to see him. But they were not wise in everything. They made a mistake. They thought Jesus would be born in a palace and may be the son of a king. So they went to ask Herod the king 'Where is he that is born "King of the Jews"?' Herod did not know the answer and he wanted his own sons to be rulers after him. Herod did not want another king. When he asked his own clever men about this they told him, 'The "King of the Jews" is to be born in Bethlehem.' This did not please Herod and he decided he would have to get rid of this king.

The wise men continued their journey and brought their gifts to Jesus. They told Joseph that King Herod might come too. Joseph was worried about this because he knew Herod could be cruel and dangerous. When Joseph went to sleep it was not long before he was dreaming. He dreamed that the wicked king was after Jesus. Then in his dream an angel of God came to Joseph and told him that Herod was coming to kill Jesus. Joseph suddenly awoke and knew that all their lives were in danger. He woke Mary up and told her to get ready for a journey. He told her of his dream and what the angel had said. Mary collected her things very quickly. She wrapped the baby up well and the three of them set off in the night. It was still very dark and they left as quietly as they could. They did not want anyone to know where they were going. To escape the king they would have to get as far away as possible. Joseph told Mary they would go to Egypt because this is where the angel had told him to go. It was a long way to journey but once they were out of Bethlehem and on the road they began to feel a little safer. It took a few days to get to Egypt and every day they were frightened that they might be followed. But at last they arrived and they lived there until the wicked Herod had died.

After Herod had died they returned to their own country but chose not to live near Jerusalem. Who can tell me where they lived and what work Joseph would do? They lived in Nazareth and there Jesus would grow up. Joseph was a carpenter and no doubt Jesus often wanted to help him with his work.

Activity

Get the children to mime the story from the visit of the wise men, Joseph sleeping, the dream of the angel, waking up and being frightened, waking Mary, packing bags, leaving as quietly as possible and setting off for Egypt.

Prayer

God, we thank you
for the escape of Jesus into Egypt.
We pray for all refugees
and those whose lives are in danger at this time.
Amen.

Song

When Jesus came from heaven (verse 1)

TORCHES

Aim

To look at the flight into Egypt.

Teaching

Can you tell me who was the ruler of the Jews when Jesus was born? It was Herod and he lived in Jerusalem. The Senate in Rome appointed Herod king and he was given the title 'King of the Jews'. After three years in power Herod was known as Herod the Builder because of all the new building work he started. He built the fortress of Masada near the Dead Sea and the Fortress Antonia, but he was most famous for the rebuilding of the Temple in Jerusalem. He began the building of the Temple in 19 BC and most of it was finished in 10 years but it was no completed until AD 64.

Herod was a powerful king but always fearful of rebellion, of someone trying to take away his power. If he was suspicious of anyone, whether they were members of his family, friends, nobles or statesmen, he would have them imprisoned or tortured or even put to death.

When the wise men visited him and asked, 'Where is he that is born king of the Jews?' you could say they made a big mistake. Herod would see this person as a threat to his rule and would seek to destroy the infant Jesus. Once he was told the king of the Jews was to be born in Bethlehem he started to scheme how to get rid of Jesus.

Maybe the wise men made Joseph worried when they told him Herod was likely to come and see Jesus. Joseph had a dream after the wise men left and in the dream an angel of God warned him that Herod would seek the life of Jesus. As soon as he woke, Joseph told Mary they were in danger and that the angel had said they should leave the country and make for Egypt. They both packed their belongings as quickly as they could and set off before Herod arrived. Fortunately neither Herod nor his men knew what the Holy Family looked like.

It was a long way to Egypt but Joseph and Mary kept travelling until they got there and felt a little safer. Here they would live until Herod had died.

Even after Herod was dead, Joseph did not feel it was wise to live near Jerusalem because Herod's son, who lived there, was just as cruel. So the Holy Family went to live in Nazareth where Joseph worked as a carpenter.

Activity

Look at a map and show the journey from Bethlehem to Egypt. Can the group think of anyone else whose life was threatened by a king and who lived in Egypt? (Moses)

On the worksheet they can learn how to make a map of places in the Holy Land.

Prayer

God, you go with us on all our journeys.
Protect us from all evil
and keep us always in your love and your care.
We ask your blessing
upon all who are refugees or homeless.
Amen.

Song

Unto us a boy is born

31

Second Sunday of Christmas

Aim

To rejoice in the mystery of the Word made flesh and in the kingdom of heaven.

Preparation

The Advent candles are still lit every week until Candlemas.

Opening activity

Have four people with lighted tapers in different corners of the church. Let a fifth person with a lighted taper stand in the centre of the church. (This is more effective if the lights are left off until the candles are lit.)

Let the fifth person begin by saying, 'The Word became flesh', and asking the congregation to say, 'and lived among us' each time he/she says it, and to say it loudly. The people with tapers come down the church in turn and light a single candle. After each one lights a candle, person 5 says, 'The Word became flesh' and the congregation respond.

1 The love of God is revealed in Jesus.
   (lights candle).
5 The Word became flesh
All **and lived among us.**

2 The light of God conquered the darkness.
   (lights candle).
5 The Word became flesh
All **and lived among us.**

3 The life of God giving life eternal.
   (lights candle).
5 The Word became flesh
All **and lived among us.**

4 The Lord is with us always.
   (lights candle).
5 The Word became flesh
All **and lived among us.**

   (Number 5 lights the central candle)
5 The Word became flesh
All **and lived among us.**

Opening prayer

O Holy Child of Bethlehem,
descend to us, we pray;
cast out our sin, and enter in,
be born in us today.
We hear the Christmas angels,
the great glad tidings tell:
O come to us, abide with us,
our Lord Emmanuel.
Phillips Brooks (1835–1893)

Opening song

What child is this

Readings

Ecclesiasticus 24:1-12
Canticle: Wisdom of Solomon 10:15-21
Ephesians 1:3-14
John 1:(1-9) 10-18

Thought for the day

St John's Gospel owes its thought patterns to Hellenistic Judaism – that is to both Greek and Jewish ideas. The combination of these two led to the belief that existence has two dimensions. Heaven is the sphere in which God is at work: this would include light, joy, love, peace, grace, spirit and truth. The created world – the Cosmos – is the sphere of Satan and it includes darkness, distress, death, all evil and falsehood. John does talk of heaven above and earth below but he does not seek to imply they are separate; rather, they are different spheres at work in the same space and in the same human being. We have in our lives the potential of heaven and its opposite.

Like God, heaven is not far away but to be experienced in the here and now. The kingdom of heaven is always at hand. Part of the understanding of the at-one-ment – the atonement – is that we are as much in heaven as on earth.

Because we so often live on the level of the cosmos alone, we have blinded ourselves to the reality that heaven is all about us. The call of John the Baptist and Jesus to repentance was a call saying, 'Turn around, you are looking at life and the world in the wrong way. The kingdom of heaven is waiting for you to enjoy it.' To say, 'The Lord is with you,' is a reality we have to make our own. God is not a long-distance phone call and heaven is not 'far, far away'. Heaven is not only somewhere we should be planning to retire to after death but also somewhere we should be entering and living in now.

St John suggests that in Jesus the glory of God is revealed: the very presence of God in an earthly life. Those who see this and believe in him have the power to become the children of God.

Question time

How can we realise the fullness of the kingdom of heaven now in our earthly life?

Do you see that the coming of God's kingdom and the doing of God's will are two parts of the same experience?

Illustration

A woman from County Kerry in Ireland was asked, 'Where is heaven?' She thought for a moment and then replied, 'About one foot and six inches above me.' She wanted to show that God and heaven are always close at hand and not beyond our reach. We have to just stretch ourselves, extend our vision, give the kingdom of heaven some priority in our life to begin to realise we are there. By giving time and attention to God we learn that 'we dwell in him and he in us'.

Intercessions

Blessed are you, Lord God,
Creator of heaven and earth.
In you and in your love
heaven and earth are one.
You have sent your Son, our Saviour,
to lead us back into your kingdom.
You have called us to work with you
and have given us of your Spirit.
Blessed are you, Father, Son and Holy Spirit.

We give you thanks and praise
that we may share in your kingdom here on earth
and that in Jesus Christ
we see our humanity and your divinity as one.
We ask your blessing upon all preachers of the word,
on all who proclaim your presence
by their actions and their love.
We pray for all who are seekers
and that we may know you better and love you more.
We remember all who are being prepared
for baptism or confirmation
and all who are seeking
to commit their lives to you in love.

Silence

Holy God, come among us:
hear us and help us.

We pray for peace on earth
and goodwill among all people.
We ask your blessing
upon all who strive for justice and peace.
We pray for the United Nations
and all who seek to bring unity and fellowship
between nations.

Silence

Holy God, come among us:
hear us and help us.

We give thanks that Jesus was born into an earthly home
and shared in our daily life.
May we know that our homes and loved ones
are part of your kingdom.
We ask your blessing on homes
where there is strife and division, deceit and distrust.

Silence

Holy God, come among us:
hear us and help us.

We give thanks that nothing can separate us
from your love.
We ask your blessing upon all
who are ill, lonely or oppressed.
We remember friends and loved ones
who are in hospital or ill at home
and all who are caring for them.
We pray also for all who despair,
all who have lost hope or any vision of your love.

Silence

Holy God, come among us:
hear us and help us.

Loving God, you invite us to delight in your presence
and to live in your kingdom.
Lord, keep us in life eternal.
We give thanks for your faithful ones departed
and we rejoice in the fellowship of all your saints.

Silence

Merciful Father,
accept these prayers
for the sake of your Son,
our Saviour Jesus Christ.
Amen.

Memory verse

To all who receive him, who believe in his name, he gave power to become children of God.
John 1:12

Suggested music

Father of heaven, whose love profound
In the bleak mid-winter
It came upon the midnight clear

CANDLES

Aim

To revise the Christmas story and to make sure the children understand it and know the various names.

Teaching and activity

Start with the activity. Have a lot of Christmas cards showing the Nativity. If possible, have one for each child. Use just the picture on the front and cut each of the pictures into three pieces. Tell the children they have to collect a whole picture each; once they pick up one piece they have to keep it and find the other two. Some children may need help.

Once they all have their cards, get them to put them together and talk about what they see. Who can see the mother of the baby? What is the name of the mother? Mary. Now, who is her husband? Yes, it is Joseph. Let us all say together: 'Mary and Joseph.'

Look at the baby in the picture. Often he looks shining bright. Do you know his name? Let us all say it together: 'Jesus.'

Some of you may be able to tell what sort of place Jesus was born in. Yes, it was a stable; perhaps on some cards there is a cow or a donkey. Put your hands up if you have a cow or a donkey on your card. Let us all say, 'Jesus was born in a stable.' Who knows why he was born in the stable? Because there was no room at the inn.

Now on some cards there are people visiting Jesus. Who came to see the baby Jesus? The shepherds came because an angel told them about Jesus. Which city did they go to? Yes, it was called Bethlehem. Let us all say together, 'Jesus was born in Bethlehem.' Some cards have angels on them because they told the shepherds about Jesus being born. What else or who else is on the cards?

If the wise men are there, tell the children that you will let them know all about the magi next week. Spend the rest of the time looking at the cards and helping the children to understand and explore the Nativity story. You may like to use a crib and figures as a further visual aid.

Prayer

Be near me, Lord Jesus,
I ask you to stay
close by me for ever,
and love me, I pray.
Bless all the dear children
in your tender care
and fit us for heaven
to live with you there.

(From 'Away in a manger'. As the words are well known, get the children to pray this with you.)

Song

Little Jesus, sweetly sleep

(If possible, play the song at the beginning and at the end of the session and then teach the children to sing it.)

LAMPS

Aim

To review the Christmas story and encourage the children to tell it.

Teaching

Use a set of crib figures, including an angel if possible. Alternatively, you can use cut-out figures from Christmas cards. Get various children to pick up a figure until all the figures are gone. A new group of children could do this after it has been done once.

Who has Mary? What does she look like? Do you remember who came to see Mary to tell her she was going to have a baby?

Hold up the angel and tell me what you think the angel said to Mary. Who wanted Mary to have this baby? God wanted her to but only if Mary said what?

Let the person who has Mary say 'Yes' to God and to the angel.

Not long after Mary said 'Yes' to God, who did she get married to? It was to Joseph.

Who has Joseph? Hold him up. Can you tell me anything about him? He was married to Mary. He was a carpenter. What does a carpenter do?

Mary and Joseph had to go on a long journey. Ask those who have Mary and Joseph to walk around the room. Where are they going? Who knows the name of the place? They were going to Bethlehem. Now they had to look for somewhere to stay. They would go to an inn.

Let us pretend Joseph and Mary are knocking on a door; let everyone knock. Now what did the innkeeper say? 'No room at the inn.' Let us all shake our heads. This made Mary very sad. The innkeeper was a kind man and he noticed Mary was sad and that she was soon to have a baby. So he was sorry for Mary and Joseph and offered them a place to stay. Where did he tell them they could stay? In a stable. What might you find there?

Now Mary and Joseph could settle down for the night. (Let the figures be placed out in front of everyone, in a stable if you have one.) We know that something special happened that night. What was it? Yes, the baby Jesus was born. Who has the baby Jesus? Let us all clap as he/she walks around the room and then puts the baby beside Joseph and Mary. Let us all be very quiet and say thank you to God for Jesus coming to earth.

Outside, above the hills, a wonderful thing happened. There was some singing. Who was singing? The angels were singing 'Glory to God in the highest'. Let us say it together: 'Glory to God in the highest.' Who heard the angels? Yes, the shepherds, and when the angels were gone what did the shepherds do? They went to see Jesus. Let our shepherds walk right round the room and then let them place the shepherds beside Jesus, Joseph and Mary.

Now we have finished, but there is still someone with a figure. Who is it? Yes the angel has still to be put near Jesus. But because people could not see the angel, let us put the angel a little way off. The angel of God is always there but most people do not know this.

Activity

There is a wordsearch on the worksheet which reminds the children once again of the story.

Prayer

Lord Jesus, we thank you
for coming to live among us.
You come to share in our lives
and to give us your love.
May we give our love to you
and know that you are with us.
Amen.

Song

Mary had a baby

TORCHES

Aim

To explore ideas of our receptivity to God.

Teaching

Some people live in poor reception areas and have difficulty with their mobile phone, or with their digital radio or even with their television. Many things can cause this. Do you know of any? You may have moved

34

too far from the transmitter. Your aerial may not be facing in the right direction. Are you sure you are pointing in the right direction? Sometimes it is amazing how a little movement away from the centre can distort our reception. It might be that you have something in the way that blocks out the picture, like a block of flats or a high hill. Many things can crowd out the picture, like overhead electric wires or an engine without a suppressor – sometimes even a tree can do it.

Strangely enough, you can be in too receptive an area where there is a lot of interference from other places. If there are too many signals, you need to try and tune in more carefully.

It would seem that Jesus lived in a poor reception area. Could someone read John 1:10, 11?

> He was in the world, and the world came into being through him: yet the world did not know him. He came to what was his own, and his own people did not accept him.

Many gave Jesus a poor reception. There was 'no room' at the inn. The Creator of time and space came into this world and people said, 'No room, we are too busy. Go somewhere else.' Herod felt that Jesus was a threat to him and tried to get rid of him. Later people would force Jesus out of the city, out of their lives and on to the cross. They refused to receive him and he became the 'scorned and rejected of men'.

But some were receptive and some still are. Listen to these words from St John: 'But to all who received him, who believed in his name, he gave power to become children of God' (John 1:12). God has given us the power to become his children, to enjoy his presence and to know eternal life. All God asks of us is to be receptive to him each day and seek to know him and his will. (Ask for suggestions of how we can become more receptive to Jesus, and look at examples from the Gospels.)

Activity

There is a wordsearch on the activity sheet concerning the various titles of Jesus.

Prayer

Dear Lord, for these three things we pray:
to know you more clearly,
to love you more dearly
and to follow you more nearly,
day by day.

Adapted from a prayer of Richard of Chichester (1197–1253)

Song

Hark, the herald-angels sing

EPIPHANY
The Epiphany

Aim

To share in the seeking and the worshipping of the wise men.

Preparation

The Advent candles are lit every week until Candlemas. Have figures of the three wise men to be carried to the crib and a star to lead them. It would be good for the children to dress as the wise men and offer gifts.

Opening activity

Have four people with lighted tapers in different corners of the church. Let a fifth person with a lighted taper stand in the centre of the church. (This is more effective if the lights are left off until the candles are lit.)

Let the fifth person begin by saying, 'The Word became flesh', and asking the congregation to say, 'and dwells among us' each time he/she says it, and to say it loudly. Let the people with tapers come down the church in turn and light a single candle. After each one lights a candle, the fifth person says, 'The Word became flesh' and the congregation respond. Person 5 lights the central candle.

1   Blessed be God, who by the leading of a star
     brought the wise men to Christ the King.
     (lights candle)
5   The Word became flesh
All **and dwells among us.**

2   Christ was proclaimed by the angels.
     (lights candle)
5   The Word became flesh
All **and dwells among us.**

3   Christ was worshipped by the shepherds.
     (lights candle)
5   The Word became flesh
All **and dwells among us.**

4   Christ was adored by the wise men.
     (lights candle)
5   The Word became flesh
All **and dwells among us.**

5   Christ is worshipped throughout the world.
     (lights candle)
     The Word became flesh
All **and dwells among us.**

Opening prayer

O God, by the leading of a star
you brought the wise men to come before Jesus.
In our seeking lead us to know you,
to love you and to worship you
this day and always.
Amen.

Opening song

We three kings of Orient are

During this hymn let the star lead a procession of the crib figures of the wise men around the church. Let children dressed as wise men follow.

At the end of verse 1 the star is placed behind the crib. The wise men can continue to process.

At the end of verse 2 the gold-bearing figure is placed in the crib and the child(ren) dressed as the gold-bearer can stand close to the crib.

Verse 3 will have the same actions with the incense-bearer and verse 4 with the bearer of myrrh.

At verse 5 the children should kneel before the crib. During the final chorus let the children stand up, bow to the Christ child and then go skipping back to their places.

Readings

Isaiah 60:1-6
Psalm 72:(1-7) 10-14
Ephesians 3:1-12
Matthew 2:1-12

Thought for the day

The shepherds were lucky because when the angels told them about Jesus their journey to the stable was not really very far. They were given directions and had a good idea where they were going. The wise men were not so lucky because their journey was to be a long one. They were often in the dark and they were not always sure of their destination. To be guided by a star is hardly an exact way of navigation and there is no fixed address they can aim for. Their journey would call for courage and the determination not to give up. It would have been easy to be put off and ask if it was all worth it. It would have been easy to choose comfort and safety, to give up when they met with obstacles. Many people would say, 'Why bother?' But in their hearts they knew they would not be satisfied until they had come before the Chosen One, until they knelt before the Christ child and offered him their gifts and their lives. The wise men knew there was more to life than comfort and security, more to life than possessions or even wisdom. The wise men were searching for a relationship with God. Theirs was a journey of faith. The wise men are an encouragement to all who are seekers and an example of our pilgrimage through life.

In their seeking the wise men went to the wrong place. They went to Herod the king and we know the sad consequence of that mistake. They had assumed a king would be born in a palace and now would have to rethink their ideas. Too often in our search for God we have gone to the wrong people or gone with fixed ideas. But if we continue to seek and do not give up on our journey of faith, we will also be able to come to the Christ and offer ourselves to him. Let us never forget that we are seeking because our God is calling us. He wants us to come before him and to rejoice in his presence.

Question time

Has your journey of faith been easy or is it often still hard and tortuous?

In this life we are all seekers, for the presence and love of our God can be explored and enjoyed more and more. Do you see yourself as a seeker and a traveller moving closer to God?

Illustration

There are many roads to God. God calls each of us and waits for our response. In the wise men we see at least three different roads. Perhaps they travelled alone and on different paths at the outset. Their faith journey brought them together.

Gold is a symbol of all of God's gifts. All things come from God and of his own do we offer. God gives us life and this wonderful world. Many come to God through thanksgiving, through gratitude for all that he gives. Gold is also a symbol of power: wealth helps people to achieve and poverty restricts people.

Frankincense is symbol of awe, of mystery and adoration. If we are sensitive to the wonders of the world and the mystery of creation, this can lead us to God. This in turn can lead us to respect all of creation because it is of God. Frankincense is used in worship and many people learn of God through the worship of others.

Myrrh is a symbol of pain and the need for relief from pain and sorrow. For many it is easy to forget God in the good times. But when we lose a loved one or become seriously ill ourselves, it makes us ask questions about our existence. As mortals we all need the salvation and healing that God gives.

Intercessions

Blessed are you, Lord our God,
for you have called us to seek you,
to know and to love you.
You have revealed yourself in Jesus Christ,
our Saviour and our God.
We come to worship you.
Blessed are you, Father, Son and Holy Spirit.

We give thanks for the wise men and the leading of a star.
We ask your blessing upon all who are seekers
and all who dedicate their lives to you.
We remember all those who lead worship
and teach of your love and salvation.
We pray today especially for the Churches of the Far East.

Silence

Lord, we seek you and call upon you:
hear us and help us.

As the wise men sought a king, we rejoice
that you are the King of kings and Lord of lords.
May your love and your will rule in our hearts.
We ask your blessing upon all leaders of people
and all who make important decisions for our world.
We pray today for all research scientists.

Silence

Lord, we seek you and call upon you:
hear us and help us.

As the Holy Family shared in an ordinary home,
we ask your blessing upon our homes.
May our homes reveal your presence
and our relationships increase our love for you.
We remember all homeless peoples,
all refugees and those who belong to homes
where there is violence or lack of love.

Silence

Lord, we seek you and call upon you:
hear us and help us.

With the gift of myrrh
there was an offering of the sorrows of our world.
We remember all who long for freedom and redemption.
We pray for all suffering people,
all who are distressed
and all who feel that no one cares for them.
We pray for the work of doctors, nurses, paramedics
and all who are involved in healing.

Silence

Lord, we seek you and call upon you:
hear us and help us.

We rejoice with Mary and Joseph,
with the shepherds and the angels,
with the wise men,
with the Church in heaven and on earth.
We commend ourselves, all peoples and the whole world
to your unfailing love.

Silence

Merciful Father,
**accept these prayers
for the sake of your Son,
our Saviour Jesus Christ.
Amen.**

Memory verse

Then, opening their treasure chests, they offered him gifts of gold, frankincense and myrrh.
Matthew 2:11b

Suggested music

O worship the Lord in the beauty of holiness
As with gladness men of old
Every star shall sing a carol

CANDLES

Aim

To show how the wise men travelled a long way to come and see Jesus.

Teaching and activity

Start with the activity. Have some Christmas cards showing the Holy Family and the wise men. If possible, have one for every three children. Use just the picture on the front and cut each of the pictures into three pieces. Tell the children to pick up only one piece of card and then search for the children who have the matching pieces. If there are one or two children who don't make a three, let older children help a younger group.

Once they have their cards, get them to put them together and talk about what they see. Who can see the mother of the baby? What is the name of the mother? Mary. Who knows what her husband is called and can you find him on your card? We all know the name of the baby; let us say it together: 'Jesus.'

Now some cards might not have had any of the Holy Family, only three men travelling. Do some cards show something in the sky? A star. If there is a star in the sky, what time of day is it? It is night. The men are using a star to guide them to where they want to go: the star is leading them and they are following. They followed the star for a long time and travelled many miles. How did they travel? Are there any cards with camels on them? The wise men travelled from the east and came to Jerusalem because they were looking for a king. The wise men went to the palace of King Herod and asked him about a king. But Herod was not pleased because he was the king and he did not want there to be another one unless it was one of his own sons. Herod did not know where this king should be born. But there were some people who did and they told Herod and the wise men that the king would be born in – who knows? Let us all say it together: 'Bethlehem.' So the wise men had to get back on their camels and go to Bethlehem, which was not very far from Jerusalem.

When they came to Jesus they bowed down to him because they knew they had now seen the King. When they saw Jesus they knew he was the one God wanted them to see. Each of the wise men brought a special present for Jesus. Can you see any of these presents on your cards? Who can tell me one of the presents? (If possible, have some gold, incense and myrrh to show the children, or have three boxes – one gold, one silver and one white. Produce these as they are mentioned.)

Gold – what could you make with gold to show that Jesus is a king? You could make a crown to put on his head. Gold is to show Jesus is our King.

Incense – what is this used for? It is usually burned and gives off a nice smell. It is burnt in some churches to show that God is with us. Incense tells us that in Jesus God is with us. Let us say together, 'God is with us.'

The third gift – myrrh – is a kind of medicine and it takes away pain. Jesus came into the world to free us from suffering and pain and so that we should enjoy living with him. Jesus is our Saviour. Let us say together, ' Jesus is our Saviour.'

Prayer

Jesus, you are our God and King.
You are always with us.
You bring us love and joy.
You are our Saviour.
Amen.

Song

Guide us, guide us little star,
we have travelled very far.
We have seen your lovely light
as we journey through the night.
Now we come to Christ our King
and our love to him we bring

Let the leader sing a line (to the tune of 'Twinkle, twinkle, little star') and then let the children echo it. Have a star on a pole for one of the older ones to carry and lead the children round the room while they sing.

LAMPS

Aim

To encourage the children to tell the story of the wise men.

Teaching

Use a set of crib figures, including a star and the wise men, if possible. Alternatively, you can use cut-out figures from Christmas cards. Get various children to pick up a figure until all the figures are gone. A new group of children could do this after it has been done once.

Who has the figure of the baby? Can you tell me who this baby is? Do you remember who came to see the baby? The shepherds came to see Jesus because the angels told them he is the Saviour. Can anyone tell me what it means to be the Saviour?

Now, who has the baby's mother? Can you tell me her name? Yes, she is called Mary. Can you remember where her baby was born? He was born in a stable, because there was no room at the inn.

Who has Mary's husband? Do you know his name? Yes, it is Joseph and he is a carpenter. What sort work does a carpenter do?

Now, who has the star? Why do you think there is a star here? It is to guide people in the darkness. The star is to show them the way. How many people were to follow this star? Let the three wise men follow the star. (Get the star to go round the room with three children following – the rest might like to follow behind them.)

Now let us look at the presents the wise men brought to Jesus. Can anyone find them on their card? Who knows what they are? What do you think these strange presents mean? (If possible, try and have some gold, incense and myrrh to show the children.)

Why do you think a wise man gave gold to Jesus?

Gold is a sign of power and wealth, and it is a good gift for a king.

Incense (at this stage it would be good to burn a little incense – an incense stick would do) is used by people who want to pray to God. Incense smoke rises upwards, as do our prayers. Incense says God is near. Why do you think one of the wise men offered the gift of incense? This gift tells us Jesus is the Son of God.

Myrrh is used like a painkiller. If you are in pain, what are you given to take the pain away? Myrrh is used to take away pain. Why do you think a wise man gave this gift to Jesus? Myrrh was given as a gift to show that Jesus would suffer pain for us. Do you know when he did this? Jesus would also bring us freedom from many troubles and sorrow.

Activity

Have a golden crown, a stick of incense, a small white box for myrrh. Make sure the children know what each is. Then play 'pass the parcels'. When the music stops, the one with gold puts the crown on their head and stands up tall; the one with the incense puts his or her hands together in prayer; the one with the myrrh pretends to cry in pain. Let the music start again and continue as before.

Prayer

Lord Jesus, we thank you
for the wise men and their gifts.
We love you as our King, our God
and our Saviour.
Amen.

Song

The Virgin Mary had a baby boy

TORCHES

Aim

To understand that God calls us to seek him, as he called the wise men.

Teaching

The story of the three wise men begins in their own homes and their own land. They were clever men and rich men, but each of them felt they needed something more in their lives. God was quietly calling them to seek him and find him. Being wise, each realised they would not be happy until they had offered themselves to God and until they knew that God loved them. This made each of the wise men seekers. They were seekers after the truth and seekers of God. This is what brought the three of them together: they would share the journey as seekers after God. I am sure the three of them knew God was near and calling them, but they also felt he was going to show them his love in special way. They also believed he had sent a star to guide them.

The problem of being guided by a star is that you have to travel in the dark; you have to travel at night. People must have thought the wise men very foolish because they slept by day and travelled by night. It was dangerous to do this, but they risked danger. It would have been easy to be put off, but they kept on their journey. They made a mistake by going to King Herod, but even their mistake did not stop them. They received guidance from the people who read the Holy Scriptures and this helped them on their road.

When they arrived at last, they each offered a special gift that expressed something about themselves and about Jesus. What were those gifts?

Gold is wonderful. It is good to have a lot of gold or money, but it cannot buy you life or health, it cannot buy you happiness or peace. In our lives we need more than success or gold. To be truly happy we need to know our God and his love. Like this wise man, we need to seek God, knowing that he wants us to come to him.

Incense is a strange gift. Do you know when you usually use incense? It is used in worship. It is used as a sign of the presence of God and that we come before him. The second wise man saw God in Jesus. God will show himself to us through and in Jesus if we seek the presence of Jesus and come to worship him.

Myrrh is a sad sort of gift but sometimes very welcome. Myrrh is to relieve pain, to ease suffering. Perhaps the third wise man knew a lot of suffering and pain in his life; maybe there were great sorrows that bothered him. He would offer his sorrows to Jesus and know that in Jesus there is joy and peace. He believed that Jesus would deliver us all from darkness and death. Perhaps also he was aware that, like all people, Jesus would not be free from suffering and pain in this world.

God calls each of us to know him and his joy. God wants us to know his Son and the love and peace that come through him. He calls us out of the darkness of life to seek him. As we come before Jesus today let us offer ourselves to him.

(You might like to explore what gift the young people would offer to Jesus as an expression of their life.)

Activity

Discuss what gifts modern wise people may bring to Christ and why.

Prayer

What can I give him,
poor as I am?
If I were a shepherd
I would bring a lamb;
if I were a wise man
I would do my part,
yet what can I give him:
give my heart.
Christina Rossetti (1830–1894)

Song

The wise may bring their learning

First Sunday of Epiphany
The Baptism of Christ

Aim

To show how Jesus is revealed as God's Son through his baptism.

Preparation

The Advent candles are lit every week until Candlemas. This week have the Candles near the font. Decorate around the font with flowers and symbols of the Trinity.

Opening activity

Have four people with lighted tapers in different corners of the church. Let a fifth person with a lighted taper stand in the centre of the church. (This is more effective if the lights are left off until the candles are lit.)

Let the fifth person begin by saying, 'We rejoice in the light', and asking the congregation to respond, 'of Father, Son and Holy Spirit' each time he/she says it, and to say it loudly. The people with tapers come down the church in turn and light a single candle. After each one lights a candle, the fifth person says, 'We rejoice in the light', and the congregation respond.

1   I light this candle in thanksgiving
for God the Creator of light.
(lights candle)
5   We rejoice in the light
All **of Father Son and Holy Spirit.**

2   I light this candle in thanksgiving
for Jesus Christ, the Light of the World.
(lights candle)
5   We rejoice in the light
All **of Father Son and Holy Spirit.**

3   I light this candle in thanksgiving
for the Holy Spirit who enlightens us all.
(lights candle)
5   We rejoice in the light
All **of Father Son and Holy Spirit.**

4   I light this candle in thanksgiving
for Mary and for all faithful people.
(lights candle)
5   We rejoice in the light
All **of Father Son and Holy Spirit.**

5   I light this candle in thanksgiving
for Jesus dispelling the darkness.
(lights candle)
5   We rejoice in the light
All **of Father Son and Holy Spirit.**

Let a child bring forward a ewer of water to be poured into the font. The congregation can then renew their baptismal vows and perhaps be sprinkled with the water.

This is a good day to use the Peruvian Gloria.

Opening prayer

Praise to you, Father, Son and Holy Spirit,
for in you we live and move and have our being.
Help us to realise that at all times we dwell in you
and you are with us and in us.
Amen.

Opening song

Songs of thankfulness and praise

Readings

Isaiah 42:1-9
Psalm 29
Acts 10:34-43
Matthew 3:13-17

Thought for the day

Throughout the Epiphany season we see how Jesus is revealed to the world. He is visited by the wise men from the East who represent the nations of the world. In today's reading we see at his baptism how the Father gives his sign of approval and how the Spirit comes upon Jesus. Next week we will see how John the Baptist points out Jesus as the Chosen One of God. The following week reveals how Jesus fulfils the prophecies of Isaiah. With Epiphany 4 we will see how the miracle of the water made into wine reveals the power and compassion of Jesus.

John the Baptist's message had four great themes: repentance, confession with baptism, judgement and righteousness. These themes have been the rallying calls of many a revival. But we know there is something more needed. Matthew is a master of understatement when he simply says, 'Jesus came from Galilee to John at the Jordan to be baptised by him' (3:13). After all that John had done, all his preaching, all his preparing the way, Jesus came. Without this, all religion is stern and forbidding, but when Jesus comes and is accepted in a church and in a life, everything changes. There is a new light and a new hope. When Jesus comes on the scene, whatever it is, it is changed.

Sadly there are many good people who are leading righteous and respectable lives who are living BC – before Christ. Even some churches seem to live as if they belonged to the Old Testament rather than the New. They need to allow Jesus into their lives and experience the joy and freedom he brings. This can be well illustrated by Saul and his harsh life before the Damascus Road and his liberated life after it.

Do not live in the BC era. Know the Lord comes and he comes to you. Meet Jesus each day in your prayers and in your daily living. Welcome him into your life.

The revelation of who Jesus is comes as Jesus emerges out of the water. The Spirit comes upon him as a sign that he is now ready for his mission. The voice of

God is heard saying, 'This is my Son, the Beloved, with whom I am well pleased.' This tells us from whom he comes and whom he reveals to us. It is worth noting that the Baptism of Jesus is one of the few times the Bible actually mentions Father, Son and Holy Spirit.

Question time

Is your life lived in the BC era without awareness or reference to Christ?

In the Baptism of Jesus we see the working of the Trinity. Do you let the Father, Son and Holy Spirit into your life?

Illustration

What a difference Jesus makes. *The Miracle of the River Kwai* by Ernest Gordon tells the story of prisoners of war building a bridge. They were overworked, often starving, exhausted and ill. The need to survive made them put themselves first and fail to see each other's needs. Then two men, Dusty and Dinty, began helping others. They put themselves out to care for and respect others. A new spirit began to spread through the camp until the place was transformed, as were its inhabitants. When questioned about their actions, Dusty read from 1 John 4:21: 'The commandment we have from him is this: those who love God must love their brothers and sisters also.' Dusty was a Methodist and Dinty a Roman Catholic, and both were full of the Presence. The lives of the men had been hell. Then 'Jesus came' and what a difference that made.

Intercessions

Blessed are you, Lord our God,
for you are our Maker, our Saviour
and our Guide.
Keep us mindful of your presence,
your love and your power,
that we may learn to rejoice in you and your love.
Blessed are you, Father, Son and Holy Spirit.

We remember before you all who are being prepared for baptism or confirmation.
We ask your blessing upon all who seek to reveal your love and your peace.
We pray for all preachers of the word
and all who reach out in mission.
We pray that the Church may share
in your mission to the world.
Lord, help us all to reveal your glory in our midst.

Silence

Holy Trinity,
hear us and help us.

We ask your blessing upon all who are beginning new ventures and new work.
We pray for all who are being asked to extend themselves through learning and the development of their abilities.
We remember those who are entering
into new relationships
and we ask your blessing
upon those who are newly married.

Silence

Holy Trinity,
hear us and help us.

We thank you for our homes and our loved ones.
We ask your blessing
upon those who are moving to a new home
or who are moving away from their families.
We remember all who are homeless,
all who live in poverty or hunger.
We pray to you for all who work
to relieve the needs and suffering of others.

Silence

Holy Trinity,
hear us and help us.

We remember before you
all who feel confused or troubled at this time.
We pray for all who are distressed
and those who are not able to cope
with what is happening around them.
May they know your presence and your power.
We ask your blessing upon all who are ill
at home or in hospital,
especially those who are fearful or lonely.

Silence

Holy Trinity,
hear us and help us.

We rejoice in the gift of life and life eternal.
We ask your blessing
upon our loved ones and friends
who have departed from us.
We remember especially today
those who have enriched our lives
by their example and goodness.
May they rejoice in glory
and may we share with them in your eternal kingdom.

Silence

Merciful Father,
**accept these prayers
for the sake of your Son,
our Saviour Jesus Christ.
Amen.**

Memory verse

A voice from heaven said, 'This is my Son, the Beloved, with whom I am well pleased.'
Matthew 3:17

Suggested music

When Jesus came to Jordan
Hail to the Lord's anointed
Christ, when for us you were baptised

CANDLES

Aim

To help the children to be aware of the revelation of Jesus through his baptism.

Teaching

Talk about the font in church and what it is for. Ask if any of the children have been to a baptism (Christening). If possible, show pictures of a baptism and of a river baptism. Do they know what happened? What was put on the person's head? Do they know how many times? Have a bowl of water and a doll to illustrate this. Three drops of water: one to tell us that God the Father loves us, one to tell us that Jesus loves us, and one to tell us that the Spirit of God loves us. Say after me: God loves me; Jesus loves me; the Spirit of God loves me.

See if the children know if they have been baptised. Tell them to ask when they go home.

One day, when Jesus was ready to begin his special work, he went down to the river Jordan, where John the Baptist was baptising people. Jesus watched as each person went into the water. They walked into the river to where John was standing and then John dipped them under the water. When they came out they looked very happy and knew that God loved them. Then it was Jesus' turn. He walked right into the river until it flowed round him and past him. The water came right up to his middle (Get someone to come out and pretend to stand in the water and show how it was up above his waist.) Now John the Baptist put his hands gently on the back of the head of Jesus and dipped him right under the water. (Demonstrate with the child.) Jesus had now been baptised.

When Jesus came out of the water two wonderful things happened. People saw the Holy Spirit of God come upon him. They said it came down like a bird, like a dove. They didn't *see* the other thing, but they *heard* a voice from heaven. It was the voice of God and it said, 'You are my Son, I love you and I am pleased with you.' Jesus was now ready to do the work he came to do.

Activity

Play 'In the river, on the bank'. Let the children stand in a circle and when you say, 'In the river', they have to jump forward. You can repeat it. If you say, 'On the bank', they have to jump backwards. If you say, 'On the river' or 'In the bank', they are not to move at all. Anyone who does the wrong thing is out.

Prayer

Father, you love me.
Jesus, you love me.
Spirit, you love me.
Help me to love you
and to know you are with me.
Amen.

Song

Father, we adore you

LAMPS

Aim

To know about the baptism of Jesus.

Teaching

Who knows what is near the door in a lot of churches? It is where babies are first brought to church. The font is made to hold water, so that when someone is being baptised they can have three drops of water put on them. Does anyone know why it's three drops? One drop for God the Father, one for the Son, and one for the Holy Spirit. In some parts of the world people are still baptised in a river and then they are usually dipped under the water three times. Do any of you know when you were baptised? Ask when you go home. Some of you may have been baptised in this church and in its font. Today I want to tell you about when Jesus was baptised.

Down in the river Jordan stood John the Baptist. They called him 'the Baptist' because he dipped all the people that came to him in the river. One by one people came to be made clean and to know that God cared for them. Some days there were lots of people waiting to be baptised.

The day Jesus came to the river Jordan there were a lot of people being baptised by John, and others were watching. When it was Jesus' turn he stepped into the river until it was above his middle. He could feel the water moving against his body and his toes on the bottom of the river. John gently took hold of Jesus' head and made him bend forward until his whole body was under the water for a moment. When Jesus came up, the water was pouring off his head but he looked very happy. Then Jesus walked back out of the river. As he did this, some people said they saw the Holy Spirit of God come upon Jesus, just like a dove descending. The people didn't *see* the next thing that happened, but they *heard* it. They heard the voice of God from heaven saying to Jesus, 'You are my Son, the one I love; in you I am well pleased.' From his baptism people began to see that Jesus was very special. From this time Jesus was ready to do the work that he came especially to do.

Activity

Play a pointing game. The first person says, 'The Father is God', and points to someone. They have to reply, 'Jesus is God', and point to someone else. The third person has to reply, 'The Spirit is God.' Now provide a new statement such as 'The Father is love' or 'The Father is good' or 'The Father is strong', getting them to repeat the same about the Son and Spirit. End with the statement 'The Father is with us', repeating for Son and Spirit.

Prayer

Father God, I love you
and I know you love me.
Jesus, Son of God, I love you
and I know you love me.
Spirit of God, I love you
and I know you love me.
May I do the work that you want me to do always.
Amen.

Song

Father, we love you

TORCHES

Aim

To show how the baptism of Jesus reveals him as the Son of God.

Teaching

Begin by looking at a map of the Holy Land and see if they can find the river Jordan. They might like to refer to the map they created on the first Sunday after Christmas. Let them also find Nazareth on the map.

Today's teaching is about Jesus when he left home to begin his ministry. We hear that Jesus went to the river Jordan. Does anyone know why? It was because John the Baptist was there. John had been called by God to prepare the way for Jesus. Now Jesus was coming to him to be baptised. John was baptising many people in the river to wash away their sins and give them a new start in life. Jesus came to John because he was ready for a new start in life: he was ready to begin his ministry and his mission.

Like the others around him, Jesus waded into the river to where John the Baptist was. When it was his turn, Jesus bowed his head and let John plunge his whole body under the water. For a moment Jesus was totally submerged. Then, as he came out of the water and walked on to the bank of the river, two wonderful things happened. The Spirit of God was seen to come upon Jesus; people said it was like a dove descending.

Then there was the sound of a voice from heaven, the voice of God, saying to Jesus, 'You are my Son, the one I love; in you I am well pleased.' Here at his baptism are revealed the power of the Spirit and the authority of God at work in Jesus. Jesus is seen as the Son of God and commissioned to do the work of God in the power of the Spirit.

Another revelation is made at the baptism: we see the Trinity revealed as Father, Son and Holy Spirit.

Activity

Encourage the group to talk about being baptised in the name of the Father, the Son and the Holy Spirit. Help them to understand that we are immersed in God: in him we live and move and have our being. How can we help each other to be aware of this reality? There is an opportunity on the worksheet to explore symbols of the Trinity.

Prayer

Father, our Creator and giver of life,
we come to you in love.
We worship and adore you.
Jesus Christ, our Saviour and rescuer from death,
we come to you in love.
We worship and adore you.
Holy Spirit, our Guide and giver of power,
we come to you in love.
We worship and adore you.
Blessing and praise to you, Holy Three,
glorious Trinity.
Amen.

Song

Father welcomes all his children

Second Sunday of Epiphany

Aim

To show the importance of bringing people to Jesus.

Preparation

The Advent candles are lit every week until Candlemas. This week, have five parents with children (or five pairs of adults) ready to bring lights from each corner of the church and from the centre.

Opening activity

Have each pair in turn come from their place. Let one give the lit taper to the other, saying, 'I give you this light to show Jesus loves you.' Taking the light, the other lights one of the Advent candles and says, 'I light this light because Jesus loves me.'

When all five have lit the candles let the ten proclaim:

Jesus is the light of the world
He is with us and loves us.

Opening prayer

Lord God,
to live without you is to walk in the darkness;
to live in awareness of you is to live in the light.
Help us to know and to reveal your love and light
through Jesus Christ our Lord.
Amen.

Opening song

Jesus our Lord, our King and our God

Readings

Isaiah 49:1-7
Psalm 40:1-11
1 Corinthians 1:1-9
John 1:29-42

Thought for the day

We continue with the Epiphany theme of the revealing of Jesus.

The day after the baptism of Jesus, John the Baptist saw Jesus coming towards him and declared, 'Here is the Lamb of God who takes away the sin of the world!' John witnesses to Jesus and to what happened at his baptism. John points people away from following him to follow Jesus. He wants people to know that following Jesus is of greater importance because Jesus is the Son of God.

The next day John was with two of his followers, and as he watched Jesus walk by he exclaimed, 'Look, here is the Lamb of God.' To describe Jesus in this way was to build on the promises of the Scriptures. Going right back to Genesis 22:8, Abraham said, 'God will provide a lamb for a burnt-offering, my son.' In doing this and in staying Abraham's hand, God rescued Isaac from death. The Passover Lamb (Exodus 12:1-13) celebrates the gaining of freedom from slavery and from death. (Compare John's statement in John 3:16.) In Isaiah, the Suffering Servant, whom the Christian Church sees as an image of Jesus, is described as 'a lamb led to the slaughter' (Isaiah 53:7).

The effect of the Baptist's words was for two of his followers to leave him and follow Jesus. As ever with seekers, they are met by the one they seek. Jesus turns to meet them. St Augustine said that we cannot even begin to seek God unless he has already found us. When we seek God, we do not go to one who hides from us but to one who has always been seeking us and comes to meet us.

Jesus asks, 'What are you looking for?' This is a good question to ask all of us: is it knowledge, security, meaning, a purpose, peace, or is it a relationship with the living God? When the disciples ask, 'Where are you staying?' Jesus invites them, 'Come and see.' The only real way to truly learn of Jesus is to abide in his presence, to stay with him. Faith is not about believing in facts; it is having a living relationship with Jesus. As an interesting aside, we are told it was about four o'clock in the afternoon. Could it be that the writer of the Gospel remembered this well and that this disciple was John who would witness to Jesus through the Gospel and, in this way, point people to Jesus?

The other disciple was Andrew. The first thing Andrew did after meeting Jesus was to go and tell his brother, 'We have found the Messiah' – that is, the Christ, the Anointed One. Andrew brought Simon to Jesus. Later he would bring the boy with five barley loaves to Jesus. Later still he would bring a group of Greeks to Jesus. Andrew is seen as the first missionary in bringing someone to Jesus. What greater service can you do than to bring someone to Jesus?

Question time

Do you spend enough time abiding in the presence of Jesus? How could you improve this?

When did you last bring someone to Jesus?

Illustration

It is often proclaimed that the Church is suffering from a crisis in the West. There is a shortage of priests, of ministers. Allied to this is a shortage of money. But more money or more clergy will not cure the crisis. The Church needs a dose of Andrews! It needs people who will abide with Christ and then bring others to Christ. The Church is not short of people and it could grow like it did of old if we would learn to abide with Christ and seek to bring others to him.

The Church grew from twelve disciples who were with Jesus and who wanted others to know him. We must learn to bring others to the One we know and love. Just think how quickly the Church would grow if we were all committed to bringing someone else to know Jesus.

Intercessions

Blessed are you, Lord our God,
for you have called us to know you
and to abide with you.
You have called us to love you and to tell of you.
Blessed are you, Father, Son and Holy Spirit,
for you have called us into life and life eternal.
Blessed be God for ever.

Father, we ask your blessing upon the Church,
that it may grow in love for you,
that it may grow in holiness,
that it may grow in size.
We remember before you
all who reach out in mission
to tell of your love and your saving power.
We pray for preachers of the word
and teachers of the faith,
and we ask that we may all share
in bringing others to you.

Silence

Lord, we pray to you:
you are our health and salvation.

Lord God,
we pray for all who are being exploited by others.
We remember the poor and the homeless
and we ask your blessing
upon all who care for refugees and deprived peoples.
We pray for all who lack any moral or spiritual guidance
and who are being led astray by people around them.

Silence

Lord, we pray to you:
you are our health and salvation.

We give thanks for those who taught us the faith
and who set us an example by their lives.
We ask your blessing upon our home,
our loved ones and all who have cared for us.
We pray for all who suffer from neglect, violence
or a lack of love.

Silence

Lord, we pray to you:
you are our health and salvation.

God, in you is our peace and our hope.
We remember in your presence
all who are ill or suffering.
We pray especially for any who feel confused by life
and who are not able to cope.
We pray for all who are caught up in drug abuse or vice.

Silence

Lord, we pray to you:
you are our health and salvation.

We give thanks for your redeeming love
and for the gift of life eternal.
We pray for all our loved ones departed
and commend them, this world and ourselves
to your unfailing love.

Silence

Merciful Father,
**accept these prayers
for the sake of your Son,
our Saviour Jesus Christ.
Amen.**

Memory verse

Here is the Lamb of God who takes way the sin of the
world!
John 1:29

Suggested music

Will you come and follow me
Jesus calls us
We have a Gospel to proclaim

CANDLES

Aim

To show how Andrew and his friend followed Jesus.

Teaching

Andrew was a fisherman. He worked on the Sea of
Galilee in a boat with his brother Simon. Because it is
easier to catch fish at night when the fish cannot see the
boat, Andrew and Simon worked at night. This meant
that during the daytime Andrew could do other things
if he was not sleeping. He went with a friend to listen to
John the Baptist. Can you remember what John the Baptist
did? He took people into the river Jordan to wash away
their troubles. Andrew and his friend found John good
to be with and they liked to hear what he was telling them.
They thought they would like to follow John the Baptist
and help him. John liked having people who listened to
him and followed him, but he wanted them to know
and follow Jesus. John told people Jesus is the Son of God.

One day Andrew and his friend were with John the
Baptist when Jesus was walking past. John pointed to
Jesus and told them that Jesus was the special One sent
from God. When Andrew and his friend heard John say
this, they decided to follow Jesus.

Wherever Jesus walked, Andrew and his friend
followed. After a while Jesus asked them, 'What are
you looking for?' They were not sure what to say, so
they asked him, 'Teacher, where are you staying?' Jesus
could see they wanted to be with him and learn from
him so he said, 'Come and see.' They went with Jesus
and stayed with Jesus all that day. When they listened
to Jesus it was wonderful. They wanted to learn more
and to be with him more. When the time came for them
to go home, Andrew went and found his brother Simon
and told him all that had happened. He told him about
Jesus and said to him, 'We have found the Christ'.
Andrew was so excited and he wanted Simon to share
in meeting this wonderful person, so Andrew brought
Simon to Jesus. It was a wonderful thing to do. Andrew
actually brought his brother to Jesus. When he came to
Jesus, Jesus looked at Simon and said, 'You are Simon,
son of John. You are to have a new name. You are to be
called Peter.' Simon had a new name, the name he

would keep as a follower of Jesus. He was so glad that his brother Andrew had brought him to Jesus and now he would be called Peter. Let us say the names of the two brothers who came to Jesus: 'Andrew and Peter.'

Activity

Play 'follow the leader'. The game is simply for the children to follow the leader wherever she/he goes and to do what she/he does. There is a picture of Andrew on the activity sheet to colour in.

Prayer

Jesus, help us to follow you
and to do what you would like us to do.
Let us learn of you and love you always.
Amen.

Song

Jesus is my friend

LAMPS

Aim

To show Andrew as a disciple and a missionary.

Teaching

Each part of Britain has a patron saint.

Who is the saint for England? George.
Who is the saint for Scotland? Andrew.
Who is the saint for Wales? David.
Who is the saint for Ireland? Patrick.

Today we are going to learn about Andrew and how he was one of the first disciples of Jesus and the first missionary. Andrew is also the patron saint of Russia.

Andrew was a fisherman, but he was also a seeker of God. He wanted to know more about God and to give his life to God. Andrew and a friend went to learn from John the Baptist. (Get the group to talk about the Baptist and the baptism of Jesus.) While they were listening to him, John suddenly stopped and pointed to Jesus and said, 'Look, there is the Lamb of God.' John also called Jesus the 'Son of God'. John wanted them to turn to Jesus and to follow him. Andrew and his friend wanted to learn more about Jesus, so they followed him. After they had gone a little way, Jesus knew they were following and asked, 'What are you looking for?' They said to Jesus, 'Teacher, where are you staying?' So Jesus invited them to come with him and see. Andrew and his friend stayed with Jesus all that day and learnt from him. They both found Jesus to be someone very special and were sure they would come back to him.

Andrew went straight to find his brother, Simon. He could not keep the good news to himself. He wanted to tell someone about Jesus. He told Simon, 'We have found the Christ.' Simon could see how excited Andrew was, so he went with him. Andrew brought him to Jesus. Jesus looked at these two men and knew they

would make good disciples. He looked at Simon and said, 'You are Simon, son of John. You are to be called Peter.' Simon was amazed that Jesus knew him but he liked his new name, for it meant 'rock'. From now on he would be called Peter and be strong for Jesus. Andrew was pleased that he had brought his brother to Jesus. Andrew was not only one of the first disciples of Jesus but also the first missionary who told the Good News that Jesus is the Christ.

Activity

Have two teams and ask them to bring certain things to the leader: a sock, a jumper, a penny. The team that brings the most things first is the winner. On the activity sheet there is an opportunity to see what Andrew brought to Jesus.

Prayer

Jesus, I thank you
for those who brought me to know and love you.
You are wonderful.
Let me learn to bring others to you.
Amen.

Song

Jesus, you are my King

TORCHES

Aim

To show the importance of bringing others to Jesus.

Teaching

For Jesus to be able to tell the Good News to all people he would need a team. John the Baptist came to prepare people for the coming of Jesus. John wanted to point people in the right direction and get them to turn to Jesus. One day, when two of his followers were with him, he pointed to Jesus and said, 'Look, there is the Lamb of God.' His followers had already heard John call Jesus 'the Son of God', so the two decided they wanted to follow Jesus. They wanted to be his followers and his disciples. It was Andrew and his friend who decided to follow Jesus, so they went after him. After they had travelled for a while Jesus stopped and turned to Andrew and his friend and asked, 'What are you looking for?' They asked Jesus, 'Teacher, where are you staying?' Jesus invited them to come with him and see. Andrew and his friend stayed with Jesus all day. They listened to him and enjoyed being with him. They were both sure that Jesus was special, the One they had all been waiting for.

Andrew was very excited and he rushed home to tell his brother, 'We have seen the Christ.' He could not keep this good news to himself – he had to tell someone. Good news is to be shared. In doing this he became the first of a large team who would tell others of Jesus.

Andrew is thought of as one of the first disciples and the first missionary because he brought Simon to Jesus. Jesus gave Simon a new name; he called him Peter, the first to have a Christian name! Thanks to Andrew, Peter also became part of the team of disciples and missionaries. They stayed with Jesus, learned about Jesus and then told others about Jesus.

Activity

On the sheet they can see how Andrew brought others to Jesus and also how we can be part of the team that stays with Jesus and tells of Jesus.

Prayer

Lord Jesus, may we know you
and, in knowing you, love you,
and, in loving you, proclaim you,
that it may be known we believe in you
and that you are with us always.
Amen.

Song

Lord Jesus, once you spoke to men

Third Sunday of Epiphany

Aim

To encourage people to listen to the call of God and to respond.

Preparation

The Advent candles are lit every week until Candlemas. Have five people bring lights from each corner of the church and from the centre. You may also like to have pictures of various people fulfilling their vocation – including fishermen.

Opening activity

The five light the candles in turn saying:

1   Jesus is the Light of the World. I give myself to him.
2   Jesus is Lord. I give myself to him.
3   Jesus is our Saviour. I give myself to him.
4   Jesus gave himself for us. I give myself to him.
5   Jesus is the Son of God. I give myself to him.
All   Jesus calls us to work with him.
      We give our lives to him.

Opening prayer

Jesus Christ, Light of the World,
you reveal yourself to your disciples.
Open our ears to your call
and help us to be faithful
and serve you all our days.
Amen.

Opening song

Give thanks with a grateful heart

Readings

Isaiah 9:1-4
Psalm 27:1, 5-13
1 Corinthians 1:10-18
Matthew 4:12-23

Thought for the day

We continue with Jesus being revealed as the Christ. Perhaps the arrest and imprisonment of John acted as a catalyst in making Jesus take up his ministry. Jesus leaves Nazareth. He leaves his home and goes to live in Capernaum. His life of ministry and his work of salvation now truly begin. This area of Galilee is the most northerly district of Palestine. It was not a large area, only 50 miles north to south and 25 miles east to west. But because it was the most fertile area of Palestine, it was densely populated. Josephus records that there were 204 communities with populations of over 15,000 people. Jesus began his mission where there were the most people likely to hear him. Surrounded by Gentile nations, it was an area open to new ideas and used to change. This would be an area open to the teaching and ministry of Jesus.

Matthew tells us that Jesus began to 'proclaim': the word he uses is that of a herald's proclamation. The herald speaks with a certainty of his message. Preachers cannot tell us anything with certainty if they have doubts themselves. The herald speaks with authority because he speaks on behalf of the king, from a source beyond himself. In this case, Jesus speaks the word of God. True preaching is concerning the word of God and not our own opinions or ideas. The message is: Repent, turn around, turn to God. If you are not looking the right way, you cannot go the right way. Seek God. If you but know it, God's kingdom is near – it is because you look in the wrong direction that you do not see it or enter it.

Jesus now calls his first disciples. It is worth noting in Matthew that the initiative comes from Jesus. This is so often true: God/Jesus calls but so often we stall. He calls Simon Peter and Andrew as they are casting a net into the Sea of Galilee, saying, 'Follow me.' Immediately they leave their nets and follow him. They do not say, 'Wait until we have finished', or 'Wait until we have sold this fish'; they leave all and follow him. If we do not respond to the call immediately, we are less likely to respond later – though Jesus calls and calls. In the same way, he calls James and John who are in a boat with their father mending their nets. Immediately they leave the boat and their father and follow him. The two sets of brothers give up their security and their homes to follow the Master.

So the ministry of Jesus begins. Jesus travels throughout Galilee, teaching in synagogues, proclaiming the Good News and healing people.

Question time

God calls all but many stall. Jesus seeks us to be part of his team, but do we follow him?

Do we see ourselves as active in the ministry of Christ?

Illustration

There are two stories of Socrates and his calling of disciples. Xenophon met Socrates on the road and the teacher barred his path with a stick. Socrates asked Xenophon simple questions about where certain things were made. Then he asked, 'Do you know where men are made good and virtuous?' 'No, I do not,' answered the young man. Socrates then said, 'Follow me and learn.'

On another occasion a man called Aeschines came to Socrates and said, 'I am a poor man, I have nothing else to offer but myself.' Socrates replied, 'Do you not see that you are giving me the most precious thing of all?'

It is in giving ourselves to God that we truly give.

Intercessions

Blessed are you, Lord our God,
for you give us life,
you give us love,
you give us yourself.
Lord, may we learn to give our life, our love,
ourselves to you,

for it is in such giving
that we open our lives to you.
Blessed are you, Father, Son and Holy Spirit.

We give you thanks, O Lord,
for all who have heard your call
and served you faithfully.
We give thanks
for those who have shared their faith with us.
We ask your blessing upon all who seek to witness
to your abiding presence and your love.
We pray for all who are seeking to fulfil their calling in life.
We pray for schools, colleges and universities.
We remember especially today
all who are being prepared for baptism,
confirmation or ordination.

Silence

Lord, hear us
and help us to serve you.

We give thanks for all who provide us with our daily food.
We ask your blessing upon all who are involved
in growing or supplying our food.
We remember before you
all who are being used as cheap labour
and we pray for fair trade and justice.
May we all use the resources of the world
with care and respect.

Silence

Lord, hear us
and help us to serve you.

We give thanks for our homes and our loved ones,
for all who have enriched us
by their love and generosity.
We ask your blessing upon all who are struggling
through debt, poverty or homelessness.
We pray for all who feel used, abused or unloved.

Silence

Lord, hear us
and help us to serve you.

We ask your blessing
upon all who are finding life difficult
through illness or oppression.
We pray for all who feel their abilities
are being wasted or thwarted
through illness or circumstance.
May we know
that in whatever circumstance we find ourselves
God still loves us and calls us to love him.

Silence

Lord, hear us
and help us to serve you.

We rejoice that we are called to life eternal.
We remember friends and loved ones
who are departed from us.
May we all share in your abiding love
and the fullness of life eternal.

Silence

Merciful Father,
**accept these prayers
for the sake of your Son,
our Saviour Jesus Christ.
Amen.**

Memory verse

And he said to them, 'Follow me and I will make you
fish for people.'
Matthew 4:19

Suggested music

Follow me
Guide me, O thou great Redeemer
God is our strength from days of old

CANDLES

Aim

To show how Jesus called the fishermen.

Teaching

When Jesus started his work he had a lot to do. He
would need help to tell people of God and his love. So
Jesus looked for people who would help him and work
with him.

Early one morning Jesus was walking by the seaside.
He saw two brothers standing in the water and throwing
their nets out into the shallow water. What do you think
they were doing? They were trying to catch fish. Jesus
watched them for a while and saw how they did not
give up. If they did not catch fish at first, they tried and
tried again. Jesus saw that they were strong men and
not afraid to work.

Now, if you remember last week, there was a fisherman and his friend who followed Jesus. Do you remember
the fisherman's name? He was called Andrew and he
had a brother. What was his brother's name? He was
called Simon, but what did Jesus call him? He called
him Peter. Jesus recognised these men and he realised
they would be good men to help him in his work.
Instead of catching fish, they could help him to bring
people to God. If you remember, Andrew had already
brought Peter to God. Jesus called to the fishermen and
said, 'Follow me, and I will make you fish for people.'

This was a special moment. Would Andrew and Peter
leave their nets and their boats and follow Jesus? The
two men thought it was wonderful and immediately
they left their things and followed Jesus.

Jesus was happy to have two such strong followers.
But Jesus needed more helpers if he was going to do all
the work he wanted to do. As they walked a little
further along the beach, Jesus saw three men in a boat:
they were James and John and their father Zebedee.
They were all fishermen and getting their nets ready to
go out and catch fish. Jesus may have recognised at
least one of them as the friend who had come with
Andrew. Jesus called the young men and immediately
James and John left the boat, their nets and their father,
and followed Jesus. Now Jesus had four men to help

him in his work. Who can tell me their names? Andrew, Peter, James and John. Let us say their names together. They would learn from Jesus and work for Jesus. They would be his disciples. Let us say what the fishermen were: 'Disciples of Jesus.'

Activity

Play a version of musical statues. The children run around. When the music stops, they must stop until the leader says, 'Follow me.' Now they follow the leader as the music plays and copy what the leader does. Then the music stops and so the game continues.

Prayer

God, we thank you
for Andrew, Peter, James and John
and that they followed Jesus.
May we also follow Jesus
and do what he wants us to do.
Amen.

Song

Fisherman Peter on the sea

LAMPS

Aim

To show how the fishermen responded to Jesus immediately.

Teaching

Begin by revising last week's story. John the Baptist had two disciples who followed Jesus and stayed with Jesus. Who were they? We know one was Andrew. The other was his friend and it is thought it might have been John. Who did Andrew bring to Jesus? His brother who had been called Simon. What did Jesus call him? Peter.

When Jesus began to do the work that he came to do, he needed some helpers. He needed friends, disciples to be part of his team. There was a lot to do and Jesus could not do it all alone. Already John the Baptist had prepared a way for him and now Jesus needed people who could work with him.

One day Jesus was walking by the Sea of Galilee. He saw two fishermen throwing a net into the sea to catch fish. Jesus knew that it took skill and patience to catch fish. He watched and noticed how strong these men were. Suddenly he realised he had seen them before. These were just the kind of men who could be part of his team. They were not afraid to work and they did not give up easily. Jesus called to them, 'Follow me and I will make you fish for people.' Andrew and Peter may not have been quite sure what Jesus meant but it would be wonderful to follow him and to work for him. They left their nets on the beach and immediately followed Jesus. They were the first two of his team.

Going a little further down the beach, Jesus saw two more young men James and John working with their father. They were getting nets ready for the next time they would be going out in their boat. Jesus realised how the fishermen often faced storms and were brave on the sea. He knew they would make good members of his team. Jesus called to them, 'Follow me.'

Immediately the two young men left their father and the boat, to follow Jesus.

Now Jesus had four men as part of his team. They would be disciples and they would become apostles, which means those who are sent out. First they would have to spend time with Jesus, to learn from him and to be with him. Then he would send them out as part of his team. Let us say the names of the four: Andrew, Peter, James and John. How many more did Jesus call? He had twelve special disciples. But Jesus calls each of us to work with him and for him. He calls us to know him and to love him, then to tell other people about him.

Activity

Play 'Simon says'. The players must do what Simon/Susan says if he/she starts with the words, 'Simon/Susan says'. But if an order is given without the 'Simon/Susan says' and anyone follows it, they are out. This is a game about listening carefully and doing what we are told.

Prayer

Lord Jesus, as the fishermen listened to you
and followed you,
help us to follow you each day
and be part of your team.
Let us show our love for you
and do what you would like us to do.
Amen.

Song

Step by step, on and on

TORCHES

Aim

To show that Jesus seeks us to be members of his team.

Teaching

Revise last week's story. Note how Andrew and a friend followed Jesus, stayed with him and listened to him. Show how Andrew is the first to bring someone else to Jesus. Make sure they know that this was Simon, whom Jesus called Peter.

At the very start of his work Jesus knew he needed others to help him. He needed a team. He needed people who would tell of him and bring others to him. Jesus was walking by the Sea of Galilee when he saw Andrew and his brother Simon Peter throwing a casting net into the sea. Fishing like this takes a lot of patience and often a lot of strength. Here were two who could join the team. Jesus called to them, saying, 'Follow me and I will make you fish for people.' Immediately the two fishermen stopped the work they were doing to follow Jesus and to work for him: two members for his team.

Soon Jesus saw two more young fishermen. They were working with their father, getting nets ready. Perhaps one of them, John, was the friend who went with Andrew to see Jesus. Jesus called these two men and they also left everything and followed Jesus. Now the team had grown to four. How many were in the original team? Twelve.

Jesus actually calls us all to be part of his team. He calls us to get to know him, to love him, and to tell others of him. Obviously we cannot really tell of him until we get to know him.

TEAM is a good word. It can stand for:

To
Each
A
Ministry

Every member of a Team has a part to play. If we do not do our share, the team is weakened.

Every one of us is called to share in the ministry and mission of Jesus.

Think upon these words and see if you are playing your part in the team:

Christ has no hands but your hands
to do his work today.
Christ has no feet but your feet
to speed folk on his way.
Christ has no lips but your lips
to tell folk why he died.
Christ has no love but your love
to win folk to his side.

Activity

They can explore the idea of being part of the Jesus Team on the worksheet.

Prayer

Jesus, we thank you that you have called us
to know you and to enjoy your presence.
Give us the wisdom and the courage
to proclaim the Good News
and tell of your saving power.
Amen.

Song

A stranger walked along the shore

(Sing at least verse one with the chorus.)

Fourth Sunday of Epiphany

Aim

To show God meets our lack of resources with his abundant power and generosity.

Preparation

The Advent candles are lit every week until Candlemas. This week have five people ready to bring lights from each corner of the church and from the centre. The congregation says the response.

Opening activity

1   I come in weakness to the power of God.
    (lights candle)

All **The Lord is my light and my salvation.**

2   I come in darkness to the light of God.
    (lights candle)

All **The Lord is my light and my salvation.**

3   I come in fear to the peace of God.
    (lights candle)

All **The Lord is my light and my salvation.**

4   I come with troubles to the healing of God.
    (lights candle)

All **The Lord is my light and my salvation.**

5   I come in need to the love of God.
    (lights candle)

All **The Lord is my light and my salvation.**

Opening prayer

Lord, you know our needs before we ask
and are always more ready to give
than we desire or deserve.
We come to you for healing renewal
and for the fullness of life eternal.
Amen.

Opening song

Joy to the world!

Readings

1 Kings 17:8-16
Psalm 36:5-10
1 Corinthians 1:18-31
John 2:1-11

Thought for the day

The first miracle recorded by St John is seen as the beginning of the saving works of Jesus, and as a revelation of his glory. The setting for all of this is a country wedding in Galilee.

Jesus' mother prompts the action in this event when she says to Jesus, 'They have no wine.' The celebrations were not meant to end but suddenly the resources ran low. How often this is true of life. We would like to go on but we run out of energy, run out of supplies, and cannot continue. We all experience that as humans our resources are limited. We rarely heed the words of Isaiah when he says, 'They that wait upon the Lord shall renew their strength.' We need to learn that all our powers and resources are gifts from God.

Mary says to the servants, 'Do whatever he tells you.' Throughout the rest of the story they do just that. This is to be seen as a major theme in the story: it is through obedience to Jesus that wonderful things can happen. We are to put our trust in his words.

The stone jars each held about 25 gallons. So the miracle created about 150 gallons of wine – or 682 litres or over 1000 bottles – and that is after they had drunk all the wine that the steward had provided. I know a lot of people who would follow anyone who could do this! But we miss the point if we concentrate on the amount of drink; this is a sign of the superabundant grace of God and how he renews and refreshes us beyond what we can hope for. Our resources are limited but God's are not.

When we scrape the bottom of the barrel or feel totally drained, it is often because we have gone on in our own strength and abilities and have not come to God or sought to do his will. In John's Gospel Jesus says, 'I came that they may have life and have it abundantly' (John 10:10).

We are told that the sign of the water made into wine revealed his glory and the disciples believed in him.

Question time

Do you spend time each day with God to be refreshed and restored in his presence?

Illustration

Charles was a relatively new Christian. He had a good home, a job and a loving family. Not long before it had been all endangered through Charles drinking too often. He said he could not help it. Whenever his resources were low, whenever he felt tired or exhausted, he turned to the bottle. His family were suffering; they did not have enough income to survive on after Charles's drinking. A friend introduced him to Alcoholics Anonymous and also to his local church. The second had an amazing effect. Charles discovered the power of the love and presence of God. Now when resources were low or when he felt exhausted, he turned to rest in God and to be renewed by him. At a Bible study he expressed difficulty with the miracle of changing water into wine. 'But,' he said, 'I know Jesus can change lives. He can turn wine into food on the table and to clothes on our backs.' Jesus has the power to renew and refresh each of us in our lives.

Intercessions

Blessed are you, Lord our God.
You give us life
and you continually renew and refresh us
with your presence and your love.

You are the strength of the weak
and the light to all who walk in darkness.
Blessed are you, Father, Son and Holy Spirit.

Lord God, may we reveal your joy and power
in our daily living.
We ask your blessing upon the Church,
that it may be obedient to your word
and seek to bring others to know your glory.
We ask you to bless all preachers
and teachers of the faith,
that they may have the power
to reveal you and your love to others.

Silence

God of love and joy,
hear us and refresh us.

Lord, our Creator,
we pray that we may use the world aright.
Let us not squander or waste the resources
you have given us
but use them to your glory and the benefit of all.
We pray for all who monitor our planet and its resources.
We ask your blessing
upon scientists and politicians
and all who work to care for and improve our world.
We remember today
all who suffer from deprivation, from poverty,
from hunger or from homelessness.

Silence

God of love and joy,
hear us and refresh us.

We give thanks for our own home
and all you have given us.
We pray for those who provide us with our food
and our daily needs.
We ask your blessing upon all who work
to provide good homes and shelter
to the poor of our world.

Silence

God of love and joy,
hear us and refresh us.

We remember today all who are running out of resources.
We pray for the fearful and the anxious,
the sad and the lonely.
We ask your blessing upon all who are ill
and cannot cope on their own.
We remember all who, through ageing or illness,
need regular care and attention.
We pray for all carers
and all who work in the health service.

Silence

God of love and joy,
hear us and refresh us.

We rejoice in life
and that you give us life eternal.
Renewing and restoring God,
we remember in your presence
our loved ones departed

and ask that they may rejoice in your presence
and in the fullness of life eternal.
We commend them, the world and ourselves
to your unfailing love.

Silence

Merciful Father,
**accept these prayers
for the sake of your Son,
our Saviour Jesus Christ.
Amen.**

Memory verse
Rejoice in the Lord, always.
Philippians 4:4

Suggested music
Jesus the Lord said, 'I am the Bread'
Rejoice in the Lord always
May the grace of Christ our Saviour

CANDLES

Aim
To show how Jesus wants us all to be happy.

Teaching
Show pictures of a wedding and, if possible, a wedding banquet. Ask the children if they know what is happening? Have any of them been to a wedding? See if any have been bridesmaids or pageboys.

What does everyone do after a wedding? (Show the banquet picture.) They have a party to show that they are happy. Often there are lots of people and there has to be a lot of food. It takes a lot to get ready for a party. (Encourage the children to talk about the planning of a party.) Everyone gets a piece of the special wedding cake, so it has to be a big cake.

Once, a long time ago, there was a wedding and everyone was enjoying it; they were all very happy. Then suddenly something sad happened: they ran out of wine. They had made this wine especially for the party and now there was none left. There was nowhere they could buy any wine, so it seemed that the party was over. Maybe more people had come to the party than they expected, or maybe they did not have a lot of wine to start with. This made the bride and groom very sad. (Get everyone to show a sad face.) Soon everyone would be sad because the party would end.

Mary heard about this. Can you guess which Mary this is? It is the mother of Jesus. Mary went to Jesus and told him, 'They have no wine.' Then she told the servants, 'Do whatever he tells you.'

Jesus looked at the bride and groom and saw sad faces. (Get everyone to show a sad face.) He was sorry for them and wanted to help them.

Jesus knew that near the door were six water pots that were nearly empty. He told the servants to fill them with water. This took some time because there was no tap and they had to get their water from a well. Let us count as the water pots are filled. Show an empty water pot (no. 1) from the activity sheet, then turn it over and show it blue and full now; repeat this five more times – 2, 3, 4, 5, 6. Six great big pots full of water. Jesus now asked them to take some water out of a pot and take it to the person in charge of the wedding. They did this and it was discovered that the water had turned into wine. Soon the bride and bridegroom knew there was a lot of wine and they were very happy. (Ask the children to show a happy face.) Jesus did not want them to be sad; he wanted them to be happy.

Jesus wants us all to be happy. He wants us to enjoy life and not be sad. Jesus would like to help us to be happy and enjoy being with him.

Activity

Sit in a circle with one person in the centre. Everyone has to look sad. They have to show sad faces. Tell them the middle person is to be like Jesus: he/she comes to make them happy. When he/she points at someone or touches them, instead of being sad, they have to smile and be glad. There is an opportunity on the worksheet to make a water pot and sad and happy faces.

Prayer

Jesus, we thank you for loving us
and wanting us to be happy people.
May we not make anyone sad
but help to make them happy.
Amen.

Song

Give me joy in my heart

(Learn at least verse 1 and the chorus.)

LAMPS

Aim

To show that Jesus comes to bring joy into our lives.

Teaching

Let us pretend we are preparing for a party: what would we need? What would you like to drink? A long time ago when people had a party they had to prepare all the food near to the time. But they had to prepare the drink a long time beforehand because they would probably make it themselves. Because they did not have the drinks we have, and water was unsafe to drink, they drank wine made from grapes and water.

Jesus went to a party with his mother and his disciples. In fact, it was a wedding party. Have any of you ever been to a wedding? Everything had been prepared and everyone was enjoying the party. There would be singing and dancing and people would be happy. Suddenly the wine began to run out. This made the bride and the groom very sad, because if there was no wine the party would soon come to an end. Perhaps they didn't have

much to start with, or maybe they did not expect as many people to come to their party. But now the wine was running out and they were sad.

Someone told Mary, 'They have no wine.' Mary told Jesus. Then she told the servants to do whatever Jesus asked them to do. Jesus looked at the great big water pots at the door and saw they were nearly empty. All the water had been used for washing. Jesus told the servants to fill the water pots. This took some time. Why? Where did they get the water?

Once they filled the six big water pots, Jesus asked them to give some to the person in charge of the feast. They took some in a cup to him. When the person in charge tasted it he was amazed. This was better wine than they had been drinking. He smiled and soon the bride and groom were smiling and then everyone was happy once more.

This was the first miracle that Jesus did and it was at a place called Cana in Galilee. It showed how Jesus had power to do wonderful things and how Jesus cared about people and their needs. Miracles are signs, or pointers, for us to notice that Jesus is God.

Activity

Get the children to play charades about full and empty, acting out, eating, drinking, filling a glass with water, filling a car with petrol. Get someone to show they are hungry. When someone guesses correctly, let them act out the next charade.

Now give them parts to act out the wedding of Cana. Have a bride and groom, servants, someone in charge, Mary and Jesus. Get the servants to draw water from a well and get everyone to show how they turn from being sad to being happy.

Prayer

Jesus, you are always ready to help us
and if we do what you ask,
you do wonderful things through us.
You are generous and give us of your goodness.
May we give our love to you each day.
Amen.

Song

Life for the poor was hard and tough

TORCHES

Aim

To show how Jesus can transform our lives.

Teaching

All the resources of the earth are limited. Though many resources are in great abundance, they are still limited. Fossil fuels are limited and we have only so much coal, oil and gas. Many things will run out unless they are renewed as we use them. If we cut down trees, we need also to grow trees; if we fish our oceans, we need to give the fish time to reproduce and to restock. As people, we have limited supplies of energy and if we overwork or do too much, we can run out of energy or strength. God has given to this earth in a generous way but he asks us to care for and respect the earth, each other and ourselves.

The story of the wedding at Cana is about how Jesus responds when his mother tells him about the resources running low at the wedding feast. (Get the group to read the story from John 2:1-11 and then to act it out.) Note how Mary tells the servants to obey Jesus in all that he says. Tell them about the water pots and how they would need filling from the well. Get the governor of the feast to show that this is the best wine.

Explore how Jesus restores other failing powers. Jesus heals the sick, cures the deaf and blind, makes the lame walk. Jesus restores life where it is fading away. Jesus gives hope and courage to us all.

This is the Good News: Jesus meets our limited resources with his abundance of power. He comes to our weakness with his strength, to our emptiness with the fullness of life. When we are in darkness, he comes as our light. When we are weary, worn or sad, he offers us

his strength and the power to renew us. The story of the wedding at Cana is not just about Jesus providing wine, but also about giving us a glimpse of the Lord as giver of life and life eternal.

Activity

On the worksheet they can explore further the idea of limited resources and how Jesus is able to meet our needs.

Prayer

Lord, we come in darkness to your light.
We come in weakness to your strength.
We come in sadness to your joy.
We come in trouble to your peace.
We come in weariness to be renewed.
Lord, change us and we shall be changed.
Amen.

Song

I've got that joy, joy, joy

The Presentation of Christ

To be used on the Sunday nearest 2 February, if not on the day.

Aim

To let the light of Christ enter our hearts and our lives.

Preparation

This is the last Sunday for the candle-lighting that began in Advent. If you do not have Advent candles, have a large candle to represent the light of Christ; last year's Easter Candle is ideal. Have a candle for each person or at least for each family to light during the service.

Opening activity

(This can be done after the Gospel, if preferred.)

Once everyone is in church put out all lights and sit in the darkness for a short time. If it is not dark, ask everyone to close their eyes. Tell them the darkness represents our world and our lives without Christ. In the darkness ask all the people to quietly invite Jesus, the Light of the World, into their lives. Quietly light the four Advent candles. As the central candle is lit, say, 'The Lord is my light and my salvation.' During the singing of a hymn let everyone come out with a candle (plus drip protector!) and receive a light from the 'Christ candle'. ('The Lord is my light' from Margaret Rizza's CD *Fire of Love* could be played.)

Once all have their candles lit, let them all hold their candles and proclaim, 'The Lord is my light and my salvation.'

Opening prayer

(To be said at the lighting of the 'Christ candle')

Come, Lord of Light:
lighten our darkness.
Lighten our lives with your love;
lighten our homes with your presence;
lighten this world with your peace.
Come, Lord of Light, come among us.
Amen.

Opening song

Christ, whose glory fills the skies

Readings

Malachi 3:1-5
Psalm 24:(1-6) 7-10
Hebrews 2:14-18
Luke 2:22-40

Thought for the day

What Mary and Joseph were doing was what all Jewish parents were required to do. By Jewish Law, Mary could not enter a holy place or touch anything holy until she had given thanks to God for her first-born and offered the accustomed sacrifice. Mary came to be purified and with Joseph to offer two doves. If they were well-off they would have been expected to offer more. The offering of two doves was known as the 'offering of the poor'. This event was being performed every day by couples and their child, and there is nothing unusual about it. When Simeon comes on the scene, however, we enter into something quite different.

Simeon looked for the 'comforting of Israel'. He had been promised he would not die until he had seen the Lord's Anointed One – that is, the Christ. Simeon takes the baby Jesus in his arms and blesses God. He knows he has the Christ in his arms, the one who is to be the glory of Israel. But there is more. The Jews thought upon the Christ as *their* Saviour; Simeon describes Christ as 'a light for the revelation to the Gentiles'. Jesus would not be the exclusive property of one nation – he came to be the Saviour of the world. Because of this even as non-Jews, we can all say, 'The Lord is my light and my salvation.'

Jesus is revealed as the Light of the World. Later as a grown man and fulfilling his ministry, Jesus will say of himself, 'I am the light of the world. Whoever follows me will never walk in darkness' (John 8:12). To refuse to accept Jesus as our Light is to walk in the darkness of the world. To accept Jesus as our Light is to have our lives filled with his light. Today the Church lights many candles to witness to this fact. The Feast of the Purification is often better known as Candlemas for this reason. Candlemas marks the end of the Epiphany season of the revealing of Christ, and now we turn towards Lent and the suffering of Christ. The Advent candles, if they are still in church, are now taken out. The next time a large candle is brought into church it is the Easter Candle. But today we rejoice in the Good News that the light of Christ is not exclusive – it is for all, it is for you. We can all say, 'The Lord is my light and my salvation.'

Question time

Can you remember the various revelations of Jesus that you have heard of in the Epiphany season?

Do you invite the light of Christ's presence to come into your life?

Illustration

The night was pitch black as the car drove along a country lane. There were no lights for miles. Suddenly the driver was aware that a rear tyre had a puncture. He would have to stop and mend it. Once out of the car he could see very little. The lights of the car did not give light where he wanted it and he had no torch. This would be a very slow job and he was not sure he could do it in the dark. It was worrying because he was a long way from any houses and it was very late at night. Fortunately, within a few minutes he saw a light coming along the road in front of him. It was a milkman on his early rounds. Though he was busy, the milkman stopped and provided light and what a difference that made. The man no longer worked in darkness but in the light.

Intercessions

Blessed are you, Lord God.
To you be all praise and glory for ever and ever,
for you are our light and our salvation.
You created light out of darkness
and have brought your light to our lives
through the birth of your Son, our Lord Jesus Christ.
Blessed are you, Father, Son and Holy Spirit,
one God for ever and ever.

As our Lord was brought into the Temple,
we ask your blessing upon the Church
throughout the world.
May we share in the mission of Christ
and show that his light is for all peoples and nations.
We remember all who are being baptised or confirmed
and all who are seeking to dedicate their lives
in your service.
We pray for all your faithful people,
that they may be lights in the world.

Silence

Lord of light and life,
hear our prayer.

Lord, we pray for the time
when the kingdoms of this world
may become the kingdom of Christ our Lord.
We ask your blessing upon Elizabeth our queen
and upon all leaders and rulers of nations.
Lord, give wisdom to all who are in authority.
We pray for all who influence our minds
through the press and the media.

Silence

Lord of light and life,
hear our prayer.

As Joseph and Mary presented Jesus in the Temple,
we ask your blessing upon our young people,
that they may be taught the faith and learn to love you.
We remember before you our own homes and loved ones.
We pray for all schools, colleges and universities.

Silence

Lord of light and life,
hear our prayer.

We remember all who walk in darkness.
We pray for those who are fearful, anxious or depressed.

We ask your blessing upon the world poor,
the persecuted, the hungry, the refugees, the homeless,
and all whose lives are in danger.
We pray for all who are ill at home or in hospital.

Silence

Lord of light and life,
hear our prayer.

We rejoice in the fellowship of all your saints
and ask your blessing upon our loved ones and friends
who are departed from us.
May they rejoice in your light
and in the fullness of life eternal.

Silence

Merciful Father,
**accept these prayers
for the sake of your Son,
our Saviour Jesus Christ.
Amen.**

Memory verse

The Lord is my light and my salvation.
Psalm 27:1

Suggested music

Faithful vigil ended
Lord, the light of your love *(Shine, Jesus, shine)*
Colours of day
This little light of mine
Christ is the world's true light
The Lord is my light (from *Fire of Love* by Margaret Rizza)

CANDLES, LAMPS and TORCHES

There is no separate teaching for the children and young people as the service has actions for all. If the groups do go out, there are candle templates for them to colour in the Candle, Lamps and Torches books.

ORDINARY TIME
Proper 1

Sunday between 3 and 9 February inclusive
(if earlier than the Second Sunday before Lent)

Aim

To look at what it means to be the salt of the earth and the light of the world.

Preparation

Have photographs and examples of various lights in the entrance or around the church. You can have a candle, a paraffin lamp, a gaslight, a torch, an electric light, safety lamp and a lighthouse. (You may like to add various packets of salt.)

Opening activity

Have a strong light and a mirror. Show how the mirror can reflect the light and make it shine in dark areas of the church.

Opening prayer

Eternal Light, shine in our hearts;
eternal Goodness, deliver us from evil;
eternal Power, be our support;
eternal Wisdom, scatter the darkness of our ignorance:
eternal Pity, have mercy upon us;
that with all our hearts and mind and strength
we may seek your face
and be brought by your infinite mercy
to your holy presence;
through Jesus Christ our Lord.
Amen.
Alcuin (735–804)

Opening song

Awake, awake: fling off the night

Readings

Isaiah 58:1-9a (9b-12)
Psalm 112:1-9 (10)
1 Corinthians 2:1-12 (13-16)
Matthew 5:13-20

Thought for the day

Matthew seeks to show Jesus as a second Moses. The flight into Egypt echoes Moses' flight into the desert; the killing of the Holy Innocents echoes the infant Moses in danger from Pharaoh. Jesus tempted in the wilderness is like Moses in the wilderness. Moses went up Mount Sinai to convey the Law to the people; Jesus ascends a mountain to teach the people. Jesus says, 'Do not think I have come to abolish the law and the prophets; I have come not to abolish but to fulfil.'

Last week we rejoiced in the Lord as our light and salvation. This week we hear our Lord asking us to be the light of the world. So he is asking us to share in his light and ministry. Jesus asks us to be the salt of the earth and the light of the world. Notice how these qualities are to be for all; they are not restricted to the Jews or to members of the Church. The Gospel is all-inclusive.

Salt was a very precious commodity in the time of Jesus. Sometimes it was used to pay Roman soldiers – the word 'salary' comes from the salt used as wages. The Romans said that salt was the purest of all things because it was made from two pure things: the sun and the sea. The very purity of salt prevents corruption – it stops food going bad. The Christian is asked to be an example: to work to prevent evil and to stop society from going bad. As this can sound negative, we must remember that salt gives taste and zest to food, it brings out the flavour and stops things being insipid. We are called to reveal the joy of living, to show that life has flavour and to stop so much insipid living. A high calling, but it is ours in Christ.

'You are the light of the world.' In the ancient world to keep a light burning somewhere was of utmost importance. If your light went out, you had to go and borrow a light from someone else. All lights receive their light from somewhere. We receive our light from Jesus Christ. The light we give out is a reflected light, a light we have received from Jesus.

Light is to be seen not hidden. We cannot keep our faith a secret but must share it with others and so bring them to the One who is the Light of all. We are called to show the light in the way we live. We are witnesses to the true Light that is come into the world. There is so much darkness and so many dark places that can overcome us without the light of Christ. We are called to bring that light to the world.

Light is often there as a guide, to warn of danger, to lead people to where they ought to be. Those who have received Christ are asked to guide and lead others to him and to the Father of light. Jesus calls us, saying, 'Let your light shine before others, so that they may see your good works and give glory to your Father in heaven' (Matthew 5:16).

Question time

What do the qualities of salt and light suggest about how we should live as Christians?

Do we see that the Gospel is for the whole world, or are we too exclusive?

Illustration

A man bought a special gift for his wife. It was a musical box that played a tune when you opened it, but it was different because it also glowed in the dark. It was meant to be seen when the days were dark or dull. As it was a present, he kept the box hidden away and all wrapped up. At last he produced it one dark evening and his wife unwrapped it with great excitement. They turned the lights off, but then it could not be seen. It did not glow in the dark, and they were disappointed. Perhaps it was broken. They put the lights back on and discovered a label inside the box that said, 'If you want me to shine all night, keep me in the sun all day.'

There was nothing wrong with the box, and once they left it in the sunlight, it glowed in the dark.

In the same way if we are to be lights in the world, we must spend time each day absorbing the light of Christ.

Intercessions

Blessed are you, Lord God,
Giver of life and Creator of love.
We give you thanks and praise
for the light of each day
and for the light of the Gospel
as revealed in our Saviour Jesus Christ.
We rejoice in the life that you give us
and we delight in your presence.
Blessed are you, Father, Son and Holy Spirit.

As we give thanks for the light of Jesus Christ
we ask that this light may shine in our lives
and in the whole Church.
We ask your blessing on all who proclaim the Gospel
and who teach the word.
We pray for all who are seeking
to revive and promote faith in you and your love.
May the Church grow in love, in witness
and in number.

Silence

Lord God of light,
scatter the darkness from our world.

We ask your blessing upon rulers and leaders
who have difficult decisions to make
concerning the world
and who are often not sure which way to go.
We pray for all who work
to bring freedom and justice to all people,
those who seek to relieve the poor
and care for the oppressed.
We pray for those who feel
that they are working in the dark
and unable to find their way.

Silence

Lord God of light,
scatter the darkness from our world.

Lord, we ask that all darkness be dispersed
from our hearts and our communities.
May we help to bring your light and life
to our homes and to all our relationships.
We ask your blessing upon our families and friends
and upon all with whom we work or play.

Silence

Lord God of light,
scatter the darkness from our world.

We remember today all who walk in darkness
and in the shadow of fear or death.
We ask your blessing upon the fearful,
the anxious and the troubled.
We pray for all who are in the darkness
of doubt or despair.
We bring before you
friends and loved ones who are ill
or who are finding it hard to cope with life.

Silence

Lord God of light,
scatter the darkness from our world.

We give thanks for the fullness of eternal life.
We ask your blessing upon our loved ones
who have entered into the fullness of your kingdom
and all the faithful departed.
We pray for the day
when we may all see you more clearly
and walk without fear in your light.

Silence

Merciful Father,
accept these prayers
for the sake of your Son,
our Saviour Jesus Christ.
Amen.

Memory verse

Let your light shine before others, so that they may see your good works and give glory to your Father in heaven.
Matthew 5:16

Suggested music

The Spirit lives to set us free
Thou, whose almighty word
Lord, the light of your love *(Shine, Jesus, shine)*

CANDLES

Aim

To tell of the passing on of the light of Christ.

Teaching

Who can remember when we all had candles in church and shared the light with each other? (Get the children to talk about the Candlemas service.)

Today I want to tell you about the Church in the olden days before we had electric lights. As it got dark sometimes the only lights in the church were the two candles on the altar. (You can see if the children understand where these candles are. If this is too strange for them, tell them of a light in church that reminds us that Jesus is always with us.) From there someone took a light with a taper or another candle and then gave the people in the front rows a light to light their lamps or candles that they brought with them. They then passed the light on to the row behind until every family had a light. People shared their light with each other. After the service it was dark outside but now people had their lamps lit from church. They went with the light and took it to their own homes: they brought the light into their houses. Sometimes they shared their light with friends and sometimes they passed on the light to people they met on the road home. The light slowly spread and gave light to the whole area. (At this point you could have the activity.)

Jesus wants us to share the light of the Good News. Jesus wants us to hear about him and to tell others about him. He wants us to be like lights in the dark and show our friends and others that Jesus is the Light of the World. Jesus wants us to know him and to tell other people that he loves them too. In that way we will pass on and share the light. Can you think of a friend you can tell about Jesus?

Activity

Play a version of pass the parcel. Pass a candle around the group (unlit for safety). When the music stops, whoever has the candle has to cross the circle and give it to someone else. The music then starts again and so it continues. At the end take the candle and light it, and say, 'Thank you, Lord Jesus, for giving us your light.'

Prayer

Lord Jesus, Light of all the World,
let your light shine in our hearts
and in our homes,
and let us share your light with our friends.
Amen.

Song

Jesus bids us shine

LAMPS

Aim

To show what Jesus meant by asking us to be 'lights'.

Teaching

Talk about the Candlemas service and the passing on of the light if this took place last week.

Show pictures of various kinds of light and, if possible, bring some examples. Have candles, perhaps an oil lamp and a torch. It would be good to have a flashing warning light or a picture of a police car or ambulance with a light. A picture of a lighthouse is also a good illustration. Have a picture of the sun and the moon.

Talk about what light is used for. If there were no sun what would happen to us and to all the living things on the earth? We would die. We all need light and warmth to live. We cannot survive without light. The sun gives us light. So does the moon, but where does the moon get its light from? It is a reflected light. The moon can give us light because it gets it from the sun; it has no light of its own.

Light helps to show us where things are and it guides us. The light from a lighthouse shows where there are rocks and dangers. The lights on a runway guide the plane safely to the ground. Police car lights and ambulance lights are there as warnings. (You could also explore the use of traffic lights.)

Jesus is sometimes called the Light of the World. Jesus brings us life. He is our guide. And he keeps us from danger. Jesus is like the sun in the way he gives us light and life. He wants us to pass on the light he gives us. Just like the moon reflects the sunlight, Jesus wants us to reflect his light. But we cannot pass on the light if we have not received it. To share the light of Christ with others, we have to spend a portion of each day with Jesus. (Explore the ways we can do this.)

Activity

Get the group to stand in a large circle. Give one a bright torch and another a mirror. The torch has to shine towards the person with the mirror. At first the person keeps the mirror turned away. When it catches the light they have to shine the reflected light on another person's feet and keep it there. If the light rises above waist level, the person with the mirror is out. When this happens the mirror passes to the next person as does the light.

Prayer

Lord Jesus, help us to walk in your light
so that we may reflect your love
and so bring others to you
and to the brightness and life
that you offer to all.
Amen.

Song

This little light of mine

TORCHES

Aim

To explore what it means to be the salt of the earth.

Teaching

The Jews often thought of the Messiah, the Christ, as being for themselves only. Some churches are in danger of almost trying to claim Christ as their own possession. The Gospel is for *all* people at *all* times and in *all* places. When Jesus wants us to reflect his light he says he wants us to be the 'light of the world'. He also says we are to be the 'salt of the earth'. We are not to work for the benefit of our own community alone but reach out to others and so share in the mission of Christ. Let us look at what Jesus might mean when he calls us the salt of the earth.

Salt was a very precious commodity, so much so that sometimes the Roman soldiers were paid in salt. From the word 'salt' we get the word 'salary.' The Greeks called salt 'Theion', meaning 'Divine'. Can we see others and ourselves as precious in the sight of God and as sons and daughters of God?

Salt is used in many foods to give them taste and often to stop them going off and becoming bad. Salt gives zest to many foods and at the same time acts as a preservative. Many foods would be insipid without salt: there is salt in ham, cheese and bread, to mention a few. Most of us feel that crisps taste much better with some salt, as does a boiled egg.

Much of life is in danger of becoming dull and insipid. Christians are called to add zest and to bring the joy of Christ into daily living. Jesus called lively and adventurous people to follow him and be his disciples. These were the people called to show the love and the power of God. Can we be sure that we still do this today, and so attract people to God by the wonderful difference it makes knowing him and his love?

As a preservative, salt stops corruption in perishable goods such as cheese and ham and some fish. Can we not only show that we believe that we are not perishable goods (see John 3:16) but also help to create an atmosphere where people are not easily corrupted or led astray? There are so many things that can quickly corrupt our minds and spirits; if we are to be the 'salt of the earth', we must help to stop this rot. Can we be sure that we stand against evil and not just go with the flow?

If you dissolve salt in water, as when cooking, it seems to disappear but it is there, hidden, pervasive although not seen. Can we sometimes see that this is the way we are called to transform the society in which we live?

Activity

Have a tasting session. Give each a drink and see if they can say what has been added to the water. Leave one with only water, one with salt, one with orange juice, one with sugar, one with coffee, etc. Some are noticeable, such as orange or coffee, but others, although hidden, nonetheless have an influence on the drink.

Prayer

Lord Jesus, you have called us
to be the salt of the earth.
Help us to fight quietly against evil
and to encourage people to enjoy life.
Let us show we belong to you
and that you give us the gift of life eternal.
Amen.

Song

Brother, sister let me serve you

Proper 2

Sunday between 10 and 16 February inclusive
(if earlier than the Second Sunday before Lent)

Aim

To discover how Jesus wants us to show respect and reverence for each other as a reflection of our reverence for God.

Preparation

Have a large printout of the Ten Commandments and the Collect for Purity from the Communion Service in the entrance. Add to this news headlines of violence, war, drug abuse and breakdown in relationships.

Opening activity

Mini Drama

Voice 1   I am good: I don't smoke, I don't swear, I don't drink, I don't go chasing after women.
Voice 2   Neither do stones. What *do* you do?
Voice 1   I am good.
Voice 2   But what do you *do*? (*pause*) It is no use being good for nothing.

Opening prayer

O God, from whom to turn is to fall,
to whom to turn is to rise,
and in whom to stand is to abide for ever:
grant us in all our duties your help,
in all our perplexities your guidance,
in all our dangers your protection,
and in all our sorrows your peace;
through Jesus Christ our Lord.
St Augustine (354-430)

Opening song

Be thou my vision

Readings

Deuteronomy 30:15-20
or Ecclesiasticus 15:15-20
Psalm 119:1-8
1 Corinthians 3:1-9
Matthew 5:21-37

Thought for the day

Matthew continues to show Jesus as a Moses figure, so today we hear of Jesus and the Ten Commandments. Jesus does not seek to abolish the Commandments but rather to look at their deeper meaning. Jesus is not challenging the Law but rather extending it to show its implications. Jesus moves from the rules about behaviour to the root cause of that behaviour. This reminds us that our God sees into the heart and mind. Our God is the God 'to whom all hearts are open, all desires known and from whom no secrets are hidden'.

These words from the mountain deserve much attention and thought as they teach us about reverence for each other, for God and for ourselves. In the Jewish synagogue the scrolls of the Law were carried around the congregation at the beginning of each service so that all might show reverence for the Law. Jesus extends that reverence for all people, always. If our relationships with each other are broken or wrong, then it is very unlikely that we have a good relationship with God. There is no cheap grace. We need to look at our lives and our attitudes.

Verses 21 and 22 are concerned not only with murder but also with thinking about murder or harming someone. Evil thoughts towards anyone are forbidden. This involves not only the killing of the body but also what is now called 'character assassination'. The anger mentioned here is that which is deep-rooted and often nurtured. We are not to treat people as if they were fools or morons. Respect for all is required.

Verses 23 and 24 state that we cannot offer gifts to God if we have bad relationships with others. It is interesting to note how often we use the same attitude towards God as we do to others. If we are not willing to listen to others, it is not likely we will listen to God. The longer we pursue a certain stance against others the deeper the division becomes (25, 26).

Once again Jesus looks at where the trouble begins. Adultery begins with the eyes and the heart. We are easily led astray by our thoughts and our deeds – and we can blame no one but ourselves. To turn away from God's ways is the road to hell (27-30).

Broken relationships and loose relationships can show that we have little respect for each other. Those who have little respect for those around them are not likely to respect God (31, 32). The issues of divorce are too complex to be dealt with in a few sentences.

We have to have a reverence for the truth. There should be no need for oaths if our word can be trusted and, if it cannot, an oath is often the belittling of God or ourselves by our words. There is a danger of double standards in our dealings if we even suggest it takes an oath to makes us truthful (33-37).

Question time

How can we as a community show respect for the people around us?

Do we take what we think seriously enough to guide it towards what God would have us do?

Illustration

How we think affects all of our lives. It is not what we do but why we do it that has great effect. There is a lovely scene in *Peter Pan* by J. M. Barrie: the children have seen Peter fly and they wish to fly too. They try to fly from the floor and from the bed but fail. 'How do you do it?' John asks Peter. Peter answers, 'You just think wonderful thoughts and they lift you up in the air.'

Too often we do not give enough direction to what goes on in our thoughts.

Intercessions

Blessed are you, Lord our God,
for you have created us in your own image:
you have called us to reflect
your love and your forgiveness to all.
You give us power to share in your grace.
Blessed are you, Father, Son and Holy Spirit.

Lord, as you reveal your love to us,
help us to show that love towards all whom we meet.
We ask your blessing
upon all who seek to reveal your grace
and to walk in the way of your laws.
We remember before you
all who preach and teach of your love.
We ask your blessing
upon all who study the Scriptures
in groups or in schools.

Silence

Lord of life and love,
hear us and help us.

Lord, as you teach us to respect each other,
help us to respect the earth and all its creatures.
Give us a reverence towards all of your creation.
Guide all who care for the resources of our planet
and the environment in which we live.
We pray for areas that have been devastated
by war or greed.

Silence

Lord of life and love,
hear us and help us.

Lord, forgive our times of anger and hatred
and help us to live at peace with each other.
May our communities be places
where no one is belittled and no one oppressed.
We pray for our homes and our loved ones.

Silence

Lord of life and love,
hear us and help us.

Lord, we remember before you
all who are suffering through violence or abuse.
We pray especially for those
whose lives are marred by their past or present sins.
We remember also today all who are struggling
with pain or chronic illness
and all who can no longer cope with life on their own.

Silence

Lord of life and love,
hear us and help us.

We rejoice that nothing can separate us
from the love of God in Christ Jesus.
We ask your blessing
upon our friends and loved ones departed.
As we rejoice in the fellowship of all your saints,
we commend this world, all peoples and ourselves
to your unfailing love.

Silence

Merciful Father,
**accept these prayers
for the sake of your Son,
our Saviour Jesus Christ.
Amen.**

Memory verse

You shall love the Lord your God with all your heart,
and with all your soul, and with all your strength, and
with all your mind; and your neighbour as yourself.
Luke 10:27

Suggested music

Lord of our life, and God of our salvation
Let there be love
Brother, sister, let me serve you

CANDLES

Aim

To show there is need for rules.

Teaching

Show some signs and see how many the children can
recognise. You can hold up a hand to mean 'halt'. You
can then beckon the children forward by drawing your
hand towards yourself a few times. You can put your
finger to your lips to mean 'silence'. (Get them to do
each of these – you could develop it into a game.) See if
the children understand the sign for a 30-mile-an-hour
speed limit and the colours of traffic lights. Why do we
have rules like these? They are not only for our safety
but to make life easier for everyone. What would it be
like if no one kept the rules? It would make the world a
very dangerous place. When we go out somewhere, we
have to go with someone like our mother or father. We
put our hand in theirs or follow them closely.

Can you remember how Jesus asked the disciples to
follow him? He asked the fishermen disciples to follow
him. Do you remember their names? Peter, Andrew,
James and John. Jesus wants us to follow him by doing
what he wants us to do. Jesus wants us to be loving and
kind, not angry or naughty. Jesus wants us to care for
others and not to call anyone bad names or be nasty to
them. If we do not do these things, we make the world,
and sometimes our homes, a sad and dangerous place.
Let us learn to follow Jesus and try to do good things
for him.

Activity

Play 'traffic lights'. The children run around. If 'red' is
shouted, they must stop immediately. When 'green' is
shouted, they have to get moving. When 'amber' is
shouted, they must continue what they are doing: if
they are running, they must keep running; if they have
stopped, they must not move. Anyone who does the
wrong thing is out.

Prayer

Lord Jesus, help us to follow you,
to be kind and loving to each other.
Lord, let us love your world and all its creatures.
Amen.

Song

Follow Jesus, follow Jesus,
walk his way, walk his way,
loving one another, loving one another,
every day, every day.
Susan Sayers

(To the tune 'Frère Jacques')

LAMPS

Aim

To show how rules are made to help and guide us.

Teaching

If you were old enough to drive along a road, there would be many rules for you to keep. Can you tell me any of them? Speed limits, keep on the left, traffic lights, wear seat belts are just some of them. All of them are for your safety and to help you to cooperate with others who are on the road. They are not really restrictions but rather to help you travel in safety and with respect for others.

Imagine a game of football without any rules. It would not matter about size of teams or the pitch or the goal area. It would not matter if you picked the ball up or scored in either goalmouth. It would become chaotic and useless and there would be little real enjoyment. The rules are there to help the game and to show the players how to act.

If you want to play a musical instrument, there are quite a lot of rules to follow. You cannot just play any note or at any speed, and if you are playing with others, you have to keep in tune and time with them. All these rules are not to spoil what we do but to help us.

In the same way God gave Moses the Ten Commandments to help people to care for each other and to help them to live in peace with each other. Sometimes the Ten Commandments were made into just two that were to cover every thing. You can find them in St Luke: 'You shall love the Lord your God with all your heart, and with all your soul, and with all your strength, and with all your mind; and your neighbour as yourself' (10:27). What do you think is meant by 'neighbour'? It is not just the people who live next door; it is everyone. These two rules are there to help us to live: love God; love one another.

Jesus wants his followers to show the love of God in their lives. He wants us to live in peace with each other and to forgive one another. Jesus wants us to be kind and not cruel or nasty to others. These are rules to help us to live together and enjoy being with each other.

They are not to stop us doing things so much as to help us all enjoy life.

Activity

Play a game of obeying the leader such as 'Simon says'. This will encourage attentiveness and obedience. You can tell them that without the rules we could not play the game.

Prayer

Jesus, we want to follow you.
Help us always to walk in your way
and to do what you would like us to do.
May we enjoy living by your rules
that give us the freedom to live
in love and peace.
Amen.

Song

You can't stop rain from falling down

TORCHES

Aim

To show that the rules of God are about reverence for God, for each other and for ourselves.

Teaching

In the book of Exodus we are told how God gave Moses the Ten Commandments to show the people how he wanted them to live; to reverence God and each other. God wanted people to reflect the love that he has for us. The Commandments are about our relationship with God, with our parents and with each other. Although they are rules, they are there to help us live life to the full rather than restrict us. (Get the group to find Exodus 20:1-17 and have ten of them read a Commandment each.)

Rules are important. Imagine how dangerous it would be to drive if there were no rules for driving. Which rules are for our safety? Wearing seat belts, 30-mile-an-hour speed limits, 'Give way' signs, etc. The rules are for the benefit of us all. If people break the rules, they endanger themselves and others.

In any sport there are rules or the game would end in chaos and no one would know who won or when to start or finish.

Rules are not meant to be negative but positive, to help us get the most out of life. Jesus did not come to do away with the rules but to show us how far-reaching they are. We should learn to live by the spirit of the rule rather than the letter, and show reverence and respect for God and for all people at all times. Jesus shows that God wants us to live in fellowship with each other, forgiving each other and not making a fool of anyone. If we want to be at peace with God, we have to learn to be at peace with each other.

Activity

Get the group to find today's Gospel, Matthew 5:21-37, and to read out the rules Jesus gave. Can they see how Jesus is extending the Ten Commandments into all that we say and do?

Prayer

Lord Jesus, guide me into the way of peace.
I give my hands to work for you.
Let my feet always be on your path.
Let me speak your praises and do your will
this day and for ever.
Amen.

Song

A new commandment

Proper 3

Sunday between 17 and 23 February inclusive
(if earlier than the Second Sunday before Lent)

Aim

To show how our lives should reflect the love of God because we are made in his image.

Preparation

Have pictures of war, violence and crime in the entrance and alongside them some pictures of peace and love. Have a poster that says, 'Love your neighbour and hate your enemy.'
Have the 'hate your enemy' crossed out and in big letters 'love your enemies' in its place.

Opening activity

Mini drama

Voice 1   Wait until I get out of school, I will get her for that.
Voice 2   I say to you: love your enemies.
Voice 3   I hate them and all that they do.
Voice 2   I say to you: love your enemies.
Voice 4   I never forgive anyone who does me wrong.
Voice 2   I say to you: love your enemies.
Voice 5   If he hits me, I will hit him.
Voice 2   I say to you: love your enemies.

Opening prayer

Lord, you love us with an everlasting love.
You hate our sins but accept us as your beloved.
Help us to show that we are loved
by reflecting the love you give us
and sharing it with all,
through Jesus Christ our Lord.
Amen.

Opening song

Let there be peace on earth

Readings

Leviticus 19:1, 2, 9-18
Psalm 119:33-40
1 Corinthians 3:10, 11, 16-23
Matthew 5:38-48

Thought for the day

Once again we hear of words from the Sermon on the Mount. Again Jesus is concerned with our relationships with each other and again Jesus wants us to learn to love as God loves us.

Life under Roman rule was one of violence and the fear of violence. The Jews limited vengeance; Jesus abolished it! Today's teaching is to help people not to react badly and also to learn how to keep cool in heated situations. All of what Jesus suggests today has sometimes been called 'the uncomfortable words'.

The law of 'an eye for an eye, and a tooth for a tooth' (see Exodus 21:23-25) was meant to limit vengeance and to restrain violence. But sadly this often meant that violence was breeding violence, as it often does. We nearly always want to hit back as hard as we can. Jesus is talking about non-retaliation and about having a generous spirit. At the same time, he is saying we should choose our way of doing things and not be forced into wrong actions by the enemy. Do not let the opposition determine how you should act. Marcus Aurelius said, 'The only way to avenge yourself is not to become like the wrongdoer.' Sometime the easiest way of getting rid of an enemy is to make him/her a friend! A generous reaction can often have profound effect.

The advice of turning the other cheek, giving your cloak as well, going a second mile, giving without hope of return, forgiving enemies and praying for those who hate you, may sound impossible but Jesus fulfilled them all in the events leading up to his crucifixion (see Lamps teaching). It is by doing these things that we are seen as the image of God and in this way reflect his love. This is what we are called to do, and in doing this we are counted as 'perfect'.

In no way does this mean we allow ourselves to be a doormat and easily trodden on. It does not mean we allow evil to triumph or have free reign: Jesus never did this. It does mean we do not lower our standards and become like our enemies. Love in this case does not mean the sort of love we have for our nearest and dearest; rather it means we will not allow bitterness and violence to take over our lives. We will not descend to the rule of tit for tat. This is a matter of our will rather than our heart. It is taking a firm stand against evil without joining its methods.

Question time

Do we allow vengeance and resentment to destroy our peace?

How can we show love towards those who hate us, without becoming a fool or a doormat to be trodden on by all?

Illustration

One of the Great Masters was painting the Last Supper. The painting was coming along well until he had a violent row with a friend. He went home full of anger and painted on to the canvas his friend as Judas. This would serve to remind him of the row between them; it would keep his anger warm. Now there was little of the painting to finish, only the central character which was the Christ. But the vision would not come. Hand and eye did not work as they should and the canvas was left unfinished. The hatred of the Judas figure was destroying peace of mind and preventing creative work. The anger in the mind left no room for vision. After weeks the canvas was untouched. He met his former friend and now felt ashamed of what he had done. He expressed sorrow to his friend and they were reunited. The artist went home and changed Judas and then painted his friend in the Christ place. The friendship had been restored and so the canvas completed.

Intercessions

Blessed are you, Lord God, King of the Universe,
for you have created us in your own image.
You have called us to reflect your love
and your forgiveness to all.
Blessed are you, Father, Son and Holy Spirit.

We pray that your Church may reflect
your love and your mercy;
that we may live as those who share
your peace and your forgiveness;
that we may seek to live in harmony and peace
with each other;
that we will be known as Christians by our love.

Silence

Living and loving God,
hear us and help us.

We ask your blessing upon all who are suffering
from acts of violence and war at this time.
We remember all who are suffering
through the anger and hatred of others.
Lord, may they not be overcome with evil
but overcome evil with good.
We pray for the work of the United Nations
and all peacekeeping forces.

Silence

Living and loving God,
hear us and help us.

Lord, we thank you
for all who have shown us the way of love
through their own self-giving and generosity.
We ask your blessing upon our homes
and all who are dear to us.
We remember before you
all who are denied human love
or who feel rejected at this time.

Silence

Living and loving God,
hear us and help us.

We remember all whose lives are being destroyed
by hatred and resentment,
all who are caught up in violence and war.
We pray for all who are suffering in our world,
especially those who feel they are on their own
without help.
We ask your blessing upon all who work
for the relief of suffering and sorrow.

Silence

Living and loving God,
hear us and help us.

We rejoice in the fellowship of your saints
and all who have reflected your image here on earth.

We pray for friends and loved ones
who have enriched our lives
and are now departed from us.
Lord, we commit ourselves, all on earth and in heaven
to you and your unfailing love.

Silence

Merciful Father,
**accept these prayers
for the sake of your Son,
our Saviour Jesus Christ.
Amen.**

Memory verse

But I say to you, love your enemies and pray for those who persecute you.
Matthew 5:44

Suggested music

Beauty for brokenness
O Lord, all the world belongs to you
Make me a channel of your peace

CANDLES

Aim

To show how love can conquer fear and violence.

Teaching

Once, high in the hill country, there was a wild dog that frightened everyone. If anyone approached it, it would snarl and growl. People said it was a mad dog and should be driven out of the area. Whenever it was seen, people shouted at it and threw sticks or stones at it. This hurt the dog and only made it wilder still. Soon everyone was saying how savage and dangerous the dog was.

One day a man came to live on the edge of the village. He was a very kind man and tried to be friends with everyone. If anyone was unkind to him or nasty, he was never unkind or nasty in return. People soon realised he was a very good man.

Once when he was out walking, the man saw the wild dog and it snarled at him. It looked fierce and hungry. The man thought it looked very thin. So he hurried home and got some meat for the dog. Then he went to look for it. Suddenly he heard it growling. But it did not frighten him. He spoke quietly to it and then gently threw the meat towards it. The dog soon gobbled it up. Every day the man went to see the dog. For a while the dog was still frightened and snarled but it soon got used to this good man and knew he would not harm it. After a while the man was able to feed it by hand. Then later still he was able to encourage it to come to his house for food. Finally, when the weather got very cold and the snow fell, he managed to get the dog to come and stay in his house. The dog did not growl at him but it often wagged its tail to show it was happy.

The people of the village did not know what had happened. They thought the wild dog had disappeared. When they asked the man, he said he did not know of a wild dog but he had found a hungry and frightened dog and he had slowly made friends with it. Then he called the dog out to him. At first the dog and the people were frightened of each other but the good man told them not to be afraid and showed them that they should all be friends.

Jesus asks us to be friends, not to be greedy or selfish, and not to be unkind to anyone. Let us all hold hands in a circle and say together, 'Jesus wants us to be friends.'

Activity

On the activity sheet they can colour in the man and his dog and the words 'Jesus wants us to be friends'.

Make sure everyone knows the name of everyone else. Form a circle and number them all one or two. The 'ones' go around the circle clockwise and the 'twos' anticlockwise. They shake hands with everyone they meet and say the name of the other child and 'you are my friend'. Let them complete the circle twice.

Prayer

Lord God, you are friends with us all,
help us to be friends with each other.
Teach us to be kind and generous,
as you are to us.
Amen.

Song

There are hundreds of sparrows

LAMPS

Aim

To show that it is better not to meet violence with violence.

Teaching

A long time ago there were some men and women who went to live in the desert so that they could have a lot of time to talk to God. They lived on their own but they had a lot of visitors.

One of these men lived alone near a well. The well was very deep and from it he drew water every day. He used the water to put on his garden and to encourage things to grow. The garden produced enough food for him to eat and he had a palm tree that produced dates. Who knows what dates are? (Have some dates and allow the children to taste them. Use unstoned dates but warn the children about the stone in the middle.)

One day the man went to meet two visitors who were coming to stay with him and he brought them back to his home and his garden. But when they got there a lion was already there. The two visitors were really frightened and started to shake with fear. They were ready to pick up sticks and stones to throw at the

lion. The man was not afraid but he was very careful. He went towards the lion and at first it backed away. He tried to show the lion he meant it no harm. The man knew the lion was hungry. He reached up to the branch of his palm tree and took off some dates. At first he threw a few to the lion and then he encouraged the lion to come to him and take some from his hand. After this the lion went quietly away. But the lion and the man had become friends and it probably would come again. The good man told his visitors: 'It is easy to make enemies and to fight with each other or with the animals, but, if possible, Jesus wants us to be friends with each other.'

Jesus wants us to be friends with each other. He does not want us to be unkind to anyone or to fight with anyone. He wants us all to try and be friends.

Activity

Play 'sea creatures'. Everyone sits in a circle. Then go around the circle giving everyone a name: Cod, Crab, Lobster, Herring. When you call out a name, for example Crab, all the Crabs have to run around the circle in a clockwise direction. If you shout, 'The tide has turned', then they have to run in the opposite direction. If you shout, 'The tide is in', they must run back to their place. The last one back is out. Repeat for the other names.

Prayer

Lord God, you love us
and want us to be friends with you.
Help us to be friends with you
and with each other.
Let us be kind and generous
to all people and all creatures.
Amen.

Song

God is love: his the care

TORCHES

Aim

To show how Jesus fulfilled his own saying about 'love your enemies'.

Teaching

Jesus says some very hard things in today's Gospel. Let us begin with verse 39. Jesus says, 'Do not resist an evil-doer.' Do you think that means we should just let people walk over us and do what they like? Surely not, for Jesus spoke against injustice, he healed illness and cast out the moneychangers from the Temple. But Jesus knew that violence tends to breed violence and hatred breeds hatred. By reacting violently when people wrong us is putting us in danger of becoming like them. St Paul understood this well in his writing to the Romans. Read Romans 12:17-21, ending with 'Do not be overcome by evil but overcome evil with good.'

Jesus asked us to do some difficult things. Some people would say they were impossible, but Jesus did all of them in the events leading up to his crucifixion.

Jesus said, 'If anyone strikes you on the right cheek, turn the other also.' Jesus twice gave himself to those who struck him: a servant of the high priest and the soldiers (see Matthew 26:67 and 27:30).

Jesus said, 'If you are forced to go a mile, willingly go a second.' Jesus went to the Judgement Hall and then to Calvary (Matthew 27:2 and 27:31).

Jesus said, 'If someone takes your coat, give him your cloak also.' Jesus gave all his garments at Calvary and his life too (Matthew 27:35 and 27:51).

Jesus asked us to love our enemies and pray for those who persecute us. At the crucifixion Jesus prayed for his persecutors and for their forgiveness (Luke 23:34).

Jesus knew that violence easily breeds violence and often we seek to return hatred with hatred. The way of Christ is to overcome evil with love, for this is the way of God. As those who are made in God's image, Jesus wants us to show the same love and forgiveness.

This is not an easy way. It does not ask us to allow ourselves to be trodden on but it does ask us to keep ourselves free from hatred and the desire for vengeance.

We are not asked to like our persecutors: we could not do that. But we are asked not to join them in their actions. Our attitude to others matters greatly.

Activity

Discuss what the above says about the danger of being in a gang or of seeking revenge. Let the group explore how it demands great will-power, but it also shows who is in control.

Prayer

Lord God, you have created us out of love
and for your love.
You ask us to show your love to all,
as you love everyone.
Help us to learn to love those who are against us
even when we cannot possibly love their actions.
Amen.

Song

Peace, perfect peace

Second Sunday before Lent

Aim

To encourage a deeper trust in God.

Preparation

Put up advertisements for expensive clothes, exotic foods and holidays in the entrance to the church. Create two posters, one that says, 'Seek you first the kingdom of God', and another saying, 'Why worry?'

Opening activity

Mini drama

Voice 1   I have been invited to a party and do not know what to wear.

Voice 2   Why worry? You are invited because we like you.

Voice 3   I think my hair is going grey.

Voice 2   Why worry? We love you for who you are.

Voice 4   I cannot make my mind up what to have for dinner.

Voice 2   Why worry? You are lucky to have a choice. Why worry? God loves each of you and cares about you. Learn to trust in him.

Opening prayer

Lord, we come to you
for peace of mind and spirit.
Teach us to rest in you and in your love
and to work for the coming of your kingdom.
Amen.

Opening song

Seek ye first the kingdom of God

Readings

Genesis 1:1–2:3
Psalm 136 or Psalm 136:1-9, 23-26
Romans 8:18-25
Matthew 6:25-34

Thought for the day

Do not worry. By saying this Jesus did not mean us to be thoughtless or careless about our future or our world. Jesus was not suggesting a reckless approach to life. But he wants us to live in a trusting and loving relationship with God. Jesus wants us to avoid the anxiety, the angst, that is life sapping, and to enjoy life. Jesus gives us seven reasons not to worry.

Matthew 6:25 – God gives us life and our lives are more than eating and drinking and dressing up. Often we set our sights too low. We are also spiritual beings.

6:26 – Birds do not pile up stores for unknown futures. We are more than the things we amass. We are not measured by what we have but who we are. We are children of God and God loves us.

6:27 – Know that worry does not extend your life – in reality it can reduce it! Be rid of worry; exchange it for trust.

6:28-30 – The lilies of the field are the poppies and the scarlet anemones. Their time is brief but their beauty is worth noticing. Though they are here today and gone tomorrow, God cares for them. Realise how much more he cares for you. Spend time to learn of God's love towards his creation.

6:31, 32 – To centre our lives on things that perish only makes us feel perishable. Jesus calls the worry about food, drink and clothing the worries of the Gentiles – that is, of non-believers. Those who know God know that he will not let them perish (John 3:16). Worry about things is often due to a lack of a living relationship with God. This is reflected in a consumer society.

6:33 – Seek God's will for yourself and the world you live in and know that God loves you and is with you. It is only when we are in harmony with God that we can be in true harmony with the world around us.

6:34 – Learn to live one day at a time, to live in the present moment. So much worry is projected fears that never happen. Do not forever plan for tomorrow but live today – this day has enough troubles to occupy us.

If we can learn to live this way, our lives will be greatly enriched.

Question time

Do we see that too much worry shows a lack of faith in God and in our long-term future?

Worry is so wearying. Do we forfeit our peace by neglecting our relationship with God? (See Isaiah 26:3, 4.)

Illustration

Imagine two people going for a walk together. Both have a difficult task to perform later in the day: a task that will take all their energy and ability.

One man cannot get it out of his mind. He turns it over and over. He does not notice the sunshine or the birds singing. He fails to notice the beauty that is all around him. He may as well be indoors and working.

The other man relaxes for a while in the sunshine. He enjoys the heat of the sun and the sound of the birds. He is aware of the good things around him. He watches a butterfly with delight. This man is being refreshed and restored, ready for the work ahead.

One carried his worries and they wore him down. The other took time off and was refreshed for the job ahead. It is too easy to let worry and anxiety prevent us from enjoying the present moment and steal any energy we have.

Intercessions

Blessed are you, Lord God,
for you are our Creator and Redeemer;
you are our Strength and Shield.
As you love us with an everlasting love

and offer us life eternal,
help us to trust in you and in your grace.
Blessed are you, Father, Son and Holy Spirit.

Lord, help us to love the world
with the great love that you have for the world.
Guide your Church,
that it may keep its priorities
and that above all it may seek you and your will
in all that it does.
Lord, increase our faith in you,
that we may reveal your presence in our lives.
We ask your blessing
upon all who are suffering for their beliefs
or who are struggling with their faith.

Silence

Lord God, hear us:
help us to put our trust in you.

Father, we thank you for the beauty of the earth,
for flowers and birds.
We pray for all who seek to conserve and protect
the world in which we live.
We ask your blessing
upon all who deal with limited resources,
upon those who care for fish stocks,
and those who deal with the rainforests.
We pray for all who are short of food
or deprived of proper homes.

Silence

Lord God, hear us:
help us to put our trust in you.

We give thanks for our lives
and your love towards us.
Lord, bless our families and friends
with your goodness.
May the way we live show our trust in you.
Let us not squander or hoard
the good things you have given us
but use them to the good and benefit of all.

Silence

Lord God, hear us:
help us to put our trust in you.

God of love and peace, we remember before you
all who are weighed down with anxiety or fear.
We pray for those who are depressed
and those who feel they can no longer cope with life.
We ask your blessing upon all who are ill
and all who suffer in any way.
May they come to know your love and your peace.

Silence

Lord God, hear us:
help us to put our trust in you.

We give thanks for your everlasting love
and we rejoice in the gift of eternal life.
Lord, we commend to you
our friends and loved ones who are departed from us.
May they enjoy your presence and your love.

We commit them, this world and ourselves
to your unfailing presence and peace.

Silence

Merciful Father,
**accept these prayers
for the sake of your Son,
our Saviour Jesus Christ.
Amen.**

Memory verse

Strive first for the kingdom of God and his righteousness.
Matthew 6:33

Suggested music

Dance and sing
Give to our God immortal praise
He's got the whole world in his hand

CANDLES

Aim

To give thanks to God for the world and for his love for us.

Teaching

God decided to make something he could love, so he made the universe out of his own love. God made the light. He made the sun, the moon and the stars, and our world.

God made water. He made the rain.

But now there had to be somewhere for things to live, so God made dry land. He made the earth, hills and valleys. What else do you think God made from his love? He made mountains and flat land; he made soil and rocks. (What else did he make with water? He made rivers, streams, ponds, lakes and oceans.)

Now the earth was ready for things to grow. So what did God make grow out of the ground? He made flowers, trees, grass, fruit and food. God saw it all and loved it.

The earth was now ready for living things. God made things to fly in the air, to swim in the sea and to live on the land. Tell me what he made to fly in the air? Now what was made to swim in the sea? And what lived on the land? God made them and loved them.

Then God thought it was time to make something special, something that would love him and work with him. Do you know what the special thing is? God made people. That means he made us, you and me. Let us all stand up in turn and say our name and say, 'God made me.' I will start: 'I am David and God made me.'

God made us all and loves every one of us. Thank you, God.

Activity

Play musical statues. At each stop tell the children what they have to be: a star, a river, a hill, a tree, a lion, themselves. When they are a river they should be allowed to move slowly. Remind the children that God loves everything. (This is not an elimination game.)

Prayer

Thank you, God, for making the world
and all that is in it.
Thank you for making and loving me.
Amen.

Song

God who made the earth

LAMPS

Aim

To show God's love in creating the world.

Teaching

Show a sheet of black paper and ask what is on it. Say this is what it was like before God decided to make the world out of his love. Read Genesis 1:1-5. Show a blank white sheet and say how God had not finished; he had only started. Now it was time to make life-giving water. Read Genesis 1:6-8. Ask for volunteers to draw rain, clouds and seas.

Now it was time for living things but they would need dry land as well as water. Out of his love God made the dry land and growing things. Read Genesis 1:9-13. Again, have volunteers to fill a sheet with plants, flowers, fruit and trees.

God then decided it was necessary for times of light and darkness, of activity and rest, of the seasons. Show the black sheet of paper again and say how God made the sun, the moon and the stars. Read Genesis 1:14-19. This time get volunteers to add to the dark sheet the evening sky with moon and stars. Can they invent a light patch to show the bright sun?

The earth was now ready for living things. God in his love created every living creature. He took a long time to do it but he created all sorts of wonderful living things. Read Genesis 1:20-25. This time the scope is limitless – perhaps everyone could add their favourite animal, bird or sea creature to a large sheet of white paper.

At last the earth was ready for God to make humans. He wanted them to know he made everything out of his love and for the humans to give their love to him and to each other. Read Genesis 1:26-31. This time let everyone draw themselves and have written under them all, 'God made us'.

Activity

The lesson is full of activity. You could also play the 'pointing game'. Start by pointing at someone who has

to say, 'My name is . . . and God loves me.' Then they point at someone else and so the game goes on.

Prayer

God, you have made all things
out of your love and for your love.
Help us to show our love to you
in the way we care for our world.
Amen.

Song

Thank you, Lord, for this new day

TORCHES

Aim

To help the group to look at their priorities.

Teaching

Roger was too tired to help his father cut the grass, or to help his mother with the washing up. He was too tired to get down to his homework. But when Lisa called and asked if he would go skating with her and then for a swim, Roger had all the energy in the world. It is interesting how we are always able to find time and energy to do certain things.

Read Matthew 6:25-34. Jesus shows how people worry about what they are going to eat and drink and about what they will wear. We spend a lot of time thinking about these things. Well, they are important to us. What else do you spend a lot of time on?

Sport
Music
Computer games
Videos
Homework
Partying

(Add to this list.) Now arrange the list in a rough order of the time given to each item.

How much time do you spend in the presence of God, in prayer and in reading the Bible? Do our actions show how low God is in our priorities? What do you think Jesus meant when he said, 'Strive first for the kingdom of God and his righteousness'? How can we do this as a group and as individuals?

One young woman was asked why she spent a full hour in prayer each day. She replied, 'I am swapping the things that pass away for the eternal.' How much time do we spend worrying about trivial pursuits that are passing and how much care do we take of our eternal life?

We feed and care for our body because that is very important, but how much care do we put into seeing that our spirit is also growing properly? It is no use having a body beautiful if we are empty inside. It is no use feeding our body if we allow our spirit to die of starvation.

Activity
There is an opportunity on the activity sheet to check how we spend our day. There is also a chance to look at Matthew 6:25-34 in greater depth.

Prayer
Blessed are you, Lord our God,
for you give us life and love.
Help us to care for our whole being,
our body, mind and spirit.
Teach us to serve you
through our care and love for others.
Amen.

Song
Morning has broken

Sunday before Lent

Aim
To show that God reveals his glory in his Son Jesus Christ.

Preparation
Have a torch to reveal dark or hidden parts of the church. If you cannot do this, shine the light carefully on different people and say, 'God's glory is revealed in you.'

Opening activity
In the style of *Antiques Roadshow*.

Voice 1   I found this old bit of twisted wire in a field.

Voice 2   Do you know it is gold and it is 3,000 years old? It is worth a fortune.

Voice 3   The people we bought the house off left this old picture. They said if we did not want it to throw it out.

Voice 2   It is by a famous painter of the Newlyn School. It is worth thousands of pounds.

Voice 3   I never realised how beautiful it was until I got rid of the dirt.

Voice 2   Many things have a hidden glory and none so much as the human being.

Opening prayer
Lord God, who revealed your glory through Jesus
to the disciples on the mountain,
give us also a glimpse of your glory
in our worship and in our lives.
Amen.

Opening song
God of grace and God of glory

Readings
Exodus 24:12-18
Psalm 2 or Psalm 99
2 Peter 1:16-21
Matthew 17:1-9

Thought for the day
The recognition of Jesus as the Christ at Caesarea Philippi and then his telling the disciples of how he must go to Jerusalem to face suffering and death is followed by the Transfiguration. It is as if, before all that happened in Jerusalem, the disciples were given this glimpse of Jesus in his glory to give them hope in the future. Matthew continues to tell the story in a way that compares Jesus to Moses. The Transfiguration happened 'six days later'. In Exodus 24:15-18 we hear of the cloud being on Mount Sinai for six days. The Lord came on Sinai in a cloud (Exodus 34:5). The face of Moses shone after he had been with God (Exodus 34:29). All of these have parallels in the experience of the disciples on the mountain. Matthew draws this out: after telling us that Jesus was

transfigured and his face shone, he three times says, 'Behold'. This is seen best in the King James Bible, Matthew 17:3-5:

> '. . . behold there appeared unto them Moses and Elijah' (17:3).

> '. . . behold, a bright cloud overshadowed them' (17:5).

> '. . . behold a voice out of the cloud which said, "This is my beloved Son, in whom I am well pleased"' (17:5).

St Matthew wants us to see not only that the face of Jesus shone like that of Moses but also that Jesus fulfils the law given to Moses and the prophecies as exemplified by Elijah.

The bright cloud is a symbol of the hidden presence of God. Even in the darkest days God is present. The cloud is a bright one to remind us of the presence. This can be compared to the pillar of cloud in the desert (Exodus 13:21, 22); the cloud that descended on the Tent of Meeting (Exodus 40:43); when the Lord came down on Sinai in a cloud (Exodus 24:15-17, 34:5). Psalm 99:7 says of God, 'he spoke to them from a pillar of cloud'. The cloud is seen as a representation of the shekinah, the hidden glory of God which is ever-present.

The voice out of the cloud is the assurance of the presence, and the voice affirms again what was said at the baptism of Jesus: that this is the Son and Beloved of God (see Matthew 3:17). As at the beginning of his ministry, so, as it comes near to a close, Jesus is affirmed by the Father. Jesus is the true icon, the true image of God. St John will write, 'The Word became flesh and dwelt among us, and we have seen his glory, the glory of a father's only son, full of grace and truth' (John 1:14).

Peter would later write, 'We have been eyewitnesses of his majesty. For he received honour and glory from God the Father when that voice was conveyed to him by the Majestic Glory saying, "This is my Son, my Beloved, with whom I am well pleased." We ourselves heard this voice come from heaven, while we were with him on the holy mountain' (2 Peter 1:16-18).

Before this revelation the disciples bowed down in fear. Jesus came and touched them and said, 'Get up and do not be afraid.' Again I prefer the King James Version which says, 'Arise, and do not be afraid', for already there are hints here of the power of the Son of God and his resurrection.

Jesus ordered them, 'Tell no one about the vision until after the Son of Man has been raised from the dead.' Again emphasising not only he is the Christ but the future resurrection.

Question time
Do we tend to let the clouds of our life hide the glory of God that is ever present?

Why do you think Jesus told the disciples not to talk about his transfiguration until after his resurrection?

Illustration

As dark clouds cover the sun, so it is easy to let the dark events of life hide from us the glory and the presence of our God. It is then we need know that, even when we lose our grip, we are in the hand of God and in the heart of his Son who says to us, 'Arise, do not be afraid.'

You might like to affirm the words written by a Jewish prisoner on a wall in Cologne:

I believe in the sun even when it is not shining.
I believe in love even when I cannot feel it.
I believe in God even when he is silent.

Intercessions

Blessed are you, Lord God,
ever present in our lives.
Through the power of your Spirit
you reveal your glory to us
in the face of Jesus Christ.
Help us to trust in you
and in the power of the resurrection.
Blessed are you, Father, Son and Holy Spirit.

Lord, guide your Church,
that in its words and actions
it may reveal your glory.
We ask your blessing upon preachers of the word
and ministers of the sacraments,
that they may help us to do your will
and to have a vision of your purpose,
and that each in our mission
may proclaim your kingdom and your glory.

Silence

God, in your goodness,
grant us a glimpse of your glory.

We remember all who have lost their way
and who feel confused by life,
especially those who feel life has no meaning or purpose.
We pray for all who are captives of vice or drugs.
We ask your blessing
upon all who are fearful,
especially those who are suffering
from persecution or poverty.

Silence

God, in your goodness,
grant us a glimpse of your glory.

Lord, change us and we shall be changed.
Transform our homes into places of your glory.
Transform our lives to reveal your presence.
Transform our minds to know your peace.
Transform our hearts to abide in your love.
May we know you are always with our loved ones
and with us.

Silence

God, in your goodness,
grant us a glimpse of your glory.

Lord, transform our darkness with your light.
We ask your blessing
upon all who are struggling with illness

or who are no longer able to cope on their own.
We pray for all who have been injured
in accidents or through violence this week.
We pray for the work of the rescue services
and all who seek to bring and maintain peace.

Silence

God, in your goodness,
grant us a glimpse of your glory.

We rejoice in your power
and in the resurrection.
We pray for friends and loved ones departed,
that they may enjoy and rest in your glory.
We seek to share in the fellowship
of all your saints in glory.

Silence

Merciful Father,
**accept these prayers
for the sake of your Son,
our Saviour Jesus Christ.
Amen.**

Memory verse

This is my Son, the Beloved; with him I am well pleased; listen to him!
Matthew 17:5

Suggested music

Glory to you
Christ upon the mountain
'Tis good, Lord, to be here
Christ, your glory

CANDLES

Aim

To show Jesus revealing the glory of God.

Teaching

On a dark, cloudy day when you cannot see the sun, where is the sun? How can you tell? Sometimes even the dark clouds have brightness shining through them, or a gap in the clouds lets you see the sun. Even when we cannot see it, the sun is always there.

Jesus' friend Peter had said that he believed that Jesus was very special and had come to help all people. Now Jesus wanted Peter and the disciples to be sure of this, so he took three disciples with him and went up a mountain. They were called Peter, James and John. (Let us say their names together.) Peter, James and John followed Jesus – do you remember what they did before they became disciples? They were fishermen on the Sea of Galilee.

Jesus took the disciples up the mountain where they could be alone. They did not want to be disturbed. While they were there the three disciples looked at Jesus while he prayed and they saw that his face and his

75

clothes became all shining bright. They knew that Jesus was talking to God the Father. They kept watching but suddenly a cloud came down and it was harder to see. They could not see anyone but they heard a voice and it was speaking about Jesus. The voice said, 'This is my Son, I love him, he makes me very happy, listen to him.' Let us say together what the voice said about Jesus:

This is my Son.
I love him.
He makes me very happy.
Listen to him.

Now, who do you think was talking from out of the cloud? Yes, it was God the Father. The disciples were a little bit frightened by the voice and they did not dare look up. They bowed their heads to the ground. But Jesus came and touched them and said, 'Get up, do not be afraid.' Then Peter, James and John got up and went down the mountain with Jesus but they knew they had seen something very special.

Activity

With a torch and a mirror show how the light can be directed by the mirror to different people or places. When it shines on any one let them say, 'God gives me his love.' (Avoid shining on their faces.)

Prayer

Lord God, thank you for sending Jesus
to show us your love and brightness.
Help us to know you are always with us.
Amen.

Song

Come on and shine

LAMPS

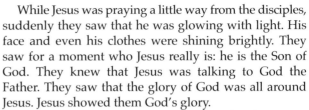

Aim

To show how Jesus reveals the glory of God.

Teaching

The disciples followed Jesus because they believed he was someone very important. They slowly learnt that he was the One sent by God and is called the Christ. One day Peter told Jesus that they knew he is the Christ. (Let us all say, 'Jesus is the Christ.') That means they believed that Jesus was sent by God to tell people of his love. But they still had something more to learn.

One day Jesus took three of his disciples up a mountain for a special reason. How many disciples would be waiting for them at the bottom of the mountain? Jesus took with him Peter and the two brothers, James and John. He wanted them to be with him while he prayed to God the Father. They were away from any other people and it was very quiet. We all need to do this sometimes so that we can say our prayers.

While Jesus was praying a little way from the disciples, suddenly they saw that he was glowing with light. His face and even his clothes were shining brightly. They saw for a moment who Jesus really is: he is the Son of God. They knew that Jesus was talking to God the Father. They saw that the glory of God was all around Jesus. Jesus showed them God's glory.

Then a bright cloud came down and hid him from their sight. But they heard a voice from the cloud. They knew that God the Father was there even though they could not see him. Perhaps they remembered how God spoke to Moses on Mount Sinai from a cloud. The voice told them, 'This is my Son, I love him. I am pleased with what he is doing. Listen to him.'

When the disciples heard this they were afraid to look and bowed their faces to the ground. After a moment or two Jesus came to them and said, 'Arise, do not be afraid.' When they looked they saw no one, only Jesus, and he was not shining but looked just like them. Jesus told them not to tell anyone about this until after his resurrection.

The three disciples wanted to tell everyone but it was their secret for the moment. Not everyone would understand but they knew that Jesus was the Christ and Jesus was the Son of God. This would help them to understand why Jesus had to go to Jerusalem.

Activity

Play the game of 'light and dark'. Someone is sent out of the room and an object in the room is chosen. The person returns and has to guess what it is. As she/he gets closer to it the group says, 'Light'; as she/he moves away from it the group says, 'Dark'. When it is found the group shouts, 'Glory!'

Prayer

Glory to you, Lord Jesus Christ,
you show us the glory of God.
We know that you are the Son of God,
that you love us and give your life for us.
Thank you.
Amen.

Song

Peruvian Gloria

TORCHES

Aim

To show how Jesus reveals God's glory.

Teaching

Get one of the group to read Exodus 24:12-18. Tell them this is Mount Sinai and here Moses received the Ten Commandments. Discuss what happened on the mountain, the cloud, the glory and the voice of God. You might also like them to read what happened to Moses when he returned from another visit to the mountain (Exodus 34:29). Tell them how the disciples would know of these stories from their Scriptures. They understood how a cloud hid God's glory and how God spoke from out of the cloud.

Jesus was worried for his disciples because they were not prepared for what might happen to them when they went to Jerusalem. So he took three of them – Peter, James and John – up a mountain. There he would pray to the Father and hope the disciples realised better who he was. Jesus moved a little way from his disciples to be alone with God. The disciples watched and saw a brightness come around Jesus. His face shone like the sun and his clothes became dazzling white. They thought they saw two men – Moses and Elijah – with Jesus. Peter spoke but as he did so a bright cloud came down and hid Jesus, Moses and Elijah from the disciples. Then they heard a voice from the bright cloud saying, 'This is my Son, my Beloved, with him I am well pleased. Listen to him!' The disciples knew this was the voice of God and they now knew for sure that Jesus was the Son of God. They had seen the glory of God and that glory also reflected in the face of Jesus. It filled them with fear and they bowed their faces to the ground.

Activity

Get the group to write code messages to each other where the word 'Glory' is a hidden word and has to be found. 'Grace loved orange, red, yellow' may not mean much but the first letter of each word spells 'Glory'. 'Jesus reveals 7-12-15-18-25' is also about glory, where the letters of the alphabet are numbered, with A as 1 and Z as 26. Let the group say how Jesus reveals God's glory to us.

Prayer

Glory to you, O God,
in sending your Son into the world.
Help us to see your glory as revealed in Jesus
and to seek to show your glory to others.
Amen.

Song

Lord, the light of your love (*Shine, Jesus, shine*)

LENT
First Sunday of Lent

Aim

To show that temptation is the norm if we are truly alive.

Preparation

Have advertisements for all sorts of things around the words, 'Are you tempted?' You might even like to add below, 'I hope so!'

Opening activity

Give out cards to everyone:

PRIORITY CARD

I will seek daily contact with God and to do his will.

I will learn how to give more and seek less.

I will not compromise by giving in to evil.

Signed............................ Dated...........

Opening prayer

Lord Jesus, you were tempted as we are
but did not give in to sin.
Help us to be faithful in our worship
and generous in our giving.
Amen.

Opening song

Forty days and forty nights

Readings

Genesis 2:15-17; 3:1-7
Psalm 32
Romans 5:12-19
Matthew 4:1-11

Thought for the day

Immediately after his baptism Jesus goes into the wilderness. Whenever Jesus had a challenge to face, he spent time alone with the Father. We all need times of stillness and quiet to discover who we are and what we aim to do.

There is a tension in Matthew 4:1 because Jesus is led by the Spirit to be tempted by the devil. The same tension is in all our lives because every moment we can choose to serve God or to turn our back on him. For Jesus the wilderness is where he takes time to sort out his priorities. We need ask ourselves, 'What are our priorities?'

Temptation is nice! If it wasn't, we would not be tempted. 'To tempt' in English usually means 'to lead astray': here in Matthew, 'to tempt' means 'to test' and does not have any connotation of good or evil. We all need times when we test our aims and our priorities or we will just drift from one thing to another. Temptation is not to do with fantasising about what we can do but rather facing up to our own potential and ability and seeing that we use them aright. We are tested, tempted, through our thoughts and our feelings, and there is nothing wrong with this. Temptation shows we are alive! But choice matters. How we use our God-given powers and freedom matters.

The temptations of Jesus are a four-pronged attack. Each temptation is meant to lead Jesus astray. The first temptation is usually not noticed, even though in Matthew it appears twice in this passage (4:3, 6) and again at the crucifixion (27:40). It is contained in the tiny word 'if'. Too often we fail because we are filled with self-doubt and doubt in God – often because we have not spent time getting to know ourselves or God!

The temptation to turn stones into bread is twofold: Look after yourself, bribe people to follow you. If you give people things, you will have a following. Jesus has come to serve and he knows that people need more than food and things: they need to know their Creator. He responds with a quotation from Deuteronomy 8:3.

In the next temptation the devil also uses Scriptures, quoting Psalm 91:11, 12. To quote or know Scriptures is not enough in itself. We need to seek to live by them. Again the temptation is twofold: give people certain assurances and force God to act. Make God do your will by being reckless and foolish and expect him to save you. Now Jesus quotes from Deuteronomy 6:16.

Often thoughts and feeling are liars! The devil offers Jesus the world – it is not his to give (see Psalm 2:8). Turn from worshipping God and worship anything else – be it football or your car – it does not matter. The devil wanted Jesus to compromise and to give in to evil, if only a little. For the moment Jesus chases the devil off with another quotation from Deuteronomy. But he knows the devil will return.

Question time

Do we recognise that we are called to use our full potential in the service of God and others?

How can you best use Lent to work out your priorities?

Illustration

One of the Desert Fathers prayed that all his passions should be taken away so that he would not be tempted. He then went to one of the Elders and said, 'You see before you a man who is not tempted and is at rest.' The Elder replied, 'Go and pray that some struggle is stirred up in you for the soul only matures through its battles against evil.' The monk did as he was asked and when temptation came he didn't ask to escape it but instead prayed, 'Lord, give me strength to get through the fight.'

Temptation is part of being alive to what is around us. We will be tempted as long as we live.

Intercessions

Blessed are you, Lord our God,
for you give us grace to defeat evil
and to resist temptation.
In our troubles you are our strength and our support.
You bring us to eternal life.
Blessed are you, Father, Son and Holy Spirit,
for ever and ever.

Lord, bless your people
who are struggling with temptation.
Guide your Church,
that it may lead others to do your will
and to live in love and peace with all.
Lord, help us to make others aware
of the deep spiritual things within our world:
that we are all called to work with you.
Help us to do your will
and so live in your kingdom.

Silence

Lord, hear us
and deliver us from evil.

We remember before you
all who are suffering through sin, violence and war.
We pray for peoples and nations
that are divided against each other
through ancient wrongs and through greed.
We pray for all who are sorely tempted to do wrong.
Lord, show us all the peace we should give
and the peace we should forgo.

Silence

Lord, hear us
and deliver us from evil.

We ask your blessing upon our homes and families.
We bring before you all who are suffering
from broken relationships and broken homes.
We pray for those who have been rejected
by their families
and all who feel they have been betrayed in love.
Bless all who work to bring reconciliation
and new hope to separated peoples.

Silence

Lord, hear us
and deliver us from evil.

We give thanks for all who share in healing
and the restoring of well being to all who suffer.
We remember all who are in pain or distress
at this time.
We ask your blessing
upon all who are separated from loved ones
through illness or disability
and all who can no longer cope on their own.

Silence

Lord, hear us
and deliver us from evil.

We give thanks for the forgiveness of sins
and the hope of eternal life.
We rejoice in the fellowship
of all the saints and the faithful
who are now in your kingdom.
We pray for our loved ones departed.
May we all at the last share in the glory
of your kingdom and your love.

Silence

Merciful Father,
accept these prayers
for the sake of your Son,
our Saviour Jesus Christ.
Amen.

Memory verse

Worship the Lord your God and serve only him.
Matthew 4:10

Suggested music

Lord Jesus, think on me
Dear Lord and Father of mankind
Be thou my guardian
O, for a heart to praise my God

CANDLES

Aim

To show that God made us and loves us even though we sometimes do wrong.

Teaching

Cut out pictures from magazines showing happy and sad people, including one of a child crying.

Look at these pictures. Who do you see in them? Yes, people, all sorts of people, happy and sad ones. Do you see this one? Why do you think the boy/girl is crying? Possibly they were naughty and did something their mummy or daddy told them not to do. They made their mummy and daddy sad and now they too are unhappy. I want to tell you what happened when God made the first people and then gave them a beautiful garden to live in.

God had made his wonderful world. But when the sun shone and the moon gave light, when the rivers were bright with water and the green grass grew, when there was fruit on the trees, birds in the air, fish in the sea and all sorts of animals on the land, God knew there was something missing. What had God still to make? Yes, there were no people. God wanted to make someone who would work with him and talk with him. He wanted someone he could give his love to, and who would also love him. God made the first people to share his love, the first man and woman, and he called them Adam and Eve. (Let us say their names together.)

God gave Adam and Eve a special garden to live in. It was called the Garden of Eden. (Shall we say that together?) God would come into the garden and talk with Adam and Eve. He loved them and they loved him. God let them have everything he had made. They had all sorts of wonderful things. There was only one thing they shouldn't do and that was to eat from the tree in the middle of the garden. They had plenty to eat; they did not even need to touch it. But one day they did a naughty thing. Can you guess what they did?

That is right, they took fruit from the tree and ate it. They did what God had asked them not to do. It was really sad, God loved them but they did not do what he had asked them to do and they did wrong. They had hurt God and so they hid themselves from him. God knew they had done wrong and he looked for them. He told them how they had spoiled what he had made by doing wrong. He still loved them but they would now have to live outside the beautiful garden in case they spoiled it even more. This made God sad and I am sure it made Adam and Eve sad. He still loved them, and he loves us even when we make him sad by doing wrong.

When we do wrong things what can we do to help put them right? We can say, 'Sorry', and promise not to do the naughty things again. We can say sorry to our parents and to God.

Activity

Play musical statues. For each bit of music suggest an animal they should be. There is an opportunity on the activity sheet for them to draw their favourite animal and themselves as part of God's loving creation.

Prayer

God, thank you for making a lovely world
and for all you have given us,
especially our mummies and daddies.
Help us not to spoil things or to hurt anyone
by doing things that are wrong.
Amen.

Song

And God said

LAMPS

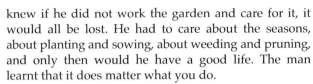

Aim

To show we have to plan for good if we want to do it.

Teaching

There was once a lazy man who had a nice garden. His father had given it to him. It had lots of nice flowers and fruit trees. There was a good vegetable patch and a pond with some fish in. But the man did not look after it. Weeds grew everywhere. When the man took out vegetables he did not bother to plant any more. He did not look after his fruit trees and did not care for the pond. He was too lazy to bother. Soon the fish started to die, the vegetables ran out, the trees did not fruit. It was all rather sad. At last the man began to suffer from hunger and he realised that the garden was a mess. He

knew if he did not work the garden and care for it, it would all be lost. He had to care about the seasons, about planting and sowing, about weeding and pruning, and only then would he have a good life. The man learnt that it does matter what you do.

Jesus knew that it matters how you do things and that it was necessary to work with God the Father and do what he wanted. So, after his baptism, Jesus went into the wilderness for 40 days to be alone, just with God. But then came temptation, and evil tried to lead Jesus away from doing what God wanted.

Evil said, 'Look after yourself first. Fill your belly with food. Fill others with food. People will follow you if you give them things.' Jesus could do it but he did not want people to follow him just to be fed. He wanted people to know they depended on the love of God for their life and not only on food. Jesus refused to give in to this temptation. Get someone to read Matthew 4:4 to find out Jesus' reply.

For the next temptation evil took Jesus to the top of the Temple and said, 'Jump. God loves you and he will look after you.' Jesus knew it would be wrong to make the Father do his will. God is not there to do our will; we are to seek God's will. Jesus wants us to follow the Father's way. Again Jesus beat temptation. Get someone to read Matthew 4:7 for Jesus' reply.

Then evil thought, 'Everyone has a price. I will offer Jesus the world.' (Do you think it really belonged to evil?) Remember evil often leads us astray by lies. Evil wanted Jesus to give himself to worldly things and to turn his back on God. But Jesus knew that it was God we should put first and love. Jesus beat the temptation. Get someone to read Matthew 4:10 to find out how.

Jesus had decided how he was to serve God the Father and defeated evil. Now he was ready for his work.

Activity

Have some Velcro darts and a dartboard. Explain how important it is to have something to aim at, and how when we miss we need to be given another chance. We all need to have aims to make sure we are going in the right direction.

Prayer

Lord Jesus, help us to fight against evil.
Deliver us from temptation
and make us strong to serve you.
Amen.

Song

We don't believe the devil's lie

TORCHES

Aim

To show that we are all tempted and that Jesus was tempted because he was also human.

Teaching

Let us pretend that you come to my house. I tell you that you can go anywhere you like, look at anything you like, explore everywhere, but you must not look in the cupboard under the stairs. As soon as I am gone I am sure there is one thing many of you will feel like doing. What is it? Yes, you would be tempted to look in the cupboard, just because you were told not to! But if you did, you would betray my trust in you. If you could not do that little thing, how could I trust you to do other things? Temptation is about what we are capable of doing, but if we give in to it we lower our standards or betray a trust. Temptation is nice – or we would not be tempted. Temptation is about our potential and how we use it.

Before Jesus began his ministry he went into the desert to be alone with God. There he was also tempted.

Round one of the fight. Jesus was tempted to look after himself – fill his belly, become a provider of famine relief. That is good but Jesus came to do more. He wanted people to look to God and spiritual things. He wanted to teach people they needed God as well as food to fill the emptiness within. Read Matthew 4:1-4. Jesus won round one.

Round two sees Jesus in the Holy City at the Temple. He should be safe there! Yet we are often tempted even in holy places. The devil wants Jesus to be a stunt man, to win people over by wonders, to force them to believe. Jesus sees that here is a danger of forcing God to act, making God do what he wants God to do. We are to try to do God's will, not make God do ours. Read Matthew 4:5-7. Round two to Jesus.

The third round is when the devil offers Jesus the world. Do you think it was the devil's to give? Temptation sounds good and nice and we can often lie to ourselves and stubbornly overlook the long-term consequences. The devil wanted Jesus to turn away from God; it did not matter what really attracted him. It is so easy to forget God and worship other things. Read Matthew 4:8-11. Jesus won round three and the devil left, but temptation is never far away. He would be back.

Activity

Let the group talk openly about temptation. Give each of them a Priority Card and let them discuss what it means for them and how they will keep it in Lent.

PRIORITY CARD

I will seek daily contact with God and to do his will.

I will learn how to give more and seek less.

I will not compromise by giving in to evil.

Signed........................... Dated...........

Prayer

Lord, help us to love you
with all our heart, mind and soul.
Forgive us when we are led astray
and deliver us from evil.
Amen.

Song

Jesus went away to the desert

Second Sunday of Lent

Aim

To see Jesus as our light and life.

Preparation

At the entrance place a photograph or drawing of some-one with a candle in a dark place. Underneath write, 'The Lord is my Light and my Salvation'. You may like also to have a print of Holman Hunt's painting 'The Light of the World'.

Opening activity

Mini drama

Voice 1 I cannot see which way to go, it is so dark.
Voice 2 The Lord is my Light and my Salvation.
         (gives a lit candle to Voice 1)
Voice 3 I feel everything is as black as night, I am so depressed.
Voice 2 The Lord is my Light and my Salvation.
         (gives a lit candle to Voice 3)
Voice 4 I really cannot see what I ought to do. I need guidance.
Voice 2 The Lord is my Light and my Salvation.
         (gives a lit candle to Voice 4)
Voice 5 The world is such a dark place, I feel lost. I could perish in this darkness.
Voice 2 God so loved the world that he gave his only Son, so that everyone who believes in him may not perish but have eternal life.
         (gives a lit candle to Voice 5)

Opening prayer

Lord, you are our light and our salvation;
let us put our trust in you.
Lighten our darkness
and drive far from us all the snares of evil,
that in you we may find eternal life.
Amen.

Opening song

All my hope on God is founded

Readings

Genesis 12:1-4a
Psalm 121
Romans 4:1-5, 13-17
John 3:1-17

Thought for the day

Normally we see Jesus working in the daytime and with crowds of ordinary people around him; today's Gospel is about a rich aristocrat who came to Jesus by night for a one-to-one meeting.

Nicodemus was leader of the Jews – that is, he was a member of the Jewish Sanhedrin of which there were only 70 members. The Sanhedrin was the supreme court of the Jews and had religious jurisdiction over all the Jews in the world. One of the things the Sanhedrin did was examine anyone charged with being a false prophet. It is amazing that such a man risked coming to see Jesus.

He came at night, perhaps out of caution. Maybe he did not want to be seen with Jesus. Possibly it was because the rabbis taught that the best time to study was at night when one was not disturbed. Perhaps he wanted to see Jesus on his own. Night might also be a symbol of his own darkness, of all the unanswered questions about his life and his relationship with God. He was a believer and a law-abiding person but perhaps he felt that there was more. Religion and law-abiding are not enough. Nicodemus knew there was something else needed. Many churchgoers find themselves in this position: it is the position of needing to move from belief to faith, from religion to the living God.

Nicodemus is courteous and says how he is impressed by the miracles of Jesus. Jesus gently sweeps this aside and comes to the need of Nicodemus. Jesus talks of the need to be born from above. Nicodemus asks if this is possible for an old man. Perhaps we should ask if it is possible for a church that has grown old to be reborn. Jesus says there is need to be born of the Spirit. We are not just earthly beings but children of God and we need to know our Father and that we belong to him. Jesus understands well that Nicodemus knows these things with his head but he has to accept them in his heart and life. Only in this way will the darkness be dispersed with the light and love of God. (See John 3:19-21.) St John wants us to know we can experience this in Jesus from the outset. John says of Jesus, 'in him was life, and the life was the light of all people' (John 1:4).

It is to Nicodemus that Jesus said probably the most famous and well-known words in the Bible: 'For God so loved the world that he gave his only Son, so that every-one who believes in him may not perish but may have eternal life' (John 3:16).

We do not hear of Nicodemus again until after the crucifixion. Joseph of Arimathea, a secret disciple of Jesus, asks to be allowed to take away the body. Nicodemus is also there, bringing a mixture of myrrh and aloes weighing about 100 pounds for the burial of Jesus – two members of the Sanhedrin showing their love and respect for Jesus. The gift is a costly one and one that shows Nicodemus in the daylight.

Question time

What do you understand by being 'born again'?

How can we show that our faith is more than law-abiding and religion?

Illustration

There are many very clever and capable people (they are often also well-off) who feel they are missing out on something of the fullness of life. Listen to the words of Federico Fellini, the Italian film producer: 'Like so many people I have no religion and I just go sitting in a small boat drifting with the tide. I just go on working, cutting, shooting, editing and looking at life and trying to make others see. Today we stand naked and defenceless, more alone than at any time in history. We are waiting for something – perhaps another miracle, perhaps the Martians, who knows?'

Fellini, like Nicodemus, is in the dark, seeking someone or something that will deliver him from the darkness, from nothingness and death. A deliverer, a Saviour, is needed.

Intercessions

Blessed are you, Lord our God,
for you have called us out of darkness
to be children of light.
The bright light of your presence
scatters the darkness within us
and is a guide on our journey.
Blessed are you, Father, Son and Holy Spirit.

We rejoice that in Christ we know
that light is stronger than darkness
and life is stronger than death.
Give your Church the courage
to proclaim the Good News to all people.
We remember all who are in doubt
or who are struggling with their faith.
We pray for those who have lost faith
and walk in darkness.

Silence

Lord, hear us:
come, lighten our darkness.

Lord of all, we bring before you
the troubles and dangers of peoples and nations,
the war-torn and the world-weary.
We ask your blessing
upon communities seeking to rebuild their lives
in peace and hope.
We pray for all rulers, governments
and leaders of people,
that they will strive for justice and peace.

Silence

Lord, hear us:
come, lighten our darkness.

Bless our homes with the light of your presence.
We pray for our loved ones and friends,
for our neighbours and our community.
May the bright light of Christ shine within us
and scatter any darkness that is around us.

Silence

Lord, hear us:
come, lighten our darkness.

We remember all who are struggling
with illness or with fear.
We ask your blessing
upon all who are in hospital,
all who have been injured
through violence or accidents.
We pray for all who are fearful of the future.
We pray also for the bereaved and the lonely.

Silence

Lord, hear us:
come, lighten our darkness.

We remember all who are nearing death
and those who care for them.
May they trust in you and in eternal life.
We commend all our loved ones departed
to your love and your kingdom.

Silence

Merciful Father,
accept these prayers
for the sake of your Son,
our Saviour Jesus Christ.
Amen.

Memory verse

For God so loved the world that he gave his only Son, so that everyone who believes in him may not perish but may have eternal life.
John 3:16

Suggested music

Lighten our darkness
Lead, kindly light
The Lord is my light

CANDLES

Aim

To show how Abram was willing to listen to God and obey him.

Teaching

When God made the world he made people so that they could love him. In every person he made a place where he could meet them. God wants us to love him as he love us. Let us all say, 'I love God: God loves me.'

Abram knew that God loved him and he wanted to do what God asked him to do. Abram was quite old and he was married to Sarai who was also quite old. They did not have any children. Abram kept sheep and goats, and lived where his father had lived before him in a place called Ur.

One day, when he was saying his prayers, Abram was sure God asked him to move away from Ur. He was not sure where God wanted him to go but he would be happy to go because he felt God would go with him. When he told Sarai, she was very surprised because Abram had always lived at Ur. But they both thought it was exciting because God had something special for them to do and they trusted in God.

So they started to pack their things and say goodbye to friends. (What sort of things do you think they would need for a journey? They certainly needed food, water, a tent to sleep in. They also took sheep and goats, maybe some camels.) It took a lot to get ready. They knew the journey might be dangerous but God had promised to be with them and protect them. Abram trusted God.

Not long before they set off, they had a visitor. He was the nephew of Abram – so do you know what that makes Abram? Abram was his uncle. His name was Lot and he was married, had a family and also a lot of sheep and goats. But Lot wanted to go with Abram. He thought it would be wonderful going where God wanted them to go. So he asked his uncle Abram and Abram said yes, they could all come.

Soon there were a lot of people walking away from Ur. There were men, women and children; there were sheep, goats and camels. They had to take a lot of food and water with them. But they wanted to do what God had asked them. They did not know where they were going but they trusted in God and set out.

Activity

Play 'traffic lights'. Let music be played quietly. (You might like to use the music from 'We are marching in the light of God'; after a while they could sing as they go.) When you call, 'Red', they must stop. 'Amber' means they must do what they were doing – if still, they must not move; if moving, they must not stop. 'Green' means move or keep moving.

Prayer

God, help us to know
you are always with us,
wherever we go.
You love us and look after us.
We love you.
Amen.

Song

Here I am, Lord

LAMPS

Aim

To show how Abram went where God asked because Abram trusted God.

Teaching

Once there was a ship on a secret mission. It set out from the harbour and no one knew where it was going, not even the Captain. He was told, 'When you get out of the harbour read the letter we have given you and it will tell you where to go next.' When the crew asked, 'Where are we going?' the Captain had to say, 'I do not know, but I trust the people who are sending us.' It was a great adventure into the unknown. The letter told him where to go next but then it said, 'There you will meet someone and they will tell you where you are to go next.' The Captain knew he was doing something exciting. He trusted those who were sending him and he knew they would be keeping an eye on him and the ship.

A long time ago the same thing happened to quite an old man. His name was Abram and he lived at Ur. He

lived where his father had lived before him and he knew nearly everyone in Ur. One day, while Abram was praying, God said, 'Abram.' He replied, 'Yes, Lord.' Then God said, 'I want you to leave Ur. I am going to give you a new land to live in. I want you to take Sarai your wife, your belongings, your sheep and goats and set off for a new land.' Abram was quite excited even though he did not know where he was to go. He was sure God would show him the way. He knew God was with him and he trusted in God.

Sarai was very surprised that they were to be moving but she also trusted in God. While they were getting ready to go, their nephew came to see them. Abram and Sarai were his uncle and aunt. He asked if he, his wife and family could also go with them. They would bring their own food, water and cattle. Abram was pleased because Lot (that was his nephew's name) would be a good help on the journey and the more of them there were, the safer it would be. God was already helping Abram by getting Lot to go with him.

Soon they set off into the unknown. There was a great crowd of them – young children and old people, sheep, goats and camels. They took tents, food and water. They set off because they trusted God and knew he would go with them.

Activity

Get the group to march around the room singing 'We are marching in the light of God'. You might like to give them directions like 'turn right', 'turn left', 'turn around', 'stop', 'start'. Get them to imagine they are a large group marching through the desert lands.

Prayer

Lord God,
we often do not know where we are going
or what will happen next,
but we know that you are always with us
and you love us.
Thank you, God.
Amen.

Song

We are marching in the light of God

TORCHES

Aim

To show Jesus as the Light of the World.

Teaching

Nicodemus was a very important person. He was a leader of the Jews. He was a Pharisee and a scholar. He was also a rich man. People looked up to him and learnt from him. But Nicodemus felt that there was something missing in his life – it was as if he was in the dark. He was clever, he had money, he was popular, but he knew that was not enough. He said his prayers, he learnt more, he was generous – but even that was not enough. There was something he was missing – really felt as if he was in the dark. Then he secretly decided what to do. He did not want anyone to know or to see him, so he planned to go in the dark. He waited until it was night. Then he wrapped his big cloak about him, hid his face and went out. He walked in the shadows until he came to where he wanted to be. He came to see Jesus – when the crowds had gone and no one would know.

In St John's Gospel Jesus is called the 'Light of the World' (see John 1:1-4, 9 and 8:12). Coming to Jesus, Nicodemus comes out of the darkness and into the Light of Christ.

Jesus saw that Nicodemus was in the dark. He saw that Nicodemus knew the truths in his head but he needed them to enter deep into his heart. Nicodemus was an honest seeker – and God comes to those who seek him. Listen to their conversation (read John 3:1-17). (There is an opportunity on the worksheet to study this passage further.)

We do not hear again of Nicodemus until the crucifixion and death of Jesus. Nicodemus now comes out in the daylight and brings 100 pounds of myrrh and aloes – a very expensive gift – for the burial of Jesus (John 19:38-42).

Activity

Encourage each member of the group to write a petition to Jesus with the refrain:

Jesus, Light of the World,
scatter the darkness from us.

Prayer

Jesus Christ,
may the light of your love and salvation
be seen in our lives and in our work.
Then may we shine as lights in this dark world.
Amen.

Song

Like a candle flame

Third Sunday of Lent

Aim
To show how Jesus fills our emptiness and our longing for God.

Preparation
Have information about the need for water for people to survive. Relief agencies such as Christian Aid will help.

Opening activity
Mini drama

Voice 1   I am bored.
Voice 2   Like a piece of wood with a big hole in it.
Voice 3   I am bored, there is nothing to do.
Voice 2   You mean you feel empty or the world is empty.
Voice 4   You need to fill a person with something.
Voice 2   Our soul is thirsting for God. He made a place in us for himself and nothing else can fill it.

Opening prayer
Lord God, our hearts are restless
until they find their rest in you.
Our whole lives we look for you, long for you.
Come, Lord, and fill us with your Spirit.
Amen.

Opening song
My God, I love thee

Readings
Exodus 17:1-7
Psalm 95
Romans 5:1-11
John 4:5-42

Thought for the day
Jesus is facing hostility from the Pharisees in Judea. So he decides to leave for Galilee: it is too early in his ministry for confrontation. To reach Galilee he travels through Samaria. In the heat of the noonday sun Jesus rests by Jacob's Well. The disciples have gone to Sychar, about half a mile away, to buy food. Jesus is thirsty but the well is 100 feet deep and he has nothing to draw water with.

Suddenly from the direction of Sychar a woman appears. What is she doing out in the midday sun? This is siesta time. She is either very disorganised or disorientated. It could be that she did not want to meet anyone. A Samaritan, a woman, and someone possibly marginalised. Jews are supposed to have no dealings with Samaritans. Rabbis are not meant to speak to women outside at all. Rabbis had also declared it was not worth teaching a woman. It is also possible that the woman was a sinner and an outcast. Whereas Nicodemus chose to come to Jesus by night, this woman comes in the heat of the day and meets him by chance.

The woman was surprised that a Jew was willing to speak to her, a woman and a Samaritan. Jesus asks for some water and the woman lowers her bucket into the well and gives Jesus a drink. Jesus asks what brings her out in the middle of the day. 'Thirst' is her reply.

Jesus saw beyond what she said and saw she had a thirst she could not quench. Perhaps Jesus learnt from her of the five husbands she had and the man she was now living with. Was her thirst for love? Was it a thirst for acceptance? Was it a need to fill the emptiness within? Maybe nothing would satisfy her for long. She would again feel emptiness, a thirst that needed quenching. Here she was, by chance, at the Well of Life.

Jesus meets her at her own level and says, 'Those who drink of the water that I give them will never be thirsty.' The woman decided to humour Jesus and asked that he gave her such water and then she need not come to the well.

Jesus asks about her husband. From what he says, the woman decides he is a prophet and could solve her problems. Jesus tells her to worship God in spirit and in truth. In response to this, the woman says, 'We must wait for the Messiah to come.' Jesus has now led her to where he wanted and says, 'I am he.'

Because the disciples return, the woman leaves Jesus but then tells the people of Sychar about him. She becomes an apostle! Many Samaritans come and believe because of her testimony.

Today there are many who thirst for life and feel empty inside. So many declare that they are bored. The evangelist Billy Graham likened such people to beautiful cars, with good engines wanting to go – but rusting away with boredom because they have nothing in their tank. They have a thirst for the eternal and cannot be satisfied with less.

Question time
What do you think the Psalmist means when he says, 'As a deer longs for flowing streams, so longs my soul for you, O God. My soul thirsts for God, for the living God' (Psalm 42:1, 2)?

Can you describe different signs of thirst for God in the community in which you live?

Illustration
Bill had tried everything to fill the gnawing emptiness that he felt inside. Whenever there was a time of quiet, the feeling of emptiness and worthlessness came upon him. He sought to escape into never having silence. Music, videos, computer games filled up his emptiness – but he knew it was still there. He tried to escape in thrills, in excitement, in sex and drugs. But underneath, the gnawing feeling was there. He felt alone and empty. One day, listening to the radio, Bill heard a poem by Francis Thompson called 'The Hound of Heaven'. The whole poem seemed to be about him. Certain lines, he said, struck home, especially these:

> 'All things betray thee, who betrayest me.'

> 'Naught shelters thee, who will not shelter me.'

And later:

'Lo! Naught contents thee, who content'st not me.'

He realised his emptiness was because he had been on the run from God. In tears this big strong man committed himself to God in prayer. He started going to church and became a much more fulfilled and contented person. He came to love the Psalms and in particular Psalms 42 and 43.

Intercessions

Blessed are you, Lord our God,
for you have made us for yourself
and for your love.
We seek your presence
and desire to give our lives and our love to you.
Blessed are you, Father, Son and Holy Spirit.

Lord, may your presence be revealed
through your Church.
May we never be satisfied with words without content,
with actions without love,
with buildings that do not convey your presence.
Lord, fill us and make us a holy people,
a fulfilled people and a missionary people.
Bless the Church,
that it may grow in outreach, in holiness
and in number.

Silence

Lord, we look for you; we long for you:
come fill us with your Spirit.

You have given us a wonderful world.
Let us not spoil it through greed or lack of respect.
We remember all who suffer from hunger and thirst.
We pray for all who do not have proper water supplies
or who have to walk miles to get water.
We pray also for all in the consumer society
who try to fill their lives with things
and are never satisfied.

Silence

Lord, we look for you; we long for you:
come fill us with your Spirit.

We give thanks for the longings that you have given us.
We ask your blessing upon our loved ones,
our families and friends.
We remember before you all who are lonely,
those who are failing in health or strength,
and all who are fearful for the future.

Silence

Lord, we look for you; we long for you:
come fill us with your Spirit.

We give thanks for the joy and freedom
you give to our lives.
We pray for all who have become captives
to vice and drugs,
all who are suffering from the misuse of alcohol.
We remember their families who also suffer.
We ask your blessing upon all who are ill
and upon those who care for them.

Silence

Lord, we look for you; we long for you:
come fill us with your Spirit.

In the power of your Spirit
you renew and refresh us.
We pray for all who are departed from us,
that they may rejoice in the fullness of life eternal.
To you, O God, and your love
we commit this world, our loved ones and ourselves
now and for eternity.

Silence

Merciful Father,
**accept these prayers
for the sake of your Son,
our Saviour Jesus Christ.
Amen.**

Memory verse

As a deer longs for flowing streams, so longs my soul for you, O God. My soul thirsts for God, for the living God.
Psalm 42:1, 2

Suggested music

Jesus, Jesus
I heard the voice of Jesus say
Is anyone thirsty
You can drink it
Father, hear the prayer we offer

CANDLES

Aim

To show how all living things need water.

Teaching

Bring plants in plant pots. If possible, bring one that is drooping from lack of water. Ask the children what all these plants need if they are not to die. Now let one of the children water the plants.

Seeds need water to grow, so does the grass, and flowers and trees. All growing things need water to grow. Where do most of them get their water? The rain. If it stopped raining for a long time, what would happen to all the plants? They would die. They need water to live.

What else needs water to live? All animals, all living things need water. *We* need water. Where do you get your water from? You are lucky. Imagine how hard it would be if you could only get it from the nearest stream. You might have to walk miles just to get some water. (Pictures from relief agencies might help here.) Sometimes people get their water from a deep hole in the ground. Does anyone know what it is called? A well. To get water from a well you need a rope and a bucket. You have to tie a rope to the bucket and then drop the bucket down the well. Once the bucket is filled with water you can pull it up again.

Once Jesus was sitting right beside a well and he was thirsty but he could not get any water. Why? He did not have a bucket to get any water. While he was sitting there a woman came to get some water and he asked her for a drink. She dropped her bucket down into the well and then gave Jesus a drink.

Jesus saw that the woman was not very happy. Just as she had helped him, he offered to help her. She was very happy and went and told other people about Jesus.

Activity

Let the children act out the story of the woman coming to the well and giving a Jesus a drink. They could also have a team game of a water race. In turn, they have to carry a cup and saucer of water without spilling to a fixed point and back to the next member of the team. Water spilt in the saucer must be put back in the cup before handing it over to the next one. The cups should begin quite full and be replenished if too much water is lost. Take care on slippery floors. If possible, have the race outside.

Prayer

Thank you, God, for water,
for rivers and streams,
for tap water and well water.
Thank you for giving us water
and for giving us life.
Amen.

Song

Sing the chorus from 'Have you heard the raindrops'.

LAMPS

Aim

To show Jesus as the 'living water'.

Teaching

What does every living thing need to survive? Air, food and water. Today we will look at water and how it refreshes us and gives us life. No one can live without water for very long. If there was no water on the earth, what would the earth become? It would become a desert: a planet without life. Water is very precious and important.

We are lucky to have a running water supply. In some countries people have to carry their water from streams and rivers. Sometimes they have to walk a long way just for water – so they never waste water. In desert countries people often get their water from a well. (Ask someone to describe what a well is and how the people get water from it.)

Once, Jesus and his disciples had walked a long way. Jesus rested by a well while the disciples went to a nearby village to buy food. Jesus wanted a drink but he could not get one. Why?

It was the middle of the day and very hot. Fortunately, a woman, with a water jar on her head, came walking to the well. She had to walk about half a mile from home to get water and the same back again. Jesus asked her if she would give him a drink. She was surprised that he spoke to her but she lowered her leather bucket and got water. She was happy to give Jesus a drink.

Jesus saw that in some way the woman felt empty and not happy. Jesus talked to her about a supply that did not run out and that was a gift from God. The woman did not understand but Jesus helped her to see he could meet her need, because he is the 'Water of Life'. (Let the children explore in their own words what this might mean.)

The woman was so excited at meeting Jesus and hearing what he had to say that she left her water pot and ran to the village to tell others about him. She brought them back with her and many believed in Jesus. The woman had become one of the apostles (or missionaries) of Jesus.

Activity

Have a team race. Each team has a plastic bucket to carry on their head. They have to run to a point, put their bucket down and then raise it again before running back to their team.

Prayer

Thank you, God, for water,
for rain, rivers and seas,
for wells, reservoirs and tap water.
We pray for all who do not have clean water
or water near at hand,
and for all who are thirsty.
Thank you for Jesus, the Water of Life.
Amen.

Song

Have you heard the raindrops

TORCHES

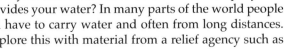

Aim

To show that Jesus is the 'Water of Life'.

Teaching

Have a member of the group read Exodus 17:1-7. Where were the people and what were they complaining about? What would happen to them if they did not get water? No living thing can survive without water. Water is very precious to the earth. In this story, who provided the water? God, through Moses, provides for the people.

Do you know the name of the water company that provides your water? In many parts of the world people still have to carry water and often from long distances. (Explore this with material from a relief agency such as

Tearfund or Christian Aid.) Sometimes water comes from a well.

Once when Jesus was going from Judea to Galilee he went through Samaria. About half a mile from the village of Sychar he came to a very famous well, known as Jacob's Well. The disciples left him there and went to Sychar to buy food. Jesus was very thirsty but he could not get any water. He was lucky because a woman with a water pot on her head came from Sychar. She was a Samaritan.

Jesus asked her for a drink of water. She was surprised because Jews did not usually speak to Samaritans, and teachers, like Jesus, did not normally speak to women in public. She gave Jesus a drink. Jesus began to tell her who he was. Jesus saw that the woman was troubled and suggested that she had a thirst for more than water. He told her how he could give the 'Living Water' and that he was the Christ, the Messiah. The woman was amazed; she left her water pot and ran back to Sychar and told how she had met the Christ. She told others of Jesus – she became a missionary seeking to bring others to Jesus.

Activity

Find out more from one of the relief agencies about how to provide clean water for a community to drink from. Show how tap water is like a dream come true for many places of the world. Get the group to talk about the meaning of Jesus as the 'Living Water'. Look also at Psalm 42.

Prayer

Lord, giver of life and love,
we thank you
for the water that refreshes and revives us.
We thank you for Jesus, the Water of Life,
who gives us life eternal.
Amen.

Song

The King of love my shepherd is

Fourth Sunday of Lent
Mothering Sunday

Aim

To give thanks for all who care for us, especially our mothers.

Preparation

Give everyone or every family a candle to light as a 'Thank you' and a prayer for their mother. Have a large box filled with sand to hold the candles in an appropriate place when they are lit. Remember, everyone has or has had a mother; let no one be excluded. You may like to give them a printed copy of the opening prayer that will be sung.

Opening activity

Invite all to come forward, in family groups or on their own, with their candle to light as 'Thank you' for their homes and especially their mothers. As people return to their seats, everyone who has come with their mother should give her a hug.

Once this is done, or during it, the opening prayer is sung.

In some churches it may be possible to go outside and let the congregation encircle the church, giving the church a family hug! If there are gaps between people, you could use lengths of string to unite them. You could sing 'Welcome to the family' or 'Bind us together, Lord'.

Opening prayer

Bless our mother, Lord, every day (x3)
O Lord, bless her now.

Keep her safe, O Lord, every day. (x3)
O Lord, bless her now.

Give her joy, O Lord, every day. (x3)
O Lord, bless her now.

(Tune: 'Kum ba yah')

(If there are lots of candles to light, different groups of children could sing this throughout the candle lighting.)

Opening song

For the beauty of the earth

Readings

Exodus 2:1-10 or 1 Samuel 1:20-28
Psalm 34:11-20 or Psalm 127:1-1-4
2 Corinthians 1:3-7 or Colossians 3:12-17
Luke 2:33-35 or John 19:25b-27

Thought for the day

It is very costly to be a mother. Mothers provide free food and shelter for their children. Mothers see their children get what they need and also protect them in times of danger. Mothers spend hours of each day looking after the house, shopping and cooking – it is good when these jobs can be shared. It is very easy to take the love and sacrifice of our mother for granted. It is the love and security she provides that gives us strength for daily life.

Today is the middle of Lent; sometimes it is called Refreshment Sunday. It is a break in the routine of Lent when we stop to give thanks for our homes and loved ones, especially our mother. This is a day when we can show that we appreciate what our mother does for us and when we can say thank you. Let us turn to our mother and say, 'Thank you', or if she is not with us, say, 'Thank you' to God for her.

Today's readings are all about mothers. The mother of Moses hid him from the wicked Pharaoh who would have killed him. To do this meant that Moses' mother risked her life. Even after three months, when she put him in a basket at the riverside, she made sure Moses was safe. She could have been killed just for loving her son.

Hannah did not think she would ever have a child but at last she gave birth to Samuel. When she later gave him to be with the priest Eli, she brought a little robe each year for her boy (1 Samuel 2:19). I am sure she sewed much love into it.

In the Gospel when Simeon met Mary he told her that Jesus would be opposed and how a sword would pierce her heart also. Mothers suffer when they see their child suffering. When one member of a family suffers all feel the pain. Think how Mary suffered when she saw Jesus on the cross.

Let this be a day when we give thanks to God for the love of our homes. It would be best if we showed how much we appreciate what our mother has done for us not only today but every day. It is a good time for families to say grace together at meals and to give thanks for the love of the ones who care for them.

Question time

Are we aware of the great gift of love that God gives to us through our mother?

God's love is seen through the love we show to each other. How can we make ourselves more aware of this?

Illustration

In J. K. Rowling's story of *Harry Potter and the Philosopher's Stone*, Quirrell, who is working for the wicked Voldemort, tries to kill Harry but is unable to do so even when he uses all the evil powers available to him. Harry asks Professor Dumbledore why Quirrell couldn't touch him and Dumbledore replies that Harry's mother died to save him, and if there was one thing Voldemort couldn't understand it was love. Love as powerful as hers for Harry left its own mark. Not a visible sign . . . but to have been loved so deeply, even though the person who loved us is gone, will give us some protection for ever.

Intercessions

Blessed are you, Lord our God,
for you have created us all.
We are your children,
loved by you
and ever under your care and protection.
We thank you for our life, your love
and all that you give us.
Blessed are you, Father, Son and Holy Spirit.

We thank you for the Church
that tells of your love
and helps people to know you.
Loving God, bless our Church,
that it may show your love to all who come to it.
We remember especially today
any who would have liked to be here
but were not able to come.

Silence

Life-giving and loving God,
hear us and help us.

We thank you for the wonderful world
that you have given us,
for the air we breathe and for water.
We thank you for all growing things and for food.
God bless all who work hard
to provide us with what we need.
We pray especially for hungry and homeless people.

Silence

Life-giving and loving God,
hear us and help us.

We thank you God for the love of our homes.
Thank you for the love and care of our mother.
We pray for families where a loved one is ill
or causing trouble.
We remember all who are suffering from lack of love,
and those who live in homes where there is tension
and broken relationships.

Silence

Life-giving and loving God,
hear us and help us.

We thank you for the confidence and joy we have
through knowing we are loved.
We ask your blessing
upon all who are lonely or neglected.
We pray for those separated from their loved ones
through illness or circumstance.
We pray for all who have been taken into care.

Silence

Life-giving and loving God,
hear us and help us.

We give thanks for your eternal love
and we pray to you for all our loved ones departed.
We remember all who have enriched our lives
by their goodness.
We commit our loved ones and all people
to your unfailing love.

Silence

Merciful Father,
**accept these prayers
for the sake of your Son,
our Saviour Jesus Christ.
Amen.**

Memory verse

Above all, clothe yourself with love, which binds everything together in perfect harmony. And let the peace of Christ rule in your hearts.
Colossians 3:14, 15

Suggested music

Bind us together, Lord
The King of love my shepherd is
In the Lord I'll be ever thankful
I come with joy

CANDLES, LAMPS and TORCHES

Today is a day for the family to worship together, to rejoice in being a family and to give thanks for their mutual love. Involve as many of the children as possible in doing things. Let them bring up the bread and wine, and take the collection. The children could carry banners expressing thanksgiving for the love of their homes and the love of God. Children could be encouraged to bring a photograph of their mother to the altar rail. Let children lead some of the intercessions and some of the readings. It should be possible for a mother and a child to share in a reading. If flowers or cards are given out, remember all of us have a mother. Encourage all to come forward. Some may like then to place their flowers or card near the candles if their mother has died and is now in God's kingdom and love.

Fifth Sunday of Lent

Aim

To show Jesus as the resurrection and the life.

Preparation

Place two posters in the entrance porch. One says, 'Death is not fatal!' The other says, 'God so loved the world that he gave his only Son, so that everyone who believes in him may not perish but have everlasting life' (John 3:16).'

Opening activity

Mini drama

Voice 1   Throw it away; it has passed its sell-by date.
Voice 2   We shall not perish but have eternal life.
Voice 3   It will not last; it is perishable goods.
Voice 2   We shall not perish but have eternal life.
Voice 4   It's worn out; it could not last for ever.
Voice 2   We shall not perish but have eternal life.
Voice 5   They are meant to be disposable, dispensed with.
All   We shall not perish but have eternal life.

Opening prayer

God, we thank you for your redeeming love.
You have sent your Son to be our Saviour.
You have rescued us from darkness and death
and given us eternal life.
To you, Lord, be praise and glory for ever.
Amen.

Opening song

How sweet the name of Jesus sounds

Readings

Ezekiel 37:1-14
Psalm 130
Romans 8:6-11
John 11:1-45

Thought for the day

In Lent we meet three events from St John's Gospel. Nicodemus was in the dark and he came to Jesus, the Light of the World. The woman at the well thirsted for life; she met Jesus by chance and found the Living Water. Lazarus was known to Jesus and loved by him but could no longer come to Jesus because he was dead. Jesus came to him and he comes as the resurrection and the life.

In St John's Gospel there are seven miracle stories. The first is Jesus meeting our lack of supplies in the changing of the water into wine. The seventh is when all our human resources are gone and Jesus comes as the resurrection and the life.

Today's miracle is in Bethany, only two miles from Jerusalem. Lazarus is ill. Jesus is beside the river Jordan, teaching and caring for people. A messenger arrives from Mary and Martha and says simply, 'Lord, he whom you love is ill.' There is no request to come because they knew he would come. Jesus continued his work by the Jordan for two days. (Jesus could not be in two places at once as he had the same limitations as any human. It is only after the Ascension that Jesus could be present at all places, at all times.)

Jesus decides to go and says to his disciples, 'Let us go to Judea again.' The disciples are worried about the dangers and Jesus tells them not to worry. Jesus tells them Lazarus is asleep (a euphemism for dead). The disciples misunderstand and say, 'Good, sleep will help him to recover.' Jesus tells them Lazarus is dead and says, 'Let us go to him.' Thomas expresses their fears and the danger when he says to the disciples, 'Let us also go, that we may die with him.'

When they arrive at the outskirts of Bethany, Lazarus has already been in the tomb for four days. Martha hears that Jesus is coming and goes to meet him. Martha says to Jesus, 'Lord, if you had been here my brother would not have died.' Jesus tells Martha that Lazarus will rise again. Martha says she believes in the resurrection on the last day. Jesus wants her to believe not in a future theory but in the reality of the resurrection in him, to believe in him. Faith is to be in the living Lord. Jesus says to her, 'I am the resurrection and the life. Those who believe in me, even though they die, will live, and everyone who lives and believes in me will never die. Do you believe this?' (John 11:25, 26). This is a question we all have to answer. It is a question about our relationship with Jesus and whether we believe in him.

Martha now goes to tell Mary. Jesus waits, possibly hoping they would have a time of quiet together. But the mourners, thinking Mary is going to the tomb, follow her. Mary kneels at the feet of Jesus and says the same as Martha: 'Lord, if you had been here my brother would not have died.' Everyone is weeping and wailing and this disturbs Jesus. Deeply moved, he asks to see where Lazarus is. 'Jesus wept.' (This used to be the shortest sentence in the Bible; it's a pity it is made longer in newer translations.) Again this shows the humanity of Jesus.

Coming to the tomb, Jesus asks that the stone sealing the entrance be moved. Martha questions the wisdom as her brother's body is in a state of decay. Jesus asks about belief. So they move the stone. Jesus now speaks to the Father and then cries, 'Lazarus, come out.' In that moment Lazarus came out in his grave cloths. Jesus says, 'Unbind him and let him go.' It is suggested that this not only means 'loose him' but 'let him go home'. Can we see these as words that Jesus speaks over the grave of each one of us?

John continues to tell us that some believed. Others reported to the opposition, the Pharisees, and they begin to plot to kill him. Caiaphas would say, 'It is better for one man to die for the people.' The crucifixion moves a step closer.

Question time

How do you show that you believe in Jesus and the resurrection?

Can you, as a Christian, witness that in Jesus death is not fatal?

Illustration

An American army chaplain tells how the raising of Lazarus affected one marine. There was a Bible study group on board a troopship returning from Japan. After studying this passage, a marine said, 'Everything is pointing at me.' The marine described how he had led a wild life and got into bad trouble. No one knew, except God. He felt guilty. He said his life was ruined and he could not face his family. He felt he was a dead man. 'But after reading this chapter, I have come alive again. I know that this resurrection Jesus was talking about is in the here and now, for he has raised me from death to life.' No doubt this man's troubles were not over, but in meeting Jesus he experienced the resurrection and the life.

Intercessions

Blessed are you, Lord our God,
who sent your Son to be our Saviour.
In your love you have opened for us
the way to eternal life
and rescued us from perishing.
Blessed are you, Father, Son and Holy Spirit.

Come, Lord, to refresh and renew your Church,
which without you is dull and dry.
Come fill the Church,
which without you is dead.
Fill the Church with your life-giving presence
and give it the power
to proclaim the resurrection to eternal life.
Lord, renew our faith in you.
Give to your Church
a new sense of mission and outreach.
Bless all preachers and ministers of the sacraments
with the joy of the Good News.

Silence

Come, Lord, revive us,
renew your people.

Come, Lord, be known
in all who share in your saving purpose.
Guide and bless all rescue workers.
We remember doctors and nurses,
ambulance workers and paramedics.
We pray for the fire service, the people on lifeboats
and all who risk their lives
in the care and service of others.
We pray for all who are carers within our communities.

Silence

Come, Lord, revive us,
renew your people.

Come, Lord, let your presence be known
in our homes and in our lives.
Bless us in all our relationships
and dealings with others.
Come, Lord, with your light and love
to lives that are struggling with poverty and debt,
with bad housing and broken-down communities.

Silence

Come, Lord, revive us,
renew your people.

Come, Lord, to all whose hope is gone,
the lost, the despairing and the deeply depressed.
We remember the over-worked, the world-weary,
the exhausted and the worn-out.
We ask your blessing
upon those who feel wrung out and dry,
all who feel numb
and those whose senses are deadened.
We pray for all suffering from deep stress or trauma
and their loved ones caring for them.

Silence

Come, Lord, revive us,
renew your people.

We give thanks for the hope of life eternal.
We remember in your presence
our friends and loved ones departed.
May we all come to know the joys of your kingdom
and the fullness of life eternal.

Silence

Merciful Father,
**accept these prayers
for the sake of your Son,
our Saviour Jesus Christ.
Amen.**

Memory verse

I am the resurrection and the life. Those who believe in me, even though they die, will live, and everyone who believes in me will never die. Do you believe this?
John 11:25, 26

Suggested music

I am the bread of life
There's a wideness in God's mercy
Christ's is the world

CANDLES

Aim

To show how Jesus gives life.

Teaching

Mary, Martha and Lazarus were friends of Jesus. (Let us say their names together.) Once when Jesus was teaching beside the river Jordan a messenger came from Mary and Martha saying, 'He whom you love is ill.' Jesus could not leave straightaway but he did leave two days later. Yet Jesus knew that Lazarus was no longer ill – he had died.

Mary and Martha and their friends were all very sad. They were crying and very upset. If Jesus had been there, he could have helped Lazarus. But now it was too late. Before Jesus came, they buried Lazarus in a cave in the hillside and then rolled a big stone against the entrance to the cave. It was very sad.

Someone told Martha, 'Jesus is coming.' She hurried to meet him. When she got to him she said, 'If you had been here, Lazarus need not have died.' Jesus told her not to worry so much because Lazarus would rise again. He asked Martha to believe in him and trust him.

Martha then went to tell Mary that Jesus was not far away. Mary went out of the house hoping to see Jesus by herself but all her friends followed her. They thought she was going to where Lazarus was buried, to cry. When she came to Jesus, she said the same thing as her sister: 'If you had been here, Lazarus need not have died.' Everyone started to cry, and Jesus also cried. They were all upset.

Jesus asked to see where Lazarus was buried. When he came to the place, he asked them to roll away the stone. Martha did not want to do this because Lazarus had been buried for four days. But, because Jesus asked, she got some of the men to move the big stone away. Jesus prayed to God the Father. Then Jesus spoke to Lazarus. Jesus called into the dark cave, 'Lazarus, come out.' Slowly Lazarus rose up and came to the mouth of the cave – he was alive again. Jesus had made him come alive. It was a miracle. What was it? A miracle.

Jesus told the people to take the bandages off him and to let him go home. Every one was very happy and said how wonderful Jesus was. Jesus had made Lazarus come alive – it was miracle.

Activity

This is a very dramatic story which the children could act out. There is an opportunity to show Lazarus coming out of the cave on the worksheets.

If you want a game, they could play 'sleeping tigers'. When the music stops they are to lie down and pretend to be asleep. They must not move at all. Anyone who moves is out. When the music starts, let them rise up and move around.

Prayer

Jesus, you are wonderful.
You made Lazarus come alive again.
We thank you for your love
and for our life.
Amen.

Song

When Jesus heard that his very good friend called Lazarus had died

LAMPS

Aim

To show how Jesus gives life to Lazarus.

Teaching

Jesus had some friends who lived at Bethany, which is only two miles from Jerusalem. He had not seen them for a while because he was away from Jerusalem and teaching near the river Jordan. While he was away, his friend Lazarus became ill. His sisters Mary and Martha were very worried about him so they sent a messenger to Jesus, saying, 'He whom you love is ill.' They did not ask Jesus to come because they knew he would.

Jesus wanted first to finish the work he was doing, then he set off. He told his disciples where they were going and they were worried. To be near to Jerusalem would put Jesus in danger from the Pharisees. But Jesus would not be put off, even though by now he knew that Lazarus had died.

When he got near to Bethany, Martha came running to meet him. She said, 'If you had been here, my brother need not have died.' Jesus was sad for Martha and told her not to worry for Lazarus would rise again. Martha said she believed he would at the end of the world. But Jesus said, 'Believe now in me, I am the resurrection and the life.'

Martha went to tell Mary. Mary hurried to see Jesus but all the people who were upset at the death of Lazarus followed her. They thought she was going to the grave to cry. When she reached Jesus she too said, 'If you had been here, my brother need not have died.' All of the people began to weep. Jesus wept.

Jesus asked to see the grave where Lazarus had been buried for four days. They showed him a cave in the hillside with a large stone closing the entrance. There Lazarus was buried. Jesus said to them, 'Take away the stone.' Martha did not want to because Lazarus had been dead for four days. Jesus reminded her to believe in him. So they took away the stone.

Jesus now prayed to God the Father. Then with a loud voice he shouted, 'Lazarus, come out.' Everyone waited and wondered. Lazarus slowly came out with bandages binding his hands and feet, and his face wrapped in a cloth. Jesus told them to unloose him and let him go home. Everyone was so excited. They had never seen anything like this before. It was a miracle.

Activity

On the worksheet are instructions to make a figure that will appear to 'come alive or rise again'. There is also a wordsearch to complete.

Prayer

Lord Jesus, giver of life,
we know that you love us.
As you gave Lazarus life,
you give us life eternal.
We give you thanks and praise.
Amen.

Song

When Jesus heard that his very good friend called Lazarus had died

TORCHES

Aim

To understand how Jesus gives us life eternal.

Teaching

Begin by telling how the people of Israel had been in captivity in Babylon for such a long time. They had lost any hope of living in freedom or returning to their own land. Let two of the young people read Ezekiel 37:1-14, one of them being the voice of God.

If possible, play 'Dem bones, dem bones, dem dry bones'.

Ezekiel had a vision of God giving new life to his people. When Jesus came, the hope of resurrection became a reality in him. Today's Gospel starts off with a friend of Jesus, Lazarus, being seriously ill and his sisters, Martha and Mary, sending a message to Jesus. It is likely the messenger took at least a day to find Jesus. Jesus had work he wanted to finish near the river Jordan and he was delayed further. The disciples were not keen to go to the Jerusalem area as Jesus' life was in danger there. But Jesus did not lack courage and a friend was ill. Mary and Martha knew he would go.

Read John 11:1-44 (you may like to add 45-53). Break it up into sections and have six readers:

> Verses 1-6: Jesus is told of Lazarus
> Verses 7-16: Jesus talks with the disciples
> Verses 17-27: Jesus and Martha
> Verses 28-37: Jesus and Mary. Jesus wept
> Verses 38-44: Jesus and Lazarus – a miracle
> Verses 45-53: Believers and opposition

This is a very dramatic story so let that be captured by the readers. If there is time, it can also be acted out. Get them to see that Jesus moves Martha from saying she believes in the resurrection to saying she believes in Jesus and that he *is* 'the resurrection and the life'. We are not called to believe in the resurrection; we are called to believe in Jesus as the Christ – only in him is the resurrection possible.

Activity

Get the group to discuss verses 25 and 26. They might like also to look at these words by Christina Rossetti:

> My life is like a faded leaf,
> my harvest dwindled to a husk:
> truly my life is void and brief
> and tedious in the barren dusk:
> my life is like a frozen thing,
> no bud nor greenness can I see,
> yet rise it shall – the sap of spring;
> O Jesus, rise in me.

Prayer

Lord Jesus, in you is life
and life eternal.
We put our trust and our hope in you
for with you is life and love.
To you be glory and praise
for ever and ever.
Amen.

Song

Jesus the Lord said: 'I am the bread'

Palm Sunday

Aim

To join in welcoming Jesus as our Saviour and King.

Preparation

Ensure that there is a palm cross for everyone. It is a good exercise to get a few of the older children together and make your own from palm leaves. You may prefer to get palm crosses from Africa and so support a village that spends a good deal of the year making palm crosses. These can usually be obtained from SPCK shops or one of the missionary societies. You can also have palm branches to wave or branches from an evergreen tree. If possible, have some English palm (willow catkins) in church. Have a few tambourines, castanets and shakers for the younger children to play during the procession.

Opening activity

Use the Liturgy of the Palms. Have two children holding trays of palm crosses and two other children to distribute them. (During the distribution everyone could sing the words 'Praise God' over and over to the tune of 'Amazing grace'.)

Get everyone to hold up their palm cross while they are blessed.

Opening prayer

Blessing of the Palms

Lord God,
we hold these palm crosses as signs
of Jesus our King riding into Jerusalem as the Messiah
and of his suffering and dying on the cross.
Bless these palms that they may be to us
a sign of his victory and of your eternal love.
May we who hold them
always accept him as our King
until we rejoice in the kingdom
where he reigns with you and the Holy Spirit,
now and for ever.
Amen.

Readings

Liturgy of the Palms

Matthew 21:1-11
Psalm 118:1, 2, 19-29

Processional

All glory, laud and honour

Let everyone join in a procession around the church (inside or out) as they sing.

Add a hymn or two that the children could sing, for example:

We have king, who rides a donkey
Hosanna, hosanna

Readings

Liturgy of the Passion

Isaiah 50:4-9a
Psalm 31:9-16
Philippians 2:5-11
Matthew 26:14–27:66 or Matthew 27:11-54

Let the dramatic readings of the Passion narratives replace the sermon today. Allow the Scriptures to speak for themselves. Use as many people as possible to share in the readings. I have provided ideas for the Liturgy of the Palms rather than comment on the Passion. I hope Holy Week will be used to do that.

Thought for the day

It is near the Passover and the last events in the life of Jesus begin in great drama. Everywhere is crowded. It is estimated that over 2 million people could make their way to Jerusalem to celebrate the Passover. Already there is a plot to take Jesus and put him to death. Jesus must be careful because it is dangerous for him to enter Jerusalem. Let us look at the courage, the claim and the call of Jesus.

We see the courage of Jesus. He was aware of the hostility and the danger. He knew he was likely to be put to death. But he did not go into hiding. He made a public declaration by his entry into Jerusalem. Jesus challenged the authorities – and does to this day. In many ways the riding into Jerusalem was an act of defiance. Yet he was not foolish. When he sent for the donkey and colt, a password is used: 'The Lord needs them.' Matthew alone talks of two creatures, a donkey and colt. He wanted to show how Jesus literally fulfilled what the prophet said: 'Tell the daughter of Zion. Look, your king is coming to you, humble and mounted on a donkey, a colt, the foal of a donkey' (see Zechariah 9:9). Even in this passage, the double mention of donkey and colt does not imply two creatures but one. It must be remembered that the donkey was considered a noble beast and was sometimes the choice of a king when he rode into a city in peace. To witness to this, the people welcomed him like a king by spreading their cloaks on the road and branches from the trees. Jehu, when he was proclaimed king, was welcomed in this manner by his friends (2 Kings 9:13) and so was Simon Maccabaeus when he entered Jerusalem after a notable victory (see 1 Maccabees 13:51).

So in his entry into Jerusalem we see the claim of Jesus. This is the entrance of a King and of the Messiah. Jesus is the Christ, the One who comes in the name (in the power and presence) of God. It is likely that he is proclaiming to be the cleanser of the Temple as Judas Maccabaeus had done 200 years before. Then people waved branches in the same way and this is the next act of Jesus (see 2 Maccabees 10:7 and Matthew 21:12-14). The cry of the people 'Hosanna' means 'save us now' and is a cry for help. It is a call for deliverance to their Saviour and their King.

The call of Jesus is not one for earthly kingship; it is for the hearts of people. Will we accept him as the

Christ, our Lord and Saviour? Will we let him rule in our hearts? His rule is one of peace and love, and yet many still turn away. Will you acknowledge his claim and hear his call to you?

Question time

How can you show that you have accepted Christ as your King?

Can you help your own community to allow the peace and rule of Christ to enrich their lives?

Illustration

In a time when in some areas even the wearing of a cross is forbidden, and when the media are often pro-other faiths and anti-Christian, one Anglican bishop made a telling comment. He was asked why the Christians did not threaten with bombings and reprisals as some did. The bishop replied simply, 'We are not allowed to react like that: we follow the Prince of Peace.'

Intercessions

Blessed are you, Lord God of our salvation;
to you be praise and glory for ever.
As we rejoice this day
in the triumphant entry into Jerusalem,
may we too be willing to walk the way of the cross.
By our lives may we witness to you
as our Lord and King
and declare your saving love to the world.
Blessed are you, Father, Son and Holy Spirit.

Come, Lord.
Cleanse your Church from any pride or greed.
Cleanse us from our sins and free us to serve you.
Strengthen our sense of mission and service.
Strengthen our sensitivity towards the needs of others.
Strengthen our faith and our vision for your world.

Silence

Saviour of the world, our Redeemer,
save us and help us.

Come, Lord.
Guide the nations into the ways of justice and peace.
Guide all leaders and rulers to care for our world.
Comfort all who are broken by war and violence.
Comfort all who are shattered
by the betrayal of loved ones;
all who feel scorned and rejected.
Comfort all who are imprisoned and wrongly sentenced.

Silence

Saviour of the world, our Redeemer,
save us and help us.

Come, Lord.
As our Saviour and Friend,
bless our homes and our loved ones with your love.
Guide us in all our dealings
and help us to live with you as our Lord.
Let your kingly rule be known in us
as it is in heaven.

Silence

Saviour of the world, our Redeemer,
save us and help us.

Come, Lord.
You were broken on the cross to make us whole.
Be with all who are suffering at this time.
Come as light to those who walk in darkness,
the despairing and the despondent.
Come as joy to all who have lost confidence
and to all who are depressed.
Come as hope to all who are ill
and fearful of their future.

Silence

Saviour of the world, our Redeemer,
save us and help us.

Lord Jesus, we remember that you died
that we might live.
You descended into the depths
to raise us to the heights.
We ask your blessing
upon all our loved ones departed.
May they rejoice in the fullness of your kingdom.

Silence

Merciful Father,
**accept these prayers
for the sake of your Son,
our Saviour Jesus Christ.
Amen.**

Memory verse

He humbled himself and became obedient to the point of death – even death on a cross.
Philippians 2:8

Suggested music

Liturgy of the Palms

Hosanna, Hosanna
Hail the coming Prince of Peace
Ride on, ride on in majesty
Clap your hands
What a wonderful Saviour is Jesus

Suggested music

Liturgy of the Passion

When I survey the wondrous cross
Meekness and majesty
O dearest Lord, your sacred head
Glory be to Jesus
O my Saviour, lifted from the earth
There is a green hill far away

CANDLES

Aim

To capture the joy of the entry into Jerusalem.

Teaching

If the children have taken part in a Palm Sunday procession, talk about it; if not, have a procession. Let the children wave streamers or palm branches and sing the chorus from 'Give me oil in my lamp'.

Show a picture of a donkey. Ask how many of them have seen a donkey or even ridden one. Has anyone noticed that there is a dark line down a donkey's back and across its shoulders? (Draw the shape for them to see). What shape does it make? It is a cross. Where have you seen a cross? Is there one in church? Why do we have a cross? We have it because Jesus died on a cross. But let me tell you what happened a few days before that, when the people wanted Jesus to be their king.

Jesus wanted to go into Jerusalem – and he wanted people to know he was their king. Sometimes kings used to ride a donkey. Jesus asked someone to lend him a donkey. He said he would send his disciples to get it. He told the man he would give them secret words to say. They would say, 'The Lord needs it.' (Let us say, 'The Lord needs it.')

Once they had the donkey, the disciples put a cloak on its back for Jesus to sit on. As they came near to Jerusalem there were lots of people and they were very excited. They believed that Jesus was sent by God, and they shouted 'Hosanna' (let us shout it), which means 'Save us' (now let us shout that).

The people started to make a carpet for the donkey to walk on. They took off their cloaks and spread them on the ground. They cut branches off the palm trees and laid them on the ground. Some waved palm branches in the air (get the children to wave streamers or palm branches – or their palm crosses). It was all very exciting. They wanted Jesus to be their king.

Let us invite Jesus to be our King. Jesus will look after us and save us because he is our Saviour.

Activity

Today the main activity is the Palm procession. Re-enact this at the end of the lesson. Get the girls to shout, 'Hosanna', and the boys to shout, 'Save us'. Let them pretend to lay cloaks on the ground. Give them something to wave. Let them all shout, 'Welcome to Jesus our King.'

Prayer

Jesus, you are our King and Saviour.
We welcome you and we shout,
'Hosanna – save us.'
We know you love us and we give our love to you today and always.
Amen.

Song

Give me oil in my lamp (chorus only)

LAMPS

Aim

To show the courage of Jesus.

Teaching

Ask the children if they know what a 'wanted poster' is. It would be good to create a wanted poster for them to see, the sort that used to be in cowboy movies: Wanted. Dead or Alive. Reward $500.

Some of the Pharisees in Jerusalem had planned to kill Jesus. They had offered a reward for his capture. The disciples knew this and did not want Jesus to go to Jerusalem because it was too dangerous. Jesus said he was not afraid and he was not afraid to die. The disciples thought it might be good to sneak into Jerusalem secretly, but Jesus wanted the people to see him and to know he was the One sent by God to be their Saviour. Jesus was very brave.

He arranged with a man to borrow his donkey. He told the man he would send his disciples to get it and they would have a password. They would say, 'The Lord needs it.' So everything was ready.

Jesus knew the road would be crowded with people and this was the time to enter Jerusalem. He sent the disciples for the donkey. When they returned with it, a disciple put his cloak over it for Jesus to sit on. They set off for the city. The disciples could see Jesus was not afraid. He wanted the people to know he was the Christ, God's Chosen One, the Saviour. (Let us say together, 'Jesus is the Christ, God's Chosen One, the Saviour.')

People were excited when they saw Jesus. He was riding like a king – he could save them. The people started to lay their cloaks on the ground to make a carpet for Jesus to travel over. Others cut down palm branches and laid them on the road – this is the welcome they would give a king. Jesus on a donkey and his disciples had become a royal procession.

The people recognised he was sent from God and they started to shout, 'Hosanna', and wave palm branches. 'Hosanna' was a shout of welcome but it also means 'Save us'. They wanted Jesus as their king to rescue them from trouble. Everyone was shouting and waving. Jesus was noticed by everyone. Jesus had challenged the authorities and he was not afraid.

Have the activity next. Then look at the shape of the palm cross. Ask them why it is in that shape. Get the children to show how much they know about the events leading up to the crucifixion and the crucifixion itself. Make sure they know the day Jesus died: Good Friday. If there is a service for them on that day, remind them and why it is then.

Activity

Encourage the group to make their own palm procession. Get them to shout 'Hosanna' and 'Save us'. As they march round the room they could sing 'We have a King who rides a donkey'.

Prayer

Jesus, we welcome you as our King.
Come rule in our hearts.
We shout, 'Hosanna',
because we know that you love us
and you are our Saviour.
Come, Lord Jesus, as King
and help us.
Amen.

Song

We have a King who rides a donkey

TORCHES

Aim

To look at the entry into Jerusalem and the events leading to the crucifixion.

Teaching

Jesus and the disciples knew it was dangerous to come to Jerusalem. The Jewish authorities had already put a price on Jesus' head. They would like to take him prisoner and kill him. The disciples were anxious about this but Jesus told them not to be fearful.

Jesus showed great courage but he was not foolish. The borrowing of a donkey and the choice of the Upper Room were both planned without everyone knowing. To get the donkey, the disciples had to give the password, 'The Lord needs it.'

Jesus set off on the donkey when the roads were full of people for the Passover. This was a public act to be seen and in defiance of those who sought his life. The people gave Jesus the 'red carpet treatment'. They laid their cloaks on the ground and strewed palm branches in the way. This was a royal welcome, though they may have been disappointed that Jesus rode a donkey for it is a symbol of peace. They welcomed Jesus as their chosen one, their liberator, and wanted him to be their saviour. Sadly their vision was only limited to freeing them from the Romans and not the greater freedom Jesus could bring. (Spend some time discussing this.) Their cry of 'Hosanna', which means 'Save us', was a cry for help.

This event would only annoy the Jewish leaders even more. They would use this to say that Jesus was in danger of leading a rebellion against the Romans. Possibly it annoyed Judas that Jesus did *not* lead a rebellion. Soon Jesus would be scorned and rejected, deserted by friends, crucified, dead and buried. Within a week Jesus would be on the cross. (Our palm crosses are to show him as our King who triumphed over death and brought us the glorious freedom of the children of God.)

Everyone wants Jesus to do what they want – to do as they ask him. They do not want a king but a puppet. Jesus is our King and he wants us to follow him, to let him rule in our hearts. He will become the scorned and the rejected, 'but to all who received him, who believed in his name, to them he gave power to become the children of God' (John 1:12).

Activity

Encourage the group to look at the Palm Sunday events and what happened in the week following. Make sure they know the main events and the names of the days. Let them look at Zechariah 9:9 and see what Jesus was fulfilling.

Prayer

Lord Jesus, you are our King.
Come and rule in our hearts
that your kingdom may come in us.
Lord, we give thanks to you
for you are our Saviour.
Amen.

Song

Hosanna, hosanna

EASTER
Easter Day

Aim

To enter into the wonder and joy of Easter.

Preparation

Involve as many children as possible in the Easter preparations. Invite the children to help decorate the church with flowers. Let the children share in preparing the Easter Garden and in covering a large wooden cross with spring flowers. Banners can be made with words such as 'Jesus is risen!', 'Christ is alive!', 'Jesus is here!'. If possible, everyone should be able to light a candle from the Easter Candle or from his or her neighbour's candle.

Opening activity

Let there be a procession where banners are carried and the flower-covered cross leads the way. Stop at the tomb for a rolling away of the stone (let a child do this). Shout, 'Alleluia, Christ is risen', with the response, 'He is risen indeed. Alleluia.' Light the Easter Candle (again let a child do this). Once more shout, 'Alleluia, Christ is risen', and have the same response as before.

After the Gospel have two women or girls come down and light two small candles to put in a sand tray. The first one says, 'I light this for Mary Magdalene who saw the Lord. Alleluia, Christ is risen.' All reply, 'He is risen indeed. Alleluia.'

The second says, 'I light a candle for Mary the mother of James who saw the Lord. Alleluia, Christ is risen.' All reply, 'He is risen indeed. Alleluia.'

All then sing the Celtic Alleluia.

Opening prayer

Glory and honour and blessing be yours,
great and mighty God.
In the resurrection you have destroyed death
and opened to us the gate of glory.
In you are life and life eternal.
We give you thanks and praise for ever and ever.
Amen.

Opening song

Jesus Christ is risen today

Readings

Acts 10:34-43 or Jeremiah 31:1-6
Psalm 118:1, 2, 14-24
Colossians 3:1-4 or Acts 10:34-43
John 20:1-18 or Matthew 28:1-10

Thought for the day

In these few verses from Matthew is an earth-changing event. Nothing can be the same once you know the risen Lord.

He begins by telling us two Marys go to the tomb, no doubt to pay their respects to the dead. One was Mary Magdalene and the other was Mary the mother of James (see Mark 16:1). We are told that these two women were present at the death (Matthew 27:56) and burial of Jesus (27:61). Their faithfulness brings them to the empty tomb.

Matthew tells of the earth shaking and the appearance of an angel. The guards shake with fear. But the two Marys are told, 'Do not be afraid; I know that you are looking for Jesus who was crucified. He is not here; for he has been raised.' They are not to look for the living among the dead. Jesus is alive. 'Come, see the place where he lay.' They are asked to believe and to go and tell the disciples, 'He has been raised from the dead.'

Now they leave the tomb with awe and wonder and great joy. They run to tell the good news. On their way Jesus meets them and says, 'Greetings.' The word Jesus used for 'greetings' is 'chairete', which means 'rejoice'. How can you do other than this if you have met the risen Lord! Knowing the risen Lord fills our lives with hope and joy.

The women worship him and hold on to him. Jesus then tells them, 'Do not be afraid; go and tell my brothers to go to Galilee: there they will see me.'

Jesus is not just a figure in history; he is the living Lord. He is not just a memory but is alive and seeks a relationship with us. Christians are not those who know *about* Christ but those who know him, meet with him and talk with him.

The sequence of this Gospel is: come and see, believe and tell. Note how they meet Jesus and worship him before they tell the Good News. Outreach and mission can only arise out of our own personal encounter with Christ. Know that the Lord is risen. The Lord is with you. Alleluia.

Question time

Do you spend enough time getting to know the risen Lord?

Worshipping and knowing Christ should make us want to share with others. How can you tell of him?

Illustration

1066 is a date we all know: the Battle of Hastings. Did you know the Normans nearly lost the battle?

The English were behind a stockade. The Normans twice tried to break through. The second time they were repelled, it was rumoured that their leader was dead. The troops immediately began to lose heart. Soon they would be in headlong flight. William pulled off his helmet and rode among his troops shouting, 'I am alive. I am still alive.' The result was immediate: new courage, new strength of heart and purpose. This time they burst through the stockade and victory was won.

How like the state of the disciples after Good Friday. They had seen Jesus die; they had lost heart. And then, on that Easter morning, Jesus said to Mary, 'Tell them I am still alive.' What a difference his appearing would make to them and to the world.

Intercessions

Blessed are you, Lord God,
by whose power our Lord Jesus is raised from the dead.
In your presence is life and life eternal.
In your power death is conquered
and the gate to eternal life is opened.
In your presence is the fullness of joy.
Blessed are you, Father, Son and Holy Spirit.

Lord, make us aware of your risen presence
in our lives.
May our worship be full of joy and awe.
Give us the courage to go out
to proclaim your love and your saving power.
Lord, as we celebrate your resurrection,
strengthen your Church
to tell the Good News to the whole world.
Bless all who are called to teach and preach
in your name.
In the power of the risen Lord,
may they lead us from darkness
to his glorious light.

Silence

Risen Lord,
**deliver us from the dominion
of darkness and death.**

Lord Jesus, as we rejoice in your risen presence,
we pray that the world may know your peace.
May we rise above division and strife,
that your victory over darkness and death
may be known in the world.
Lord, show us the peace we should give,
the peace we should share
and the peace we must forgo.

Silence

Risen Lord,
**deliver us from the dominion
of darkness and death.**

Risen Lord, you appeared to the two Marys
and sent them to tell the disciples.
Help us to show your presence in our homes
and in all our dealings.
Let us walk and work in your presence
and seek to reveal your glory in the world.
We ask you to bless all our loved ones and friends
and keep us ever in your love.

Silence

Risen Lord,
**deliver us from the dominion
of darkness and death.**

We remember all who walk in darkness
and who are heavily burdened.
We pray for all who have lost hope and who despair.
We ask your blessing
upon all who are chronically ill

and those who can no longer cope on their own.
We pray for all who are approaching death
and their loved ones who are caring for them.

Silence

Risen Lord,
**deliver us from the dominion
of darkness and death.**

Risen Lord, we ask that we might share
in your resurrection
and triumph over darkness and death.
We ask your blessing
upon our friends and loved ones
who are departed from us.
May they have a share with your saints in glory.
This day we rejoice that death is conquered:
we are free, for Christ has won the victory.

Silence

Merciful Father,
**accept these prayers
for the sake of your Son,
our Saviour Jesus Christ.
Amen.**

Memory verse

I know that you are looking for Jesus who was crucified.
He is not here, for he has been raised.
Matthew 28:5, 6

Suggested music

Christ the Lord is risen again
The strife is o'er, the battle done
Peruvian Gloria
Thine be the glory
This is the day
Walking in a garden
Jesus lives! thy terrors now
The angel rolled the stone away

CANDLES

Aim

To celebrate that Jesus is risen.

Teaching

Show the children a real egg. Ask if they know what is inside. Sealed up in this egg is a little chick and one day it will break out. If the mother hen cares for an egg, it will hatch. This means that one day the little chick will be able to break out of the shell and be seen by its mother and by anyone who is around.

Who knows what happened to Jesus on Good Friday? He was crucified – he was killed on a cross. This made his friends very sad, including two women with the same name – Mary Magdalene and Mary the mother of James. They watched when Jesus was taken down from the cross and they were there when Jesus was buried.

Does anyone know where Jesus was buried? It was in a cave, in large hole in a rocky hillside. Then they found a large stone and rolled it over the opening to the cave. It took a few men to do it. The women were watching and they were very sad because Jesus was in the dark, cold tomb.

The next day they did not go to where Jesus was buried but they did on the Sunday. Mary Magdalene and Mary the mother of James went to where Jesus was buried. They thought they would go near the big stone. But when they got there the stone had been moved. It had been rolled away. The two Marys did not know what to think. They looked into the cave and an angel of God told them that Jesus was not there – he had risen. Jesus had broken out of the tomb and was alive. Then they knew that they had to go and tell the disciples. They started to hurry away but as they went Jesus met them. His was alive. He talked with them. They hugged him. Jesus was really alive.

Jesus told them to go and tell his friends, the disciples, that he was alive and that he would soon meet them. The women were so excited. They ran to where the disciples were and said, 'Jesus is alive. He is risen.' They were all so happy: Jesus is alive. He is risen. (Let us say this together.) Now let each of us say it to the person next to us until everyone has said, 'Jesus is alive. He is risen.'

Activity

Have an Easter egg hunt – outside if practical. Alternatively, you could hide a few small Easter chicks (easily obtainable from craft and stationery shops). It is good to hide only enough for one each and they have to be shared out when all are found.

Prayer

Jesus, we are happy that you are alive,
that you have risen.
Thank you for the resurrection
and for being our friend.
Amen.

Song

Jesus has risen from the dead, from the dead,
from the dead,
Jesus has risen from the dead
on this Easter morning.

(To the tune of 'Here we go round the mulberry bush')

LAMPS

Aim

To enter into the joy of Easter.

Teaching

Begin by talking about what happened on Good Friday. Make sure the children know the events, and that Jesus was crucified, dead and buried. Explain how it would be dangerous for the disciples to be near. Tell them that

the two Marys were at the crucifixion and at the burial of Jesus, and how it made them very sad. Talk about how Jesus was buried in a cave in the hillside and a great stone rolled to close the entrance and that it was then sealed up so that no one could get in. Say how the women could not go to the tomb on the Sabbath (Saturday).

On the Sunday, very early in the morning, the two Marys went to the tomb. They wanted to show their love for Jesus and show their sorrow at his death. When they got to the tomb the large stone was rolled away and Jesus was not lying in the tomb. An angel of God asked them why they were looking for Jesus who was crucified – he was not there because he has been raised. The angel invited them to look at the empty tomb. They saw that Jesus was not there. The angel told them to go and tell the disciples, 'Jesus is risen.' They were amazed and began to run to tell the disciples but as they went Jesus met them. They hugged him and gave their love to him. Then Jesus sent them to the disciples. He said, 'Go and tell them I have risen from the dead and I will meet them.' The women were so excited. They had seen the risen Lord. They had to tell the disciples the Good News. When they got to the disciples they said, 'Jesus is risen.' And they told how they had seen him.

Let us say together, 'Jesus is risen.' Now let us say it again and add, 'Alleluia.'

Activity

Print out in large letters (one letter to an A4 page): A, A, E, E, E, I, I, I, U, U, S, S, S, S, L, L, L, J, R, N.

Ask the children to take the letters and make a sentence for a poster – all should have at least one letter. The clue is that it is about today. If they struggle, tell them it starts with a name. If they continue to be stuck, get them to put it in order by telling them it is the Good News that 'JESUS IS RISEN. ALLELUIA.'

Prayer

God our Father, we thank you
for the resurrection of Jesus,
that he is alive and is our friend.
Jesus, we know that you are alive
and we are happy to say,
'Jesus is risen. Alleluia.'
Amen.

Song

The women went to Jesus' tomb

TORCHES

Aim

To show how we should share the Good News of the resurrection.

Teaching

Has anyone been abroad? What happens when you arrive in another country or when you return home?

You have to go through Customs. Do you know what question is asked by the Customs? It is: 'Have you anything to declare?' To this there are three answers: 'No' because you have nothing, 'Yes' because you have, and 'No' when you refuse to tell. With the last answer you are in danger of losing what you are carrying.

Have someone read Matthew 28:1-10. Let the group now discuss the Resurrection. Note how in Matthew the first appearance is to Mary Magdalene and the other Mary (see also Mark 16:1). They went to pay their respects to the dead. We are told that these two women were present at the death (Matthew 27:56) and burial of Jesus (27:61).

Now they are faced with the empty tomb. They are told that Jesus is not there because he has been raised. They are invited to see for themselves and then 'Go and tell'. This Good News cannot be kept to themselves; they must share it with others. There is an urgency to 'tell'. The women run – which is very unusual in the Holy Land – to tell the disciples. Suddenly Jesus meets them on their journey. They hold on to him and worship him. Then Jesus tells then to 'Go and tell'.

We really cannot keep the Good News to ourselves. We have something to declare! Jesus Christ is risen. Death is defeated. God in his love has redeemed us and given us eternal life. If we do not tell the Good News, we are in danger of losing the awareness of it ourselves. Worship of the risen Lord should always lead to telling the Good News, to outreach and mission.

Activity

Stand in a circle in twos with hands at your side. All say, 'Christ has died', while you stretch out your arms to make the shape of a cross. Then slowly lower them and bow down low to the ground. Shout, 'Christ is risen', as you raise your hands high. Shake hands with your partner and say, 'Alleluia.' Now go round the circle, one clockwise and the other anti-clockwise. The clockwise say, 'Christ is risen', and the anti-clockwise say, 'Alleluia'. Once they meet their partner they go round again, this time saying the other words. When they get back to their places everyone says, 'Christ will come again.' You may have to practise this to get it to flow but it is worth it.

Prayer

God, we thank you for those who have told us
the Good News of your love
and that Jesus is risen from the dead.
As we know the risen Christ,
let us tell others about this wonderful miracle.
Amen.

Song

Risen! Risen! Jesus is risen!

Second Sunday of Easter

Aim

To continue to rejoice in the presence of the risen Lord who comes to us.

Preparation

Have the Easter Candle ready, plus sand tray and 13 candles.

Opening activity

Have a child light the Easter Candle. Proclaim, 'Alleluia, Christ is risen', and let all respond, 'He is risen indeed. Alleluia.'

Then let one girl or woman light a candle from the Easter Candle and say, ' I am Mary Magdalene. Alleluia, Christ is risen.' All respond, 'He is risen indeed. Alleluia.'

A second girl or woman says, 'I am Mary the mother of James. Alleluia, Christ is risen.' All respond, 'He is risen indeed. Alleluia.'

The candles are now placed in the sand tray.

After the Gospel, have ten people come down and light ten small candles to put in a sand tray. Once all the candles are lit, the ten say together, 'We are the ten disciples and we have seen the Lord. Alleluia, Christ is risen.' All respond, 'He is risen indeed. Alleluia.'

Let Thomas appear from a pew: 'Do not forget me. I doubted but I have also seen the Lord. Alleluia, Christ is risen.' All respond, 'He is risen indeed. Alleluia.'

(You may like to explain why there are only eleven disciples and who is missing.)

Opening prayer

Lord Jesus Christ,
who made yourself known
to the disciples after your resurrection
and to Thomas amid his doubting,
come and be known among us.
Fill our darkness with your light
and our doubt with your love,
today and always.
Amen.

Opening song

Jesus, stand among us

Readings

Acts 2:14a, 22-32
Psalm 16
1 Peter 1:3-9
John 20:19-31

Thought for the day

Last week's Gospel ended with the two Marys going to tell the disciples they had seen the Lord. They had a message of joy and hope.

Today's Gospel starts on the evening of the same day. Ten disciples are locked in for fear of the Jews, frightened to go out or to let anyone in. Closed doors do not hinder Jesus. He comes and gives them the typical Jewish greeting: 'Shalom' – 'peace and well-being be yours'. As it is a common greeting, Jesus is almost saying, 'Hello, I'm back!' Jesus shows them his hands and his side that still have the wounds of the crucifixion. The disciples are full of joy in his presence.

As God sent Jesus, now Jesus sends out his disciples. To enable them to go boldly, Jesus again offers them his peace. Then he breathes on them and says, 'Receive the Holy Spirit.' Just as God breathed life into Adam and Eve, Jesus breathes life into his new creation. Just as the Spirit gave life to the dry bones in the valley, and God gave hope to the people of Israel (Ezekiel 37), so Jesus gives new life and courage to his disciples.

Thomas was not there. When he returns he hears what has happened and sees the excitement of the disciples but refuses to accept their word only. Thomas wants to see Jesus – seeing is believing!

It is worth noting:

1. Thomas stayed with those who had the experience; he remained with the disciples. He listened to what they had to say. He prayed with them, ate with them and no doubt questioned them. It is through the believing community that most people encounter the risen Lord.
2. Thomas was not afraid to express his doubt – for that is how he really feels. But he did not depart from the disciples because he was truly seeking. The surest way to belief is to mix with real believers. It may be doubt but it was not rejection. Thomas kept an open mind.

There lives more faith in honest doubt,
believe me, than in half the creeds.
In Memoriam, Tennyson (1850)

Jesus comes again and once more says, 'Peace be with you.' How often do we let the peace of the risen Lord enter our lives and hearts? We believe it, but do we give it the opportunity to happen?

Thomas is now invited to reach out and put his finger in the nail holes and his hand into the wounded side. Thomas needs no more proof and says to Jesus, 'My Lord and my God.' Here, almost at the end of St John's Gospel, is the declaration that Jesus is God. Jesus is not just a good man; Jesus is a man but Jesus is also God.

There are many who have not seen Jesus – but they are blessed by their belief in him. This belief is a relationship with the unseen yet ever-present Christ.

Question time

How often do we let the peace of the risen Lord enter our lives and hearts? We believe it but do we give it the opportunity to happen?

How can our community of the faithful help others to come to know the risen Lord?

Illustration

As a result of an explosion a small group of miners were trapped underground in a confined area. The phone to the surface still worked and they indicated they were all alive but they feared there was not enough air. It was realised that they would die without help – instant help. There was not much hope of getting them out alive. There were tons of earth to be removed and it was calculated it would be too late by the time it was done. With a special drill the rescue team bored a hole to where the men were and then pumped air into the cavern. Though it took another three days to get them out, the men were found to be well and in good spirits. When one of them was asked what it was like he replied. 'A bit like the resurrection. We were sealed in a tomb unable to get out. Then we were given new air, the breath of life from the air pumped in to us. And then we were rescued and raised into the light.'

Intercessions

Blessed are you,
God and Father of our Lord Jesus Christ.
To you be glory and praise for ever.
By raising your Son from the dead,
death has been destroyed
and new life has been restored.
In him the victory over sin and the grave is won.
As you call us to newness of life,
may our lives reflect his glory.
Blessed are you, Father, Son and Holy Spirit.

Lord, bless your Church,
that it may reveal your presence
and the power of the resurrection.
May each church community
show signs of new life and joy in you.
Through our relationship with you
may we bring others to be faithful.
We ask your blessing upon
all who are seekers,
all who are new in the faith
and all who are struggling with doubt and darkness.

Silence

Lord, be known among us;
make haste to help us.

Lord, bless the world with your peace,
the peace that it cannot achieve on its own.
We pray for peace between nations and peoples.
We ask your blessing upon all peacemakers
and the work of the United Nations.
We pray for all who live in fear for their lives
and all who have lost confidence in themselves
or the world around them.

Silence

Lord, be known among us;
make haste to help us.

Lord, bless our homes and families
with the joy of your presence.
May our homes be ever open to you and your love.
We remember today all who suffer
from poverty or homelessness.

We ask your blessing
upon all who live amid strife and fear
and all who are unable to rejoice in life.

Silence

Lord, be known among us;
make haste to help us.

Lord, bless all who feel restricted
by what is happening around them.
We remember all who live in violent or deprived areas.
We ask your blessing upon all who are ill
or who have been injured through accidents,
and upon those who care for them.
Lord, give them courage and hope in their troubles.

Silence

Lord, be known among us;
make haste to help us.

Lord of life and life eternal,
bless our loved ones departed,
that in fellowship with all your saints
they may rejoice
in the fullness of your presence and glory.

Silence

Merciful Father,
**accept these prayers
for the sake of your Son,
our Saviour Jesus Christ.
Amen.**

Memory verse

He showed them his hands and his side. Then the disciples rejoiced when they saw the Lord.
John 20:20

Suggested music

Low in the grave he lay
Breathe on me, Breath of God
Love's redeeming work is done
We have a gospel to proclaim

CANDLES

Aim

To rejoice with the disciples that Jesus is alive.

Teaching

In the evening when it was dark, ten of the disciples locked themselves in a room. They were too frightened to go out. They thought that the people who killed Jesus might kill them. Who remembers how Jesus died? Do you remember what we call that day? When Jesus died it made the disciples very sad.

Now they were talking in quiet voices and remembering the wonderful things Jesus had done. They checked the door to make sure it was locked – yes, it was. Suddenly without anyone opening the door Jesus was there. He was not dead. He was alive and wanted to talk with them. Jesus is really alive! The disciples became very excited and very happy. They thought they had lost their best friend but they had not because he was alive and there with them. Jesus wanted them to tell everyone that he was alive. Let us say together, 'Jesus is alive.'

Now Thomas was not there when Jesus came. When Thomas came to the other disciples, what did they say to him? That's right. Let us all say together, 'Jesus is alive.' Thomas said he could not believe it. He had seen Jesus die. He had seen Jesus buried. He could not believe it.

'I will only believe it if I can put my finger in the hole in Jesus' hand made by the nail. I will only believe it if I can put my hand in his side where the spear made a hole.'

The disciples tried to convince Thomas that Jesus was alive but he wanted to see for himself. A whole week after Jesus had risen from the dead – who knows what we call the day Jesus rose again? – a whole week later the eleven disciples were all together in a locked room. Jesus came again and all the disciples were happy. Jesus said to Thomas, 'Thomas, come, reach out and touch my hand, put your hand in my side.' Thomas was amazed, it was Jesus and Jesus was alive. Thomas said to Jesus, 'My Lord and my God.' (Let us say to Jesus, 'My Lord and my God.')

Now Thomas would join the other disciples and tell people that Jesus was alive. Let us say it once again: 'Jesus is alive.'

Activity

Encourage the children to act out the story with ten disciples, plus Thomas and someone as Jesus. Start with the ten and locking the door, then Jesus coming and the disciples all excited. After Jesus leaves, let Thomas arrive. Let each disciple in turn say to Thomas, 'Jesus is alive.' Thomas can shake his head or say, 'I cannot believe it.' Now let Jesus appear and invite Thomas to touch his hand. Have Thomas kneel down at the feet of Jesus and say, ' My Lord and my God.' Let them all end by saying, 'Jesus is alive.'

Prayer

Jesus, you are alive
and always ready to help us.
We thank you that you rose from the dead
and make those who follow you happy.
Amen.

Song

Celebrate Jesus

LAMPS

Aim

To rejoice with the disciples in the presence of Jesus the risen Lord.

Teaching

Begin by looking back to Good Friday. Make sure the children know what happened on Good Friday. Not only was Jesus crucified; he died and was buried in a tomb.

Do they remember last week's Good News?

What were the names of the women who went to the tomb? Yes, they were both called Mary. They were Mary the Magdalene and Mary the mother of James. Who can tell what happened? What do we call the day when Jesus rose again?

Tell the group that they can act today's Good News after they have listened to it.

The same day, in the evening, ten disciples had locked themselves in a room. They were afraid that the Jews might come for them next. They were in hiding out of fear. But Jesus the risen Lord cannot be locked out! Suddenly he was there among them. He was not a ghost but the living Lord. Just as Mary had told them, Jesus was alive. They forgot their fear and were really joyful. It was wonderful: Jesus, who was dead, was alive. This was something they would want to tell everyone.

After Jesus had gone Thomas came and they told him, 'We have seen the Lord. Jesus is alive.' Thomas said he doubted it. He had seen Jesus die. He had seen him nailed to a cross. He had seen a spear thrust into his side. He had seen Jesus buried, and when you're dead you're dead. But the ten disciples kept telling him about Jesus and how they saw him. Thomas said, 'I will believe when I can put my finger in the nail hole and my hand in his wounded side.'

It was the next Sunday, a week after Easter, that Jesus came to the disciples again. This time Thomas was with them. Jesus spoke especially to Thomas and said, 'Put your finger here and see my hands. Reach out your hand and put it in my side. Do not doubt but believe.'

Thomas was overcome with wonder and joy. He looked straight at Jesus and said, 'My Lord and my God.'

Jesus told him that God blesses those who have not seen him but believe in him. The eleven disciples would want to tell as many people as they could that Jesus was alive.

Activity

Act out today's Gospel. Have ten disciples meet Jesus and each in turn tell Thomas either, 'I have seen the Lord' or 'Jesus is alive'. After the meeting of Jesus with Thomas let the scene end with the whole group saying, 'Christ is risen. Alleluia'. You may like to explore why there are only eleven disciples at this stage.

Prayer

Lord Jesus, you are unseen yet always near.
I believe in you.
I trust you.
I love you.
Help me to tell others of you
and of your resurrection.
Amen.

Song

Sing and rejoice

TORCHES

Aim

To rejoice in the risen Lord.

Teaching

Go back over the events of Good Friday. Check that they know the details of the crucifixion, the death and burial of Jesus. It is important that they all know these events clearly.

Then revise last week's teaching and how the two Marys met the risen Lord. Twice they are told to go and tell. Such good news as this no one can keep to themselves. Again make sure they know it is called Easter.

The same evening the disciples are fearful; they are anxious in case they are hunted out and persecuted. There are ten of them. Judas is dead. Thomas has gone elsewhere. Because of their fear they lock the door. Fear often stops people moving about freely. But even locked doors are no barrier to Jesus. Suddenly he is there with the disciples. He gives the usual greeting of 'Shalom', meaning 'peace'. Jesus is alive and with them. He brings peace to their troubled minds and hearts. He gives the fearful disciples courage, for he lives. He shows them his hands and his sides – in case they need proof it is him. The disciples are full of joy. Jesus gives them a commission: 'As the Father sent me, so I send you.' Then he breathes on them and says, 'Receive the Holy Spirit.' They are given new life and power.

Compare this with:

• God breathing life into his creation (Genesis 2:7)
• God breathing life into the dead bones (Ezekiel 37:1-10)
• The prayer of Psalm 51:10

They were to go out with the life of Jesus within them. They would slowly learn that wherever they went Jesus was there. Now once again he was hidden from their sight.

When Thomas returns they tell him all of this, how they have seen the Lord and that he is alive. Thomas doubts it. It is too hard to believe it is true. He had seen Jesus dead and buried. He says openly, 'I doubt it.' He will only believe if he can see for himself, if he can touch the nail holes and put his hand in the wounded side.

Again the following Sunday, Jesus is seen by them and this time Thomas is there. Jesus greets them all again with the word 'Peace'. Then he speaks to Thomas and says, 'Put your finger here and see my hands. Reach out your hand and put it in my side. Do not doubt but believe.' Thomas answers, 'My Lord and my God!' Jesus tells Thomas that God blesses those who have not seen him but believe in him.

Activity

This is another good scene to act out. Let Thomas be vociferous in his doubt. Jesus can appear by all of them suddenly turning around and finding he is there and has been there all the time. There is an opportunity to look at this event in depth on the activity sheet.

Prayer

Lord, when we walk in darkness
be our light.
When we lose hold on you
keep us in your firm grip.
When we are troubled
give us your peace.
When we are weary
breathe into us the power of your Spirit,
that we may witness to you
and your resurrection.
Amen.

Song

Lord Jesus Christ, you have come to us

Third Sunday of Easter

Aim

To show that we meet Jesus the risen Lord in various ways.

Preparation

Have a large Easter Candle and fifteen small candles and a sand tray.

Opening activity

Have someone light the Easter Candle and proclaim, 'Alleluia, Christ is risen', and let all respond, 'He is risen indeed. Alleluia.'

Then let two girls or women say, 'We are the two Marys. We light candles for we have seen the Lord. Alleluia, Christ is risen.' All respond, 'He is risen indeed. Alleluia.'

Now have eleven people say, 'We are the eleven disciples. We light candles for we have seen the Lord. Alleluia, Christ is risen.' All respond, 'He is risen indeed. Alleluia.'

After the Gospel have two people (possibly a married couple) come down and light two small candles to put in a sand tray. They say, 'We are the disciples on the Emmaus Road and we have seen the Lord. Alleluia, Christ is risen.' All reply, 'He is risen indeed. Alleluia.'

Opening prayer

Abide with us, Lord, at the opening of the day.
Abide with us in the journeying of our lives.
Abide with us in darkness and in light.
Abide with us in our homes and in our church.
Lord, abide with us always,
in time and to eternity.
Amen.

Opening song

Jesus, stand among us

Readings

Acts 2:14a, 36-41
Psalm 116:1-3, 10-17
1 Peter 1:17-23
Luke 24:13-35

Thought for the day

This is yet another appearance of the risen Lord on Easter day.

Cleopas and his companion – perhaps his wife – were making for Emmaus, seven miles west of Jerusalem. They were walking towards the setting sun at the close of day. They were a sad couple, having seen the death of a loved one, Jesus. In his dying they had lost hope; they were very much in the dark. (Compare the people of Israel in the valley of dry bones in Ezekiel 37:1-10.) As they were talking to each other, Jesus came near and went with them along the road. Jesus asked them to tell him what they were talking about.

They said how they were talking about the crucifixion and death of Jesus. They also told how they were astounded by the women who had reported that Jesus was alive. They told of the empty tomb. All of this was not enough to raise their hopes; they needed more than other people's stories and empty tombs.

Jesus walked with them and talked with them. He shared the Scriptures with them and helped them to understand about the suffering of the Messiah. Jesus the risen Lord can make sense of our experiences of life.

Jesus did not force himself upon them. He walked ahead as if going on. He turned back because they invited him: 'Stay with us, because it is almost evening.' Jesus is often passing by but will only stay if invited. God has given us a most wonderful and dangerous freedom called free will. The choice is ours. We can choose to ignore him, reject him, squeeze him out of our life, or we can invite him in, ask him to abide, share with him, put our faith in him and put our hopes on him. Jesus passes by not only in church but in every encounter, in 'mouth of friend and stranger'.

Now Jesus is revealed to them in the breaking of the bread. In our Holy Communion, Jesus is revealed; and in our communion with each other. Jesus is in church but he is also at home in our homes. At an ordinary meal, in an ordinary home, Jesus is there.

The two realised how their hearts 'burned' in his presence. Darkness had been replaced with light, sadness with joy and despair with hope. They were no longer on the sunset road but facing the dawn of a new life. They turned to Jerusalem in the direction of the rising sun, wanting to share the Good News. This is the way the Good News grows – in sharing it. It grows in us and in the world. In sharing we discover, like them, that people have had similar experiences and others know the risen Lord, not as a figure in a book but as the living Lord.

Question time

Do we take to heart that Jesus is known through the Scriptures and the Holy Communion?

To balance this, do we realise we can often meet Christ in the stranger? In the other who comes to us we can meet the great Other.

Illustration

The Church in the Outer Hebrides rejoiced in the living Lord who could be met on the road and in the guise of a stranger. The following is an old poem from the Hebrides and now used by the Iona Community:

I saw a stranger at yestere'en.
I put food in the eating place,
drink in the drinking place,
music in the listening place,
and in the sacred name of the Triune
he blessed myself and my house,
my cattle and my dear ones,

and the lark said in her song,
'Often, often, often,
goes the Christ in the stranger's guise;
often, often, often,
goes the Christ in the stranger's guise.'

Intercessions

Blessed are you, Lord God,
for you are with us in our journeying
and in our resting.
You are to be found in our homes
and our daily lives.
You, Lord, are our hope and our strength:
in you we trust.
Blessed are you, Father, Son and Holy Spirit.

Lord, make yourself known to us
in church and through the Scriptures.
May we know you in the breaking of the bread,
in the break of day
and when our hearts are breaking.
Help us to see that you travel with us on the road of life
and you never leave us.
Fill us with your Spirit,
that we may proclaim the Good News
and tell others of your love.
We remember today
all who are suffering because of their faith,
those who live in fear
and those whose lives are restricted.

Silence

Lord, abide with us:
stay with us and help us.

We remember before you all travellers
and those who provide transport.
We ask your blessing
upon those who feel they are going into the dark
and to the end of life.
We pray for political prisoners
and the work of Amnesty International.
We remember all who are captive
to doubt, fear or sin.

Silence

Lord, abide with us:
stay with us and help us.

Lord, may we be at home with you in our homes.
When our hearts burn within us,
may we know that you are near.
Help us to know you are with us
in all our dealings with others.
We remember today all who are lonely or feel rejected
and all who feel they are missing out on life.

Silence

Lord, abide with us:
stay with us and help us.

We pray for all who have lost vision and hope,
for all who are struggling with life.
We remember the broken-hearted,
those suffering from broken relationships,

all who are broken by illness or trouble,
all who can no longer cope on their own.
Lord, may they know you in their breaking
for you alone can make us whole.

Silence

Lord, abide with us:
stay with us and help us.

Lord as in you we are born anew,
we remember before you the faithful departed.
We rejoice in the fellowship of all your saints.
May we share with them
and all our loved ones, both here and departed,
in the joy and fullness of life eternal.

Silence

Merciful Father,
**accept these prayers
for the sake of your Son,
our Saviour Jesus Christ.
Amen.**

Memory verse

They told what had happened on the road, and how he
had been made known to them in the breaking of the
bread.
Luke 24:35

Suggested music

A brighter dawn is breaking
In the garden Mary lingers
Now the green blade riseth
Abide with me

CANDLES

Aim

To show Jesus is with us and with all who want to be
his friends.

Teaching

Listen to my voice. Can you see the words? No, but
they are there. Smell these flowers. Can you see the
smell? No, but it is here.

No one has seen the wind. But we know it is real.
When you talk to someone on the phone you cannot see
them but you know they are there and listening to you.
We cannot see Jesus but we know he is with us. He is
always there and wants to be our friend.

As it was getting dark two people were walking
down a road. They were both very sad because they
had seen Jesus die and thought they would never see
him again. They talked about Jesus, and one of them,
who was called Cleopas, said how he would miss Jesus
and all the wonderful things he did.

While they were walking and talking, someone came
to them and asked them, 'Why are you so sad?' Cleopas
told him it was because the wicked men had killed

Jesus and they would not see him again. The stranger told them not to worry and he explained to them why Jesus had to die. They began to feel a little better.

When they got near their house with the stranger it was nearly dark. The stranger looked as if he had a long way to go. Cleopas invited him to his home: 'Come and stay and have a meal with us.' Because he was invited, the stranger said he would stay.

When they sat down to eat, the stranger took the bread and gave thanks to God: 'Father God, thank you for this bread.' He then broke the bread to share it. At that moment they knew it was Jesus who had walked with them, talked with them and shared a meal with them.

Suddenly they could not see him but they did know Jesus is alive and he was with them.

They hurried back to Jerusalem to tell the disciples. When they got there they found out that the disciples had also seen Jesus. They were all very excited because Jesus was alive and he was with them. Later Jesus would meet the disciples again and say, 'I am with you always.'

Activity

There is an opportunity on the worksheet to make the three figures of this story from pegs, so that they can tell the story when they go home.

Prayer

Be near me, Lord Jesus;
I ask you to stay
close by me for ever,
and love me, I pray.
Bless all the dear children
in your tender care,
prepare us for heaven,
to live with you there.

(From 'Away in a manger')

Song

Jesus is a friend of mine

LAMPS

Aim

To show how Jesus is a friend in our journeying through life.

Teaching

If it is practical and you have plenty of helpers, take the children on a walk. Ask them to use their ears. What can they hear but not see? Can they hear a bird? A car? The wind? Maybe they can hear voices? Now let them use their noses. What can they smell? Flowers? Smoke? Food? Even though they cannot see them, they are there. All of us are breathing in air and breathing out again – we cannot see it but it is there. Jesus is also always there. (If you do go out you may be able to walk and sing 'We are marching in the light of God'.)

Two people were walking home from Jerusalem. Their journey was seven miles. That is as far as (. . .) is from here. We will not walk that far. As they walked they talked. But they were both very sad because they were friends of Jesus and they had seen him die on the cross and then buried in the tomb. They were sad because they would miss their friend.

While they were walking and talking, Jesus came and talked with them and helped them to feel better. They did not realise it was Jesus. But in his presence they felt a lot happier. Jesus talked about the Scriptures which showed them how Jesus knew he would die.

When they got to their home, Jesus looked as if he was going to go further on. He would not assume he could join them. They would have to invite him into their home. They asked him to stay and soon began to prepare a simple meal. At supper Jesus took the bread and said a thank-you prayer to God the Father. Then he broke the bread to share it. At that moment they knew it was Jesus. He had been with them all along the road. He was in their home. 'Jesus is alive and with us.' (Let us say this together: 'Jesus is alive and with us.')

At that moment Jesus seemed to have gone from them. But they knew he would be with them on the road and in their home. They hurried all the way back to Jerusalem – another seven miles – to tell the disciples the Good News: 'Jesus is alive.'

When they got there, the disciples were also excited because Mary had seen Jesus in the garden and ten of the disciples had seen Jesus in the room where they were together. They wanted everyone to know that Jesus was alive. We can meet him wherever we are.

Later they would see Jesus yet again and he would tell them, 'I am with you always.' Jesus is with us as we walk and as we talk. He is with us in our homes and at our meals. Jesus is there with us in church. Jesus comes if we invite him and he wants to be our friend.

Activity

If possible, the main activity today should be the walking and talking together.

Prayer

Lord Jesus, risen from the dead,
help us to know you are alive,
you are with us
and you love us.
Through our prayers
may we make you one of our friends
and know that you are with us to help us.
Amen.

Song

Jesus is my friend

TORCHES

Aim

To look at the different ways we meet Jesus.

Teaching

Read Luke 24:13-35 with one of the young people speaking the words of Cleopas.

Jesus comes and shares in our journey through life, even though often he may be unrecognised. Jesus will not force himself upon us. If we choose, we can ignore him but he is there and always there. Very often we do not recognise him or we fail to invite him into our lives. Yet he comes . . .

in our walking (verse 13)
in our talking (verse 14)
into our sadness (verse 17)
in the events of life (verses 18-20)
when we lose hope (verse 21)
in proclaiming the Good News (verses 22-24)
looking at Scripture (verses 25-27)
by invitation (verses 28, 29)
in our homes (verse 30)
at a meal (verse 30)
in Communion (verse 30, 31)
in the warmth of his presence (verse 32)
in the fellowship of believers (verses 33, 34)
in the telling of our experience (verse 35)

It is a good idea to make the above into a quiz by putting them in a random order with the group searching the passage for the answers. When they find an answer, let them tell it in their own words and then read the verse or verses from the Bible. After they have an understanding of the story, ask the group to act it out and show how the risen Lord is made known to us today.

Activity

There is a wordsearch on the activity sheet and also an opportunity to look again at the ways in which Jesus comes to us. They can add to this list from their own experience.

Prayer

Lord, make us aware that you are with us
and you never leave us or forsake us.
May we learn to share with you
and to invite you into our daily lives.
May we know your presence
in the breaking of the bread
and in our fellowship with each other.
Amen.

Song

Alleluia, alleluia, give thanks to the risen Lord

Fourth Sunday of Easter

Aim

To know we have life and eternal life through Jesus Christ our Lord.

Preparation

In the entrance have pictures of different gates and entrances. Print in large letters, 'Jesus said: "I am the gate. Whoever enters by me will be saved" (John 10:9).' You may like to have a photograph or a painting of a shepherd caring for sheep.

Have a large Easter Candle and six small candles and a sand tray.

Opening activity

Have someone light the Easter Candle and proclaim, 'Alleluia, Christ is risen', and let all respond, 'He is risen indeed. Alleluia'.

In turn have six people recite a verse each from Psalm 23. Before they say their verse, let them light a candle from the Easter Candle. Once all six have said a verse, they say together, 'Alleluia, Christ is risen', and the congregation responds, 'He is risen indeed. Alleluia'. Then they place the candles in the sand tray and go back to their places.

Opening prayer

Praise and glory to you, Lord our God.
Through Jesus we have life and life eternal.
He has opened for us the gate of glory.
In our lives help us to know him
as our guide and shepherd
and follow where he would lead us.
Amen.

Opening song

Jesus calls us: o'er the tumult

Readings

Acts 2:42-47
Psalm 23
1 Peter 2:19-25
John 10:1-10

Thought for the day

The uplands of Judea were more suited to rearing sheep and goats than to growing crops. The shepherd was a familiar figure and was seen as a strong rugged character. Life for the shepherd was not easy. He had to make sure his sheep did not get lost and this kept him alert and watchful. He cared for his sheep and had to give account to the owner for them. Out in the country there was always danger from wild animals; wolves and hyenas prowled at night. There was the added danger from thieves and robbers who were always ready to rob a flock.

To protect the sheep, they were often penned in a sheepfold. This was usually a stonewall structure with briars on the top of the wall. The entrance was a single opening. There was no gate on the entrance but the shepherd acted as gatekeeper and stayed across the entrance to protect the sheep. In a sense no one could enter except going through the shepherd. Anyone trying a different way was obviously not to be trusted. So when Jesus describes himself as the 'gate' and the 'shepherd', this is one and the same person.

Often flocks were mixed together so that the shepherds could have strength in fellowship. When the sheep then had to be separated, the shepherd would call his and they would follow him. There were often one or two leaders of the flock that encouraged the others to follow. The shepherd knew his sheep and they knew him. They actually had a relationship with each other. Note how the shepherd in Judea does not drive his sheep; he leads and they follow.

Jesus came to a world of darkness and despair. People 'erred and strayed like lost sheep'. There were those who had got themselves trapped and could not free themselves. Others were in danger of being robbed of their well-being, their joy and even their life. Jesus came that we might have life and have it abundantly; that we may have eternal life – that even death could not rob us of our being. He would descend to all the troubles we experience. He would be betrayed, deserted, rejected, crucified and buried for our salvation. He would give his life for us.

He knows us and wants us to get to know him. He will not force himself upon us but calls each of us by name. He is the gate to life and to eternal life. Salvation is through Jesus. We come to the fullness of life through Jesus. We enter into eternal life through Jesus Christ our Lord.

Question time

Do we realise the depth of meaning in the words 'through Jesus Christ our Lord'?

Do we put enough trust in the Good Shepherd to be our leader and guide?

Illustration

There is an old Jewish legend about why God chose Moses to be a leader of his people. When Moses was in the wilderness and caring for the sheep of his father-in-law, Jethro, a young lamb strayed away and got lost. Moses searched for it until he came to a deep dark ravine where it had gone down to find water. When Moses got to it he said, 'I did not know you ran away because you were thirsty. Now you must be very tired.' He took the lamb and put it on his shoulders and carried it back to safety. God said to Moses, 'Because you have cared for and brought back one of a flock belonging to man, you shall lead my flock Israel.'

Intercessions

Blessed are you, Lord our God,
for in your Son Jesus Christ
you have triumphed over darkness and death
and opened to us the way to eternal life.
Through Christ our Saviour
you have given us new hope and joy.
As we rejoice in his presence
may we give glory to you.
Blessed are you, Father, Son and Holy Spirit.

We give thanks for Jesus the Good Shepherd
and we pray for all who are called
to share in his ministry as shepherds
and guides of your flock.
We pray for all bishops, priests and deacons,
for preachers of the word
and ministers of the sacraments.
We ask your blessing
upon all who are involved in pastoral care
and those who seek out the lost and the straying.

Silence

Hear us and help us,
through Jesus Christ our Lord.

Loving God, we pray for all who express your love
in the way they care for others.
We pray for all who are striving for justice
and the relief of poverty.
We remember all social workers, carers
and good neighbours.
We ask your blessing
upon all who feel at the mercy of circumstance
and who are unable to manage on their own.

Silence

Hear us and help us,
through Jesus Christ our Lord.

Lord, bless our homes and our loved ones.
May we show respect and care for the world around us
and not be caught up with selfishness and greed.
Help us through our love for each other
to reveal your love in the world.

Silence

Hear us and help us,
through Jesus Christ our Lord.

We give thanks that through Jesus
we can walk with confidence and hope.
We ask your blessing upon all who struggle
in darkness and fear,
all who feel lost
and those who are captives to vice and sin.
We remember friends and loved ones who are ill
and all the struggling people of our world.

Silence

Hear us and help us,
through Jesus Christ our Lord.

We rejoice in the risen Lord and the promise of eternal life.
Lord, bless our loved ones departed.

May they share with your saints in glory.
To you and your unfailing love
we commit ourselves and the whole world
in time and for eternity.

Silence

Merciful Father,
**accept these prayers
for the sake of your Son,
our Saviour Jesus Christ.
Amen.**

Memory verse

Jesus said, 'I am the gate. Whoever enters by me will be saved.'
John 10:9

Suggested music

The Lord's my shepherd
Jesus the Lord said: I am the bread
Will you come and follow me

CANDLES

Aim

To show that Jesus the Good Shepherd cares for us.

Teaching

Who knows what is woolly and goes 'Baa'? Yes, it is a sheep or a lamb. What do you call the person who looks after sheep? He is called a shepherd. (Let us say it together: 'A shepherd.')

When Jesus lived in Judea, if you were a shepherd, you had to be very brave and strong. The shepherd had to protect the sheep against wild animals like wolves or hyenas (who knows what these animals are like?). He had a club to frighten them off and a sling with which he could throw stones at them. It was even more dangerous when there were robbers. Sometimes the shepherd had to risk his life for the sheep.

Because most robbers and wild animals waited until it was dark, the shepherd often put his sheep in a safe place called a sheepfold. (Draw one for the children to see.) It was usually a circle of stones with room on the inside for all the sheep. On the top of the stones the shepherd put prickly branches to stop anyone climbing in. All the sheep went through the opening in the circle. There was no proper gate to lock but the shepherd sat or stood in the opening and was ready to chase off anything that would harm the sheep. The shepherd was the gate and only when he moved could the sheep get out or someone in.

Jesus said he is the Good Shepherd and he cares for us. He loves us and knows our names. We are like his sheep. If anything is going to really harm us, Jesus will stand between the trouble and us. If we get lost or are in danger, Jesus wants to protect us and keep us safe. (Show a picture of the Good Shepherd.) Jesus wants us to be his friends and to follow him. Then Jesus is able to care for us and give us his love.

Activity

Create a small safe area in the room by drawing a circle with chalk or using chairs to make a circle. While the music plays, the children move around the room. When it stops, they must run to the safe place. Before the last two enter, the leader blocks the way because they are designated wild creatures. They have to go around the outside of the circle, growl and look fierce. The leader prevents them from entering the safe place. When the music begins let the whole thing start all over again.

Prayer

Jesus, you are the Good shepherd
and we are your sheep.
You love us and protect us
and rescue us from trouble.
Jesus, Good Shepherd, we love you.
Amen.

Song

Jesus is our shepherd

LAMPS

Aim

To show the courage of the Good Shepherd.

Teaching

Some people are very brave and do dangerous work to help others. Can you tell me of anyone who does dangerous work in caring for others? The fire service, the ambulance crews, the lifeboat people and mountain rescue teams are some of them. Sometimes they have to work in the dark and in great danger to themselves. Sometimes they are risking their own life to save others.

In the days of Jesus one of those involved in dangerous work was the shepherd. It was not easy looking after sheep in the hills of Judea. (If possible, show a picture of an eastern shepherd.) The shepherd was responsible for the sheep and had to see that they came to no harm. But in the hill country were wild animals, wolves and hyenas, animals that would kill and destroy sheep. Even worse than wild animals were robbers who were out to steal the sheep. The robbers sometimes worked in gangs and were very dangerous. The shepherd had to be very brave.

The worst time was at night because then the wild animals and the robbers would try and sneak up on the sheep. Often, to keep them safe, the shepherd put the sheep in a sheepfold. (Show a picture or describe the sheepfold.) There was only one way in and out. There was not a proper gate at the entrance but only the shepherd. Sometimes he put some prickly bushes over the entrance to stop anything going in or out. But he

stayed there all night. He stood between the sheep and trouble. He stood between the sheep and danger. He stood between the sheep and anything that would threaten them. In the morning, after removing the prickly hedge, he would call his sheep and they would follow him to where there was food and water.

Activity

Send one person out of the room – he or she is the shepherd. While they are out, choose a wolf. Now sit everyone in a circle, including the wolf. The wolf 'kills' the 'sheep' by winking at them. When a person is winked at they fall gently backwards and lie still. The shepherd has to spot the wolf before it does too much harm. When the wolf is discovered, he or she goes out of the room while a new wolf is chosen.

Let the children decide who were really good shepherds and why.

Prayer

Lord Jesus, we thank you for brave people
who risk their lives for others.
We ask you to keep them always in your love and care.
Lord Jesus, you are the Good Shepherd.
We thank you that you love us
and gave your life for us.
Amen.

Song

Loving Shepherd of thy sheep

TORCHES

Aim

To show how we come to God through Jesus Christ our Lord.

Teaching

Imagine you want to go to a special performance of a musician you like or a team you support. This is a very important event to you but for some reason you put off getting a ticket. When you ring the box office they tell you that all tickets are sold out. There is no way you will get a ticket unless there are a few cancellations and there is a waiting list. It does not look good for you. Now you tell a friend how disappointed you are. He says to you, 'Don't worry, I can get you in. I know the person in charge and they always keep me a few places unless I say I do not want them.' You could not get in no matter how hard you try but now you can through your friend. Sometimes it is not what you know – even what you can do – but who you know.

Read John 10:1-10. In Judea, being a shepherd was a dangerous job. You had to protect the sheep against wolves, hyenas and even robbers. The sheep's safety depended on the shepherd. In the evening the shepherd often penned his sheep in a stone pinfold. This was usually circular with a single entrance. On top of the wall were placed a lot of thorn bushes to keep the invaders out. The shepherd also used thorn bushes to block the gate and keep the sheep in. Then he remained at the gate all through the night. There was no real gate, only an opening but no one could get in or out except through the shepherd. When Jesus says he is the Good Shepherd who lays down his life for the sheep and also says he is the gate, there is no contradiction. Jesus cares for us, protects us and lays down his life for us. He came that we might have life and have it more abundantly (John 10:10). Not only does Jesus do this for us but he is also the gate – the entrance – to eternal life. Through his offering of himself, through his obedience to the Father, through his resurrection from the dead, he has opened for us the way to eternal life. Through Jesus is our salvation. Note how we end most prayers: we ask them 'in the name of Jesus Christ' or 'through Jesus Christ our Lord'. In Christianity it is not *what* you know but *who*. We have faith in Jesus Christ our Lord.

Activity

Have the group read Psalm 23 dramatically and then again without using a Bible. Let individuals learn a verse. Get each of them to compose a prayer ending with 'through Jesus Christ our Lord'.

On the activity sheet there is an opportunity to look at today's Gospel in greater depth.

Prayer

Father, we thank you for Jesus the Good Shepherd;
through his death he has destroyed death,
and by his rising to life again
has opened for us the gate of glory.
May we know his love and protection in our lives.
We ask this through Jesus Christ our Lord.
Amen.

Song

The King of love

Fifth Sunday of Easter

Aim

To show Jesus is with us on the journey of life and prepares the way for us.

Preparation

Have the Easter Candle plus three small candles and a sand tray. In the entrance have a sign that says, 'ONE WAY ONLY'.

Opening activity

Someone lights the Easter Candle and proclaims, 'Alleluia, Christ is risen', and let all respond, 'He is risen indeed. Alleluia'.

In turn three people light a candle and say their words:

1. I light this candle for the risen Lord who is the way and leads me into the fullness of God's kingdom.
2. I light this candle for the risen Lord who is the truth and without whom the world has no purpose.
3. I light this candle for the risen Lord who is the life and who gives me eternal life.

Then the three say together, 'Alleluia, Christ is risen', and let all respond, 'He is risen indeed. Alleluia.' Now place the lit candles in the sand tray.

Opening prayer

Lord God, whom to know is eternal life
and whose service is perfect freedom,
grant us to know Jesus
as the way, the truth and the life;
that we may walk in your way,
see the world in your truth
and come to the fullness of eternal life.
We ask this through Jesus Christ our Lord.
Amen.

Opening song

Thine for ever! God of love

Readings

Acts 7:55-60
Psalm 31:1-5, 15, 16
1 Peter 2:2-10
John 14:1-14

Thought for the day

There are dark days ahead. The disciples are in the Upper Room. Judas has gone out to betray Jesus. Jesus has told Peter how he will deny him. A world of darkness, fear, sadness and chaos is soon to come upon them. They will lose hope and lock themselves in. Jesus did not promise them an easy time. Now he calls on them to trust in God the Father and in himself, to hang on by putting their faith in him and their hand in his.

'In my Father's house are many dwelling places.' This can mean resting places on our journey where we will find refreshment and comfort. Such places help us to progress and develop. God's world is not static, nor is the kingdom of heaven.

'Many dwelling places' can simply mean there is room for all. The world may close its doors, society may lock us out, but God has room for us. 'If it were not so, I would have told you.'

Jesus says, 'I go to prepare a place for you.' He goes on ahead for us to follow. He goes before us to make the way easier. He is like a trailblazer who goes on ahead to make sure it is safe for us to go down that road. Jesus is like a pilot boat that goes before to guide a vessel into the safe harbour: he leads us into the fullness of God's kingdom. He goes to prepare a place for us. That is like us saying we have a reserved seat with our name upon it: there is a place in heaven that is specifically for us.

Jesus will come to us and take us to himself so that we are one with him and his kingdom. This is not a put-off but for us a present reality. It is expressed well in this affirmation:

I am in the heart of Jesus.
Jesus is in my heart.
Jesus is in heaven.
Heaven and where I am, are one.

This idea of a Way into the kingdom is confusing to Thomas (and to many of us!). Thomas seeks clearer directions. Jesus tells Thomas he is the Way to God. He could have given complex directions on how to find God – like getting directions in a strange area. Someone says, 'Turn right, then left, then second right, last exit at the second roundabout and across the third.' By now you feel well and truly lost. Then someone else says, 'I am going that way. I will show you and go with you.' Jesus says, 'I am with you always', and he says, 'I am the way'. He is our companion on the journey and through him we come to life eternal.

Question time

Do we acknowledge that we travel through life in the presence of our Lord and accept his guidance?

To be in the heart of God is to be in his kingdom. What does this mean for you?

Illustration

Often when we are feeling lost it is because we have wandered from him who is the Way. More than any book of directions, we need to know God is with us on our journey.

And I said to the man
who stood at the gate of the year:
Give me a light
that I may tread safely into the unknown.
And he replied:
Go out into the darkness

and put your hand in the Hand of God.
That shall be to you better than a light
and safer than a known way.

(From *Desert* by Minnie Louise Haskins, 1908, and
quoted by King George VI in his Christmas broadcast, 25 December 1939.)

Intercessions

Blessed are you, Lord God,
for in your Son Jesus Christ
you have opened for us the way to glory.
In him the world is seen in greater depth
and in him is the gift of eternal life.
Lord, ease our troubled hearts
and help us to put our faith in you.
Blessed are you, Father, Son and Holy Spirit.

Lord God, teach us to walk in your way
and to rejoice in your truth,
that we may know the fullness of life eternal.
We ask your blessing upon all spiritual leaders,
preachers of the word
and ministers of the sacraments.
We pray for all who are new to the faith
and all who are growing in a deeper awareness
of your presence.
May we all know that
wherever we go and whatever happens
you are with us and ready to lead us.

Silence

Lord, guide our journeying:
be with us always.

Lord God, we ask your blessing
upon all leaders of nations and peoples.
We pray for your guidance
in the decisions they make this week
concerning the well-being of the world
and of the communities they serve.
We remember before you
all who strive for justice and peace in our world.
We ask for your protection
upon all who are seekers or travellers.

Silence

Lord, guide our journeying:
be with us always.

Lord God, we give thanks
for all who have taught us
and guided us into the ways of truth,
those who shared with us
their faith and their vision of life.
We ask your blessing upon all schools,
colleges and universities.
We pray for our own homes and loved ones
and ask that our homes may show
your abiding presence and love.

Silence

Lord, guide our journeying:
be with us always.

Lord God, we ask your blessing
upon all who feel confused about life
and all who have lost their way.
We pray especially for all who are caught up
in the darkness of despair
and those involved in drugs or vice.
We pray for those who live a lie
and cannot face the truth.
Lord, bless all who are suffering
from broken relationships
and who are troubled in heart.
We remember all who are ill
and fearful for their future.

Silence

Lord, guide our journeying:
be with us always.

Lord God, in your Son you have prepared for us
a place in your kingdom.
Lead us into the fullness of life and joy
in your presence.
Bless all our loved ones departed,
that they may rejoice with your saints in glory.

Silence

Merciful Father,
**accept these prayers
for the sake of your Son,
our Saviour Jesus Christ.
Amen.**

Memory verse

Jesus said to him, 'I am the way, and the truth, and the life. No one comes to the Father except through me.'
John 14:6

Suggested music

You are the peace
Guide me, O thou great Redeemer
Thou art the way

CANDLES

Aim

To show that Jesus is ready to help us as we travel through the world.

Teaching

Let's pretend we have a long journey to do. It will sometimes be dark and sometimes dangerous. There will be swamps and thick forests, and it will be easy to get lost. What will we need for the journey?

We will need food and a light. We will need a map and some directions. (Show a map and a compass.) Even with all these things to help us, it will still be easy to get lost. What else can we do?

We can ask someone to tell us the way: someone who knows the way and has been there. But sometimes directions are very hard to follow. I know someone who was going on a journey and he was not worried or frightened; he was looking forward to it. I thought he must have a secret that made him brave, so I asked him. He told me he would not get lost because his brother was going with him and he would show him the way. He was very lucky, wasn't he?

Jesus knew that soon he would have to leave his disciples. Soon wicked men would kill him and make his disciples frightened. The disciples would feel lost and not know what to do. But Jesus told them not to worry. Why do you think they need not worry? What happened to Jesus after he was dead and buried? He rose again and came to his disciples. The disciples need not worry because they had a friend in Jesus and Jesus would be with them and help them on their journey and when they were worried.

Let us remember that Jesus is alive and wants to help us. Jesus does not want us to get lost or in trouble. He wants to help us to find our way and to know that God loves us.

Activity

Play 'hot and cold'. One person is sent out of the room and the rest then choose something for her to guess. When she returns as she moves about the other players say, 'Cold' when she is far away from the object and 'Colder' if she moves further away. They say, 'Warm' and 'Warmer' when she is getting near, and 'Hot' when she is very close. Let them have three chances to say what the object is.

Prayer

Lord Jesus,
show us the way you would like us to go.
Help us to follow you
and to show your love to others.
Amen.

Song

We are marching in the light of God

LAMPS

Aim

To show how Jesus wants to be our guide and the way to fullness of life.

Teaching

Begin with the activity. Discuss which is better: to have directions or a person to guide us. Why is it better?

Have you ever wanted to play a new game but could not understand the rules? Sometimes rules and directions are very hard to follow. If you are lucky enough to have a friend who knows the rules, it is far easier to learn from them and much more fun. It is the same with learning to play a musical instrument, to use a camera or a computer. It is far easier to have someone show you the way than to give you directions. People are always

better at showing us how to do something than a list of instructions. It is far better to have a good teacher than a lot of books about a subject.

Jesus knew that trouble was soon coming. Judas had gone out into the night to betray him. It would not be long before Jesus is taken prisoner, crucified, dead and buried. Then what would the disciples do? They would feel quite lost without their leader. Jesus told them that trouble was ahead and that he would be taken from them, but he told them not to worry. Be prepared for these things to happen but do not worry because I will come again and show you the Way to live and to work for God. Jesus did not give them a book of directions – he promised to show them himself.

Activity

Create an obstacle course out of chairs and boxes. Tell the group the chairs and boxes represent dangers to life. Let them suggest what the dangers are. They could be swamps or bombs, wild animals or cliffs. Now blindfold one or two of them. Tell the blindfolded ones they have to negotiate the course without bumping into anything. If they bump into more than three things, they will be out. They are allowed to have directions from the group.

Now instead of directions give those who are blindfolded someone to be their guide. Let that person help them to avoid the hazards and to travel safely.

Prayer

Lord Jesus, you are the Way.
Help us to know you are with us
and to seek to follow you
and do what God would like us to do.
Amen.

Song

I am the Way, the Truth and the Life

TORCHES

Aim

To show how Jesus seeks to be our companion and guide.

Teaching

Picture a large ship waiting to come into the harbour. There is a great storm out at sea and the ship needs the safety that the harbour offers. But around the harbour entrance there are shallow areas where the ship could run aground, and there are hidden rocks that are a great danger. The captain and the navigator look at the charts and realise the dangers. One mistake could cause a lot of trouble. To venture in alone is a risky business. Then out of the harbour comes a special little boat; it is a pilot boat. The person in this boat knows the dangerous channels and the safe way into the harbour. The sea is very rough but the smaller boat reaches the large ship and leads it safely into the harbour.

Jesus told his disciples of the troubles ahead. Judas had already left them to betray Jesus. Soon Jesus would be taken captive and killed. The disciples would feel lost and in great danger. They were troubled. Jesus said to them, 'Do not let your hearts be troubled. Believe in God, believe also in me.' Whatever happened, Jesus wanted them to put their trust in him and in God the Father. True, Jesus would be taken from them but for a purpose. He would go away. But he would prepare a way for his disciples. He would go ahead and make sure there was a safe way for them. Then he would come back and lead them so that they could come to where he had gone. Like a pilot boat, Jesus would lead them.

The disciples could not really understand this. How could Jesus lead them if he was taken away from them? How could he help them if he was killed? What do you think they would have to experience to make them realise the truth of Jesus' words?

Slowly after the resurrection they would discover Jesus is there and can be found in the garden, in the upper room, on the road, on the beach, in Galilee. In fact, they would realise they were not alone for he would still be with them and would go with them wherever they went (see Matthew 28:20).

In the same way we can discover that the risen Lord is with us. He is with us wherever we are and whatever happens to us. He is ready to be our friend and our guide, to lead us to the fullness of life and life eternal.

Like the disciples, we may not know what lies ahead, how life will go or when things will happen to us but we do know who is with us at all times.

Activity

If possible, give the group an exercise in orienteering. Give them map references for them to follow from place to place. If this is too difficult, have a couple of large road atlases or street maps and ask them to find the easiest way from A to B. Tell them how much easier it would be if they had someone who had travelled that way before.

Prayer

Lord Jesus,
we do not know what might happen to us,
we do not know where we might have to go,
but we do know you are with us
and you will guide us on our journey through life.
Lord Jesus, as you seek to be our friend,
let us welcome you each day.
Amen.

Song

Jesus the Lord said: I am the bread

Sixth Sunday of Easter

Aim
To show that the love of God asks for our response in actions.

Preparation
Have the Easter Candle plus three smaller candles and a sand tray. In the entrance display statements about love from popular songs.

Opening activity
Have someone light the Easter Candle and proclaim, 'Alleluia, Christ is risen', and let all respond, 'He is risen indeed. Alleluia.'

Now three people in turn light candles and say a sentence:

1. I light this candle for the love of the Father as revealed in sending his Son Jesus Christ.
2. I light this candle for the love of Jesus as seen in his sacrifice for us.
3. I light this candle for the Spirit of God who abides with us in love.

The three then proclaim, 'Alleluia, Christ is risen', and all respond, 'He is risen indeed. Alleluia.'

They now place the candles in the sand tray and go back to their seats.

Opening prayer
God, in your great love you have created us.
With that same love you redeem us
and abide with us.
Lord, may we rejoice this day in your love
and seek to serve you all our days.
Amen.

Opening song
Love divine, all loves excelling

Readings
Acts 17:22-31
Psalm 66:7-18
1 Peter 3:13-22
John 14:15-21

Thought for the day
St John's Gospel is about the love of God as revealed in Jesus Christ (John 3:16). God has created us out of his love, by his love and for his love. God wants us to love him as he loves us. But he will not force himself upon us. We have the freedom to ignore God and go against him if we so choose. The Christian way of life is one of love rather than law. We seek to do what is right not because of a set of rules but out of love. If we do not love, we are not likely to walk in the ways of God. Devotion comes before obedience. This is what Jesus is telling the disciples when he says, 'If you love me, you will keep my commandments.'

St Augustine of Hippo understood this when he said, 'Love God and do what you will.' He knew that in our love for God we would do nothing to offend him or cause him sorrow. We cannot say we love a person if we cause them constant heartache, grief or anxiety. If we are inconsiderate or unkind towards someone, then we do not truly love them. If we use someone for our own ends and are with them for what we can get out of them, that is not love. We should never take the love of our loved ones for granted. Love demands sensitivity, a willingness to give and even a willingness to serve. This service or obedience is what is described as the 'perfect freedom' because it is what we do out of love. This type of loving service is seen in the sacrifices and work that loving parents do for their children and for each other.

Love is God's gift of himself to us and our response is to love him in return, and in this way our love grows. 'They who have my commandments and keep them are those who love me; and those who love me will be loved by my Father, and I will love them and reveal myself to them' (John 14:21).

Faith is not a set of beliefs or keeping a book of rules; it is a living loving relationship with Father, Son and Holy Spirit. In today's Gospel we hear mention of the Father, Son and Holy Spirit and how the Spirit of God abides in us. We are not alone in the world, for the Spirit is with us and Christ comes to us. We must learn to be aware of and to rejoice in their presence and their love.

Question time
Do we spend enough time each day expressing our love for God?

How can we better express our love for each other in the daily routines of our homes?

Illustration
How often do we fail to realise the cost of love in our homes? How our parents spend much of their lives giving themselves and what they have to us? Many of the household chores that are done for us are done not out of compulsion but out of love. But we should never take this for granted and the only way to respond to such love is to love in return. This, of course, would mean taking our share in the household tasks! Love is expressed in action. We do not do it because we have to – or because it is a rule of the house; we do it out of love for each other. True devotion is taking on some of the routine of caring for our home. Our failure in this work shows a lack of sensitivity and personal response to love.

Intercessions
Blessed are you, Lord our God,
for out of your love you have made all things.
You come to us and give yourself to us.
Help us to be aware of your love in our lives
and to give ourselves to you

in love and in doing your will.
Blessed are you, Father, Son and Holy Spirit.

Lord, as you abide in us,
let our lives show your love for all of your creation.
We remember all Christians
who are being persecuted for their faith
or have to suffer scorn and mockery
from those with whom they live.
We pray for all who witness to you
amid danger and opposition.
We ask your blessing upon all who are new to the faith.
We pray for those who have recently been converted
and for those who have been baptised and confirmed.

Silence

Lord of life,
be known to be among us.

Lord, we remember all places where people are suffering
from tyranny or lawlessness.
We pray for all who are oppressed
or used as cheap labour.
We ask your blessing upon all who strive
for justice, freedom, peace and fair trade.

Silence

Lord of life,
be known to be among us.

Lord, may our homes reflect the love we share.
Keep us sensitive to the needs of each other.
May we be ready to take our share
in the work of our own home.
We remember before you
all who feel unloved and unwanted.
We ask your blessing
upon all homeless people and refugees.
We pray for all who are suffering
from broken relationships and broken trust.

Silence

Lord of life,
be known to be among us.

Lord of light, we ask your blessing
upon all who are struggling with darkness and fear.
We remember those who have been involved
in accidents or in acts of violence this week.
We pray for all who have suddenly become ill
and those who are in hospital.
We pray for all who anxiously await
the results of a medical examination.

Silence

Lord of life,
be known to be among us.

Lord of life,
we rejoice in the power of the resurrection
and we remember before you
all your saints and martyrs.
We ask your blessing
upon our loved ones and benefactors
who have now departed from us.
May we all abide in your presence and eternal love.

Silence

Merciful Father,
accept these prayers
for the sake of your Son,
our Saviour Jesus Christ.
Amen.

Memory verse

If you love me you will keep my commandments.
John 14:15

Suggested music

Great is thy faithfulness
We have a gospel to proclaim
Love's redeeming work is done

CANDLES

Aim

To show how God loves us and wants us to love him.

Teaching

At home, who provides you with food and looks after you? Who sees that you have clothes to wear and that you have clean things? Who works hard so that you can be comfortable? Do you think they have to do all this? Why do they do it?

Your mother and father do it because they love you. They want you to be happy and to enjoy life because they care for you. Every day they spend much of their time working to provide for you. The more they love you, the more they enjoy caring for you. If we love them, we should see what we can do to be useful in our homes. We should tidy up our own things and help when we can. (Explore ideas from the children of how they can be helpful at home.) By helping we show our love for all who live in our home.

Sometimes we do things that our mother or our father does not want us to do and it upsets them. Sometimes we can make them sad by being naughty. But they still love us, feed us and care for us. Even when we do things that hurt them, they still want to give their love to us. We are very lucky if we are loved like this.

God, who made us all, also loves us. He made this wonderful world for us to live in. He gave us life and he gives us his love. He would like us to love him and to make him our friend. How can we be friends with God and give him our love? We can talk to him each day. What do you call talking to God? Yes, praying. We can say our prayers each day, knowing that God loves us and then we can give our love to God. We can also show our love by caring for God's world and not doing things that would make God sad. (Explore with the children how they can do lovely things for God.)

Activity

Play 'stuck in the mud'. Have one who is 'it'. Whenever a person is tagged, they have to stand still with their legs apart and arms outstretched and shout for help. A friend who has not been tagged can crawl between the other's legs and set them free. This is a good exercise to see how friends can help us.

Prayer

Jesus, you have sent the Spirit of God to help us,
and you have promised to come to us.
Help us to know you love us
and to give our love to you.
For you are here and your Spirit is with us. Amen.

Song

There are hundreds of sparrows

LAMPS

Aim

To show the group that God is always with us.

Teaching

If you had to go on a dangerous journey in the dark, what would you like to have with you? The best thing would be a companion, someone who knew the way and could help you to avoid the dangers. It would be good if that person offered some light and support for the journey.

When we know we have a companion and are loved, it drives away fear. But if we suddenly find we are on our own and our loved ones are far away, then we get fearful and troubled.

When Jesus told his disciples he was going away they began to get worried and anxious. He told them not to worry because he was going away to prepare a place for them so that when he came again he could show them the way. He promised to return to them and not leave them alone. Jesus also promised to ask the Father to send another helper to be with them: the Spirit of truth. They would not be able to see the Spirit but they would know the Spirit of God is with them and stays with them always. Jesus told them they are not like orphans who have no helper; they are not alone in the world because the Spirit of God is with them. God loves them and his Spirit is with them and in them.

We cannot see the Spirit but the Spirit is there. We cannot see the air but if it was not there we would die. We cannot see the wind but we know when it blows. We cannot see the scent of a flower but we can smell it when it is near. The Spirit of God is always near and wants to be our helper and friend.

How can we make friends with the Spirit of God? By remembering he is with us and wants to help us. By speaking to him each day and trusting him at all times.

We could say each day, 'The Lord is here: his Spirit is with us.' Let us say this together: 'The Lord is here: his Spirit is with us.'

Activity

Encourage the group to make statements about life and the presence of the Spirit by saying:
'When it is dark the Lord is here.'
All respond, 'His Spirit is with us.'
'When I need help the Lord is here.'
All respond, 'His Spirit is with us.'
'When I need loving the Lord is here.'
All respond, 'His Spirit is with us.'
'When I am in trouble the Lord is here.'
All respond, 'His Spirit is with us.'

Prayer

Lord God, you care for us and love us.
You never leave us but are always there,
ready to help us and give us strength.
Help us to love you
and put our trust in you each day.
Amen.

Song

God is love: his the care

TORCHES

Aim

To encourage the group to explore the meaning of the word 'Advocate'.

Teaching

Jesus has told his disciples about the dangers that lie ahead of them. Judas has gone out to betray him. Jesus has told Peter that he will soon deny him and the disciples will desert him through fear. They are all very sad at this news and are anxious about being separated from Jesus. Jesus has inspired them, guided them and given their lives meaning: they cannot imagine life without him. Jesus wants to ease their worry and says to them that he will pray to the Father and the Father will send another Advocate to be with them for ever. This is the Spirit of God. Not only will the Spirit of God be with them; it will abide in them. Like the very air we breathe. We cannot see it but it is all around us and within us. So is the presence of the Spirit around us and within us. The disciples are not left helpless or like orphans because the Spirit of God is with them and Jesus himself will come again to them. Jesus tells them because *he* lives they will also live – they would not truly understand this until after the resurrection. Sometimes the Church expresses this truth in just a few words: 'The Lord is here: his Spirit is with us.' It is a great pity if we do not let the truth of those words sink into our minds and hearts. It is good to start each day and every important event with these words at least in our minds: 'The Lord is here: his Spirit is with us.'

Let us look at some of the meanings of the word 'Advocate'. The Greek word is *parakletos* which is hard to translate. It definitely means 'helper' or one who stands by you at all times. When a ship is in distress at sea, a lifeboat comes and stands by. It is there ready to help if help is needed, ready to rescue if rescue is needed. Often in the record books of lifeboats the entry is 'stood by'. The Spirit of God is our helper who stands by and is ready to come to our help if we call upon him.

The word can also mean 'Strengthener'. Just as the lifeboat gives new courage and hope to those in trouble, so the Spirit of God gives us hope and strength in our distress. The Authorised Version of the Bible uses the word 'Comforter' which means 'with strength'. The Spirit brings us strength. When we are confirmed we seek the 'firmness and strength of the Spirit'.

'Advocate' can also mean someone who is called to give witness in our favour or to plead our cause. Again this means standing by us in trouble.

Encourage the group to develop these ideas of the working of the Spirit.

Activity

Affirm the presence of God in our lives at all times by saying, 'The Lord is here: his Spirit is with us.' Get each member of the group to make a statement about life or the Spirit and end it with 'The Lord is here', with the group responding, 'His Spirit is with us'.

Prayer

Come, Holy Spirit of God,
fill our lives with your presence,
strengthen us through your power
and guide us in your goodness.
May our lives show
that you are with us and within us always.
Amen.

Song

Spirit of God, unseen as the wind

Ascension Day

Aim

To affirm that the presence of the ascended Lord is always with us.

Preparation

Have the Easter Candle and six small candles to be lit from the Easter Candle, plus a sand tray.

Opening activity

Have someone to light the Easter Candle and proclaim, 'Alleluia, Christ is risen', and let all respond, 'He is risen indeed. Alleluia.'

Six people in turn light a small candle from the Easter Candle and say a sentence:

1. I light this candle for the risen Jesus
    who appeared in the garden.
2. I light this candle for the risen Jesus
    who was seen on the road.
3. I light this candle for the risen Jesus
    who was known in the breaking of the bread.
4. I light this candle for the risen Jesus
    who came to the closed room.
5. I light this candle for the risen Jesus
    who shared a meal on the seashore.
6. I light this candle for the risen Jesus
    on the mountain in Galilee.
1. Jesus is with us always.
    Alleluia, Christ is risen.

All **He is risen indeed. Alleluia.**

The six people with candles put them in the sand tray and return to their seats.

Opening prayer

Lord, may we rejoice in your ascension
and show in our lives
that we know you are with us always.
Help us to walk in your ways and do your will,
that it may be seen that we dwell in you
and you in us.
Amen.

Opening song

Hail the day that sees him rise

Activity

This takes place after the Gospel at the Easter Candle. (This can replace the intercessions.) There is a diagram of a traditional Easter Candle at the end of today's resources. If you want to add the crown of thorns, the nails and the spear hole to the candle before the service, you could use five drawing pins. Different people could do a section each. You can also have a crown of thorns made from barbed wire or a thorn bush, two nails for the hands, a single nail for the feet and a spear for the side.

Affirm the Alpha and Omega

God, you are the beginning and end of all things.
All things are made by you and for your love.
You are the Alpha and the Omega.
Creator of time and space;
Saviour beyond time and space;
Spirit within time and space.
We worship and adore you.

Withdraw the incense grain for the crown of thorns (or touch the top of the candle)

The head that once was crowned with thorns
is crowned with glory now.

(Show the crown that is to be put on a table for display)

O dearest Lord, thy sacred head
with thorns was pierced for me;
O pour thy blessing on my head
that I may think for thee.

Lord, we remember before you
the troubled in mind,
all who have painful memories,
the depressed and the despairing,
the mentally disturbed.
Lord, keep our minds strong
in the knowledge and love of God
and help us to proclaim your presence and love.
Ascended Lord, may our minds ascend
to where you are in glory.
Alleluia.
Alleluia.

Withdraw the grains of incense for the hands (or touch two places further down the candle)

(Show the two nails and place them with the crown of thorns)

O dearest Lord, thy sacred hands
with nails were pierced for me;
O shed thy blessing on my hands
that they may work for thee.

We remember in your presence
all whose hands are idle.
We pray for those who are unemployed
and redundant,
those who are disabled
and all with waning or failing powers.
We remember all who are tempted to misuse
the power that God has given them.
Lord, we are always in your presence:
may we live to your praise and glory.
We are in the hands of God.
Alleluia.
Alleluia.

Withdraw the incense grain for pierced side of Christ (or move further down the candle)

(Show the spear and then place it with the crown and the nails)

Time and again the humans break the heart of God.
Yet God never ceases to love us.

O dearest Lord, thy sacred heart
with spear was pierced for me;
O pour thy spirit in my heart
that I may live for thee.

God we remember before you
all who are betrayed in love,
the broken-hearted and the deserted,
the rejected and the lonely.
We thank you for our loved ones and our friends.
Ascended Lord,
as you love us with an everlasting love,
help us to love you and show your love
in our love for each other.
Alleluia.
Alleluia.

Withdraw the incense representing the feet (or place your hands near the base of the candle)

(Show the nail that held his feet and place it with the other symbols of Christ's death)

He who was firmly fixed is set free.
He is let loose on the world.

O dearest Lord, thy sacred feet
with nails were pierced for me;
O pour thy blessing on my feet
that they may follow thee.

Lord, we remember before you
all who are striving for freedom,
all who are held captive.
We ask your blessing
upon all who seek to do your will
and to bring in the glory of your kingly rule.
We rejoice for death is conquered.
We are free.
Christ has won the victory.
Alleluia.
Alleluia.

Extinguish the Easter Candle.

(Place the unlit candle with the other symbols)

The Lord has gone up on high.
Alleluia.
Alleluia.

Hail the day that sees him rise. Alleluia!
See, he lifts his hands above. Alleluia!
See, he shows the prints of love. Alleluia!
Hark! His gracious lips bestow, alleluia!
blessings on his Church below. Alleluia!

Jesus said, 'I am with you always.'
Alleluia.
Alleluia.

'I go to prepare a place for you
that where I am you may be also.'
Alleluia.
Alleluia.

Lord, we remember in your presence
all who are in the dark.
May they come to your love and light
and know you as their ascended Lord and friend.
We remember all our loved ones departed
and rejoice that we are all united in you.

The Lord is here. Alleluia.
Alleluia.
His Spirit is with us. Alleluia.
Alleluia.

Readings

Acts 1:1-11* or Daniel 7:9-14
Psalm 47 or Psalm 93
Ephesians 1:15-23 or Acts 1:1-11
Luke 24:44-53

* The reading from Acts must be one of the readings for the day

Thought for the day

From Easter Day onwards the disciples not only rejoiced in the presence of the risen Lord but actually saw him in various places. The women saw Jesus in the garden. The travellers on the road to Emmaus found that he walked with them and was made known to them in the breaking of the bread. Jesus appeared in the room to ten disciples and a week later was seen again when Thomas had joined them. Jesus shared a meal with them by the Sea of Galilee. He walked and talked with Peter and John. Finally he is with them on the mountain of the ascension. The disciples were learning that he was with them wherever they were and whatever they were doing.

The ascension brings us to a change. Jesus enters into the cloud and is gone from their sight. But we know that this is no ordinary cloud. This is the cloud that represents the hidden glory and the hidden presence of God, who is unseen yet ever near. In returning to the Father, Jesus leaves our sight but not our presence. St Matthew's Gospel captures this in the last words of Jesus, and the last words of his Gospel: 'Jesus says, "And remember I am with you always, to the end of the age"' (Matthew 28:20b).

The longer ending to St Mark's Gospel tells of the abiding presence in this way: 'So then the Lord Jesus, after he had spoken to them, was taken up into heaven and sat down at the right hand of God. And they went out and proclaimed the good news everywhere, while the Lord worked with them, and confirmed the message by the signs that accompanied it' (Mark 16:19, 20).

The disciples were in no doubt they were not left alone but, as he had promised, Jesus was with them and worked with them and through them. The great message of the ascension is this: 'The Lord is here; his Spirit is with us.'

Question time

Do we spend enough time rejoicing each day in the presence of our Lord?

How can we show that we are called to be the 'body of Christ' to the world?

Illustration

If the disciples were asked after the ascension, 'Where is Jesus now?' their reply would be very like the one that Longinus made to the wife of Pilate in John Masefield's *The Trial of Jesus*. Procula asks, 'Do you think he is dead?' To which Longinus replies, 'No, lady, I don't.' When asked, 'Then where is he?' Longinus replies, 'Let loose in all the world, lady.'

In the ascension we come to know that the Jesus who was limited by time and space is now able to be with all peoples at all times and in all places.

Memory verse

And remember I am with you always, to the end of the age.
Matthew 28:20b

Suggested music

Alleluia, sing to Jesus
Come, let us join our cheerful songs
O dearest Lord, thy sacred head
He is exalted
Be still, for the presence of the Lord

CANDLES, LAMPS and TORCHES

As this is a working day and a school day, I have assumed there will be no separate teaching for the children and young people. However, I feel, if the opportunity is there, the children should be encouraged to go up onto the church tower or a high place and release balloons with tags on them celebrating the Ascension. I have included in the Candles, Lamps and Torches books suggestions for tags and banners that could be made during the sermon if the young people withdraw. It is important that some of the young people are involved in the words and actions of this day. I have also included a hymn for each group.

This is an important event in the life of Jesus and, if missed on Ascension Day, the material could be used on the Sunday following.

Song

Candles – I'm singing your praise, Lord
Lamps – Jesus isn't dead any more
Torches – He is K-I-N-G

Crown of thorns

O dearest Lord, thy sacred head
with thorns was pierced for me;
O pour thy blessing on my head
that I may think for thee.

O dearest Lord, thy sacred hands
with nails were pierced for me;
O pour thy blessing on my hands
that I may work for thee.

Spear
hole in
side

Nail holes
in hands

O dearest Lord, thy sacred heart
with spear was pierced for me;
O pour thy Spirit in my heart
that I may live for thee.

Nail hole
for feet

O dearest Lord, thy sacred feet
with nails were pierced for me;
O pour thy blessing on my feet
that they may follow thee.

Christ has no hands but your hands to do his work today.
Christ has no feet but your feet to speed folk on his way.
Christ has no lips but your lips to tell folk why he died.
Christ has no love but your love to win folk to his side.

Seventh Sunday of Easter

Aim

To show that eternal life comes from abiding in God and knowing he abides in us.

Preparation

Have a few clouds made out of dark card with the invitation to open them and see what is behind them. Have a bright shining sun behind one. Behind others have words such as 'I am with you always', 'The hidden presence of God', 'God unseen yet ever near', 'Jesus is at the right hand of God'. Place a large vase full of chestnut blossom in church.

Opening activity

Who looked behind the clouds? If you did not look, you would not see what was there. On Ascension Day the Easter Candle was put out and removed. Who knows why? It is because the risen Lord has ascended. He is out of sight but not out of our presence. If we look for him we will find him – or he will find us. It is said that when the Easter Candle is put out, the chestnut tree puts out its candles to remind us that Jesus is near.

Opening prayer

Blessed are you, Lord our God,
for we are always in your hands.
You uphold us and protect us.
We rejoice that as Jesus is at the right hand of God
he is ever present and ready to help us.
Blessed are you, Father, Son and Holy Spirit,
one God for ever and ever.
Amen.

Opening song

Christ, whose glory fills the skies

Readings

Acts 1:6-14
Psalm 68:1-10, 32-35
1 Peter 4:12-14; 5:6-11
John 17:1-11

Thought for the day

Like Moses (see Deuteronomy 31–33), Jesus prays at the end of his earthly life. This prayer is a 'last will and testament' that shows certain key ideas. Jesus prays in the typical Jewish fashion, eyes open and looking towards heaven.

In the first part of his prayer Jesus asks that his 'hour' will glorify the Father. In St John's Gospel the 'hour' is not one event but is made up of the life, death, resurrection and the appearances of Jesus. 'Glory' and glorification echo the Old Testament idea of glory as revealing God's power. To see God is to experience his power and his will (see Exodus 16:10; 24:7). When God's glory is revealed through people, it is because they do his will and manifest his power. Jesus reveals the hidden glory of God.

More than this, Jesus has the power to give eternal life. Through Jesus we have life eternal. The way to eternal life is to know God and to know Jesus Christ. Let us be aware that eternal life does not mean a quantity so much as a quality. Eternal life is a certain quality of life. It is life lived in awareness of the presence and power of God and of his Son Jesus Christ. This would make St John say, 'Whoever has the Son has life; whoever does not have the Son of God does not have life' (1 John 5:12). The Old Testament understood well about the relationship of knowing God and life: 'by knowledge the righteous are delivered (Proverbs 11:9). Wisdom is 'a tree of life to those who lay hold of her' (Proverbs 3:18). Hosea hears God saying, 'My people are destroyed for lack of knowledge' (Hosea 4:6). Amos is aware of this when God says, 'Seek me and live' (Amos 5:4). Habakkuk dreamed of a time when 'the earth will be filled with the knowledge of the glory of the Lord, as the waters cover the sea' (Habakkuk 2:14).

Though it is very necessary to know with our minds, this knowledge of God demands of us an intimacy of the deepest sort of relationship with him. It is to know him in a way that we become one with him (see Genesis 4:1). The fullness of life depends on maintaining a relationship with the Father and the Son. If we break with that relationship, we are in danger of no longer having eternal life. God does not break that relationship with us, and if we turn to him, he will welcome us home. Our joy is to know we can abide in him and he abides in us – and in this is eternal life.

Question time

Though the Lord is unseen, he has invited us to abide in him as he abides in us. How can we make this a daily awareness in our lives?

Do you really take to heart the words, 'The Lord is here: his Spirit is with us'?

Illustration

In his diary for 1922 Shackleton writes of his Antarctic expedition:

> When I look back on those days, with all their anxiety and peril, I cannot doubt that our party was divinely guided both over snowfield and across storm-swept sea . . . I know that during that long racking march of thirty-six hours over unnamed mountains and glaciers of Southern Georgia it seemed to me we were not three but four. I said nothing to my companions on the point but afterwards Worsley said to me, 'Boss, I had a curious feeling in the march that there was another person with us.'

Do we affirm in our lives that our Lord is with us and travels with us wherever we go?

Intercessions

Blessed are you, Lord our God,
for you have raised your Son
from the darkness of death
to the fullness of life eternal,
to your right hand on high.
By his death he has destroyed death;
by his rising to life again
he has restored to us eternal life;
by his ascension
he has opened for us the gate of glory.
Blessed are you, Father, Son and Holy Spirit.

As we rejoice in the ascension,
we give thanks for men and women of vision,
for those who have shared their faith with us.
We remember all whose lives are clouded
by doubt or despair.
We pray for those who feel life is dull,
that they may come to know
the joy of the presence of the ascended Lord.
Lord, empower your Church
to proclaim the Good News of your saving acts.

Silence

Lord, with us always,
hear us and help us.

As we rejoice in your presence,
we remember all who feel lonely
and neglected in our world.
We ask your blessing on all who are oppressed
and those who are struggling to survive.
We pray for all who are caught up in violence and war,
and for those not at peace with each other,
with themselves and with you.

Silence

Lord, with us always,
hear us and help us.

As we rejoice in your love,
we remember our loved ones,
our homes and families.
We pray for our community and neighbourhood.
We ask your blessing
upon all who strive to brighten the world
by their dedication and goodness,
by their faith and willingness to sacrifice.

Silence

Lord, with us always,
hear us and help us.

As we rejoice in your power,
we remember all whose powers are waning,
the elderly and the infirm
and all who are disabled.
We ask your blessing upon all who are ill
or who have been injured in accidents.
May they find courage and hope in you
and in your abiding love.

Silence

Lord, with us always,
hear us and help us.

We rejoice that you are our great High Priest
who ascended into heaven,
and that you are at the right hand of God
making intercession for us.
May our loved ones departed
and all your faithful
rejoice in you and rest in the glory of your kingdom.

Silence

Merciful Father,
accept these prayers
for the sake of your Son,
our Saviour Jesus Christ.
Amen.

Memory verse

Abide in me as I abide in you.
John 15:4

Suggested music

Christ's is the world in which we move
Come and celebrate
Give to our God immortal praise

CANDLES

Aim

To know the ascended Lord is with us always.

Teaching

Who can tell me what happened to Jesus after he died and was buried? He rose again. Let us all say together, 'He rose again.' Do you know the name of the day when Jesus rose again? It is called Easter Day. Let us say together, 'On Easter Day, Jesus rose again.'

Who can remember some of the places where Jesus was seen after he rose again? (List these on a board or flipchart.)

1. In a garden, to Mary Magdalene and the other Mary
2. On the road to a place called Emmaus, to two disciples
3. When he broke bread to share it
4. In a room to ten disciples (Who was missing?)
5. In a room to eleven disciples
6. On the beach, where he cooked some fish
7. On a mountain where a cloud hid him from the sight of the disciples.

Who knows the name of the day when Jesus was hidden from their sight? It is called Ascension Day because we think of it as the day when Jesus went up into heaven. Ascension means 'going up'. But Jesus was not really leaving his disciples. They had been learning that wherever they went, Jesus was there.

Jesus was with them always. They could not see him but they knew he was there and he had promised them, 'I am with you always.'

When the sun hides the clouds, has the sun gone away? No, it is there even when big dark clouds hide it. Jesus is with us even though we cannot see him – he is always there and wants to be our friend. Jesus still helped the disciples in their work even though they could not see him. Jesus wants to help us and wants us to know he loves us and is always there.

Activity

On the activity sheet they can make a cloud and hide Jesus behind it. When Jesus is revealed the children should say, 'Jesus is there, always there.' Have a game where a number of objects are hidden around the room before the children come in and then get them to find the objects. Hide a picture of Jesus behind a cut-out cloud.

Prayer

Jesus, you are our friend and are always with us.
Even though we cannot see you,
you are still with us and love us.
We come to give our love to you.
Amen.

Song

Give me joy in my heart

LAMPS

Aim

To know that Jesus is with us always.

Teaching

Tell a story of the rescue of someone who fell down a deep dark hole. They could not get out by themselves and if they were left there they would die. But someone heard their cry for help. The rescue service came and a man was lowered into the dark. It was a dangerous place and he had to be very careful. He came right down to where the person was. For a while he looked after and gave comfort to that person. Then when he was ready he strapped the two of them together and gave a signal. At the top they knew it was time to lift the rescuer up again as he would bring the person with him. He had gone down to bring the person up to a safe place.

The story of Jesus is like this. Because the people of the world were troubled by darkness and their lives were in danger, he came down from heaven to be seen by the people and to help them. He came right down to where they were. He came down and was born in a stable. What do you call the birth of Jesus? The Nativity. When do we celebrate it? At Christmas.

Jesus came right into the world's troubles and entered even death and went down into the grave. What is the name of the day that Jesus was crucified died and was buried? It is Good Friday.

Jesus did not come just to die but to bring us eternal life. So he needed to rise again from the dead, so that we

could also rise. What do you call the day when Jesus arose again? It is Easter Day.

Jesus was seen many times after his resurrection – in the garden, in a room, on the road, by the seaside, on a mountain. The disciples were learning that Jesus is with them always. Now it was time for Jesus to return to God the Father; he was to go up to God from where he came. Who can tell me what we call the day when Jesus went up to God the Father? It is called 'the Ascension'. Let us listen to how it happened. (Let someone read Acts 1:9.) But the disciples knew that even though they could not see Jesus, he is always with them. The cloud hid him from their sight but he is always there. (Get someone to find the last words of Jesus from Matthew 28:20.) To remind us that Jesus is with us we will write these words 'I am with you always'.

Activity

Create a hidden message on a cloud from Jesus which says, 'I am with you always'.

Prayer

Lord Jesus, you are with me,
always with me.
Though you are hidden,
help me to know you are always there
and ready to be my friend.
Amen.

Song

God is love: his the care

TORCHES

Aim

To explore the reality of the hidden presence of God.

Teaching

Let different people read Acts 1:9-11; Luke 24:50-53; Matthew 28:20; Mark 16:19, 20.

What event does each of these passages tell us about? The Ascension. Do you know what ascension means? It means going up. Jesus, who had come down to earth and descended even into death, arose again and, after being seen for forty days, ascended into heaven. Yet the disciples knew he was still with them. Which words do you think they would remember as the last words of Jesus? 'I am with you always.'

The Ascension is difficult to describe. It was not the leaving of Jesus but only that his abiding presence would no longer be seen – just as the presence of the Father is not seen. In the telling of the Ascension there are three things to remind us of the abiding presence: the cloud, the sitting at the right hand of God and the promise.

The cloud is a symbol of the hidden presence of God. Just as the cloud can hide the sun which is always there, God is always there even though we cannot see him. In the story of Moses we hear of God going before the Israelites in a pillar of cloud (Exodus 13:21-23). When Moses went up on Mount Sinai, God descended in a cloud (Exodus 34:5). Then when the glory of the Lord descended to the Tent of Meeting, the Lord was hidden in a cloud (Exodus 40:34). This cloud was known as the shekinah and was a symbol of the hidden glory of God. It is from this cloud that God speaks at the Transfiguration of Jesus (Matthew 17:1-8). So at the Ascension, when Jesus enters the cloud he is becoming part of the hidden glory of God. This is also what St Luke means when he says Jesus was taken up into heaven.

St Mark describes Jesus as sitting at the right hand of God (Mark 16:19). The right hand of God is a symbol of the power of God. Often in early art the hidden presence of God was depicted as a hand reaching out of the sky. There is an ancient Proverb, well known in Israel, which says, 'The right hand of God is everywhere.' To be at the right hand of God means that God is present at all times, in all places and to all people.

We can add to this symbolism the promise of Jesus that is recorded in Matthew 28:20: 'Remember, I am with you always, to the end of the age.' The Gospels and Acts are in no doubt about the abiding presence of Jesus. Mark says simply that after Jesus was taken up into heaven he continued to work with the disciples (Mark 16:19, 20).

In the Ascension we celebrate the abiding presence of our Lord.

Activity

On the worksheet they can look again at the symbolism of the Ascension and at the Scripture passages. It is good to create clouds that reveal Jesus' hidden presence.

Prayer

Lord, we rejoice that you are here
and that your Spirit is with us.
As you abide with us,
help us to know you
and abide in your presence and love
and to seek to reveal your glory in the world.
Amen.

Song

Christ, be with me

Pentecost

Aim

To proclaim and enjoy the fact that 'his Spirit is with us'.

Preparation

Have streamers of red, yellow and white for small children to wave. You may like to have a banner with the words 'His Spirit is with us' in large letters. Have twelve candles to be carried in the procession and a sand tray ready for the candles at the front of the church.

Opening activity

Start off a procession with the males of the congregation declaring, 'The Lord is here', and the females of the group replying, 'His Spirit is with us'. This could be sung three or four times reaching a crescendo and then another three or four times in diminuendo. The congregation could go around the church singing 'The Spirit lives to set us free'. When the hymn is over let twelve people light candles from the altar candles. Each in turn will declare, 'The Lord is here', and all respond, 'His Spirit is with us. Alleluia'. The candles are then placed in the sand tray.

Opening prayer

Come, Holy Spirit of God,
fill our emptiness with your presence.
Come, Holy Spirit of God,
fill our darkness with your light.
Come, Holy Spirit of God,
fill our weakness with your power.
Come, Holy Spirit of God,
make us aware that we are in your presence
and you are in us.
Amen.

Opening song

Come down, O Love divine

Readings

Acts 2:1-21* or Numbers 11:24-30
Psalm 104:25-35, 37
1 Corinthians 12:3b-13 or Acts 2:1-21*
John 20:19-23 or John 7:37-39

* The reading from Acts must be used as the first or second Reading

Thought for the day

Pentecost is 50 days after the Passover. As the Passover is usually in April, Pentecost comes in June. Because the weather is better then, it is possible there are more pilgrims from other countries at Pentecost than there are in April. The disciples are also in Jerusalem. Their number is now made up to twelve again as they have appointed Matthias in place of Judas Iscariot. The disciples are doing what Jesus asked them: they were waiting in Jerusalem for the power of the Holy Spirit (Acts 1:4-8).

The disciples were all together in one place when suddenly from heaven there came a sound like the rush of a violent wind. Tongues of fire seemed to rest upon each of them; they were all filled with the Holy Spirit.

We will never know quite what happened at Pentecost but the results are seen in the change that came over the disciples. At one moment they were hesitant, frightened, unable to speak out, and they probably felt drained and powerless; then, they were ready to go out, bold and courageous, ready to proclaim the Good News, full of the Holy Spirit and his power.

In the first thirteen chapters of Acts there are more than 40 references to the Holy Spirit, empowering, moving and guiding people. The Acts of the Apostles has been rightly called the Gospel of the Holy Spirit. The longing that Moses expressed in Numbers 11:24-30 is fulfilled, for the Lord has poured his Spirit on his people.

The symbolism used is to help us realise the presence of the Spirit in the lives of the disciples, although their own actions are the true testimony.

The wind is the hidden presence of God, not seen but felt. It is the same word that is used for 'breath' and for 'spirit'. Whatever happened at Pentecost, new life was breathed into the disciples.

Fire is a symbol of the presence, as in the burning bush. It is a sign of a strong power at work and a sign of enlightenment. At Pentecost the disciples were given new vision and power.

That same Spirit is offered to us, is with us, but can only work if we respond to his coming. Let us celebrate that the Lord is here and his Spirit is with us.

Question time

Do we make sure we wait upon the coming of the Spirit and that our lives are open to him?

How can we, as part of the Church, reveal the working of the Spirit in our lives?

Illustration

For a long time the flute seemed to lie around the house. It was not played and it gathered dust. Occasionally, someone would get it out and struggle to play a tune. It was decided that is was not a good instrument, perhaps useless and should be got rid of. This was mentioned to a friend of the family when he came to dinner. He asked that he might be able to handle it and play it. Mother had to dust it down before she gave it to him. Somehow it looked special as soon as it was in his hands. Once he started to play, the family were amazed at the beautiful sounds and music. This was a wonderful instrument and responded beautifully in the master's hands. It was just waiting for the touch of the master.

In many ways the disciples were like this until they were filled with the Spirit.

Intercessions

Blessed are you, Lord our God.
To you be praise and glory for ever.
As your Spirit moved over the face of the deep,

bringing life to the world,
and as the same Spirit filled the disciples at Pentecost,
come to us, refresh us and renew us.
Blessed are you, Father, Son and Holy Spirit.

Holy Spirit of God,
moving in the deep of creation,
come into the depths of our lives,
guide us and empower us.
We ask your blessing upon the Church,
that it may have the courage
to proclaim the Good News and tell of your power.
May the Church be seen as Spirit-filled
through its display of the gifts of the Spirit.
Guide us,
that each of us may use our gifts and talents
to your glory and the benefit of each other.

Silence

Holy Spirit of God, come:
refresh us and renew us.

Holy Spirit of God,
giving life to dry bones,
we ask your blessing
upon all who feel threatened or who have lost hope.
We remember before you
refugees, homeless and oppressed peoples.
Give your strength
to all who seek to bring liberty and justice.
Guide the leaders of nations
and all who are in positions of authority
into the ways of peace.

Silence

Holy Spirit of God, come:
refresh us and renew us.

Holy Spirit of God, kindle the hearts
which without you are dull and cold.
Bless us in all our relationships,
strengthen our love for each other,
give joy to us as families in our homes
and in our dealings with each other.
We pray for all who seek to restore broken relationships.

Silence

Holy Spirit of God, come:
refresh us and renew us.

Holy Spirit of God, Breath of Life,
we ask your blessing
upon all who feel hindered or isolated
through illness or disability.
We remember those in constant pain
and all who are finding life difficult.
We pray for all who are despairing and depressed.

Silence

Holy Spirit of God, come:
refresh us and renew us.

Holy Spirit of God,
Giver of life and life eternal,
we rejoice in your renewing and restoring power.
We ask your blessing upon our loved ones departed,

that in you they may know the fullness of life
and the joy of your presence.

Silence

Merciful Father,
**accept these prayers
for the sake of your Son,
our Saviour Jesus Christ.
Amen.**

Memory verse

When you send forth your spirit, they are created; and
so you renew the face of the ground.
Psalm 104:31

Suggested music

Breathe on me, Breath of God
O Breath of Life, come sweeping through us
Spirit of the living God

CANDLES

Aim

To show how the Holy Spirit gives power and strength
to the disciples.

Teaching

Begin by showing a power drill (without any drill bits,
and at this stage without the power pack) or some other
power tool. Ask the children if they know what it is. If
someone is able to answer, let them come out and
demonstrate. Because it does not work let them just make
the sound and pretend. But sadly it does not work. Does
anyone know what the drill needs? Produce the power
pack and clip it in place. Now let someone else demonstrate how it works.

Ask about toys that have batteries or power packs.
What happens when the batteries or the power pack
runs out of power? Sometimes you can still make things
work but it is not as good.

After Jesus had ascended to God the Father (who can
remember this from last week?) the disciples felt they
had lost a lot of their power. Jesus still wanted them to
work with him but they felt they were unable to do it.
They did not have the power. But they remembered
what Jesus had said to them. He told them to wait in
Jerusalem until they had received power from God. It
was now ten days since Jesus had gone from their sight
and they were still waiting. They were all together in
one room.

Suddenly there was a noise like a strong wind blowing.
(Let us make the sound of the wind.) The noise got
louder – they could not see the wind but it filled the
house and it filled them. They were being filled with the
Spirit of God. They were given new power and strength.
Now they would be able to go out and tell people about
Jesus. Now something else wonderful happened. There
was something like flames of fire in the room and it
came to rest upon each of them. It did not hurt them

because again it was really the Holy Spirit of God filling them with power and ready to help them. The disciples did not have the power before but now they did. Now they could go out and tell others about how wonderful God was.

Activity

Let the children make crowns of fire that they can wear when they return to the service. Get the children to act out the events of Pentecost. Have a group of disciples; others can be the wind. The wind should touch each of the disciples after going around the room. A group with crowns of flames can then run around the room and put the crowns on the disciples' heads. Once this is done the wind and the fire sit down and the disciples then move around the room to a piece of music.

Prayer

God, we thank you for the Holy Spirit
and the power he gave to the disciples.
Come to us, Spirit of God,
and give us the power to work for you.
Amen.

Song

I'm a pow, pow, power pack

LAMPS

Aim

To know that the Spirit gives power to all the disciples.

Teaching

Show the children a bicycle pump and ask how they would use it. It is for putting air in tyres. If a tyre is flat, the bike will not work properly and you will spoil the wheel if you keep using it. If a tyre needs more air, what would you do? Get someone to come out and give a demonstration with an inner tube or using a balloon. You may like to give them all a balloon to blow up using their mouths.

Who can remember what happened at the Ascension? Because Jesus was gone from their sight, the disciples felt quite flat. They felt they did not have the power to do what Jesus wanted them to do. They needed more power and courage. But they did remember what Jesus told them. He told them to wait in Jerusalem until they had received power from on high. They were not sure what this meant but they waited in Jerusalem. It was ten days since the Ascension.

It was the festival of seven weeks. If you have seven weeks plus one day, how many days is that? It is fifty, so the festival was also called Pentecost because it was fifty days after the Passover, and Pentecost means fifty days. They were all together in Jerusalem. The city was crowded with people who had come for the festival. The disciples were all in one room. Suddenly there was

a sound. It was quiet at first but it got louder; it was the sound of a strong wind and it filled the house where the disciples were. It not only filled the house but it filled the disciples. The disciples knew it was the Spirit of God, for whom they had been waiting. They were filled with the Spirit. They no longer felt flat. The Spirit filled them with power and courage. Then something else happened – there were flames of fire moving in the room and a flame seemed to rest upon each of them. Again they knew that it was the Spirit of God coming to them and inspiring them, giving them power to go out and tell others of Jesus and the love of God.

Activity

If possible, it would be good to have some helium-filled balloons and release them from the church tower. Get the children to make banners that show the Spirit of God at work as wind and flames. Encourage them to act out this story.

Prayer

Spirit of God, unseen as the wind,
come and fill us, your disciples.
Fire of heaven, strong and powerful,
come and fill us with your light,
that we may know you and your love.
Then let us tell others of your power
and of the presence of God.
Amen.

Song

Spirit of God, unseen as the wind

TORCHES

Aim

To show how the Spirit guides and empowers the disciples.

Teaching

Have you ever been in the doldrums? There is actually no such place but sailing ships could suddenly find themselves in the doldrums. It was a place in the ocean where the wind dropped altogether and there was no movement of the sails. When sailing ships did not have engines it meant the ship was stuck for a while. Sometimes people feel in the doldrums when they run out of energy or inspiration. All you can do then is wait, wait until energy is restored and you can get going again.

Jesus knew that once the disciples could not see him they would feel in the doldrums. They would not be sure what to do and they would not feel powerful enough or wise enough to do anything. Jesus knew this but he wanted them to continue his work, so he told them to wait in Jerusalem until they received the Holy Spirit. The disciples waited in Jerusalem and it was now the day of Pentecost. Pentecost means 50 days. It was 50 days since the Passover – so it was 50 days since Jesus was condemned and crucified. The disciples had to be patient; they did not know how long they would have to wait, but they trusted Jesus. So they waited.

Suddenly there was a sound like the wind in the house where they were. It filled the house and it filled them. They knew this is what they had been waiting for. Now they would be given power and energy to do the work God wanted them to do. It would be the power of the Spirit. It is interesting that the same word is used by the disciples for breath, for wind and for spirit – none of these can be seen but we know when they are with us. With the sound of the wind came something like flames of fire resting upon each of the disciples. They knew the Spirit was inspiring them and enlightening them. Now they were Spirit-filled, they were ready to go out and tell others. Get the group to read Acts 2:1-17.

Read also Acts 5:32 and say how it is the person seeking to do God's will who is most likely to know the Spirit of God and grow in the power and strength of the Spirit.

Activity

Encourage the group to talk about how the disciples were given the Holy Spirit and to act it out. Encourage them to understand the importance of waiting upon God and seeking to do his will.

Prayer

Come, Holy Spirit of God, fill us with your love.
Come, Holy Spirit of God, fill us with your power.
Come, Holy Spirit of God, fill us with your light.
Come, Holy Spirit of God, fill us with your inspiration.
Then may we bring others to know you
and to love you.
Amen.

Song

The Spirit lives to set us free

ORDINARY TIME
Trinity Sunday

Aim
To encourage everyone to be Trinitarian in their faith and their prayers.

Preparation
Have symbols of the Trinity around the church – a painting of the hand of God with Jesus, and the Holy Spirit – a dove; a triangle; a Celtic knot of three parts; words such as 'One in Three: Three in one'. You might like to include an icon such as the Rublev 'Icon of the Trinity', although this will need some explanation. If possible, have some clover or shamrock.

With the help of the congregation it is good to display some baptism cards or certificates.

Decorate the font and have some water in it.

Opening activity
All profess their faith:

Do you believe in God the Creator
who made heaven and earth,
who made us out of love?
I believe and trust in him.

Do you believe in God the Son,
who shared in our humanity,
who died and rose again for us?
I believe and trust in him.

Do you believe in God the Holy Spirit,
who is the Lord and giver of life,
who sustains us in our need?
I believe and trust in him.

This is the faith of the whole Church.
I believe and love one God,
Father, Son and Holy Spirit.

Now let all process to the font while a quiet piece of music is played.

Using a spray branch dipped in the water, sprinkle the people and say aloud, 'You are baptised – totally immersed – in the presence, power and love of Father, Son and Holy Spirit.' All respond, 'Amen, alleluia.'

Opening prayer
Father, Son and Holy Spirit,
in you we live and move and have our being.
We are immersed in your love
and in your abiding presence.
You are always with us and ready to help us.
Glory to you, Father, Son and Holy Spirit.
Amen.

Opening song
Father in heaven

Today is a good day to sing the 'Peruvian Gloria'. You can also sing the creed in the words of 'We believe in God'.

Readings
Isaiah 40:12-17, 27-31
Psalm 8
2 Corinthians 13:11-13
Matthew 28:16-20

Thought for the day
The word Trinity does not appear in the Bible. Even so, the experience of God as Father Creator, as Son Redeemer, as Spirit Guide and Strengthener can be known and shared. At the baptism of Jesus there is the voice of the Father and the descent of the Spirit. The Trinity is there to be experienced.

When Jesus tells of his return to the Father, he promises the coming of the Spirit of God. Once again this is mention of Father, Son and Holy Spirit.

At the very end of Matthew's Gospel, the risen Jesus comes to the eleven disciples. There is his presence to be experienced. He tells of his power, his authority.

He gives the disciples a purpose, a commission. They are to 'Go and make disciples of all nations, baptising them in the name of the Father, and of the Son and of the Holy Spirit.' Here again we have the Trinity.

We must remember this is not a formula to be used at a service but a way of life. The reality of God as a Trinity – Three Persons in One God – is there for us to experience and to share with others. We are asked to immerse people in the Trinity, in the power, in the presence and in the peace of Father, Son and Holy Spirit. We are to know for ourselves and to encourage others to be aware that our lives are lived in this Triune presence.

At the end of his second letter to the Corinthians, St Paul has those words we often use: 'The grace of the Lord Jesus Christ, the love of God, and the communion of the Holy Spirit be with all of you' (2 Corinthians 13:13). We are not to see this as a request but as a reality, a reality that we need be aware of and live. If these words are used at the end of a service or a meeting, they are to remind us that we are in the presence of the Trinity and we go out and live in that presence. Remember today and each day that you are immersed in the Holy Three.

Question time
Do you affirm your immersion in the Holy Trinity each day that you dwell in him and he in you?

If you are a parent or a godparent, do you immerse your child or godchild regularly in the presence and power of God?

Illustration

In the Hebrides, the islands off the west coast of Scotland, it was often difficult for a priest to get to some of the communities to baptise a new-born child. It became the tradition for the midwife to do a form of baptism that was known as the 'birth baptism'; later the child would be baptised in church and this was known as the 'great baptism' or the 'church baptism'. One such midwife said, 'When the image of the God of life is born into the world I put three little drops of water on the child's forehead. I put the first little drop in the name of the Father, and the watching-women say, "Amen." I put the second little drop in the name of the Son, and the watching-women say, "Amen." I put the third little drop in the name of the Spirit, and the watching-women say, "Amen." . . . All the people in the house are raising their voices, with the watching-women giving witness that the child has been committed to the blessed Trinity.'

Here is part of such a baptism prayer:

In the name of God,
in the name of Jesus,
in the name of the Spirit,
the perfect Three of power.

The little drop of the Father
on thy little forehead, beloved one.

The little drop of the Son
on thy little forehead, beloved one.

The little drop of the Spirit
on thy little forehead, beloved one.

To aid thee, to guard thee,
to shield thee, to surround thee.

Intercessions

Blessed be God, Father, Son and Holy Spirit,
the Three in One,
the holy and wonderful Trinity
bound together in one eternity of love.
Blessed be God the Creator of all things.
Blessed be the Christ, our Saviour and Friend.
Blessed be the Spirit within us, our Guide and Strength.
Blessed be God for all that he is and all he has done.
Blessed be the One and the Three.

Holy God, we ask your blessing
upon all who are baptised and confirmed in the faith,
that they may witness to your presence and love.
We pray for preachers and teachers,
that they may seek to reveal
the mystery of your being with us.
Lord, guide the mission and outreach of your people.

Silence

Holy God, Holy and Strong One,
hear us and help us.

Holy God, we give thanks for your whole creation.
Guide and bless all who work in research
and who seek to discover the mysteries of your world.
We remember all scientists and explorers.
We pray for all who are at school, college or university.

We ask your blessing upon all who provide us
with our daily needs.

Silence

Holy God, Holy and Strong One,
hear us and help us.

Holy God, be among us
in our homes and in our work.
Surround our loved ones and ourselves
with your love and protection.
We ask your blessing
upon all who are recently married
and those who have a new child in their family.

Silence

Holy God, Holy and Strong One,
hear us and help us.

Holy God, you are ever ready to help us.
We ask your blessing upon all doctors, nurses
and those caring for loved ones who are ill.
We remember all ill and suffering peoples,
the poor and hungry of our world.
We pray for all who feel they are without help or hope.

Silence

Holy God, Holy and Strong One,
hear us and help us.

Holy God, giver of life and life eternal,
we rejoice in your presence
and ask your blessing upon our loved ones
who are departed from us.
May they share with your saints
in the fullness of your glorious kingdom.

Silence

Merciful Father,
accept these prayers
for the sake of your Son,
our Saviour Jesus Christ.
Amen.

Memory verse

The grace of the Lord Jesus Christ, the love of God, and the communion of the Holy Spirit be with all of you.
2 Corinthians 13:13

Suggested music

May the grace of Christ our Saviour
Thou, whose almighty word
Father, Lord of all creation

CANDLES

Aim

To get the children familiar with the idea of three persons in the Trinity.

Teaching

Can anyone remember what happened when Jesus was baptised? The voice of God was heard to speak and the Holy Spirit was seen coming down like a dove. God the Father who made the world, Jesus Christ the Son of God our Saviour, and the Holy Spirit of God were all known at the baptism of Jesus.

Who knows if they were baptised and where?

Do you know where the font is in church? The word 'font' is like 'fountain' because it holds water. Water is put in the font so that it can be put on the head of any-one who is being baptised. Sometimes we call it being 'christened' because it is when we are brought into the Christian Church. All who are baptised receive three drops of water on their head. (You may like to act this out with a doll.) Does anyone know why it is three drops?

One is because God the Father made us and loves us. Let us say together, 'God the Father loves us.'

The next drop is for Jesus who died and rose again and loves us. Let us say together, 'Jesus Christ loves us.'

Who is the third drop of water on our head for? It is for the Holy Spirit who loves us. Let us say together, 'The Holy Spirit loves us.'

Now let us put the three together and say:

God the Father loves us.
Jesus Christ loves us.
The Holy Spirit loves us.

When we are baptised it is to show that God loves us and God is with us. Now let us say:

God the Father is with us.
Jesus Christ is with us.
The Holy Spirit is with us.

Although we cannot see God, he loves us and is with us, so we can say:

God the Father is here.
Jesus Christ is here.
The Holy Spirit is here.

We can also say:

The Father is God.
Jesus is God.
The Spirit is God.

Activity

Divide the children into two groups. The first group repeat what you say the Father is but say instead, 'Jesus is . . .'. The other group will say, 'The Spirit is . . .'.

After each group speaks let everyone clap their hands twice before the next group speaks. With a little practice you should be able to get up a good rhythm.

Prayer

God our Father, we thank you
for making the world.
Jesus, we thank you
for loving us.
Holy Spirit, we thank you
for being our friend.
Thank you, Father, Son and Holy Spirit.
Amen.

Song

Father, we adore you

LAMPS

Aim

To encourage the children to think of the three persons of the Trinity.

Teaching

When the people of the Hebrides (show on a map or tell how the islands are off the West coast of Scotland) said their prayers they liked to pray to the Trinity. Who knows what Trinity means? Tri = 3. Unity =1. Tri-unity or Trinity means three in one, and we use it to describe our God as Father, Son and Holy Spirit. The Father is God, the Son is God and the Holy Spirit is God – Three – and yet there is only One God. We can never fully understand this but we can talk about the Trinity and pray to the Trinity. If you are going to pray to the Trinity, what would you need in your prayers? You would need to speak to Father, Son and Holy Spirit. Here are three examples from the Hebrides (have each of these prayers read by members of the group):

Come I this day to the Father.
Come I this day to the Son.
Come I this day to the Holy Spirit powerful.

The peace of God be to you,
the peace of Christ be to you,
the peace of the Spirit be to you
and to your children,
to you and your children.

My walk this day is with God.
My walk this day is with Christ.
My walk this day is with Spirit.
The Threefold all-kindly,
Ho! Ho! Ho! the Threefold all-kindly.

When you were first brought to church and to the font to be baptised, do you know the words that were said over you? 'I baptise you in the name of the Father, and of the Son and of the Holy Spirit.' You are immersed – are in the presence of – God the Father, Son and Holy Spirit always. So it is good to pray to the Three-person God. It is a good way to start each day. You can say something like:

I am in the presence of God the Father.
I am in the presence of Christ the Saviour.
I am in the presence of the Holy Spirit.

(Let us say this together.)

Now let us change the word 'presence' for 'love'; then we will change 'love' for 'light'.

After doing this encourage the group to suggest a word that can be used or another Trinitarian prayer.

Activity

Divide into three groups. The first group will make a statement about the Father, such as 'The Father is God.' The second group will say, 'Jesus is God.' The third group will say, 'The Spirit is God.'

After each group speaks let everyone clap their hands twice before the next group speaks. With a little practice you should be able to get up a good rhythm. See how many prayers and affirmations they can make to the Trinity.

Prayer

Father, you are our Creator.
Jesus, you are our Saviour.
Spirit, you are our Guide.
We thank you for your love
and your presence with us
today and always.
Amen.

Song

Father, we love you

TORCHES

Aim

To explore the experience of the Trinity.

Teaching

The word Trinity cannot be found in the Bible but the experience of the working of God as Father, Son and Holy Spirit can. We cannot grasp the full meaning of the Trinity with our mind – that is like trying to contain the sea in a small container – but we can hold the Trinity in our heart for it is made for the eternal. The Trinity is beyond our understanding but not beyond our experience or our loving.

Let us do a bit of detective work and look for evidence in the Bible.

In Genesis 1:1-3, at the very beginning of the Bible, we are introduced to the Creator God. This concerns God the Father, yet even here in verse 2 we can see a hint of the Spirit of God at work.

In John 1:1-4 we have what sounds like Genesis but John introduces us to the 'Word of God'. In verse 14 John will tell us that the Word became flesh and in this way he tells us of the birth of Jesus. The Gospels are about Jesus as the Son of God.

In Luke 1:35, at the annunciation of the angel to Mary, we hear of the Holy Spirit and the promised birth of the Son of God.

At the baptism of Jesus, the voice of the Father is heard and the Spirit comes upon Jesus (Matthew 3:16, 17). You may also like to look at the beginning of the Temptations (Matthew 4:1-3).

At the ascension, Jesus asks his disciples to baptise in the name of the Father and of the Son and of the Holy Spirit (Matthew 28:20).

To his disciples Jesus promised the Holy Spirit, whom the Father will send (John 14:25, 26). He asked the disciples to wait for the coming of the Spirit promised by the Father (Acts 1: 4, 5). Pentecost sees this fulfilment and the experience of the Spirit (Acts 2:1-4). The Acts of the Apostles is full of the disciples working in the power of the Spirit.

In Ephesians we have a wonderful prayer that is Trinitarian in its outlook (Ephesians 3:14-19).

St Paul ends his second letter to the Corinthians with words that are now well known: 'The grace of our Lord Jesus Christ, the love of God and the communion of the Holy Spirit be with all of you' (2 Corinthians 13:13). This is not a request but a reality. The Trinity is to be experienced and known in our daily lives.

Activity

Encourage the group to write their own prayers to the Trinity. Let some of them be used for group prayers at the end of the session with different groups saying the lines to Father, to Son and to Holy Spirit.

Prayer

Father, you are here with us and we love you.
Jesus, you are here with us and we love you.
Spirit, you are here with us and we love you.
Amen.

Song

Father God, we worship you

Proper 4

Sunday between 29 May and 4 June inclusive
(if after Trinity Sunday)

Aim

To encourage the building of a relationship with our God.

Preparation

Have notices in the entrance of exemption clauses in house insurance policies. 'Premiums are higher if built on clay'; 'Is your house in a flood plain?'; 'Have you had a structural survey?'; 'Is your building on land liable to subsidence?' – show photographs of tumbledown houses and collapsed buildings.

Opening activity

Mini drama

Builder   I have a lot of good things and I would like to share them. Would you two build me a couple of houses, no expenses spared? (*Builder exits*)

Man 1   I chose the best I could find. I knew what he would want. I dug deep foundations. Used the best materials I could get. I built a super house.

Man 2   He is a fool in his generosity. I cut a lot of corners and pocketed the money. I used cheap materials and put it up quickly. I painted over the cracks and hid the defects. I had time to relax and to party. Who cares? He will not know. What does it matter if it falls down later? (*Builder returns*)

Builder   I forgot to tell you, the house is yours. It is for you to live in.

Opening prayer

O God, the strength of all who trust in you,
without whom nothing is strong, nothing is lasting,
we seek to know you and to love you,
for in this is life and life eternal,
through Jesus Christ our Lord.
Amen.

Opening song

Christ is our cornerstone

Readings

Genesis 6:9-22; 7:24, 8:14-19
or Deuteronomy 11:18-21, 26-28
Psalm 46 or Psalm 31:1-5, 19-24
Romans 1:16, 17, 3:22b-28 (29-31)
Matthew 7:21-29

Thought for the day

Today's Gospel is the end of the Sermon on the Mount. The words that precede today's Gospel are 'you will know them by their fruits' (Matthew 7:20). Words are not enough; our relationship with God is shown in the way we live. No amount of religious acts or fine words can replace the doing of God's will. If we want to be part of the kingdom, we have to live by the rule of its king. We need notice every time we pray the Lord's Prayer that we say, 'Your kingdom come: your will be done.' God's kingdom will only come in us if we do his will.

Some of the toughest words in the Gospels are 'I never knew you'. Jesus is saying we need a relationship with him. This is the foundation of the kingdom and this is the way to eternal life – a relationship with Jesus. This is not just saying prayers and saying his name; it is having a living vital relationship with him.

Jesus compares the person who does his will to a wise builder who builds on the rock. Throughout the Old Testament the 'rock' is a symbol for God's protecting presence, God's sheltering. The wise person builds their life not only on the knowledge of God but on a relationship with him. This is far-sighted and means that whatever happens the person will survive in God.

The foolish person lives for quick results and for ease. Such a person does not have far-sighted vision but lives short-term. There is no building of a deep relationship with God. Life is measured by wealth, possessions, popularity, personal achievements, health and strength. All these are good things but not safe or lasting foundations. The danger for such a person is one day to hear the words, 'I never knew you.'

We all need to think about our future, our long-term future. This is in no way life-restricting but in fact life-enhancing. None of us want to live in a rickety, falling-apart structure when we can have a house of firm foundations.

Question time

Can you sing with confidence, 'Christ is our corner stone, on him alone we build'?

Do you see God and doing his will as the basic foundation of your life?

Illustration

In the last century the cathedral at Winchester had restoration troubles. Great cracks were appearing in the structure. Experts suggested building buttresses to hold the cathedral up; others suggested great metal tie-bars to be placed across the cathedral to stop its walls falling outwards. One man insisted that they were only dealing with the symptoms of the trouble and the real cause was much deeper: he wanted to look at the foundations. He sunk a shaft into the ground and looked. He discovered the cathedral was built on a peat bog. The builders had laid tree trunks over the watery land and the cathedral was built on these. Due to improved drainage in the city the peat had dried out and shrunk. In many places there was a space between the cathedral and the ground below it. A man was employed for five and a half years to work underground in the removing of peat and putting in its place concrete blocks. Even a cathedral is only as firm as its foundations.

Intercessions

Blessed are you, Lord our God.
You are our refuge and strength,
an ever-present help in trouble.
We seek to put our trust in you
and to do your will,
that your kingdom may come in us
as it is in heaven.
Blessed are you, Father, Son and Holy Spirit.

Lord God, help us to build our lives
on a firm foundation:
to put our trust in you and your saving love.
Strengthen your Church when it is beset
by the storms of the world,
that it may remain firm in the faith
and obedient to you.
We pray for all who are seekers,
looking for meaning and purpose in their lives
and in the world.
We remember all who are being persecuted for their faith.

Silence

Lord, your kingdom come,
your will be done.

We ask your blessing
upon all who teach and influence others,
upon those who set standards
and offer ways of living to our society.
We pray for all who are involved in government,
in broadcasting and in the press.
We remember all whose lives
have been caught up in floods, famine or war,
all who feel fragile and endangered.
We pray for all who help others to rebuild their lives.

Silence

Lord, your kingdom come,
your will be done.

We give thanks for those who have provided us
with security and protection.
We ask your blessing upon our homes
and our loved ones.
We pray for the places where we work
and for those with whom we spend our leisure time.
We remember all homeless and stateless people.

Silence

Lord, your kingdom come,
your will be done.

We bring before you
all whose world has fallen apart this week.
We remember those who have lost loved ones,
who have lost freedom, employment
or who have had their homes repossessed.
We pray for all who have been involved in accidents
or who have suddenly become ill.
We ask your blessing upon those who are close to death.

Silence

Lord, your kingdom come,
your will be done.

We ask your blessing upon our loved ones
who have departed from us –
passing through that great flood we call death.
May they rejoice in your welcome
and in your kingdom.

Silence

Merciful Father,
accept these prayers
for the sake of your Son,
our Saviour Jesus Christ.
Amen.

Memory verse

God is our refuge and strength, a very present help in trouble.
Psalm 46:1

Suggested music

Thy way, not mine, O Lord
As for me and my house
When we walk with the Lord

CANDLES

Aim

To encourage good listening through the story of the wise and foolish builders.

Teaching

When Jesus noticed that some people were not listening to what he was saying, and others were listening to him but not doing what he asked, he told them a story. It was about two men who we building their own houses. One was a wise man and the other was a foolish man.

The wise man thought about the years ahead and wanted to build a good house. He wanted a house that would be strong and protect him against the storms and the darkness. He wanted a house that would not tumble down or fall apart. So he built it carefully and slowly. Do you know the first thing he did? He cleared away the soil and dug down to rock. He wanted to build his house on rock so that it would be strong. It was hard work but he knew it would be worth it. When he had finished building he knew he had done his best. Let us say, 'The wise man built his house upon the rock.'

Now we will sing it three times and as we do we will put one hand on top of the other and reach higher and higher until we make the shape of a house.

One day it started to rain. The rain came tumbling down and because it kept raining the waters rose up and the floods came up. Let us say, 'and the rain came tumbling down.' Now let us say it again and add, 'and the floods came up.' We will sing, 'and the rain came tumbling down, and the rain came tumbling down and the floods came up.' As we do it we will show with our hands the rain coming down and the floods coming up.

As the waters rose, the man the in house watched but he was not terribly worried because he had built on the rock and his house was safe. The floods came up 'and the house on the rock stood firm'. (The children can finish by showing the shape of a house by making a triangle shape with their hands above their heads.) Let us say this line then we will sing it. Now let us put it all together and sing 'The wise man built his house upon the rock'.

Who remembers what the other man was? He was foolish. He did not look ahead but wanted an easy way to build his house. He did not build on rock because it meant hard work. He found an easy place to build. He built in a hollow and on sand. Let us say, 'The foolish man built his house upon the sand.' Now let us sing it three times and with our hands show how he built it up. We can now show how the rain came down and the floods came up as we sing. What do you think happened to the house? The floods hit it and broke it and it collapsed, 'and the house on the sand fell flat'. Let us say it together. Now we will sing it and when we say, 'fell flat', let us fall to the ground.

Activity

Have the children sing the whole song through with the actions.

Prayer

Lord Jesus, help me to listen to you
and to do what you want me to do.
I love you, Lord Jesus,
and want you to be my friend.
Amen.

Song

The wise man built his house upon the rock

LAMPS

Aim

To look at building our lives on a firm foundation.

Teaching

If you were asked to build a house, how would you begin? Would you start with the roof or with the upstairs rooms? No you start on the ground. In fact, you would start by digging *into* the ground. You have to start with foundations on which the walls will stand. Would you build on land that shook like jelly? Would you build on land that flooded? Would you build on a sandy beach? Why not? Because if you do not make your foundations strong, then your house will not be strong. Your foundations have to be very strong and lasting; they have to stand against floods and storms.

Jesus told people that if they did not listen to him and do what God wanted them to do, they were like a house with bad foundations. What would happen to such a house? Listen to this story. Get someone to read Matthew 7:24, 25. Then get someone else to read Matthew 7:26, 27.

If someone does not do what Jesus asks them to do, is that person wise or foolish? Jesus wants us to get to

know him and to work with him. He wants us to listen to him, to hear what he is saying and then to do what he asks of us. He wants us to show others how God loves them as he loves us. But we cannot do this if we do not get to know Jesus or if we do things that he does not want us to do.

If we do not listen to our teachers, we will not learn properly and we will miss out on many things. If we do not listen to advice, we will run into danger. In the same way, if we do not listen to the words of Jesus, we will not build our lives on firm foundations.

Activity

Play a listening game like 'Chinese whispers' where a sentence is passed around the group to show how well or how badly people listen to what is said. You may like to split the group into two and get them to build a pyramid of playing cards. Give one group a very wobbly surface to build on and the other a very firm steady table. Let the group discuss who fares best.

Prayer

Jesus, help me to listen to your word
and seek to do your will.
May I show that I love you
by doing what you want me to do.
Amen.

Song

I'm gonna build my house on solid rock

TORCHES

Aim

To look at our vision of life.

Teaching

Some people are very short-sighted; they live for the moment only and do not plan for the future or think about how their actions now influence their lives, sometimes for ever. Jesus noticed that some people did not really listen to him. They sometimes spoke as if they knew him but had never bothered to get to know him. Obviously we cannot really speak about Jesus if we do not get to know him. The way to get to know him is to spend time with him and to listen to his words. But it is easy to put off – we would rather be on our PlayStation or at a party; we would rather be playing sport or out with our friends. Jesus wants us to enjoy all of these things but he also wants us to have a relationship with him. It would be terrible to hear Jesus say to us, 'I never knew you.'

Jesus tells a story about two builders. One is short-sighted and takes the easy way out without thinking about the future. The second makes sure of starting on a firm foundation. The first one can laugh at the second because his house is looking good while the second is still digging into the ground. The first one can relax and play while the second is still building. But later when the storms come, life is different. The man who built on sand finds his house crumbling and his life falling apart. The one who built on rock is secure and protected against the storm. Now the long-term planning has paid off and the short-sightedness has cost the other man dearly.

Often we are in danger of spoiling our future by what we are doing now, and, even worse, we are in danger of losing out on the eternal by our present attitude to life.

Activity

Explore the dangers of short-sightedness in our lives, our education, and in our attitudes towards each other, to the world and to God. (Spend a good part of this time letting the group suggest the dangers of not listening to and not respecting each other, the need to listen if we are to learn. They may like to discuss why some courses are called 'foundation courses'.) How can we build on foundations that will last?

Prayer

Lord God, grant that we do not lose sight
of things eternal as we live our daily lives.
Help us to remember your abiding presence and love.
Lord, may we always be ready to do your will
in caring for this world and for each other.
Amen.

Song

Anyone who hears

Proper 5

Sunday between 5 and 11 June inclusive
(if after Trinity Sunday)

Aim

To look at the power and love of Jesus

Preparation

Have photographs of people who are rejected, barred or who are outcasts. Display them around the text 'Anyone who comes to me I will never drive away' (John 6:37b).'

Opening activity

Mini drama

Voice 1   Just look at that, Jesus is inviting a collaborator and tax man to join his team. Disgraceful.

Voice 2   Look, now he is spending time with a superstitious woman who should have stayed at home. I would tell her.

Voice 3   Look again, he goes with a man who comes to him only because he is desperate. What can Jesus do with the dead?

Voice 4   Jesus shows the power and the love of God at work in all who turn to him.

Opening prayer

Lord Jesus, as you called Matthew to follow you
and as you called a young girl back to life,
help us to hear and to heed your call.
May we learn to follow you
and to come to that life which is eternal.
Amen.

Opening song

Immortal love, for ever full

Readings

Genesis 12:1-9 or Hosea 5:15–6:6
Psalm 33:1-12 or Psalm 50:7-15
Romans 4:13-25
Matthew 9:9-13, 18-26

Thought for the day

In today's Gospel we see various facets of the power of Jesus at work. Jesus is able to call people from all walks of life, if they will respond. Matthew is so unlikely and he is working in an unlikely place. Matthew belonged to a priestly family but had preferred to make money and work for the enemy who occupied the country. Matthew was a collaborator. Because of his work as a tax collector, Matthew was hated by many and banned from the synagogue. Yet no matter how Matthew filled his pockets with money, he still felt an inner need. Matthew was not at ease or at peace with himself. Jesus had the power to see this and to call Matthew from his work to follow him. Jesus saw the potential of the man who could keep the accounts, and in time Matthew would give us a fine account of the life of Jesus. Matthew was changed through the power of Jesus.

The leader of the synagogue was desperate. He had tried every way he could to bring healing to his daughter but no one had been able to help. The little girl should have been entering into the fullness of life but her life was ebbing away. The leader came to Jesus as a last resort but he at least acknowledged that Jesus could do something. He believed that Jesus could restore life. Jesus saw the faith of the man. We shall see that Jesus has the power over life itself. While Jesus was going to the house the little girl died. But Jesus had the power and took her by the hand. With her hand in his she arose.

While he had been going to the leader of the synagogue's house, a woman interrupted his journey. This woman thought she could steal a cure from Jesus by touching one of the tassels on his cloak. She should not have been there because of her illness. Because she was suffering from haemorrhages she was counted as unclean – and anyone she touched would be counted as unclean. She was rather superstitious thinking she could steal a cure. But she recognised that Jesus did have power. Jesus had the power to restore her life to its fullness. Because of her faith in him Jesus healed her and so revealed his power.

If we truly believe in Jesus, we will respond to his call. We will allow him to enrich our lives and transform us by his power.

Question time

Do we truly seek to follow Jesus and do the will of God or are we trying to make God do what we want?

Knowing that Jesus has the power to give us life eternal, do you seek him out each day?

Illustration

Jim had all the money he needed. It seemed whatever he did turned to gold. He had a great home and a lot of friends. He was able to spend a good deal of time enjoying himself. But Jim had an emptiness that nothing could fill. The more he tried to fill it with action, things or parties, the more it gnawed at him. He told a friend and the friend introduced him to a poem called 'The Hound of Heaven' by Francis Thompson. The line that worried the rich man was 'All things betray thee, who betrayest Me'. The friend had the sense to tell him that he need not worry, for the hunger that he felt was none other than the calling of God in his life. 'Listen to God, respond to God and you will soon feel different.' Jim did as advised, he did not change his way of life or his friends, but he turned to God each day, started to worship each Sunday at his local church. He did not change but God changed him and he was now a far richer man than he had ever been.

Intercessions

Blessed are you, Lord our God,
for out of your love
you call us to know and to love you.

Lord, may we come to know you,
and in knowing you, love you,
and in loving you, serve you,
whose service is perfect freedom.
Blessed are you, Father, Son and Holy Spirit.

Lord, as you have called us
make us worthy of our calling.
We ask your blessing
upon all who seek to fulfil their calling in life.
We pray for those
who are called to proclaim the Gospel
and to give account of you.
We pray for preachers and evangelists.
We ask your guidance
upon all who are called to witness to you,
to your power and your love.

Silence

We come to your love:
heal us and raise us up.

We remember before you
all who suffer from rejection and scorn.
We pray for homeless people,
for refugees and the world poor.
We ask your blessing
upon all who are used as cheap labour
or who are abused by taskmasters.
We pray for all who suffer from injustice
or the lack of fair trade.

Silence

We come to your love:
heal us and raise us up.

We give thanks for our homes and our loved ones.
As we ask your blessing upon them,
we remember homes where there is sorrow
and suffering.
We pray for those who are struggling
due to the illness of a loved one,
those who have got deeply into debt
and those who feel drained and exhausted.

Silence

We come to your love:
heal us and raise us up.

We give thanks
for all who work in the healing professions,
and we pray for our own doctors and health workers.
We remember all who are denied healing and help
through poverty or war.
We ask your blessing upon all who are caring
for a loved one who is terminally ill,
and for the work of hospices.

Silence

We come to your love:
heal us and raise us up.

We give thanks for all you have lifted from death
into the fullness of life eternal.
We rejoice with all the faithful departed
who are where sorrow and pain are no more.

To you, to your power and love,
we commit this world, our loved ones and ourselves
now and for ever.

Silence

Merciful Father,
**accept these prayers
for the sake of your Son,
our Saviour Jesus Christ.
Amen.**

Memory verse

Anyone who comes to me I will never drive away.
John 6:37b

Suggested music

O Lord, all the world belongs to you
When God almighty came to earth
What a friend we have in Jesus

CANDLES

Aim

To show how Jesus made a little girl well and how Jesus loves us.

Teaching

Welcome anyone back who has been ill. Talk about how mothers and fathers are very sad when they have a child who is ill and how they feel happier when their child gets better. Today I want to tell you how Jesus made a little girl well again when no one else could help her.

The little girl's daddy looked after a church. He made sure that it had someone to take the services and that it was tidy and ready for people to come and pray. One day when he came home from church, he found that his little girl was poorly. The little girl had to go to bed and her mother asked the father to get a doctor to help the girl get better. But the little girl did not get better. Soon she could not keep awake, she could not eat, and then what do you think happened? The little girl died. Her mother and father were now very sad indeed.

Someone told the father that Jesus was near and maybe he could have helped. The father knew in his heart that Jesus could have helped and even now Jesus could still help. The Father ran to where Jesus was and told him, 'My daughter has just died, but come and lay your hands upon her, and she will live.' Some people tried to tell him not to bother Jesus: if the little girl was dead, he had come too late. But Jesus looked at the man and saw how he loved his daughter. He saw also how the man believed in him and that he could do what the man asked. Jesus and his disciples went with the man to his house.

When they got there everyone was crying and some were playing sad music because the little girl was dead. Jesus told them to stop crying for he would awaken the little girl. But they laughed at him because they did not believe it was possible. Jesus asked the crowd to leave the house so that it could be quiet. He loved the girl's parents and the little girl and still wanted to be able to help them. He went into the room were she was. She was lying very still upon the bed. Jesus took hold of her hand. At first it was cold but in his hand it began to get warm. Now Jesus said to her, 'Get up.' The girl opened her eyes and she got up.

Jesus had shown his love and his wonderful power in making a little girl well again. She was able to join her mother and father and enjoy life again.

Activity

Begin by asking all the children except one to lie quietly on the floor. They must not move. They should keep their eyes closed. Tell them they are to stay like that until someone comes and touches their hand. The one child still standing will go around the children touching their hand and encouraging them to stand up. After the story get the children to act it out. When the children sing the song let them reach as high as they can when they sing, 'So high you can't get over it', then crouch down low as they sing, 'So low you can't get under it', and open their arms wide as they sing, 'So wide you can't get round it'.

Prayer

Jesus, we thank you for loving us
and being our friend.
We ask you to look after and help
all the ill or sad children.
Amen.

Song

Jesus' love is very wonderful

LAMPS

Aim

To show the love and power of Jesus at work in healing the woman who came to him.

Teaching

Once there was a woman who became ill. Before she was poorly she used to go to the market to shop. She went to the church to say her prayers. She enjoyed going to see friends and have them come back to her house to see her. She liked being with people and meeting people.

One day she realised that she was not very well. She found that she was bleeding and the bleeding would not stop. It was not dangerous to her life but she wanted it to stop. She went to the doctor and he tried some medicines but she did not get better. Then the doctor told her that she had to stay at home. If she went out, she had to keep away from other people. She could not visit friends and they should not come to her house. She was told that she could not go to the market and she could not go to church. All of this made her very lonely and very sad. It was believed that if she touched anyone, it made that person unclean. If she sat on a seat, it made it unclean. So she was not allowed to go anywhere.

The woman became very sad and prayed to God for help. But she did not seem to get better. Then one day she was told that Jesus was in her town. She was not really allowed to join the crowds that went to see him but she thought, 'If I could but touch even the hem of his coat, I am sure his power would make me better.' The chance came as Jesus passed near her house. She came out and into the crowds. She knew she should not but she wanted to touch Jesus. She did not even want to stop him, just touch him. She sneaked up behind Jesus and touched his robe. As she did this, Jesus stopped. The crowd stopped. It felt as if the whole world stopped. Jesus wanted to know who had touched him. He felt as if some power had gone out from him. The woman was now afraid. What would Jesus say? Had she made him unclean? What would the crowd say? Surely they would be angry that she was there. But before anyone could get angry Jesus spoke to her very kindly and gently and said, 'Your faith has made you well.' Because she had believed in Jesus, in his love and in his power, she was healed. No one could complain at her being there because she was made well. Jesus in his love for her had given her the power to be healed. Now she could do all the things she used to do. She would never forget the love of Jesus or his mighty power.

Activity

Play a game of tag. When one is touched they then help to touch others until all are tagged. You might like to tell them that this is a game called 'Contagious'! It is about contact.

Prayer

Jesus, we thank you for your love
and your power to heal.
We ask your blessing
upon all who are ill or suffering
at this time.
Amen.

Song

Step by step

TORCHES

Aim

To look at Matthew and his calling.

Teaching

Not many people like having to pay tax. If you knew that the tax man was charging extra to make money for himself, that would make you like him even less than before. Many Jews disliked tax collectors because they were working for the enemy of occupation: they were working for the Roman Empire.

One type of tax was like our VAT: it was collected on goods as they entered or left the city. The money was collected near the city gate so no one could dodge it. There were often arguments here and a lot of haggling.

One of the collectors was a man called Matthew. He was very good at maths and at accounts. He knew how to add up and usually in his own favour. Matthew came from a priestly family, so he could have done work in the church, but he preferred making a lot of money. Because he was a tax collector for the Romans he was excluded from his church. He was not liked. Matthew became rich and had a lot of possessions but he was beginning to see that this was not everything. He felt as if there was something missing in his life.

Then one day Jesus came along. Perhaps Matthew aimed at taxing Jesus. But as Jesus did not have anything to tax he would not be able to. Yet Jesus still came to the tax place. He could see that Matthew needed to change, to be challenged, so he said to him, 'Follow me.' Probably Matthew had already heard of Jesus and his work. Here Jesus was calling him, calling him to leave what he was doing – to leave his accounts and to follow Jesus into an unknown way of life.

Activity

Today's Gospel is about Jesus working with 'untouch-ables' – the tax collector, the 'unclean' and the dead. Get the group to look at each in turn and say why they think it important that each of these events is recorded. This is a good Gospel passage to act out.

Prayer

Lord Jesus,
friend of the friendless
and help of the helpless,
we come to you in faith.
We trust in you,
in your love and in your power.
Lord Jesus, help us to hear your call
and to follow you.
Amen.

Song

One more step

Proper 6

Sunday between 12 and 18 June inclusive
(if after Trinity Sunday)

Aim

To show that those whom Jesus calls he also sends out.

Preparation

Create two posters for the entrance, one which says, 'JES S needs U to do his work'; the other, 'JES needs US to reach out.' Have a display of various examples of the outreach of the Church among the poor, the dispossessed and the suffering. You may like to add to these the question 'Will you go for Jesus?'

Opening activity

Mini drama

Voice 1 I love the peace and quiet of the church.
Voice 2 (*in a stage whisper*) Jesus says, 'Go.'
Voice 3 I love to escape from the busyness of life.
Voice 2 (*in a stage whisper*) Jesus says, 'Go.'
Voice 4 I come to meet a few friends.
Voice 2 (*in a stage whisper*) Jesus says, 'Go.'
Voice 5 I enjoy the music and the liturgy.
Voice 2 All the benefits of coming to church are good but Jesus says, 'Go out and make disciples.'

Opening prayer

Lord God, you have called us
to know you, to love you and to proclaim you.
May we live in awareness of you
and, in the power of your Spirit,
tell of your love in all the world,
through Jesus Christ our Lord.
Amen.

Opening song

Jesus calls us

Readings

Genesis 18:1-15 (21:1-7) or Exodus 19:2-8a
Psalm 116:1, 10-17 or Psalm 100
Romans 5:1-8
Matthew 9:35–10:8 (9-23)

Thought for the day

Today's Gospel shows Jesus going about doing his daily work: he is teaching, proclaiming the good news and healing the sick. Jesus is aware of how harassed and helpless so many people are – you can see it in their faces and in their actions. Look at people in any street and you can see the same distress and stress on their faces. Jesus feels for them; he had compassion for them. He sees that they are like sheep without a shepherd, wandering with no one to guide them or protect them. He wants to help all of them. Jesus is aware of the great harvest to be won and says to the disciples, 'The harvest is plentiful but the labourers are few; therefore ask the Lord of the harvest to send out labourers into the harvest.' Such a prayer should come with a health warning, for the reply from God is, 'Whom shall I send?' and the answer should be, 'Here am I, send me.'

Jesus calls his twelve disciples to him, to learn of him, to be with him, to love him, but also to send them out. Jesus gives of his power to his disciples but for them to give to others. Here in Matthew 10:2 we see the other title of the chosen: they are 'Apostles', those who are sent by him. Jesus sends them to be heralds and healers, to proclaim the good news and to care for the distressed. Jesus needs his disciples to continue his work. Jesus warns them of the dangers: the task will not be easy and there will be opposition. But they will have the power of the Spirit so they are not to worry.

In Matthew's Gospel the last words of Jesus are still saying, 'Go': Jesus sends all whom he calls. Let it be said, though, he does not send out before he calls people to him. We cannot speak in his name if we do not know and love him. Coming to him and then going out in his power into all the world is what makes us the true Church of God. It is then we are seen as

the one (united in him)
holy (belonging to God)
catholic (for all people, at all times and in all places)
and
apostolic (sent out by him in the power of the Spirit)
Church (called by him and answering his call).

Our God is a calling God, seeking a response from each of us: he is a sending God. In Jesus we hear the command, 'Go, therefore, and make disciples of all nations, baptising them in the name of the Father and of the Son and of the Holy Spirit.' With this sending is the promise, 'I am with you always' (Matthew 28:19, 20).

Question time

How does your church show signs of being apostolic?

Mission – going out – is not for ministers and priests only; it is for all God's people. How can you help to put this into action?

Illustration

Picture yourself coming to your own community and all the lights are out. The only light is coming from the church. You go to see where the light is coming from. It is coming from near the altar, so you approach the light. You see it is coming from a man sitting in a chair. You are about to ask him what he is doing and you see it is the Christ. You kneel before him. He does not move because he is a captive. He is tied to the chair, a prisoner. You ask him, 'Why are you tied, what has fixed you here?'

He replies, 'I am stuck here because my people will not reach out in love. My people do not proclaim the good news. My people do not help in the healing of the nations. They have fastened me in the building.'

'Lord, how can I set you free?'

'By going out in my name and working with me in all the world.'

You offer yourself to his service, saying, 'Here I am, send me.' At that moment the Christ is freed and the lights begin to come on again.

Intercessions

Blessed are you, Lord our God,
for you have called us into life and to love you.
You have called us to proclaim your love and power
in all the world.
Lord, send us out in the power of your Spirit,
that we may tell of you and your abiding presence.
Blessed are you, Father, Son and Holy Spirit.

Lord, we ask your blessing upon your Church,
that we may show signs of being One in you,
Holy and dedicated to being apostolic
as we reach out to all peoples.
We pray for all who are reaching out to others
in your name and in love.
Bless and guide all who preach the word
and all who share in your healing ministry.
We remember those involved in a pastoral ministry
and those who work to relieve the distress and sorrow
of people and nations.

Silence

Lord, as you have called us,
hear us and help us.

We pray for all who are called to govern
and all who influence the minds of others.
We pray for leaders of industry
and great multi-national companies
and for all they work with.
Lord, help us to show our care for the earth
and our respect for the individual
in all that we do.
We remember those whose lives are blighted
by the greed or insensitivity of others.

Silence

Lord, as you have called us,
hear us and help us.

We give thanks because you show us your love
through those who love us.
We ask your blessing
upon our homes and our loved ones.
We pray for homes where there is stress and distress.
We remember all who are finding it difficult to cope
and those who are deeply in debt.
We pray for all who are seeking to help those in need.

Silence

Lord, as you have called us,
hear us and help us.

We give thanks for all involved in the healing ministry.
We ask your blessing upon doctors and nurses
and all the emergency services.
We pray for those who are good neighbours and carers
in their local community.

We remember all who are frustrated
through illness or a disability,
and all who are struggling with life.

Silence

Lord, as you have called us,
hear us and help us.

We rejoice in the fellowship of all your saints,
in all who have heard your call and done your will.
We ask your blessing upon our loved ones
who are departed from us.
May we all share in the joy of your love
and your kingdom.

Silence

Merciful Father,
accept these prayers
for the sake of your Son,
our Saviour Jesus Christ.
Amen.

Memory verse

The harvest is plentiful, but the labourers are few; therefore ask the Lord of the harvest to send out labourers into his harvest.
Matthew 9:37, 38

Suggested music

Here I am
Will you come and follow me
Forth in the peace of Christ we go

CANDLES

Aim

To show how Jesus needs helpers to do his work.

Teaching

When your mother or father has a lot of work to do, how can they make it easier? It is easier if they get help. Sometimes when there is a lot of work we need other people to help us. (See if the children can give an example – such as if we are carrying something heavy or there is a big room to tidy.)

Jesus soon had a lot of work to do. He wanted to tell people about how God loves them. He was sorry for people who were sad or ill and wanted to help them. But soon there were so many people coming to Jesus that he hardly had time to eat or rest. He needed some helpers. Jesus decided to ask some people to follow him and be his disciples. Disciples would learn from Jesus and help him to do his work.

Do you remember how he went to the Sea of Galilee? He saw the fishermen and he called two lots of brothers to follow him. This was 2 + 2 – how many is that? Yes, four fishermen disciples. Can you remember their names? Peter and Andrew, James and John. Let us all say their names together. Then Jesus called on someone who was a tax collector. Does anyone know his name? It begins with M. (Is there someone in the group with this name?) Now that is five. Jesus wanted to have twelve disciples. So he had to choose some more. Do you know the names of any more of them? (See Matthew 10:2-4.) (They may know of Doubting Thomas or the disciple who betrayed Jesus.)

Jesus wanted the twelve disciples to follow him, to be with him and to learn from him. So they had to travel with him and share in what he did. Once they had learnt what Jesus was doing, then they could share in the work. They could also teach about the love of God and care for people who were ill or troubled. But they could only do this if they followed Jesus and worked with him first. When they were ready, Jesus sent them out to help to do his work. When they went out they were not just disciples, they were also apostles. Let us say together: 'apostles'. To be an apostle means to be some-one sent by Jesus. Jesus wants us to be his disciples and learn from him but he also wants us to be his apostles. He wants us to go out and tell others about him.

Activity

Scatter the names of the children around the room on postcards. Encourage them to find their name. Some may need a little help. Once everyone has found their name, call the names out and after each name say, 'Follow me.' They then must come forward and stand beside you. Now play 'Simon says'. They must do what you tell them as long as you start with the words, 'Simon says'. If you do not say, 'Simon says', they must do nothing. This is about learning to listen carefully and do what you are asked.

Prayer

Lord Jesus, you have called us
to know you and love you.
Help us to listen carefully and learn of you,
to follow you
and then we can tell others about you.
Amen.

Song

Fisherman Peter

LAMPS

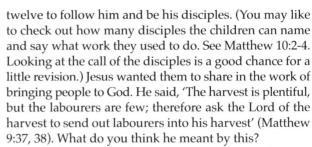

Aim

To discover Jesus wants to send out those whom he calls.

Teaching

Once Jesus had left his home and started teaching and healing people he saw how sad and troubled people were. Soon there were so many people coming to Jesus that he could hardly look after them all. Jesus needed some helpers. He needed helpers to tell of God's love, to care for the sick and the distressed and to look after the aching and the anxious. Jesus could not do all this work on his own. It was too big a job for one. So Jesus called

twelve to follow him and be his disciples. (You may like to check out how many disciples the children can name and say what work they used to do. See Matthew 10:2-4. Looking at the call of the disciples is a good chance for a little revision.) Jesus wanted them to share in the work of bringing people to God. He said, 'The harvest is plentiful, but the labourers are few; therefore ask the Lord of the harvest to send out labourers into his harvest' (Matthew 9:37, 38). What do you think he meant by this?

Once the disciples had spent some time with Jesus learning about him and about the love of God, Jesus decided they were ready to be sent out to share in his work. Jesus wanted to send them out to teach and to heal. Jesus warned them it could be dangerous but not to worry because the Spirit of God – the Holy Spirit – would be with them to help them. When they went out they were given a new name. They were not just disciples, not just learners, because now they were being sent out. They were called Apostles because 'apostle' means 'one who is sent'.

Explore ideas of being sent. Sent into raptures by one we love. 'Sent' by a pop star or a football star and so we 'follow' them, we collect information about them, we try to be where they are, to listen to them or watch them. We want to tell other people about them.

We are called to be apostles, to be sent by Jesus. How can we show that Jesus sends us out in his power?

Activity

Scatter a lot dried peas on the table or the floor. The group is split into teams and each is given a straw. They have to choose a leader who will have the most to do. When they are ready the leader has to collect ten peas by sucking them on to his straw and placing them in a saucer. The team can count as they do it. Then the whole team has to work together to harvest another 20 peas. How much easier it is with helpers: we can harvest the peas much faster.

Prayer

Lord Jesus,
as we learn to know you and love you,
send us out in the power of your Spirit
to live and work to your praise and glory.
Amen.

Song

God, you can use me

TORCHES

Aim

To look at the hallmarks of the Church.

Teaching

As soon as he started his ministry Jesus was aware of the needs of so many people. They needed to be told of the love of God, they needed to know someone cared for them, and many needed healing. The work was too much for him to do alone. Jesus called twelve men to help him. They were to be his disciples. They would travel with him, learn from him and work with him. One day he said to them, 'The harvest is plentiful, but the labourers are few; therefore ask the Lord of the harvest to send out labourers into his harvest' (Matthew 9:37, 38). He saw they were ready and he wanted to send them out to do the work he was doing. He wanted them to be more than disciples; he wanted them to be apostles, which means 'those who are sent'. He wanted them to go out into all the world and to reach out to others telling them the Good News of the Gospel. His last words to them in St Matthew's Gospel are 'Go, therefore, and make disciples of all nations, baptising them in the name of the Father and of the Son and of the Holy Spirit.' With the sending is the promise, 'I am with you always' (Matthew 28:19, 20).

When we talk of the Church, we do not mean a building but the people whom God has called. He has not just called us to be with him, though we must start by being with him: he has called us to go out in his name.

All precious metals should have hallmarks to show they are genuine and not fakes. The hallmarks should be a sign of the real article. Hallmarks usually tell you who made it, where it came from and that it has certain qualities. Every time we say the Creed we tell of the hallmarks of the Church. We say, 'We believe in one holy catholic and apostolic Church.' Let us say this together.

One means there are not lots of churches; there is one Church and it is all the people whom God has called. Not only is it the Church on earth, it is the Church in heaven. In God we are all one.

Holy means it belongs to God, is dedicated to God, seeks to serve God. As part of the Church you have to show signs of holiness.

Catholic is not about denominations. The Church is catholic because God has called it to be for all people, at all times and in all places. The Church cannot be exclusive. It is not a club; it is there to reach out and show the love of God to all.

Apostolic tells us that the Church has a mission. It is sent by God to do his will. It is a herald of the Good News and is asked to bring healing to the people of the world. The Church is there to worship God and to go out and reveal him to others.

Church describes not bricks and mortar but people who hear and answer the call of God. The Church is a living organism made up of all its members.

These are the hallmarks of the Church. As you are the Church, are these hallmarks found in you?

Activity

Explore further how the group can display the hallmarks of the Church in their daily life. Divide the group into five and give them each a hallmark of God's people – ONE, HOLY, CATHOLIC, APOSTOLIC, CHURCH – and ask them to mime it to the rest of the group.

Prayer

Lord God, you have called us
to be your people and to belong to you in love.
Help us to show your love to all people.
Send us out
to tell of your presence and your kingdom
in the world.
Amen.

Song

We have a gospel to proclaim

Proper 7

Sunday between 19 and 25 June inclusive
(if after Trinity Sunday)

Aim

To show how God cares for us, and how this should drive away fear.

Preparation

Have photographs or notices about the loss of bird life, the destruction of the rainforest, the pollution of the air and under each in bold letters have 'GOD CARES'.
You may like to show a suffering animal, a suffering person and again 'GOD CARES'.

Opening activity

Mini drama

Voice 1 Do you realise that by using so much fuel we contribute to global warming?

Voice 2 I don't care.

Voice 3 Do you not see that by pulling out hedgerows we are spoiling the birds' habitats?

Voice 2 I don't care.

Voice 4 Surely you know that being cruel to animals is wrong.

Voice 2 I don't care.

Voice 5 Do you not see that cheap clothing is produced by almost slave labour?

Voice 2 I don't care.

Voice 6 God cares all the time and you can hardly believe in him if you do not care.

Opening prayer

O God, as you created all things
out of your love and for your love,
help us to show your loving care
for the world and for each other.
May we show respect and awe
towards all your creation
and seek to protect it where we can.
Amen.

Opening song

Praise, my soul, the King of heaven

Readings

Genesis 21:8-21 or Jeremiah 20:7-13
Psalm 86:1-10, 16-17
or Psalm 69:8-11 (12-17) 18-20
Romans 6:1b-11
Matthew 10:24-39

Thought for the day

It is worth remembering that Matthew is a Jewish Christian. He sees Jesus as the fulfilment of the Jewish hopes and Scriptures, as a link with their history. It is likely that the Gospel was written after AD 70, after the destruction of Jerusalem and its Temple. Because of the rebellion of the Jews, the Roman general Titus reduced the city and the Temple to ashes and rubble. It was so completely destroyed that a plough was drawn across the city. This was a time of tribulation when people's faith was deeply challenged. It was a time when Christians were being persecuted for their faith and needed words of encouragement. By the time the Gospel was written Jesus had not only been scorned and rejected, crucified, dead and buried, but he had risen again. This is the context in which to read today's Gospel.

Jesus talks about the relationship between him and his disciples. A disciple cannot hope for an easier life than Jesus. If Jesus has been maligned and called 'Lord of the dung' (one understanding of Beelzebul), the disciples could not hope to escape. Jesus does not promise an easy life but he does offer life eternal.

Now we come to one of the great themes of the Bible. Jesus says, 'Have no fear, do not fear.' In a world of darkness and trouble it is easy to fear and to lose hope but we are not left alone because our Lord is with us. In this passage fear is mentioned four times.

Do not fear them (10:26, 27). Jesus tells us that nothing goes unnoticed, nothing is hidden or secret; God will triumph. Jesus tells us to speak out without fear. Jesus is there even in the dark.

Do not fear those who kill the body but cannot kill the soul (verse 28). No matter how much people seek to destroy us, Christ gives us the gift of life eternal. We are more than mere bodies. Our human bodies are forever dying but we as a person survive. For the Christian death is not fatal! We shall not perish but have everlasting life (see John 3:16).

But rather fear him who can destroy both body and soul in hell (28). The Jews well understood that 'the fear of God is the beginning of wisdom'. This is not terror but awe, not being afraid but having great respect for. Because it sounds like a threat, the following words are important (29-31): God values each of us, cares for all his creation, so 'Do not be afraid'. Learn that God loves you and cares for you. Then you may know that 'perfect love casts out fear'.

Question time

Do our anxiety and fear show a lack of faith in the loving God?

Do we show a disrespect for God when we are careless with his creation?

Illustration

Because Jesus says we need to fear God, he adds the balance of the fact that God values us and loves us. He talks of the sparrows. He says in Matthew's Gospel, 'Are not two sparrows sold for a penny? Yet not one of them falls to the ground without God noticing.' St Luke gives this in a slightly different form: 'Are not five sparrows sold for two pennies? Yet not one of them is forgotten in God's sight.' It would seem if the buyer was willing to buy four sparrows for two pence, a fifth was thrown in for free. It was as if the sparrow had no value at all! But God noticed and cared; God cares for all his creation.

When Jesus talks of one falling to the ground, it is easy to think of its death, and most people would not notice. But it may just mean land on the ground, to descend from flying. If God notices the small action of the sparrow, will he not all the more care for us?

Intercessions

Blessed are you, Lord our God,
for you created this world out of your goodness
and pour your love upon it.
All things are precious in your sight
and all are valued.
Blessed are you, Father, Son and Holy Spirit.

God, our Protection and strength,
we bring before you
all who are suffering for their faith,
all who are mocked, scorned, rejected
and in danger.
We remember those imprisoned
and those who suffer physical harm.
We pray for all who seek to proclaim your love
and to help in the healing of nations.
We ask your blessing
upon the Church to which we belong
and pray that we may use aright
the resources you have given us.

Silence

God, in your love and mercy,
hear us and help us.

God our Creator,
we ask you to bless and guide
all who work for the conservation of the earth
and for the care of each creature.
We pray for those involved in the protection
of endangered species
and we pray for those who seek to preserve
the rainforests and their inhabitants.

Silence

God, in your love and mercy,
hear us and help us.

We give thanks for the comfort and security
of our homes.
May we always be aware of the needs of others
and the danger of seeking the cheapest goods.
We ask your blessing upon our families and friends,
that they may know of your love and care.

Silence

God, in your love and mercy,
hear us and help us.

Loving God, we remember in your presence
all whose lives are endangered at this time.
We pray for those who have been involved in accidents
or acts of violence.
We remember those who have been driven off their land
or out of their homes.
We pray for all who are suffering in any way.

Silence

God, in your love and mercy,
hear us and help us.

Lord, you care for us in life and in death
and you offer us life eternal.
We ask you to give joy and peace
to our loved ones departed
and to all your saints.
May we come one day with them
to share in the fullness of your glory.

Silence

Merciful Father,
**accept these prayers
for the sake of your Son,
our Saviour Jesus Christ.
Amen.**

Memory verse

Do not be afraid; you are of more value than many sparrows.
Matthew 10:31

Suggested music

Do not be afraid
Why should I feel discouraged
March on, my soul, with strength

CANDLES

Aim

To show how God cares for his world and for each of us.

Teaching

Get the children who can read to read a line each of the hymn 'Who put the colours in the rainbow?' If this is too difficult, read it slowly and let them reply to each line 'God.' (This should be fun for them to do even if they just do the response.)

When God made the world he saw all that he had made and was pleased that it was a good world. God loved everything he had made from the smallest of his creatures to the largest. Who can think of a small animal that God loves? Can you think of a small bird? You may be able to think of a small fish. Now let us think of the large creatures that God loves. Tell me the name of a very large animal, a large bird and a large fish. God loves all of these because God loves the world that he has made. God notices when a bird lands on the ground or when a fish swims in deep water. God sees all his wonderful creatures and cares for each one. Because God loves them, he wants us to care for them. It would make God sad if we were unkind to any of his animals or we spoiled anything he had made because God loves all of them.

This means that God also loves us; he loves you and me. God cares for us and wants to be our friend. He knows when we are happy and when we are sad. He knows when we are fit and strong, and he knows if we are ill. God cares for us. Because he cares for us and loves us, he wants us to care for each other. Remember, as God cares for the tiny sparrow in our garden, he will also care a lot about us.

Activity

Play 'Musical statues'. When the music plays they have to be a large animal and when it stops they have to be absolutely still. When it starts they have to be a small animal and so on. Anyone who cannot keep still when the music stops must sit out and watch the others perform.

Prayer

God, thank you for a wonderful world
and all that is in it.
We thank you for the birds, the fish
and the land animals,
for the beautiful earth.
We thank you for making us and loving us.
Amen.

Song

There are hundreds of sparrows

LAMPS

Aim

To show that God loves all of his creation and us in particular.

Teaching

Who has a pet at home? (Find out the variety of pets and their names, if the children feed them and take them out.) Do you look after it and love it? It is not good to have a pet if we do not care for it. If we went away on holiday, we could not leave it without food; we would have to make sure it is still looked after. Who looks after your pet if you go away? It would be terrible if we were unkind to our pet or neglected it. If we have a pet, it needs our love and our attention.

When God made the world he made it all out of his love and for his love. God loves everything that he has made. He loves the tiniest of his creatures and the greatest. (Explore which are the tiniest of God's creatures and which are the largest.) God cares for each of his creatures and knows where they are and what is happening to them. God cares if they get into trouble or are in danger. Because God loves each of them, he wants us to look after his world and the creatures in it. God does not want creatures to suffer through our greed or carelessness. (You could explore the idea of conservation work and the work done to rescue endangered species.) God wants us to learn to love the world with the love that he has for the world.

We must remember that God made each of us. Through our parents he gave us life and he loves us and cares what happens to us. God cares how we deal with each other and does not want us to be unkind or cruel.

He wants us to care for any who are in trouble or in need and to show that he cares for them. God provides for us all, for every creature and we must not take others' share and make it our own.

Get someone to read Matthew 10:29 and get the group to talk about what it means.

Let us thank God today for loving us, for being with us, and always being ready to help us.

Activity

Explore a conservation project such as 'Save the panda' or a local bird or butterfly. Find out why it is important to save it. God does care for his creatures: he loves them and he dearly loves us.

Prayer

God, help us to love the world
the way you do.
Teach us to respect all creatures
and not to make any suffer
through our greed or neglect.
May we know at all times
that you love us.
Amen.

Song

'Cheep!' said the sparrow

TORCHES

Aim

To affirm that God is with us and cares for us at all times.

Teaching

Who can remember what it means to be 'an apostle'? It a person who is sent. Jesus chose his disciples so that when they were ready he could send them out to do the work he wanted done. Before Jesus sent them out he gave them some warnings: if people had called him names, the disciples could not hope for better treatment. If they had opposed him, they would not be friendly to his disciples. Jesus was aware of the dangers and wanted to warn his followers that life would not be easy. It is a mistake to think that once we follow Jesus, life becomes easy; it can become more dangerous and we can face more not less opposition. There are always those who will mock or try to dissuade us in our mission.

Although this is so, Jesus says, 'Have no fear of them.' Truth will prevail; Jesus and God will prevail. Nothing is hidden from God and he cares for us constantly. What we hear him tell us to do in the quiet of prayer we are to go out and proclaim, for he has called us to tell the Good News – this is our mission.

We are to remember who is in ultimate control. It is God. We are also to remember that we are destined for God's eternal kingdom. We are in his service and should not fear those who cannot take our eternal life from us. Many a Christian martyr has witnessed to the fact they might lose their life but they did not lose eternal life because they remained faithful to God. The knowledge that we have eternal life gives us courage and hope.

Jesus said we should fear God. This is about awe and respect and the knowledge that in God's hands is eternal life. Jesus does not mean we should be frightened of God because God is a God of love and care. For this reason Jesus tells us how God cares for the sparrows. Sparrows of very little value – almost worthless – in the eyes of the world but God cares for them. If God cares for the sparrows, does he not all the more care for us? In our mission we should be aware of the presence, the knowledge and love of God at all times.

Jesus warns there can be much opposition, even sometimes within our own homes. If we play for safety, we will never venture very far. If we do not risk, we may never gain. But those who go out in the name of Jesus will gain life eternal. Get the group to read Matthew 10:38-39 and to spend the rest of the session discussing what it means for them.

Activity

Play 'Chinese whispers'. Pass around a statement about the love of God. See how it changes in its telling. Tell the group how we are to proclaim Christ rather than whisper about him.

Prayer

Lord God, as you have called us
to know you and to love you,
help us to tell of your love
and your saving power,
through Jesus Christ our Lord.
Amen.

Song

God is love: his the care

Proper 8

Sunday between 26 June and 2 July inclusive

Aim

To show how through hospitality Christ can be proclaimed and accepted.

Preparation

Display a few notices near the door that are unwelcoming, for example, 'No Strangers', 'Keep Out', 'Private', 'Members Only' – but cross them out in red. Have a large 'WELCOME' sign and another that says, 'We are open to all who come.' Have two young people ready to welcome and shake hands with all who come today.

Opening activity

Four people are at the front of the church; the fifth stands at the back.

Voice 1 I do not know what she comes for. I do not like her.

Voice 2 What is she doing here? She has never been a friend of mine.

Voice 3 If you knew what she was like, you would not be seen with her.

Voice 4 I invited her and welcomed her. She needs the Gospel like any of us.

(The four wave to her and all shake hands with her or hug her.)

Voice 5 Thank you for your welcome. I did not know the church could be so friendly.

Opening prayer

O Lord our God,
you welcome us into your presence
and offer us your love.
You are accepting and forgiving.
Help us to show that same love to others
by being welcoming
and telling them of you.
Amen.

Opening song

O Lord, all the world belongs to you

Readings

Genesis 22:1-14 or Jeremiah 28:5-9
Psalm 13 or Psalm 89:1-4, 15-18
Romans 6:12-23
Matthew 10:40-42

Thought for the day

Jesus is still talking about mission when he talks about the disciples being welcomed. Jesus has previously been talking about the hostility they will experience; now he talks of hospitality. If all had been hostile to the Gospel, the disciples would not have survived to tell the message and Christianity would not have grown. But many people were longing for the Good News and readily welcomed the disciples. We need to be on our guard and not express hostility towards people when we can extend hospitality and welcome.

Hospitality was a characteristic of the Middle East. Among the Jews it was typified by Abraham and Sarah who welcomed the three strangers and found they had welcomed angels: they had welcomed God (Genesis 18). The writer to the Hebrews says how we should be hospitable when he says, 'Do not forget to show hospitality to strangers, for in so doing some have entertained angels without knowing it' (Hebrews 13:2). The meeting of people also involves the 'shekinah', the hidden presence of God.

Hospitality was often a sign of a relatively secure community. From the Hebrides comes a lovely statement:

I saw a stranger at yester'en.
I put food in the eating place,
drink in the drinking place,
music in the listening place,
and in the sacred name of the Triune
he blessed myself and my house,
my cattle and my dear ones,
and the lark said in her song,
'Often, often, often,
goes the Christ in a stranger's guise.'

The disciples are to go out in the name of God. They are to be his representatives, his image, his icon to the world. The Jews believed that to receive an envoy of the king was to receive the king. To welcome a messenger of a friend is the same as welcoming the friend. Not all doors are closed to Jesus; many long to hear the Good News. We are his disciples and if we do not take the message, how will people hear?

Question time

How can the Church be more hospitable to strangers?

Do we see friendship and hospitality as a good chance to tell the Good News or show it in our lives?

Illustration

The selfish giant banned the children from his garden. He built a wall around it and put up a notice saying:

> # TRESPASSERS
> ## WILL BE
> # PROSECUTED

From that time spring did not come to the giant's garden; it remained in winter. By keeping himself to himself, there was no warmth in the place.

Only when the children sneaked back did spring return with them. It was then that the giant realised his hostility to the children had kept him in the cold.

(Read the full story of the Selfish Giant in *The Happy Prince* by Oscar Wilde, Puffin Books.)

Hostility brings about isolation. Hospitality opens us to the warmth of relationships.

Intercessions

Blessed are you, Lord our God,
for you have called us to be your people,
to represent you and to show your love.
By the power of your Spirit
enable us to live and work to your praise and glory.
Blessed are you, Father, Son and Holy Spirit.

We give thanks for all who have gone out in mission
and proclaimed the Good News in word and deed.
We remember especially
those who brought the Gospel to our land.
We ask your blessing upon preachers of the word
and on all who witness to you
by their lifestyle and example.
We pray for all who have never heard the Gospel
and those who are afraid to commit themselves.
We ask you to protect all missionaries
who face hostility.

Silence

Loving God,
hear us and help us.

We remember all who live in a hostile environment,
those who are suffering from war or oppression.
We ask your blessing
upon all who seek to bring peace and healing
to the divisions of our world
and all who strive to bring freedom and justice
to nations and individuals.
We remember the work of the United Nations
and Amnesty International.

Silence

Loving God,
hear us and help us.

Father, we thank you for the love of our homes
and ask your blessing upon our families and friends.
We remember all who suffer
from rejection or violence in their homes.
We pray for all who have been taken into care
or those living on the streets of our cities and towns.

Silence

Loving God,
hear us and help us.

Father, we give thanks for your healing love.
We remember before you all suffering people,
the ill and the hungry,
the world poor and the unemployed.
We ask your blessing upon all who are terminally ill
and those who are caring for them.
We pray for helpers who feel exhausted
or who feel they are not appreciated.

Silence

Loving God,
hear us and help us.

We give thanks that, through Christ,
the way to the fullness of your kingdom
is open to us.
We pray for our loved ones departed.
We commend them to you
as we do the world and ourselves.

Silence

Merciful Father,
**accept these prayers
for the sake of your Son,
our Saviour Jesus Christ.
Amen.**

Memory verse

Whoever welcomes you welcomes me, and whoever welcomes me welcomes the one who sent me.
Matthew 10:40

Suggested music

Colours of day
We have a gospel to proclaim
Brother, sister, let me serve you

CANDLES

Aim

To encourage the children to be open and welcoming.

Teaching

We all like having friends. Tell me the name of one of your friends. Do you share together and play together? Wouldn't it be sad if we did not have any friends? Let me tell you a story about a selfish giant.

The children used to enjoy playing in the big garden. It was far nicer than the dusty streets. But the selfish giant built a wall around the garden and put up a notice:

TRESPASSERS
WILL BE
PROSECUTED

The giant was very selfish and the children had nowhere to play. Then spring came all over the country and the trees blossomed but the giant's garden stayed cold and covered in frost and snow. Spring did not come and neither did summer.

One morning when the giant awoke he found spring had come. The children had crept back into the garden through a hole in the wall. Now the sun was shining and the birds were singing. One tree in the furthest corner of the garden was still in winter and a little boy was crying because he could not get up into the tree. The giant realised how selfish he had been. He went out and lifted the little boy into the tree and immediately it blossomed. The giant was sorry for being so selfish and he knocked the wall down and the children were happy in his beautiful garden. (See the story of the Selfish Giant in *The Happy Prince* by Oscar Wilde.)

Jesus wants all of us not to be selfish but to be kind and welcoming to people. If we are not friendly, it makes for a sad and troubled world. If we were without friends, it would be very sad. Can you think of ways we can show we are friends? (Let the children suggest.)

We could welcome people and invite them to join us. We could give them a friendly wave. We could shake hands or give them a hug. We could let them share in our games or share our sweets with them.

Jesus wants to be our friend. He wants us to spend some time with him and with his friends. How can we show we are friends of Jesus? (Let the children make suggestions.)

We can be friends with Jesus by saying our prayers every day and doing what we know he would like us to do. Jesus wants us to listen carefully to what people tell us about him and he wants us to know he is with us always.

Activity

Get the children to each have a partner. Then the whole group makes a circle. The partner on the right goes anti-clockwise around the circle and the other goes clockwise. They are to shake hands with everyone they pass using each hand in turn and say, 'Hello'. When they come back to their partner they are to hold both hands and swing around twice. Finish by getting them all to join hands and say, 'We are all friends of Jesus.'

Prayer

Jesus, friend of little children,
be a friend to me;
take my hand,
and always keep me close to you.
I will seek you
and will meet you every day.
Jesus, always be my friend
and never go away.
Amen.

Song

Welcome, welcome

LAMPS

Aim

To show how the Church can grow.

Teaching

It is good to see how you are growing up. You are getting bigger and learning more. It is exciting to be able to grow. Some of us like to grow things in our garden, just for the joy of seeing them grow. Sometimes people plant trees that will take a long time to grow but they know that other people will benefit.

Johnny was a preacher of God's word in America. He went from farm to farm to tell people of the Good News. At one farm he noticed that when the apples were crushed to make cider, the pips were thrown away. What a shame, thought Johnny. What do you think he could do with the seeds? He could collect them and plant them as he went around the farms. He often collected seeds and planted them near farms. He built little fences to protect them. In time the seeds grew to trees and started producing apples. Even when Johnny was long gone people were able to enjoy what he had done. But it was not only apple seeds Johnny had sown; he had sown the seed of the Good News in people's homes and hearts. A lot of people had to be thankful for Johnny because he introduced them to Jesus, as well as giving them apple trees. They often thanked God for the man they called Johnny Appleseed. Through Johnny the Church grew.

Jesus needed help to make the Church grow from the very beginning, and so that is why he chose twelve disciples. They would be sent out and make other disciples and teach others of Jesus. If each of the twelve all made just one disciple, how many would that be? Now if each of the 24 made one disciple, how many would that be? If each of the 48 made one disciple, how many would that be? That is how the Church grew quickly because they all told others about Jesus.

If the Church is to grow today, it needs us to invite others to come and learn of Jesus. We have to welcome them. We have to tell our friends how wonderful Jesus is. If we do not tell them, then maybe they will never know. Jesus needs each of us to be a disciple and an apostle so that people may learn to love him and the Church can grow.

Activity

Let each one choose a partner. Then they have to tell the other one about Jesus for a minute. After a minute the second one has to try and do the same. Before they start it might be a good idea to tell them they should talk of the love of Jesus, his resurrection and how he is with us always.

Prayer

Jesus, you are wonderful.
Help us to tell others of your love
and your saving power.
Show us how to share with our friends
the Good News that we have learnt.
Amen.

Song

Welcome to the family

TORCHES

Aim

To show how we should seek to reveal Christ to others.

Teaching

Jesus is still talking to his disciples about sending them out. Can you remember the name for one who is sent out? Apostle. Jesus wants his friends to be apostles. He has warned them that not everyone will be kind to them and sometimes they will be in danger, but there are people who will welcome them and this is how the number of believers will grow, how the Church will grow.

Jesus could not possibly reach out to everyone, so he asked the help of disciples and made them apostles. They were to be his representatives; through them people would get to know Jesus. When people welcomed them, Jesus was also being welcomed. In a wonderful way Jesus is with each of his disciples. Jesus is with us.

How will some of our friends learn about Jesus if we never speak of him, if we cannot tell them how wonderful Jesus is? Jesus wants us to be his missionaries, his apostles. Jesus wants us to show that we love him and that he is with us. When anyone receives the Good News from us, they not only receive the Good News; they receive Jesus. Jesus comes through us to be with our friends. Think hard about these words:

> Christ has no hands but your hands
> to do his work today.
> Christ has no feet but your feet
> to speed people on his way.
> Christ has no lips but your lips
> to tell them why he died.
> Christ has no love but your love
> to win them to his side.

Without our sharing in Jesus' work, the Gospel will not be heard by many. It is through you and your actions that the Church of God can grow. We must remember the Church is in the business of growing and we must help it grow.

Activity

Explore how the Gospel came to our land and, if possible, how it came to the area in which you live. Is there a famous bringer of the Gospel to your area? You could at least explore the sending of Augustine to Kent and the story of Gregory seeing slaves in the market place. There is a wordsearch of the names of some of the early saints of our land.

Prayer

Lord Jesus, you have called us to be apostles
and to go out and tell others of you.
Give us strength and wisdom to do this
and help us to know that you are with us always.
Amen.

Song

We'll walk the land

Proper 9

Sunday between 3 and 9 July inclusive

Aim

To encourage people to respond to the welcoming call of Jesus.

Preparation

Print a large invitation card to put in the entrance.

```
┌─────────────────────────────────────┐
│     YOU ARE INVITED                  │
│  TO COME THIS DAY BEFORE             │
│    THE KING OF KINGS                 │
│                                      │
│        Please respond                │
└─────────────────────────────────────┘
```

Opening activity

For seven voices

Voice 1 Come to the Palace and enjoy a feast with the Queen.
Voice 2 Can't come, it's my night out with the lads.
Voice 3 Come to Wembley and see the Cup Final.
Voice 4 Too busy. There's something on TV I want to watch.
Voice 5 Come and enjoy a night out at the theatre.
Voice 6 Can't, I'm going to cut the lawn.
Voice 7 Feeble excuses. They were invited. They who excuse themselves exclude themselves.

Opening prayer

Lord, among all our troubles and worries
you call us to come to you and rest.
May we find in you a sure refuge and strength,
that we may do what you want us to do
and become the people you want us to be.
Amen.

Opening song

The King is among us

Readings

Genesis 24:34-38, 42-49, 58-67 or Zechariah 9:9-12
Psalm 45:11-18 or Song of Songs 2:8-13
or Psalm 145:8-15
Romans 7:15-25a
Matthew 11:16-19, 25-30

Thought for the day

Jesus talks about how poor some people are at responding; in fact, they are often perverse in their unwillingness to react. There were obviously some days when he thought that he was in a poor reception area. Jesus said people were sometimes like petulant children who refused to cooperate, they were given music and invited to dance but they refused; so they were called to join the mourners and show sadness, and they refused this also. Because John the Baptist came fasting and out of the desert, they called him a mad man. When Jesus shared in their eating and drinking, they called him a glutton and a drunkard. People avoided being moved by either man. But those who excused themselves from the company of Jesus excluded themselves, and so it still is today.

Jesus sends out an invitation: 'Come to me, all you that are weary and are carrying heavy burdens, and I will give you rest' (Matthew 11:28).

> Come to me, enjoy my presence, my company.
> Come to me and receive my power and peace.
> Come to me and know of my healing love.
> Come to me, on whom your life depends.
> Come, all who labour, in field or factory,
> in shop or office, in school or sweatshop.
> Come, all who labour in vain and for nothing.
> Come, all who are carrying heavy burdens,
> with personal problems, with fear, with doubt,
> with debt, with guilt and sin.
> Come to me and I will give you rest.
> Come, let me revive you, refresh and restore you.
> Come and learn to be resurrection people.

The invitation stands; it is for you, but will you accept it? Think seriously about these words from a hymn:

> What a friend we have in Jesus,
> all our sins and griefs to bear!
> What a privilege to carry
> everything to him in prayer!
> O what peace we often forfeit,
> O what needless pain we bear,
> all because we do not carry
> everything to God in prayer!

Question time

Do we see that Jesus invites us personally to come to him for rest and refreshment?

How often do we struggle alone when help is at hand, both human and divine?

Illustration

From *Pilgrim's Progress* by John Bunyan:

He ran . . . till he came to the place somewhat ascending and on that place stood a cross . . . Just as Christian came up . . . his burden loosed from his shoulders and fell from off his back . . . I saw it no more.

Then Christian glad and lightsome said with a merry heart, 'He has given me rest by his sorrow and life by his death' . . . it was very surprising to him that the cross should ease him of his burden . . . Then Christian gave three leaps for joy, and went on singing,

> 'Thus far did I come laden with my sin
> nor could ought ease the grief that was within
> till I came hither: what place is this,
> must be here the beginning of my bliss,

must here the burden fall from off my back,
must here the strings which bound it crack.
Blest Cross! Blest Sepulchre! Blest rather be
the man who was put to shame for me.'

Intercessions

Blessed are you, Lord our God,
for you are a very present help in trouble.
You are more ready to hear than we to pray,
and willing to give us more than we desire or deserve.
We come to you for rest, for renewal,
for the strength to do what you would have us do.
Blessed are you, Father, Son and Holy Spirit.

We give thanks for the Church throughout the world.
We remember today all who are weary in their service
and all who are in danger of losing faith.
We pray for priests and pastors
who are working in difficult areas and with little support.
We ask your blessing
upon all who are seeking to share the burdens
of those with great responsibilities.
We pray for all who are carers
and who are giving support to others.

Silence

Lord, we come to you:
renew us and give us peace.

As we rejoice in the gift of life,
we remember the world-weary,
the overwrought and the anxious.
We pray for all who are laden with troubles or guilt.
We ask your blessing
upon all who are overworked or oppressed
and those who are fearful for the future.
We remember those who have lost the joy of living
and all who cannot easily relax.

Silence

Lord, we come to you:
renew us and give us peace.

We give thanks for our friends and loved ones,
for those who share our joys and our sorrows.
We remember all who have been a support
and comfort to us.
We pray for families where there is tension and stress
and we remember all who feel lonely and without help.

Silence

Lord, we come to you:
renew us and give us peace.

We give thanks, O Lord, for continual support
and we pray for all who feel uncared for or unwanted.
We remember all who are at the point of breaking
and all those who have broken down.
We ask your blessing upon all who are ill
and are finding life difficult.
We pray for all who seek to be a help and a support.

Silence

Lord, we come to you:
renew us and give us peace.

We ask your blessing
upon all who have found their rest in you.
We remember our friends and loved ones departed.
May they find in you rest, renewal
and the joy of the resurrection.

Silence

Merciful Father,
**accept these prayers
for the sake of your Son,
our Saviour Jesus Christ.
Amen.**

Memory verse

Come to me, all you that are weary and are carrying heavy burdens, and I will give you rest.
Matthew 11:28

Suggested music

O my Saviour, lifted from the earth
I heard the voice of Jesus say
All you who seek a comfort sure

CANDLES

Aim

To show how Jesus wants to share with us and help us.

Activity

Have a box containing about a dozen books for each team. The box should feel quite heavy. Let everyone feel the weight of the box and, if possible, gently lift it. Tell them they are going to have a race carrying the box. Let them feel a little anxious as they prepare for the race. Now tell them before the race begins to empty the box. It will be a lot easier to race with if it's empty.

Teaching

Having started with the activity talk about how much harder the race would have been if we had to carry all that weight. We would have all been much slower and we would not have found it so much fun. I could see that some were getting worried about carrying such a heavy box. Wasn't it good when you were told you could take the books out?

Sometimes people have very heavy things to carry, like shopping or heavy cases. How can they get help? They can put them on wheels! But that is not always possible. They could get other people to help them. Heavy weights get much lighter if they are shared. (You could show this by putting four books into each box rather than twelve.) We can often help each other and at home so that no one has too heavy a load or too much to do. (Explore how they can lighten the load at home.)

Jesus always wanted to help people and to stop them struggling with their troubles. He invited them to come to him for help.

Once four men came carrying a man who was poorly. The man was a heavy load but the four shared it and did not mind because the man was their friend. They had to carry him up some stairs and on to a flat roof. He felt heavier as they took him up the stairs. Then they had to lower the man through a hole in the roof to get to where Jesus was. They found that heavy work. Jesus made the man well again. Not only was he better but his friends no longer had to carry a heavy load.

Jesus does not want us to carry anything too heavy by ourselves; he wants us to share. Jesus wants us to come to him when we are troubled by something or frightened. If we get worried or feel upset, it feels like a heavy load. Jesus wants us to come to him and talk to him. Then the worries and the troubles will get lighter because he will help us.

Give one of the children a heavy box but be careful about the weight. Tell them they should carry the box all day and ask them how difficult it would be. It would be hard to enjoy playing and even hard to eat something. You would become very tired. Now give me the box. You do not need to carry it. Isn't that better?

In the same way Jesus wants to help us. He is always ready to listen to us because he loves us. He does not want us to feel troubled but wants us to enjoy ourselves. Let us remember to talk to Jesus each day and let him share our lives.

Prayer

Jesus, you are our friend.
You are always ready to help us.
You are ready to listen to us
and always love us.
We come to you and find rest.
Thank you.
Amen.

Song

Jesus is my friend

LAMPS

Aim

To understand how Jesus offers to lighten our burdens.

Teaching

When Jesus lived in Nazareth he probably learned to work with Joseph in his workshop. Can you tell me what was Joseph's work? He was a carpenter. Jesus would learn to work with a saw and a hammer, how to shape and smooth wood and make it into tables and chairs. They would make farm implements and ox-yokes. In the days before tractors many farms used oxen to draw their ploughs and to pull their carts. Often the oxen had to pull heavy loads, so it was important that their yoke fitted properly around their neck and shoulders or it would hurt. Some people made rough yokes or ill-fitting yokes and this chafed the skin of the ox and often caused sore areas. It was important to have a well-fitting yoke. In Palestine ox-yokes were made of wood: the ox was brought to the carpenters and measurements were taken. The yoke was then roughed out to size and the

ox was brought back to have it tried on. The yoke was then adjusted to fit so that it would not rub or put undue stress on the ox. Often oxen are yoked together so that an older one can help a younger one, or just to make the burden lighter.

There is an ancient story that says Jesus made the best ox-yokes in all of Galilee because he cared about the ox. People came from all over to buy ox-yokes from him. It was said that Jesus had a notice above his work place that said, 'My yokes fit well'.

Jesus often noticed how people were troubled and burdened with care. They were being chafed more than an ox and he wanted to help them. Jesus could ease the burden an ox was given and he offered to ease our heavy load too. But people put off. He invited them to come to him but they did not bother. Like so many people today: Jesus invites them to come to him for ease and rest and they refuse or cannot be bothered. Listen to his words: 'Come to me, all you that are weary and are carrying heavy burdens and I will give you rest' (Matthew 11:28).

These are words Jesus says to us. He offers to be our friend, to help us when we are troubled, to comfort us when we are distressed. Jesus promises us rest and renewal if we come. He is willing to share our load. But he can only do it if we come to him and spend time with him. In our prayers we learn to be yoked to Jesus. Jesus is then able to take the strain and the stress from us. Let us come to him each day.

Activity

Give everyone a stone. Tell them it is a worry stone. They have to think of it as a trouble, a fear or a worry they are carrying. During a piece of music they are to bring it and lay it near the foot of a cross to remind them that Jesus loves us, cares for us and is ready to help us.

Prayer

Lord Jesus, we come to you
because you are the Holy and Strong One.
You are more ready to help us than we know
and more ready to hear than we are to ask.
Jesus, we come to you.
Amen.

Song

Jesus is a friend of mine

TORCHES

Aim

To show how Jesus invites us to come to him when we are burdened.

Teaching

Picture yourself with a heavy load to carry. You may feel like Atlas who carried the world on his shoulders. See yourself straining under the weight and beginning to feel stressed. You struggle until you are exhausted and the load just gets heavier. Now notice that your father or a friend is close at hand. They have been waiting to help you but wanted to be invited. The wanted to share in carrying your burden but you kept yourself to yourself. Now see how much easier it is with someone to share. A load shared is a load halved and so made much lighter.

Love also lightens a load. There are many things in this life we can bear as long as we know we are loved. Without love much becomes unbearable. Love gives us strength. There is a song called 'The road is long' and it is about someone carrying someone else but he sings 'He ain't heavy, he's my brother' (If possible, listen to this song by Rob Russell, originally recorded by the Hollies.)

Jesus offers us his help and rest from our labours and burdens. He offers us his love and his companionship. But we need to accept it because he will not force himself upon us. Think upon these words: 'Come to me, all you that are weary and are carrying heavy burdens and I will give you rest' (Matthew 11:28).

Let us look at 'Footprints' and see in it the wonderful help that is offered to us.

One night a man had a dream. He dreamed he was walking along the beach with the Lord. Across the sky flashed scenes from his life. For each scene he noticed two sets of footprints in the sand; one belonged to him, and the other to the Lord.

When the last scene of his life flashed before him, he looked back at the footprints in the sand. He noticed that many times along the path of his life there was only one set of footprints. He also noticed that it happened at the very lowest and saddest times in his life.

This really bothered him and he questioned the Lord about it. 'Lord, you said that once I decided to follow you, you'd walk with me all the way. But I have noticed that during the most troublesome times in my life, there is only one set of footprints. I don't understand why when I needed you most you would leave me.'

The Lord replied, 'My son, my precious child, I love you and would never leave you. During your times of trial and suffering, when you see only one set of footprints, it was then that I carried you.'

Activity

Get the group in twos to mime carrying heavy loads and seeking help from various sources. This can include mechanical help. The rest of the group has to guess what is being mimed. Then ask them all to mime how they would seek help from Jesus. Talk about this afterwards.

Prayer

Lord Jesus, we come to you.
You invite us to come for rest, renewal
and restoration.
We come for your help and for your love.
Amen.

Song

What a friend we have in Jesus

Proper 10

Sunday between 10 and 16 July inclusive

Aim

To encourage more receptivity in our hearing and receiving of the Word.

Preparation

Display the work of the Bible Society and their logo (Bible Society, Stonehill Green, Westlea, Swindon SN5 7DG; www.biblesociety.org.uk). You may also like to have work of the Bible Reading Fellowship available (BRF, First Floor, Elsfield Hall, 15-17 Elsfield Way, Oxford OX2 8FG; www.brf. org.uk).

Opening activity

Show a soil testing kit and say how it works by showing how the soil is capable of a good reception of certain seeds. Pretend to do a test on people (you must be careful and make sure you have their permission): 'No, too acidic'; 'Far too sour'; 'Too hard'; 'Full of all sorts'; 'Receptive and good soil ready for sowing.'

Opening prayer

Lord, open our ears and hearts to your Word.
Let it get into our lives,
deeply into our being,
and then grow and bear fruit.
May we make room for your Word to grow in us
and then bring others to hear and receive you.
Amen.

Opening song

Alleluia, alleluia give thanks to the risen Lord

Readings

Genesis 25:19-34 or Isaiah 55:10-13
Psalm 119:105-112 or Psalm 65:(1-8) 9-13
Romans 8:1-11
Matthew 13:1-9, 18-23

Thought for the day

Matthew introduces us to a turning point in the ministry of Jesus. Up to this point Jesus has been teaching in the synagogues; now he is teaching on the seashore. The doors of the synagogues are beginning to close, even though the ordinary people want to hear him. Some minds and hearts are shutting Jesus out. At this stage Jesus begins to use parables, good earthly images that challenge us and ask us to go deeper into their meaning. Jesus wants us to ask, 'What does that mean for me? Is this a story about me?'

At the point where some are refusing to hear him, Jesus tells the parable of the Sower. He had already warned his disciples that life would not be easy. No doubt there was a danger they would feel it was all a waste of time. Yet Jesus told them that there was also a welcome awaiting them in many places. Maybe some labour is lost but the harvest is still bountiful. No farmer expects every seed to germinate – some are blown away, some eaten and some choked by weeds – but the majority grows and produces a harvest. It must be said, of course, if there is no sowing, there will be no harvest.

In our lives we need to look at what is needed for the Word of God to grow. We are not the seed of this parable but the soil. The seed is the Word of God and this will grow in us, given the opportunity.

The seed must be able to get in. If it is denied entry, it will not grow. Closed minds and closed doors, the unwillingness to listen and prejudice all prevent the entry of the Word. If we cannot listen and give our attention, then we will not hear. The footpath of the parable is caused by the regular passage of feet; it is hardened and unreceptive, and in the same way regular habits can prevent us from hearing properly.

The rocky ground is shallow ground. Shallowness is a greater danger of our age. We know about many things but of little in depth. We do not stay long enough with a thing to learn of it. Like butterflies we flit from one thing to another. To grow we need good roots.

Then there are the thorns that choke out the life of the growing seeds. The seed needs room to grow. Busyness, hyperactivity, crowded lives, cares, anxieties – yes, and having so many things – can fill our days and leave no room for the Word of God. We all know this but do we learn from it?

But if the Word is allowed entry and given some depth, it will grow. If we give space and room, it will produce fruit. We will be greatly enriched and be part of the great harvest of God.

Question time

What habits prevent you from having a living relationship with Jesus?

How can you make room in your life for your faith to grow?

Illustration

In India 150 years ago, in the area of Dornakal, there was a man called Venkaya who could neither read nor write. He heard from a friend about a new religion that was of a God that loved everyone. One day as he watched the Hindu pilgrims bathing in the river he was asked by one of their leaders why he was not bathing. He said he no longer believed enough in the Hindu ways. The leader asked if he was a Christian and Venkaya said, 'No, but I would like to be.' The leader told of an English Christian preacher who could help him. Venkaya sought out Mr Darling who was a missionary with the Church Missionary Society. At that moment Mr Darling was deeply distressed: he had spoken of Christ for eight years and had not had one convert. Now, amid much opposition, Mr Darling taught and then baptised Venkaya and sixteen other outcasts. The seed was beginning to grow. In his old age and quite blind,

Venkaya sat by the roadside to tell others the Gospel story. Through his preaching 500 converts were baptised. His work continues to bear fruit.

Intercessions

Blessed are you, Lord our God,
for you come to us
and seek to make your home with us.
Let our doors and our ears be open to you.
Let our hearts find their rest and their joy in you,
that we may grow in grace and live to your glory.
Blessed are you, Father, Son and Holy Spirit.

We ask your blessing
upon all who proclaim the Good News.
We pray for preachers and evangelists,
for teachers in schools and Sunday schools.
We remember all at theological colleges.
May we hear and receive your word,
that it may grow in us and that we may serve you.
We pray for all who have never heard
or who have closed their minds to the Gospel.

Silence

Loving God,
hear us and help us.

We give thanks for the harvests of our world
and for all who provide us with food and our needs.
We pray for farmers and all who work in agriculture.
We ask your blessing
upon all who suffer from a bad harvest.
We remember the world poor and the hungry.
We ask your guidance upon all who work for Fair Trade.

Silence

Loving God,
hear us and help us.

We give thanks for our homes
and pray that you will always be at home
in our homes and our hearts.
We pray for the young who are growing in the faith
and for their nurture.
May we all make room
in our lives and in our days
to know you and your love.
We remember all who are struggling
with their relationships
and pray for all who have hardened their hearts.

Silence

Loving God,
hear us and help us.

We ask your guidance upon all
who are caught up in the cares of this world,
who are over-wrought and anxious.
We remember those who are fearful
of what the future holds,
for all who are lost in materialism
and know no standards but those of wealth.
We pray for all who have become poor in spirit.
We ask your blessing upon all who are ill or suffering
and their loved ones who care for them.

Silence

Loving God,
hear us and help us.

We give thanks for your saints in glory
and pray that our loved ones departed
may know the joy of your kingdom.
We commend this world, our families and ourselves
to your unfailing love.

Silence

Merciful Father,
**accept these prayers
for the sake of your Son,
our Saviour Jesus Christ.
Amen.**

Memory verse

Let anyone with ears listen!
Matthew 13:9

Suggested music

We have a gospel to proclaim
Lord Jesus, once you spoke to men
Praise we now the word of grace

CANDLES

Aim

To encourage the children to listen to the Word.

Teaching

Jesus wanted to tell everyone that God loves them. But not everyone would listen. Some said they were too busy to listen. Some said they did not want to meet Jesus and some even asked him to leave their town. There were some people who closed their doors to Jesus. But because a lot of people wanted to hear him, Jesus spoke to people in the open air at the seaside or on a hillside. Jesus knew if people did not listen, they would not hear what he had to say. When he started to speak to them he said, 'Listen.'

What do we have to do to listen properly? Which part of our body is for listening? If we fill our ears with loud noises, or cover our ears up, we will not hear properly. Let us see how still and quiet we can be. The next thing we need to do is to give all of our attention to the speaker. If you are scribbling or talking while someone is speaking, you are not going to listen carefully. We look at the speaker and we try and think about what they are saying. Then we will hear properly.

Here is a little story Jesus told people about listening. Listen to it very carefully and I will ask you about it afterwards. (Read Matthew 13:3b-9.)

What was the first word Jesus said? 'Listen.' He was talking about a man sowing seeds in a field. The man was scattering the seed. Who knows what happened to the first lot of seed? It fell on the path and the birds ate it. The seed could not get into the ground. Just like words that cannot get into people if they do not listen.

Where did the next seeds fall? It was rocky ground and it did not have much soil. The seed got in but soon it stopped growing. If we do not think about what we are told, we are like that seed and we do not learn.

What happened to the next seeds? They were among thorns, weeds. What did the weeds do? They stopped the seed from growing. If our minds are too busy to listen, then we might not really know what we are told to do.

But most of the seed was in good soil and it grew. If seed is given the chance to grow, it will. If we want to learn about Jesus, we have to listen to what he says and what we are told about him.

Jesus ended the story by saying something we can all do. Can you tell me what he said? He said, 'Let anyone with ears listen!'

Activity

Play a quiet game like 'Sleeping tigers'. They pretend they are sleeping tigers in the jungle. One person counts to ten while they lie down to sleep. After this anyone who moves is out. If they are very still, get them to run around for a while and start again.

Prayer

Loving Jesus, let me be
still and quiet, close to you,
learning of your love for me,
giving all my love to you.
Amen.

Song

Two little eyes to look to God

LAMPS

Aim

To tell the story of the sower and get the group to talk about listening.

Teaching

Let us be very quiet and listen. What sounds can you hear? How still and quiet can you be? Sometimes it is very hard to hear someone speaking. Can you give examples? When very loud music is being played or when we have our ears covered up. Sometimes it is hard to hear sounds because we have closed a door and shut them out, or we have just not listened.

Not everyone listened to Jesus. Soon some people were closing their doors to him and they would not be able hear him. Jesus told a story about listening and began by saying, 'Listen!' So let us listen carefully to the story and when we have finished I will ask you all about it. (Read Matthew 13:3b-9.)

Who was working in the story? It was a farmer. What was he doing? He was throwing seeds all around his

field so that they would grow. Who can tell me what happened to some seed?

Some fell on the path – what happened to it? Yes, the birds came and ate it up and it did not grow.

Some seed fell on rocky ground and did not have a lot of soil. What happened to that seed when the sun shone? It shrivelled up and died because it did not have enough water.

Some seed fell among weeds, among thorns and thistles. What did they do the seed? They stopped it growing because they crowded it out.

Poor farmer, he had lost a lot of seed. But what happened to the rest? It fell on good ground and grew. So the farmer would be happy.

Now, Jesus ended the story by saying what? 'Let anyone who has ears listen!'

Who has ears? Put your hand up if you have. Are you sure you were using them and listening? Jesus wanted us to think about listening to him and how some people do not listen. (Encourage the children to make comments on the different soils and show that Jesus was talking about how we let him into our lives or let him be kept out.)

Activity

Play 'Chinese whispers'. You might like to start with 'God gave us two ears and one mouth so that we should listen twice as much as we speak.'

Prayer

Lord Jesus, we want to be like the good soil
and be ready to receive your word
and learn what you want us to do.
May we never close our hearts or ears to you.
Amen.

Song

The sower

TORCHES

Aim

To look at how receptive we are to each other and to Jesus.

Teaching

If you use a mobile phone, you will know that some areas are not good for reception. A mobile does not work well in a tunnel. You cannot really listen to a phone message and to your CD player or iPod at the same time. If you have your phone locked away in your locker at school, you are not likely to hear it.

Jesus began to be shut out of the synagogues and started to teach in the open air. There were people who refused to hear him and there still are. Jesus did not exclude them; they excluded themselves from his love and his power. Some did this in an obvious way and others through their own habits or busyness. Jesus wanted to speak to people but some were not receptive.

Because of this Jesus told a story about a sower and the different kinds of soil. As he told it, he wanted people to listen carefully and consider if the story was about them. (Read Matthew 13:3b-9.)

This passage begins and ends with the same word. What is it? This is not just about receiving words but the Word of God, and the Word of God is not just the Gospel; it is Jesus himself. Do you give Jesus your undivided attention or do you let other things crowd him out?

Let us consider in turn the different soils and how they reflect our attitudes not only to Jesus but also to each other.

The seed on the path did not even get in: it found no entry. There are those who do not listen. Like words that go in one ear and out the other! How good are we at giving our attention? (Discuss.) This is often 'hardened ground': people do not hear what they do not want to hear. If the seed is to grow, the soil needs to be able to be disturbed. Some people put up a notice: 'Do not disturb.'

The rocky soil was shallow: it had no depth. The seed could not get proper root. How often are we shallow in our listening, letting our attention shift and flit from one thing to another? (Discuss.) The seed needs not only to get in but into the depths, and so it is with the Word of God in our lives.

The seed among the thorns are choked. No two things can occupy the same space at the same time. We often fail to listen because we are preoccupied. We are too busy, involved in something else. What do you think this verse means when it talks of cares and riches? (Discuss.)

Fortunately, there is a lot of good seed about. People do listen to each other and give each other their undivided attention. People are open to receiving the Word of God and letting Jesus into their lives. Do you hear what this is saying to you?

Activity

Play 'Just a minute'. Let one member of the group speak on a subject for a minute. They repeat themselves, someone is allowed to interrupt and then take up the subject. The person speaking when the minute is up gets a point. (You will need a stopwatch or egg timer for this game.)

Prayer

Lord, you speak to us
and we hear better if we can keep silent.
We come to you in the stillness
and seek your guidance.
Like the child Samuel, we say,
'Speak, Lord, for your servant is listening.'
Amen.

Song

In the morning early

Proper 11

Aim

To show that although good and evil are woven into our lives, we must at some stage weed out the harmful.

Preparation

At the entrance place a bowl of flowers with cuttings from magazines about caring and good actions. Have a bowl of thistles and cuttings about murders, drug peddling and oppression.

You may also like to have an advertisement for a selective weed killer!

Opening activity

Interview a gardener:

Why did you become a gardener?

How do you recognise weeds? Do you sometimes have to wait until they become established?

How do you get rid of them?

Can you really keep your garden weed free?

Opening prayer

Lord God, you created us out of your goodness.
Yet we err and stray
and do what you do not want us to do.
Father, forgive us,
weed out our sins,
guide us
and keep us true to you.
Amen.

Opening song

O Lord, my God

Readings

Genesis 28:10-19a or Wisdom of Solomon 12:13, 16-19 or Isaiah 44:6-8
Psalm 139:1-11, 22, 23 or Psalm 86:11-17
Romans 8:12-25
Matthew 13:24-30, 36-43

Thought for the day

This story of the field with good seed and weeds is only in St Matthew's Gospel. Here Jesus is talking about the problem of evil in the world and how it is difficult to get rid of it. If you have ever done any gardening, you will feel for the person who asks, 'Where, then, did these weeds come from?' A friend of mine gave me some useless advice: 'If you want to find out which are weeds, pull everything out and wait: the weeds are the ones that will come back.'

In the parable, Jesus suggests it is an enemy that has sown the weeds. The weeds are tares and the trouble is they look like wheat. This is because it is a degenerate sort of wheat: it is wheat that has gone wrong.

The Jews had a legend that said the tares, also known as 'bearded darnel', had their beginning in the time of wickedness before the flood. It was a time when all creation went astray and brought forth things contrary to their nature. This was a time when perverse and wicked things happened. This is when the tares came into existence. It is for this reason the Jews often called tares 'bastard wheat'.

In their early stages of growth wheat and tares look very alike. It is only when they mature, when they have headed out, that you can distinguish them. Tares must not be left with the wheat because they are poisonous. They produce a narcotic that causes dizziness and sickness. Yet if pulled out too early, you may pull out the wrong plants. There is a right time to do it and it often takes patience and then discernment.

There is certainly much about life in this little story. All of us are a mixture of good and evil. It is not the way God wants us to be. Wickedness in individuals and society needs to be rooted out. We all know that one bad apple can spoil them all. But we do need sensitivity in dealing with people – for all have some good in them. Think how the early Church nearly rejected Saul. Because of his record in persecuting Christians people were rightly cautious. But, as Paul, the convert had a wonderful record in spreading the Good News. Early judgements are often in danger of being rash. There is a danger we will get rid of the lively and the adventurous in early judgements. It all takes discernment. We must learn to discern and, when the time comes, to separate out, just as we do to the weeds in our gardens. Corrupt people corrupt, and perverse people cause perversity. It matters what we do and who we mix with, and, remember, if we are careless, evil triumphs.

Question time

Do we take the presence of evil in our society seriously?

How can we as a Church stand against some of the evils of our times?

Illustration

They were known as the terrible twins at school. They were disruptive in class and caused no end of bother in the playground. They were encouraging other children to be disruptive too. Staff meetings talked about them, offered ideas to help them, but all were determined to keep them in the class if possible. Teachers used their skill and discernment in dealing with them. It was only in the third year that it became obvious that it could not go on. By then it was also obvious it was not both of them but just one who was the real trouble. They were put in separate year groups. Now one settled down and worked hard. The other continued to be trouble at school and at home. The school finally had to remove the disruptive one from the normal class. They were reluctant to do so but it needed doing. Though they were twins with apparently equal opportunities, one caused trouble all his life; the other became a doctor and a healer.

Intercessions

Blessed are you, Lord our God,
for you have given us a world full of beauty and wonder
and have created us in your image.
Yet we have abused the world and marred your image.
Lord, in your goodness, heal your world and restore us.
Blessed are you, Father, Son and Holy Spirit.

We give thanks
that you have called us to work for you.
Through your Spirit
give us the gifts of wisdom and love in all our dealings.
We ask your blessing upon the Church
where it is working among the oppressed
and rejected peoples of our world.
Give your Church courage to stand against evil
and work for the good of all.

Silence

Lord, guide us
and help us.

We give thanks
for the balance and harmony of your creation.
We pray for all who are working to stop pollution
of land, sea and air;
all who work to protect
the species and the harvests of our world.
We ask your blessing upon those
who seek to care for the rain forests.
We pray for all who strive for justice
and for the social welfare of all people.

Silence

Lord, guide us
and help us.

We give thanks
for our loved ones and our homes
and ask you to bless and protect us.
We remember all who are forced to live
in slums or shantytowns
and those who live on the streets of our cities.
We pray for all whose relationships have broken down,
especially those full of anger or guilt.

Silence

Lord, guide us
and help us.

We pray for all who have suffered
through the wickedness or evil of others.
We remember victims of crime, violence and abuse.
We pray for all whose memories are scarred.
We ask your blessing on households that have suffered
because one member has gone astray.
We pray for all who are ill and in need of care.

Silence

Lord, guide us
and help us.

We give thanks that you are a loving and forgiving God;
in you we can be healed, restored and renewed.
We ask you to bless our loved ones departed,

that they may know and rejoice in your love.
We commit ourselves and all of creation
to your saving power and love.

Silence

Merciful Father,
**accept these prayers
for the sake of your Son,
our Saviour Jesus Christ.
Amen.**

Memory verse

Teach me your way, O Lord, that I may walk in your truth.
Psalm 86:11

Suggested music

Come, ye thankful people, come
Fight the good fight
Lord, the light of your love (*Shine, Jesus, shine*)

CANDLES

Aim

To tell the story of the wheat and the tares.

Teaching

Jesus told a story about weeds. Who knows what weeds are? They are plants that grow in the wrong place and spoil what we want out of the garden. Some weeds can look very pretty but most weeds are ready to invade our gardens and take over. Some weeds grow very fast and so our little seeds do not have the chance to grow. Sometimes weeds grow around other plants and stop them from growing properly. Other weeds are greedy and take all the goodness out of the soil and so other plants starve. Then there are weeds that grow very tall and keep other plants in the shade and stop them getting sunlight. Some weeds are poisonous and dangerous to touch or eat. Who can tell me the name of any weeds?

What does your mother or father do in the garden if they find a lot of weeds? They will dig them out or try to get rid of them. There are some weeds that come back even though we think we have got rid of them. A gardener has to keep a look out for weeds. (At this stage it would be good to show some weeds, like thistles and nettles, convolvulus – bind weed – dandelion and buttercup.)

Jesus told a story about a farmer who sowed good seed in his field. The seed was to grow so that it could be made into bread. But while he slept an enemy came and sowed bad seed – weeds. The weeds were poisonous – who knows what that means? The farmer knew he would have to pull out the weeds, but they were mixed with the good growing plants and if he pulled up the bad, he might pull up the good as well. So he let them grow together until the harvest. At the harvest he gathered the good seed and put it in his barns. What do you think he did with the weeds? He pulled them out and put them into the fire to burn them. That would get rid of them. Maybe you have a bonfire in your garden sometimes to get rid of weeds?

Jesus wants us to show how we love God and care for each other. He does not want us to be greedy or to spoil things for other people. Jesus wants us to be kind and to share. But if we do selfish or naughty things, it is like letting weeds grow in our life. Jesus wants us to keep wrong things out of our lives and to grow good.

Activity

Get the children to plant seeds in small plant pots or yoghurt cartons with holes in the bottom. Fill the pots with compost and give the children a quick-growing seed such as cress or radish, and then get them to take the pots home to look after. For dramatic results, dried marrowfat peas soaked for a couple of days before planting give excellent growth.

Prayer

God, we thank you for good seeds,
for the seeds of flowers, fruit and vegetables.
We thank you for seeds from which trees grow
and seed from which bread is made.
May we grow to love you and to do good
and be part of your kingdom.
Amen.

Song

God, you can use me

LAMPS

Aim

To look at the story of the tares and wheat.

Teaching

Let us look at a few opposites. What is the opposite of good, right, kind, loving, peaceful, happy? Often we want to do one thing and the danger is we do the opposite. We are like a field where good seeds are sown but where weeds also grow. Can you remember last week's story and the different soils into which the good seed fell? (Look again at the story of the sower and how the seeds need to get in, have depth, have space and not be choked by weeds.)

Today we will listen to another story of Jesus about seed. (Read Matthew 13:24-30.)

What kind of seed did the farmer sow? He sowed wheat and it was good seed. Just like when God made the world and he saw that it was good.

But while the farmer slept, what happened? An enemy came and sowed bad seed: he spread weeds all over the field. No one knew because the seeds were so small and were not noticed. Even when they were growing, both seeds looked the same. But the weeds were poisonous: they would make people dizzy and sleepy; they would make them ill. One of the farmer's workers asked, 'Where, then, did these weeds come from?' Can you remember the answer? 'An enemy has done this.' The

workers wanted to pull the weeds out but the farmer said, 'Wait.' He did not want the good plants to be harmed by pulling out the weeds. Yet he did want rid of the weeds. He told the workers to wait until the harvest and then gather the good wheat into one place and to take the bad weeds to bind them up and burn them.

Jesus wants us to know we are like a field because in our lives are good things, but the opposite is there as well. We have hidden weeds that stop us being good and kind and loving. Sometimes we are the opposite of what God would like us to be. The best way to keep weeds out of our gardens is to fill the garden with good things like flowers and vegetables. Empty gardens always grow weeds. The best way to do good things for God is to fill our lives each day with good things and kind things and to keep out the opposite that tries to grow in us.

Activity

Play a game of opposites. The children run to music. When the music stops you give a command but they must do the opposite. If you say run, they must stand still. If you say stand, they must sit. If you say be quiet, they must talk. Stop the music and tell them how difficult it would be if we lived like that. Now get them to do what is asked. Anyone failing to do so is out.

Prayer

God, we thank you for our good and beautiful world.
You have made all things for us to enjoy
and to care for.
May we always do what you want us to do
and be kind and good to each other.
Amen.

Song

The Spirit lives to set us free

TORCHES

Aim

To explore the meaning of the parable of the tares and the wheat.

Teaching

Look at the creation story, especially Genesis 1: 4, 10, 12, 18, 21, 25, 31.

What is the refrain that runs throughout the story? 'God saw that it was good.' God made a good world for us to enjoy and for us to care for. Yet, somehow, through the freedom that God gave to his creation, his creation sometimes worked against him and his goodness. This way the opposite of goodness entered the world. What are some of the names we have given to this opposite of goodness? Badness, evil, sin, crime, the devil – all are putting a name to what goes against what God wants and often what we would really like.

Listen to the story Jesus told the crowd. (Have some-one read Matthew 13:24-30.)

Notice how the farmer sows good seed. Under the cover of darkness an enemy comes and sows weeds. These seeds are poisonous, they will make people ill and cause sickness and dizziness so that people do not function properly. These seeds are meant to spoil the quality and the goodness of what has been sown. It is not unknown for this to happen in the ancient world. An enemy would come secretly and ruin the good work someone had done. (You might like to explore modern parallels – such as spreading a computer virus.)

The problem with tares is that you cannot tell they are there to start with; even when they begin to grow they look harmless. Only later does the trouble begin. Then it is too late to pull them out without endangering the good seed. But one day they will need to be separated from the good seed or they will do great harm. In the end the weeds are gathered and burned.

For the rest of the session explore how this parable relates to us and the mixture of good and evil that makes up all our lives. As in gardening the best way to get rid of weeds is to plant more good seeds. If we let evil grow, it is in danger of poisoning not only our lives but also the lives of others.

Activity

Let the group explore areas of evil influence and where bad seeds seem to be sown. How can we do something about it? You might like to bring examples of crime and acts of evil from newspapers.

Prayer

Lord, on the way of goodness,
if we stumble, help us and bring us back.
Give us the courage to stand against evil
and to seek what is good.
May we seek your will
and work for the coming of your kingdom. Amen.

Song

Abba Father

Proper 12

Sunday between 24 and 30 July inclusive

Aim

To show how we need to sow, to search for and to sift out the kingdom.

Preparation

Put up notices about people finding hidden treasure or having an object of which they did not know the value. Add to this a notice: 'SEEK AND TREASURE LIFE ETERNAL'.

Opening activity

Have a mini treasure hunt for 'pearls of wisdom'. Print on postcards short texts such as 'God is Love'. Hide about a dozen of these around the church. Get the congregation – or just the children – to find them. When they are found, let them be read out.

Opening prayer

Lord God, we seek to know you and your kingdom.
May our faith, though small,
grow in awareness of you, the great God.
Let us never lose sight of things eternal
in our daily dealings and actions.
Amen.

Opening song

New every morning

Readings

Genesis 29:15-28 or 1 Kings 3:5-12
Psalm 105:1-11, 45b or Psalm 119:129-136
Romans 8:26-39
Matthew 13:31-33, 44-52

Thought for the day

In today's Gospel we are given five parables about the 'kingdom of heaven'. The first is the parable of the mustard seed, which is a symbol of smallness and yet grows into the greatest of shrubs. This tiny seed grows so much that the birds are able to nest in its branches. Not only is this a sign of growth from small beginnings but also of hospitality. Every kind of bird is a symbol of all the nations. Though the kingdom is hidden and starts from what appears to be small beginnings, its growth potential is there – though we do need to sow it.

It is the same way with yeast. It is amazing how a small amount of yeast can transform dull and heavy dough. The contrast between unleavened bread, which is hard like a water biscuit, and leavened bread, which it soft and light, is due to the transforming power of the yeast. Do we see the joy of sharing in the transforming power of the kingdom? Yeast in the ancient world was usually added from a former batch of bread. Do we see how in each generation we have to hand on the transforming power of God? Let us remember the yeast is a disturbing element in the dough; it will not let it lie low but makes it rise and be active. There are times when we are called to disturb a situation that has become too dull and settled.

The hidden quality of the kingdom is shown in the next two parables. The treasure hidden in a field was lying there waiting to be discovered. It has the possibility of enriching life beyond the wildest dreams of the finder. He is willing to sell all that he has for it. Do we realise that it is well worth trading the temporal for the eternal? There is little use in treasure if we have lost our soul in the gaining of it.

The treasure was stumbled upon but the pearl was sought after. How much time do we spend seeking to enrich our lives with things of God? Is not some of the great discontent of our age due to the loss of our awareness of God's love and abiding presence? Surely we should be happy to give up minor treasures and beauty for the greatest beauty and treasure of all. Are you aware that many of our deepest longings are related to the call of God?

Like fishermen, we are always hauling into our lives things both good and bad. Once ashore, the fishermen sort out their catch and the bad is thrown out. This takes discernment and practice. Sometimes in our daily living we seem to have no discernment at all; we take on board the good and the bad and carry them around with us. To be part of God's kingdom we have to begin to get rid of all that is destructive or against the life in the kingdom.

Jesus asked, 'Have you understood all this?' They answered, 'Yes' (Matthew 13:51).

How about you?

Question time

Are you aware of the hidden work of God forever transforming our lives?

Do you see that the kingdom needs your cooperation, your sowing and handing on?

Illustration

Every so often we hear of someone finding a great treasure. These days metal detectors are often used to go over fields and ancient sites to turn up all sorts of wonderful things. Sometimes it is the work of archaeologists who patiently, carefully and slowly remove piles of debris before they get to the treasure they are looking for.

In 1947 a Bedouin shepherd boy was looking for a sheep that had strayed. Spying a cave in the cliff face, he decided to come back with a friend and explore. In the cave they found large earthenware pots with scrolls inside wrapped in linen. They were treasure indeed, for they were the Dead Sea Scrolls and the place was Qumran. In time the scrolls were sold and the boy compensated. All the caves in the vicinity were searched and more scrolls were found. A sect of Jews around the time that Jesus lived had written the scrolls. Many insights into the world that Jesus lived in have come from the deciphering and reading of these scrolls – they are a treasure indeed.

Intercessions

Blessed are you, Lord our God,
for you have given us of your kingdom.
You invite us to share in your Godly rule
and in the riches of life that is eternal.
Lord, teach us to seek you
until we know you and love you
and are aware of your transforming power
in all the world.
Blessed are you, Father, Son and Holy Spirit.

We ask your blessing upon all who seek
to proclaim the Good News of your kingdom.
We pray for preachers of the word
and ministers of the sacraments,
for evangelists
and all who witness in their daily lives
to your presence and power.
We remember those
who quietly transform their surroundings
for the better
and those who show others of your kingdom
in their midst.

Silence

Lord, your kingdom come,
in us as it is in heaven.

Lord we ask for the gift of discernment
in those who influence the lives of others.
We pray for all who are involved in shaping our world
through government,
through broadcasting and the press.
We ask your blessing upon all who teach
and all who are set up as examples
for our young people to follow.

Silence

Lord, your kingdom come,
in us as it is in heaven.

We give thanks for the great riches you have given us
through our home and loved ones.
May we always appreciate the care and attention
that have been shown to us.
As we have richly received, so may we share;
as we are loved, so may we love.
We pray for homes where there is tension
and a breakdown in relationships.

Silence

Lord, your kingdom come,
in us as it is in heaven.

May we not lose sight of things eternal
among all that happens in our lives.
We ask your blessing upon all who find life dull,
all who are depressed or have lost hope.
We pray for all who struggle with illness
or difficult circumstances.

We remember those who are in hospital
and all who cannot cope on their own.

Silence

Lord, your kingdom come,
in us as it is in heaven.

We give thanks
for the promise of your kingdom and life eternal.
We rejoice in the fellowship of all your saints
and commend our loved ones departed,
this world and ourselves
to your unfailing love.

Silence

Merciful Father,
accept these prayers
for the sake of your Son,
our Saviour Jesus Christ.
Amen.

Memory verse

The kingdom of heaven is like treasure hidden in a field, which someone found and hid; then in his joy he goes and sells all that he has and buys that field.
Matthew 13:44

Suggested music

O Lord, my God
Teach me, my God and King
God is good, God is great

CANDLES

Aim

To show that those who know Jesus have a great treasure.

Activity

Hide chocolate money in a container (box), enough for one piece per person including the teacher. Have a few containers with things of no use in, such as screwed-up paper, sawdust or bits of rusty metal. Go on a treasure hunt with the children and let them find the useless containers. Finally get them to 'discover' the treasure box and share out the treasure.

Teaching

After the activity, talk about hidden treasure and how exciting it must be to find something very special. (You may be able to tell a local story of finding treasure.) Jesus once told a story of a man who found a treasure.

There was a man who went to work in a field. He would have to work hard for very little money. After a while he noticed a stone that needed moving and started to do it. Under the stone he found a pottery jar. It was quite large and it had a cover like a lid over it. He became excited and wondered what was in the jar. First he looked around to see that no one was watching. Then he took the lid off the jar and found it was filled with gold coins, lots and lots of money. There was more money than he had ever seen. He became even more excited. He kept very quiet because he did not want anyone else to see what he had found. I do not think you will be able to tell me what he did next. Can anyone guess?

He put the lid back on. He covered it with soil and put the stone back over it. All the time he was very happy for he had found a treasure. Now he would be rich and so would his family. But before he could claim the treasure he would have to buy the field and he did not have any money. What could he do? He started to sell everything he had. He sold the old donkey, the little bits of jewellery his wife had; he sold their pots and pans, their chairs and their table. Soon their house was empty. People said he had gone mad. He had an empty house and owned nothing, though he now had enough money to buy the field.

The field was not a good piece of land; it was full of stones. It did not look as if much would grow there so the man was able to buy it. Now he had a little field that seemed useless. People said he was crazy, wasting his time and his money. But the man knew he had done the wisest thing he had ever done. He knew what no one else knew: the field had a hidden treasure. Now he was able to dig up the treasure and it was his. He could buy back his donkey and the jewellery. He could get another table and chairs. He would share what he found with his family and friends and they would all be very happy.

Jesus told people that knowing God and loving him was like finding a great treasure. For God is always ready to help us and to love us. It is like having a treasure we can share and get other people to know how wonderful it is to be loved by God.

Prayer

God, you are wonderful
and all things belong to you.
You give us all that we have
and you give us your love.
From out of your treasures you give to us.
Thank you, God.
Amen.

Song

Praise God from whom all blessings flow

LAMPS

Aim

To show how we should seek God's kingdom and be willing to put ourselves out to find it.

Teaching

Begin by showing a pearl or a string of pearls. Ask if the children know what they are and tell them how pearls were once very precious. Even now a good pearl is very, very expensive.

Where do pearls come from? They come from oysters and not all oysters make pearls. In fact, not many oysters make pearls. An oyster makes a pearl when it gets a tiny bit of grit into its shell that it cannot get rid of. To stop the grit rubbing and hurting it the oyster wraps pearl around the grit to make it smooth and harmless. But not many oysters do this, and often the pearl is very small or not a good shape. Only sometimes do you get really good big pearls and they are expensive.

Not long ago someone was very lucky. They bought some oysters from a supermarket. They were going to have them for a meal. When they opened one of the oysters they found a pearl. They were very excited and told the supermarket, although they had bought the oyster so the pearl belonged to them not the shop. It was not a big or expensive pearl but it was theirs and they had it set in a ring to be worn.

Jesus told a story about a rich merchant. He was someone who bought and sold pearls. He would travel around where fishermen and tradesmen sold pearls in the market place. They would argue about price and in the end he would buy the pearls. The merchant sought the best pearls.

One day he came across the best pearl he had ever seen. There was not another like it. The pearl had a beauty of its own and it seemed to glow. The merchant knew it was very special and that he must have it. But it would not be easy to get because the man selling it also knew it was very special. The merchant was aware that this pearl was special to him. He had spent his life looking for such a beauty. He could not lose it now. It was worth more than anything he could think of, so he went and sold all the pearls he had. Then he sold all the things he had collected. Then he went and bought the pearl. He didn't have many other things but now he was happier than he had ever been.

Jesus asks us to seek the kingdom of God, for to us it is a great treasure. Without God we are poor, but once we find God and know of his love, we are rich. Once we find this great treasure, it is good to share it with others.

Activity

On the activity sheet are pictures showing how a pearl is made. There is an opportunity to place 'pearls' in shells for others to find. The children may like to act out today's story.

Prayer

Lord God, you are wonderful,
greater than all treasures.
We are happy to know you love us
and are with us.
Help us to do what you would like us to do.
Amen.

Song

For the measure

TORCHES

Aim

To look at the potential for growth of God's kingdom.

Activity

Have a time of seed recognition. Include easy seeds like a dried pea, acorn, a conker, if possible. If you cannot find many seeds, you can use fruit such as apples and oranges with the seeds in them. You could cut or peel to show the seeds. Have a few very small seeds such as a dandelion clock or a thistle head. You may also like to look at one of Christian Aid's 'Growing for the Future' campaigns.

Teaching

Talk about the amazing potential wrapped up in a seed. Look at an apple seed or an acorn and talk abut how if it is given the chance, it will grow. In this tiny package is the potential for a tree. An amazing plan is held within this tiny seed. But if it is not given the chance to grow, it will not grow. If it is put in a drawer or left on a shelf, it will not reach its potential. Seeds have to be sown to grow.

When Julian of Norwich, who lived in the fourteenth century, held a tiny hazelnut seed in her hand, she wondered how it could survive. How could such a small thing endure in this great universe? She came to three conclusions:

> God made it.
> God loves it.
> God keeps it.

It was at the same time she said that God is our Maker. God loves us and keeps us.

Now let us look at what Jesus says about the kingdom of heaven. (Have someone read Matthew 13:31, 32.)

Jesus compares the kingdom of heaven to a tiny seed, something so small it is hardly noticeable. It would be easy for you to ignore it. But if you sow the seed in your field – that is, into your heart and mind, into your life – then it will grow. Like a tiny seed, the kingdom has great potential but we have to give it the opportunity to grow. It is about our relationship with God and our understanding of him.

This week let us remind ourselves each day that we are in God's presence and his kingdom seeks to grow in us and through us. Let us remind ourselves of what Julian of Norwich discovered and say each day:

> God, you made me.
> God, you love me.
> God you care for me.
> Thank you, God.

Prayer

God, you are our Creator.
You surround us with your love and care.
We seek to help your kingdom grow in us each day,
that it may grow in all the world.
Amen.

Song

God is love: his the care

Proper 13

Sunday between 31 July and 6 August inclusive

Aim

To show that the compassion of Jesus can reach out to others through our willingness to give and share.

Preparation

Have a display of people growing food as a result of the help of Christian Aid. Have an extra collection point for anyone to give to this project.

Opening activity

Two readers:

1. In northern Senegal it is the desert that is growing. Once-green areas are baked dry, brown and cracked. There is little vegetation and life is a struggle.
2. Mamadou Diop who lives in Senegal says, 'A drought of the heart is as devastating as a drought in the land.' Selfishness and greed can soon destroy a community, leaving it cracked and dry. It stunts the growth of love and kills off hopes of progress.
1. Will you help to water the earth, to feed the hungry?
2. To bring love and hope to where you dwell?

Opening prayer

Lord God, as you have given to us,
help us to be generous towards others.
May we see that the resources we have
are not wasted or squandered
but are used to your glory and the benefit of all.
Amen.

Opening song

Let us praise God together

Readings

Genesis 32:22-31 or Isaiah 55:1-5
Psalm 17:1-7, 16 or Psalm 145:8, 9, 15-22
Romans 9:1-5
Matthew 14:13-21

Thought for the day

Today's Gospel is set in times of trouble. John the Baptist has been beheaded. Jesus withdraws to the wilderness. The wilderness is often a symbol of chaos. Suddenly, in a life where all seems to be going well, chaos breaks in. But Jesus also chose the wilderness because it would give him space to think and commune with God.

We need to remember that when chaos seems to take over, God does not leave us. God was with the Israelites in the wilderness and provided them with manna, with refreshment and with his presence (Exodus 16:13-35). God fed Elijah, a widow and her son (1 Kings 17:8-16). God supplied Elijah with food and his presence when he felt he wanted to die (1 Kings 19:1-18). God fed a hundred people with only twenty barley loaves and a few fresh ears of grain (2 Kings 4:42-44). Matthew sees that the people are in wilderness times. The feeding of the five thousand wants us to recognise that God is able to transform the wilderness. As in the days of Moses, even so now God provides for his people.

By blessing the bread, Jesus reminds the people of the divine presence. The words Jesus used were most likely the same as every Jew used before meals, 'Blessed are you, Yahweh, our God, King of the Universe, who brings forth bread from the earth.' Let us remember every time we say grace we are acknowledging not only the goodness of God but his presence with us. When Matthew says that Jesus took the bread, blessed it, broke it and gave it, he wants us to think also of the Last Supper (Matthew 26:26).

By the feeding, Jesus shows his concern for the welfare of the people. Though Jesus had sought solitude, he is ready to help those who have come out to find him. His compassion is for those who have sought him out and are in danger of fainting through hunger. Hunger is not what God wants for his people. The faithful are called to relieve hunger out of their resources, even though those resources may be small. God wants to help us but first we need to make the moves we can out of what he has already given us. In giving they are to trust in God (cf. Matthew 25:34-40). Jesus challenges his disciples to give, and when they do, he gives to them and they then give to others. Jesus does his work through his disciples, through us. He waits for us who have received to help him to give to the hungry.

It is wonderful to hear that they gathered up what was left over. God gives to us richly but he does not want us to waste what he has given us. This has much to say to our modern world.

Question time

Do we recognise the importance of saying grace at meals?

How does our church show its concern for the hungry and oppressed?

Illustration

This is the story of the 'long spoons'. Someone was given a vision of what life is like. She went into a room where there was a lot of food to be eaten but only by a long spoon. The spoon was so long that the people could not get it to their mouths and food was being spilled and wasted. Everyone looked frustrated and hungry. It looked like a picture of hell.

Then she went into another room where there were still long spoons and the same system. Here everyone was feeding someone else. They were reaching out and feeding a neighbour. Here there was much laughter and fellowship. It felt more like heaven than hell.

She thought long on this and realised that there is enough in the world for everyone's need but not for their greed.

Intercessions

Blessed are you, Lord our God,
for you provide food for our daily needs
and for all creatures.
You give food, resources and talents
for us to share with others and give you glory.
Blessed are you, Father, Son and Holy Spirit.

We ask your blessing
upon all who hunger and thirst
for righteousness and the coming of your kingdom.
We remember all who feel their lives are parched and dry
and who suffer from spiritual hunger.
May the Good News be brought to all
who feel empty and that life is meaningless.
We bring before you all who go out in mission
and all who seek to proclaim your love.

Silence

Renewing and refreshing God,
hear us and help us.

We ask your blessing
upon all who lack the necessary resources for well-being.
We pray for all who are suffering
from hunger and poverty,
all who struggle due to injustice and greed.
We remember all who have lost crops and livestock
through famine, drought or war.
We pray for the work of Christian Aid
and for all who seek to bring relief
to the hungry and poor.

Silence

Renewing and refreshing God,
hear us and help us.

We give thanks for our loved ones,
for all who have cared and provided for us.
We ask your blessing upon all who work
to give us what we need.
We pray for all farmers and food providers,
for shop workers
and all who bring our food to the markets.
We ask your blessing upon our families
and our neighbours.

Silence

Renewing and refreshing God,
hear us and help us.

We remember all who feel weary with life,
drained of energy and no longer able to cope.
We pray for all who struggle against great odds.
We ask your blessing upon all who feel alone
and that no one cares for them.
We pray for all who are ill at home or in hospital.

Silence

Renewing and refreshing God,
hear us and help us.

We give thanks that you give life and life eternal,
that you are a renewing and restoring God.
As we rejoice in the resurrection,

we ask your blessing upon our loved ones departed.
May they know the peace and glory of your kingdom.

Silence

Merciful Father,
**accept these prayers
for the sake of your Son,
our Saviour Jesus Christ.
Amen.**

Memory verse

The Lord is near to those who call upon him, to all who call upon him faithfully.
Psalm 145:19

Suggested music

Guide me, O thou great Redeemer
I, the Lord of sea and sky
When I needed a neighbour

CANDLES

Aim

To show how Jesus cares for people.

Teaching

One day Jesus and his disciples went away in a boat across the sea to a quiet place. They went there because they had been very, very busy and needed to have a rest. Jesus wanted some time to talk quietly with the Father God. It would be nice to be quiet. But people had watched the disciples cross the sea and they hurried around by the seashore. The people wanted to be with Jesus and to listen to him. They wanted to see him make ill people well again. The people came in crowds, sat down on the grass and Jesus talked to them. Someone counted them and said there were over 5000 people – it was great big crowd.

Because the people had walked a long way and had stayed with Jesus, by the afternoon they were hungry. They would have a long walk home and Jesus was worried that they did not have anything to eat. The disciples were going to send them away. Jesus said that the disciples could give them some food. But the disciples were amazed because they only had five loaves and two small fish. They felt there was not enough even for them and Jesus was asking them to share with the crowd of 5000. They thought that it was not possible but when Jesus asked them to do something they always tried to do it. Jesus cared for all the people and he did not want any of them to be hungry. Jesus wanted to help them.

Jesus asked the disciples for the food. He took the five loaves and two fish. He held them in his hands and looked up to heaven. Jesus said a prayer to God the Father. Jesus thanked God for the bread, then he broke the bread in pieces and gave it to the disciples. The disciples then went around the crowd giving them bread, making sure everyone had plenty. There were 5000 people but the bread did not run out. All ate and were filled. Everyone could go home after the meal and they would tell of the wonderful thing that Jesus had done. Jesus had been sent by God the Father and he had fed the big crowd with five loaves and two small fish.

Activity

There are five loaves and two fish for the children to colour on the activity sheet.

If you want a game, hide five cut-out loaves and two fish around the room before you begin and get the children to hunt for them after Jesus asks the disciples to provide food. When the loaves and fishes have been found, continue with the story.

Prayer

Lord Jesus, we know that you love everyone
and care if people are hungry.
Help us to always be kind
and ready to share with others.
Amen.

Song

5 0 0 0 + hungry folk

LAMPS

Aim

To show how Jesus cares for people in their weakness and their hunger.

Teaching

Jesus and the disciples have been very busy caring for people and telling them of God. Now they were tired and needed a rest. To get away from the crowds they got into a fishing boat and crossed the top edge of the sea. But people saw where they were going so they hurried on foot around the edge of the sea to follow Jesus.

Jesus wanted a time of quiet and prayer but soon people started to arrive where the boat had landed. Crowds came and some were tired for they had hurried and travelled for hours. The people wanted to be near Jesus, to hear him and to be helped by him. Jesus really wanted a rest but he did not send them away. He spoke to them and told them of God. There were over 5000 people. That is a very large crowd.

When Jesus had finished speaking, the disciples asked him to send the people away. But Jesus saw that the people were tired and hungry. He saw that they needed something to eat. He said to the disciples, 'The people need not go away. You give them something to eat.' The disciples could hardly believe it. They had hardly enough food for themselves, and they told Jesus they did not have enough food for everyone. 'We have nothing here but five loaves and two fish.' Jesus said, 'Bring them to me.' The disciples wondered what he would do but they obeyed Jesus.

Jesus asked all the people to sit on the grass. When they were all still he took five loaves and two fish in his hands and gave thanks to God the Father for providing them with food. Then he broke the bread and gave it to his disciples. He told them to give it to the people. Again the disciples did as Jesus told them. It was a miracle, it was wonderful; the bread did not run out and everyone was fed. Everyone had plenty and there was even a lot left over. The people were all amazed.

Jesus knew that now that they had been fed the people could travel home a lot easier. Just as Moses had got food from God in the desert, Jesus provided food for those who followed him.

Activity

Explore the idea of saying 'Thank you'. Get the children to sit in a circle and pass a plate around. (You might like to use a paper plate with five loaves and two fish drawn on it.) As they receive the plate they have to say, 'Thank you, God, for . . . ' (*adding a word*) before they pass the plate on.

Prayer

Jesus, we know that you love us
and care for us.
We pray for all the hungry people in our world.
Show us how we can help them
to know of your love and care.
Amen.

Song

Jesus the Lord said: I am the Bread (verse 1)

TORCHES

Aim

To show how Jesus meets our emptiness and cares for our bodies as well as our spirit.

Teaching

Jesus and the disciples were very busy telling people of the love of God. Jesus saw how many felt empty and uncared for. So he spent hours and hours healing and helping people. The time came when Jesus and the disciples needed a rest. Jesus wanted some time to be quiet and alone and talk to God the Father. For this reason, Jesus and the disciples left the crowds and sailed across the top edge of the lake. They would sail away from the towns and land in a deserted area.

The trouble was people could see the boat and they started to hurry around the top edge of the lake. The quickest kept the boat in sight and others followed. Jesus wanted quiet and a time for prayer but instead he got a crowd. Someone said there was over 5000 people.

Jesus knew the people had followed because they wanted to hear more about God. They wanted help and healing. Jesus wanted quiet but he did not send them away. He talked to them of God. By the end of the day everyone was tired and hungry. Many of them had a long walk home. Jesus had fed their minds with the word of God; he had filled their spirits with the love of God. But now they were hungry. The disciples told Jesus to send them away and let them seek food in the villages they had passed. But Jesus was worried for them. He cares for the whole person including their body. Jesus' healing miracles shows how he cares for the body (ask for examples). Now he asked the disciples to feed them. The disciples looked at their supplies. They had only five small loaves and two fish. That would not go very far. Jesus said, 'Bring them to me.' By now the disciples knew they should obey Jesus and they brought the small amount of food. Jesus now asked them to get all the people to sit down on the grass. He then said a prayer of blessing over the bread, he gave thanks and broke it and gave it to the disciples. They were to share it among the people. They did this and everyone was fed. It was a miracle. It cannot be explained. Jesus fed them all. Can you think of another time when God provided food in the wilderness? Some people thought Jesus was like a second Moses. It was only after the crowd was fed that Jesus sent them back to their homes.

Jesus still cares for our whole being, our bodies as well as our minds and spirits and is concerned if any part of us suffers from hunger or distress.

Activity

Explore ideas of how we can help the poor and needy of the world. Show how disciples of Jesus are still seeking to feed the hungry. Use Christian Aid or Tearfund material to develop this thinking.

Prayer

Lord, you have given us a rich world
where there is enough for everyone's need
but not for their greed.
Help us who have received plenty
to be generous with others
and so express your care for us all.
Amen.

Song

Who took fish and bread

Proper 14

Sunday between 7 and 13 August inclusive

Aim

To show that our God cares and is with us in the storms of life.

Preparation

Have posters from the Royal National Lifeboat Institution (Head Office, West Quay Road, Poole, Dorset BH15 1HZ) or from the Mission to Seafarers (St Michael Paternoster Royal, College Hill, London EC4R 2RL). You might like to have a lifeboat collecting box with a blue flower display.

Opening activity

Listen to 'When you walk through a storm' (You'll never walk alone).

Have two readers and let the music continue quietly as they speak.

1. Elijah was exhausted but God refreshed him.
2. Elijah wanted to die but God gave him new hope.
1. Elijah was given rest and refreshment.
2. Elijah's life is in turmoil –
1. earthquake,
2. wind,
1. and fire,
2. but God is there and waiting to speak.
Both In the storms of life God is standing by, wanting to help and waiting for us to turn to him.

Opening prayer

Lord God,
when the days are dark and we are weary,
when the stress and the storms increase
and we are in danger of being overwhelmed,
hear us and help us.
May we know you are always with us
and ready to help us,
through Jesus Christ our Lord.
Amen.

Opening song

Lead us, heavenly Father, lead us

Readings

Genesis 37:1-4, 12-28 or 1 Kings 19:9-18
Psalm 105:1-6, 16-22, 45b or Psalm 85:8-13
Romans 10:5-15
Matthew 14:22-33

Thought for the day

Jesus has been with the five thousand plus, caring for them and feeding them. He has been pouring out him-self in caring for them, and now he needs to have the quiet time to be alone with God. It is for this he came into the wilderness. He sends the crowds away, back to their homes. He sends the disciples off in their boat and he goes up a mountain to pray. We need to keep contact with God especially when our lives are at their busiest. We need time for rest and renewal or we face trouble.

Jesus was alone in the evening, meeting God in the stillness. In contrast to this, the disciples were now caught up in a storm; they were being battered by waves and the wind was against them. It is amazing how in a short distance we can find we have moved out of peace and into trouble. There are many storms that can so easily overtake us. In this frail craft that we call life there is always the danger of being overwhelmed.

In the hour of their need Jesus came to them. No doubt he had realised the wind had suddenly become fierce and the disciples could be in difficulty, so he came to them. There is no way we can easily explain this. Some believed Jesus walked along the shoreline and in the surf; others that Jesus walked on water. Whatever, you need be aware that in the storms of life Jesus is there and ready to help. What wonderful words to hear in the midst of a storm: 'Take heart, it is I; do not be afraid.'

There is that lovely picture of Peter acting on impulse as ever, seeking to come to Jesus over the waves and Jesus saying, 'Come.' With eyes on Jesus, he steps out but soon he notices the wind and waves and begins to sink. Is not this the story of many of our lives? Peter calls out, 'Lord, save me.' Jesus is as ready as ever and reaches out and Peter is saved.

The image of a boat on a stormy sea is an ancient image of the Church in the world. It is the logo for the World Council of Churches. Today's Gospel is meant to reassure us in times of storm and trouble. Our faith may be small but it is in a great God and he always stands by ready to help.

Question time

Are we aware of the presence of God enough to find strength from him in times of trouble?

Amid all the troubles of our world how can we witness to the peace and love of God?

Illustration

At lifeboat stations there is usually a record of rescues and of the wonderful bravery of those who went out in the storms to help others. Sometimes, instead of a record of rescue, it simply says, 'Standing by'. That is when the lifeboat was there and ready to help if needed. The crew were keeping a watch and were ready to come to the aid of a troubled vessel if called to do so. How often our God is like that – 'standing by', always ready to help those who call upon him.

Julian of Norwich lived through stormy times. It was the time of the Black Death, the Peasants' Revolt, the battles of Crécy, Poitiers and Agincourt. She saw four kings sit on the throne of England. As a young woman, she had nearly died but she could write:

He did not say, 'You shall not be tempest-tossed; you shall not be work-weary; you shall not be distressed.' But he did say, 'You shall not be overcome.'

Julian was deeply aware that God is 'our maker, our lover and our keeper'. Amidst the storms of life, Julian was aware of the presence, the love and the power of God.

We need to learn to put our hand into the hand of God who never leaves us or forsakes us.

Intercessions

Blessed are you, Lord our God,
for you are a very present help in trouble.
You are ready to hear our cry
and come to our aid.
Lord, help us not to be afraid
but to put our trust and hope in you.
May we ever rejoice in your love and care.
Blessed are you, Father, Son and Holy Spirit,
one God for ever.

Lord, you have created us out of love
and for your love.
We ask for your protection
in the troubles and storms of life.
Bless all Christians who are struggling
against great odds.
We pray for those who are suffering
from persecution, violence or ridicule.
We remember those whose lives are at risk
and those who are exhausted.

Silence

Lord, in the storms of life,
hear us and help us.

We give thanks for the work of the Mission to Seafarers
and those who go out in lifeboats.
We pray for all whose work is upon the sea.
We ask your blessing upon fishermen,
merchant seamen and the Royal Navy.
We remember today all who are caught up
in storms, in earthquakes, floods or droughts.

Silence

Lord, in the storms of life,
hear us and help us.

We give you thanks
for the safety and protection of our homes.
We pray for all who are struggling
with problems of debt
or whose relationships are breaking down.
We pray for the work of Shelter
and remember all who are homeless
and living on the streets of our towns and cities.

Silence

Lord, in the storms of life,
hear us and help us.

Lord, we pray for your blessing
upon the world-weary, the worried and worn,
all who feel overwhelmed and unable to cope.
We remember all who are ill at home or in hospital
and those who care for them.
We pray especially for any involved in accidents
or whose illness finds no cure.

Silence

Lord, in the storms of life,
hear us and help us.

Lord, stand by us when the last great storm
seeks to overwhelm us
and we feel we are sinking beneath the waves.
Help us to know that in you we will not perish
but have everlasting life.
To you we commit all our loved ones departed:
may they rejoice in your presence and in your peace.

Silence

Merciful Father,
accept these prayers
for the sake of your Son,
our Saviour Jesus Christ.
Amen.

Memory verse

Lord, save me.
Matthew 14:30

Suggested music

Will your anchor hold
Calm me, Lord
Eternal Father, strong to save

CANDLES

Aim

To show how Jesus cares for us when we are in trouble.

Teaching

Who can remember last week's story? Jesus needed a rest but crowds and crowds of people came to see him. He talked to them, helped them and fed them. Now he was very tired. He sent the people away and then the disciples. Can you remember how the disciples travelled last week? They went away in the fishing boat. Jesus stayed by himself to pray to God the Father. While he was praying it got dark. Later the wind started to blow, gently at first. Let us make the sound of the gentle wind. Then the wind got stronger and stronger. Can you make the sound of a strong wind? Whoosh! The wind was blowing over the sea and the sea was getting angry – it was making big waves. Whoosh! – the wind was making the sea get into the little boat. Let us make the sound of the strong wind and clap to make the sound of a wave hitting the boat. It was now very dark and stormy, and the disciples were frightened. Even the fishermen disciples thought the boat might sink. They were all getting very wet.

Jesus knew the wind was strong and the waves were big and he was worried for his disciples. They were in a storm and they needed his help. Jesus set out to go to them. He did not have a boat but he was able to walk to them on the waves. When they saw Jesus coming they were frightened – they thought it must have been a ghost because it was still stormy. But Jesus told them not to be afraid. He had come to help them. Peter was almost sure it was Jesus but said, 'Lord, if it is you, let me come to you across the water.' Jesus said to Peter, 'Come.' Peter got out of the boat and on to the sea. But as soon as he took his eyes off Jesus he noticed the waves and the wind and he began to sink. 'Help!' he shouted. 'Lord, save me.' Jesus reached out with his hand and rescued Peter. Then they both got into the boat and the storm calmed: the wind stopped blowing and the waves went down.

Activity

There is an opportunity to make a boat on a stormy sea. This is a good story for the children to act out. You can use a sheet with a slit in the middle for a stormy sea. The disciples can stand in the slit while others enjoy sending waves to them.

Prayer

Jesus, when we are afraid,
when it is dark or stormy,
help us to know that you are with us
and care for us.
We thank you for rescuing Peter
from the stormy sea.
Amen.

Song

Wide, wide as the ocean

LAMPS

Aim

To show how Jesus cares and is the Saviour.

Teaching

Has anyone been in a boat at sea when it is stormy? It can be very frightening. The sea is so large. The fishermen of Brittany have a short prayer which says, 'Lord, the sea is so large and our boat is so small.' It is very easy for the sea to overwhelm a little boat in a storm.

Jesus and the disciples were very tired after the feeding of the 5000. The people went back to their homes and Jesus sent the disciples off in the boat. It was evening and would soon be dark. Jesus wanted to be alone with God the Father. He wanted to spend time in prayer speaking to the Father and quietly enjoying being with him. Meanwhile the disciples were resting on a calm sea.

When it became dark a great wind arose. It came sweeping down the hills and hitting the sea. Soon the waves were getting higher and higher. It was a very stormy night. The disciples were soon in trouble. They could not use the sail on the boat because the wind was too strong. They had to pull on the oars. While some were rowing others were trying to keep water out of the boat. All of the disciples were now soaking wet. They really felt they were in trouble. Even the fishermen disciples were afraid.

Jesus was well aware that the wind had increased. He could see that the waves were rising and he knew the disciples would be having a difficult time. Though Jesus had wanted to stay in the quiet place, he cared for his disciples and knew they needed his help. Jesus decided to go to them and help them.

It was now early in the morning. It was just getting light when the disciples saw Jesus walking towards them. It was not possible, they thought: it must be a ghost. The disciples started to cry out in fear: they were frightened. But Jesus said, 'Do not be afraid, it is I.'

Peter spoke out, 'Lord, if it is you, command me to come to you on the water.' Jesus said, 'Come.' So Peter climbed over the side of the boat and started walking on the water. He looked at Jesus in amazement. Then he felt the wind rushing against him. He looked at the waves and he began to sink. Peter was very frightened and cried out to Jesus, 'Lord, save me.' As soon as he called, Jesus reached out his hand and caught him. When they got into the boat, the wind ceased and the waves grew calm. The disciples were amazed at all that had happened. They worshipped Jesus, saying, 'Truly, you are the Son of God.'

Activity

This is a great story to act out. Have sound effects for wind and waves. Get 'disciples' to sit on the floor and attempt to row for the shore. Show Jesus in the stillness and the stillness that comes with him. Have Peter sinking in the waves and Jesus taking him by the hand. Peter rises! Let all acknowledge Jesus as the Son of God.

Prayer

Lord, may we come to you in the stillness
and trust in you in the storms.
Help us to know you are always with us
and ready to offer us your helping hand.
Amen.

Song

He's the man who calmed the sea

TORCHES

Aim

To know our God is with us – even in the storms of life.

Teaching

Look at the story of Elijah after his battle with the false prophets. Tell the group how Elijah had stood alone against 450 false prophets and won because he was not alone. God was with him and helping him.

But after this Elijah is exhausted. While feeling worn he hears that Queen Jezebel is out to kill him. He could face 450 men but he runs from one woman! Have someone read dramatically 1 Kings 19:4-8. Note how God sees to Elijah and ensures that he is refreshed. God gives Elijah strength to go on. When human resources run out, God is still there ready to help.

Now read 1 Kings 19:9-18. God is already there and waiting for Elijah. God asks what Elijah thinks he is doing. Poor Elijah – he escaped from Jezebel and now he has to face a great storm of wind, earthquake and fire. After all this Elijah heard God speak to him again in the still small voice. God gave Elijah strength to return and work for him. Alone we are not able, but with God much more becomes possible. Abraham Lincoln used to say, 'God plus one is a majority.'

Now look at the story of the stilling of the storm. Again, Jesus and the disciples are exhausted due to hard work. Jesus seeks to be alone with God the Father. The disciples are sent away. It is night and a storm arises on the sea. The wind increases and the waves grow higher. The disciples are buffeted by the storm. They lower the sail and pull on the oars but for all their effort they are in danger of sinking. Jesus is aware of their need and comes to them in the storm. (He still comes to the storm-tossed and weary.) The tired disciples are spooked! They think it is a ghost! But in the storm Jesus speaks to them. He says, 'Take heart, it is I; do not be afraid.'

Peter speaks out, 'Lord, if it is you, command me to come to you on the water.' Jesus says, 'Come.'

With his eyes fixed on Jesus, Peter begins to walk the waves. Suddenly he is aware of where he is, in the deep. He looks at the waves and feels the wind and he begins to sink. He cries out to Jesus, 'Lord, save me.' Immediately Jesus reaches out his hand and Peter rises out of the water. When they get into the boat the wind ceases and all is calm again.

Activity
These two stories are full of symbolism. They speak to us about our life and our faith. We will not escape the storms of life, or weariness or loss of confidence, but we need to know we are not alone. Let the group discuss this and say how it relates to them.

Prayer
Alone with none but you, my God,
I journey on my way.
What need I fear, when you are near,
O King of night and day?
More safe I am within your hand
than if a host did round me stand.
Attributed to St Columba

Song
O the dark waves were raging

Proper 15

Aim

To show that God's love is not exclusive but is offered to all people, in all places and at all times.

Preparation

Have two young people at the door sharing in the welcome given to all who come today. Have a map of the world and photos of different races and ethnic groups. Put these around the text: Jesus said, 'Anyone who comes to me I will never drive away.' (John 6:37). Beneath you may like to add, 'God loves all and welcomes all'.

Opening activity

Two speakers:

1. Should we let John join us?
2. No, he is not good enough.
1. How about Peter?
2. No, he is too impulsive.
1. Andrew could come.
2. What does he know?
1. Well, there is James.
2. I doubt it!
1. I wonder why we have no other friends or helpers.

Opening prayer

Lord,
your love is greater than the smallness of our minds
and deeper than all our knowledge.
You love every one of us with an everlasting love.
Help us to reflect your love
in the way we deal with all who come to us,
through Jesus Christ our Lord.
Amen.

Opening song

Lord, the light of your love (*Shine, Jesus, shine*)

Readings

Genesis 45:1-15 or Isaiah 56:1, 6-8
Psalm 133 or Psalm 67
Romans 11:1, 2a, 29-32
Matthew 15:(10-20) 21-28

Thought for the day

The exclusiveness of the Jews could not portray the inclusiveness of the love of God. The Jews would restrict God's love; Jesus would show its wideness. Jesus had been talking about how it is not foods that make a person unclean. Now we find him among the Gentiles and he is showing that contact with them does not defile anyone.

This is the only time we hear of Jesus outside Jewish territory. He is in the land of the Phoenicians who were great sailors and traders. The Phoenicians were the first to navigate by the stars. They traded with the whole of the Mediterranean and it is likely they made their way to Britain to get tin from Cornwall.

Jesus was here to avoid the hostility of the Scribes and Pharisees and of Herod. He was also avoiding the wrong kind of popularity that the crowds were bestowing upon him. This is an attempt the escape trouble for a while so that he can prepare himself and his disciples.

Here a Canaanite woman comes to Jesus for help. To converse in public with a woman who was also a Gentile was breaking the regulations of the Jews twice over. The woman comes out of love for her afflicted daughter. She has heard somehow that Jesus is a healer. She does not just ask, she shouts. She shouts, 'Have mercy on me, Lord, Son of David, my daughter is tormented.' She obviously has some faith in Jesus. It may be small, it may be poor, but it is in his ability and power. It does not matter how small our faith is if it is in a great God. Not only does she have faith, but she is persistent, she is not easily put off. (Compare the nagging widow and the judge, Luke 18:1-8.) She begins by following and shouting, and she ends on her knees, kneeling and praying.

From the beginning the disciples wanted Jesus to help her only in order to get rid of her. But Jesus wanted to open her awareness of him and his power. Jesus rebuffs her on her approach. He says it is not right to throw the children's bread to the dogs. The Jews called the Gentiles dogs as a disrespectful way of speaking of them. Probably our nearest is to call someone a bitch. But Jesus, though making a point of how he was sent to the Jews, speaks more kindly than it sounds. The word he uses is the diminutive word that means puppy or house dog. The woman, possibly still on her knees, answers that even the dogs are allowed the crumbs from their master's table. This witty reply seems to delight Jesus. Although he was for the Jews first, that was because he had to start somewhere. Jesus is for all people, in all times and at all places. Jesus rejoices in the faith of this Gentile woman. In her is a sign of the universality of the love of God as revealed in Jesus. Only at the end of the Gospel, when he has completed his mission to the Jews, does Jesus send the disciples out into all the world (Matthew 28:19, 20).

Question time

Are we sure that our Church is not exclusive in its actions?

How can we express the inclusive love of God to those who feel outcasts and rejected?

Illustration

We may hate what a person does but we need to learn not to hate the person. It is said that God hates sin but loves the sinner. The more exclusive we become in our dealings, the smaller our world and our heart. God's love is not exclusive.

There is a story of a young man who tried to join a famous London club. He had tried for months and was refused entry for one reason or another. The club was determined to be exclusive. The man's background, place of schooling, position in society did not suit. He was a good man but firmly kept out. In his prayers he asked why this was so. Then, in a vision one night, Jesus came and spoke to him and said, 'I would not worry, you have tried for months to get in; I have tried for years and they have kept me out!'

See Matthew 25:45.

Consider Edwin Markham's words:

> He drew a circle that shut me out –
> Rebel, heretic, thing to flout.
> But love and I had the wit to win –
> We drew a circle and brought him in.

Intercessions

Blessed are you, Lord our God,
for you have created us all out of love
and for your love.
Even when in our sin and foolishness
we go against you and leave you,
you are there and seek us out in love.
Blessed are you, Father, Son and Holy Spirit.

Loving God, may your Church throughout the world
show your love for all peoples and nations.
Bless all who seek to heal divisions
and to do away with prejudice.
Give courage to all who reach out to those in need
and who seek to welcome the rejected.
May your Church reflect your saving love.

Silence

Lord of life and love,
hear us and help us.

Loving God, we ask forgiveness
for the sin and arrogance that divides us
and creates barriers between nations and peoples.
We pray with love for all minority groups,
for those who are judged by their race, colour or history.
We remember all who are refugees, homeless
or outcasts of society.
We ask your blessing upon all who work
to bring a new unity and understanding
between divided peoples.

Silence

Lord of life and love,
hear us and help us.

Loving God, we thank you for our homes
and for all who have accepted us
in love and generosity.
We ask your blessing upon our homes
and the community in which we live.
We pray for all who are suffering
from broken relationships
and all who feel estranged
from the world around them.

Silence

Lord of life and love,
hear us and help us.

Loving God, we give thanks
for our health and well being.
We ask your blessing upon all who are ill
at home or in hospital.
We remember today all who suffer
from autism or schizophrenia
and all who are mentally ill.
We ask your blessing upon all
who are separated from their loved ones through illness
and all who feel rejected.

Silence

Lord of life and love,
hear us and help us.

Loving God, in your redeeming love
you accept us and welcome us.
We ask you to give joy and peace
to all our loved ones who have departed this life:
may they know the fullness of salvation.
To you and your love we commit the whole world,
our loved ones and ourselves.

Silence

Merciful Father,
**accept these prayers
for the sake of your Son,
our Saviour Jesus Christ.
Amen.**

Memory verse

Let the peoples praise you, O God; let all the peoples praise you.
Psalm 67:5

Suggested music

O Lord, all the world belongs to you
There's a wideness in God's mercy
God is love: let heaven adore him

CANDLES

Aim

To show how God cares for all his world and everyone in it.

Teaching

Start by playing the song 'Who made the twinkling stars?' *(Kidsource)*. Then teach the children to respond to each verse by saying the fourth line as you read the verses. Finally teach the children to sing it.

God made the world and all that is in it. He made it out of his love and he wants it all to love him. He wants us to care for and love the world because he made it so special. God made all sorts of different people, big ones and small ones, brown ones and white ones, boys and girls, men and women. He made us all different but he wanted us to show love and kindness to each other.

Both Johnny and Jean were given beautiful plants in their rooms. They both said they liked them. Johnny could not be bothered to water his or to make sure it did not get too hot or too cold. He did not care for it. Jean looked after her plant: she watered it and moved it when the sun was too hot and she made sure it was warm when the weather got cold. Very soon Johnny's plant was looking sad. Then it looked bad. Then it lost its flowers. Then it lost its leaves. Because he did not give his love to it and care for it Johnny's plant died. Jean's plant was very happy – it had shiny leaves and lots of beautiful flowers. Their mother decided that it was no use giving Johnny plants if he did not care for them but she often gave Jean a new plant to look after.

God does not want us to lose any of the beautiful things of the world through our greed or carelessness. God wants us to care for each other as he cares for us all.

You might like to tell how the life of the panda is threatened because of people spoiling where it lives, and how we need to show that we care for it. The World Wildlife Fund (www.wwf.org.uk) can supply information.

Activity

Play a game that excludes people. Everyone with brown shoes is out, anyone wearing green, anyone with white socks. Continue until all are out. You will need a list of how you got them out so that you can start again by saying you invite in all with brown shoes, all wearing green, etc.

Prayer

Lord God, thank you for making the world
and all that is in it,
for all the wonderful plants and animals,
for all the people,
and thank you for making me.
Amen.

Song

Who made the twinkling stars?

LAMPS

Aim

To encourage them to love the world as God loves the world.

Teaching

Find out where various foods come from. It might be helpful to have a few labels or stickers. Look at tea, coffee, cocoa and sugar. Then look at various fruits – oranges, apples, and bananas. You may like to look at rice, paper and clothing. Look where these places are on a map or globe. If possible, show a few pictures or photographs of people harvesting food or making things for us (Traidcraft or Tearfund can help with this).

We get our food from all around the world. We depend on people from other countries to provide us with many of the things we enjoy. Think what you could not have if you were limited to things we could grow and make in this country. If the people decided they would not grow things for us and not send things to us, we would have to do without many things. But for the world to be a happy place and a good place we all need to share and work together.

We have to make sure that we are not making people work for very little money and that we care about how things are made. We should all care for each other and for the world. God made us to belong to one world and wants us to show our love for the world and for each other. God does not want us to be greedy or selfish but to be ready to share and help any who are in need. God loves all that he has made. He loves you and me, he loves all people and all creatures. It matters very much to God if we waste, spoil or hurt anything in his world.

If there is time, you can explore the loss of the rainforests and how this affects not only the people who live there but the animals and even the world climate.

Activity

Have a map of the world on card, and on the other side have a face of Jesus or any face. Cut the map into various triangles and get the group to put it together. It they find it hard, show them how easy it is if they turn the map over and do the face first.

Prayer

Thank you, God, for a wonderful world.
Teach us to care for each other
and for all that you have made.
May we not spoil or hurt anything
of your wonderful creation.
Amen.

Song

He's got the whole world

TORCHES

Aim

To show how the love of God in Jesus is for all people at all time and in all places.

Teaching

What do Daleks say? 'Exterminate!' They try to get rid of people by exterminating them! If the Daleks had their way, there would be no humans left.

Occasionally we quite like to get rid of people. We avoid their company or make sure they do not know where we are going. Sometimes we decide to get rid of people who are a nuisance. But if we live in a world where we avoid contact we can live in a very lonely world.

Jesus and the disciples had gone out of the Jewish territory to the land of the Phoenicians. Look it up on a map. Because they lived by the Mediterranean Sea, the Phoenicians were great sailors and some probably sailed as far as Cornwall. Jesus went there to avoid trouble for a while. While he was there a woman came shouting after him, 'Have mercy on me, Lord, Son of David, my daughter is tormented.' The disciples wanted to be rid of her. They wanted Jesus to send her away. Why should Jesus bother? She was not a Jew, and she was only a woman! It is not right to waste time with Gentiles or talking to a woman, and it was against the customs of the Jews anyway.

Although Jesus was a Jew and was sent first to the Jews, here he showed God's love for all. He had work to do and it had priorities but Jesus showed compassion for this woman and her daughter. It would have been easy to send her away – except by now she was kneeling at the feet of Jesus. The woman's faith might not have been very great but it was in a great God. Her understanding might be little but she knew that love is able to accept and save.

Jesus told the woman that it is not fair to take the children's food and 'throw it to the dogs'. In many ways this must have sounded quite rude, but it would depend on how it was said. The Jews called the Gentiles 'dogs' and meant it as a term of contempt. Jesus uses the word for 'puppy' or 'pet dog'. His words did not put the woman off. Jesus did not seek to exclude her. The woman's reply – 'Yes, Lord, yet even the dogs eat the crumbs that fall from their master's table' – pleased Jesus. He was pleased with the faith she had shown and said, 'Woman, great is your faith.' Jesus healed her daughter as she had asked.

Here we see the outreach of Jesus beyond the Jewish territory. Jesus is dealing with a non-Jew who is also a woman. Only at the end of Matthew's Gospel will we see Jesus extending this outreach when he sends the disciples out into all the world. Jesus is not exclusive, even though as a human his mission was limited. Jesus reveals God's love for the whole world (John 3:16).

Activity

Have an elimination game. If you have a group of, say, 10 or 16, start by getting them into groups of 3, then 4, 5, 6, 3, 2, etc., so that there is always one person left out. (You will need to work this out according to your numbers.) Let the groups chant, 'Eliminate them!' When there are three left, complicate it by telling them the last one is the real loser! The last one has lost by eliminating all her/his friends.

Prayer

Lord God, we rejoice in your love
for us and for all people.
May we learn to reveal your love
in our dealings with others
and so help to bring them to know and love you.
Amen.

Song

God is love: his the care

Proper 16

Sunday between 21 and 27 August inclusive

Aim

To show that Jesus is the Christ, our Saviour.

Preparation

Have photographs in the porch of well-known people. Cover the bottom or top half of each photograph and see if people can guess who they are. Include a photograph or painting of Christ on the cross but show only his hands and feet. Have a crucifix and a floral decoration with the words, 'Who do you say that I am?'

Opening activity

'Who's who' in the Gospels

Who was the first fisherman disciple?
Who was the disciple called 'Rocky' or the 'Rock'?
Who had sisters called Mary and Martha?
Who betrayed Jesus?
Who first saw Jesus when he rose again?
Who doubted the resurrection?
Who did the disciples say Jesus is?
Who is our Saviour?

Opening prayer

Lord Jesus, you are our Saviour and our God.
You came down from heaven
to lift us up into your kingdom.
May we put our trust in you
and know you as our friend and Redeemer.
Amen.

Opening song

Amazing grace

Readings

Exodus 1:8–2:10 or Isaiah 51:1-6
Psalm 124 or Psalm 138
Romans 12:1-8
Matthew 16:13-20

Thought for the day

As in last week's Gospel, Jesus is outside Galilee (and Herod's jurisdiction). He is about 25 miles north of the Sea of Galilee and in the area of Caesarea Philippi. At this stage Jesus is still avoiding conflict. There are already those who are plotting and planning to kill him. He needs time to be sure the disciples know fully who he is and to be prepared for what lies ahead. Before he sets out for Jerusalem and the cross, he needs to be sure of the awareness of the disciples.

You can imagine them sitting by a campfire in the evening and in a pagan area. Jesus asks them who people say that he is. A few answers tumble out. 'Some say John the Baptist come back.' Perhaps they put this one first because it is a bit hilarious: some of the disciples knew both John and Jesus. They were well aware of them at work at the same time.

Elijah was the next in people's minds. This could be far more likely and had to be looked at. It was believed that, before the Christ came, Elijah would return. Malachi declared the promise of God: 'Lo, I will send you the prophet Elijah before the great and terrible day of the Lord comes' (4:5). These are almost the last words in the Old Testament and to this day the Jews look forward to the coming of Elijah before the Christ comes.

'Jeremiah,' said some. This may sound strange to us but there was a tradition that, before the coming of the Messiah, Jeremiah would return. It was believed that Jeremiah had hidden the ark and the altar of incense that were in the Temple before the exile. He had hidden them in a cave. Before the Christ came, Jeremiah would come and produce the goods.

All of these were precursors of the Christ. The people were not yet aware enough. Jesus then asked the disciples the big question, 'But who do you say that I am?' Jesus does not want to know what they have been told; he wants to know about their own relationship with him and their vision of who he is. For the Christian it is not enough to know *about* Jesus; we need to know him, to have a relationship with him. Faith is not so much about belief but about a living relationship with Christ.

It is good to look at the first three Gospels and hear the response of Peter:

> You are the Messiah, the Son of the living God. (Matthew 16:16)
>
> You are the Messiah. (Mark 8:29)
>
> The Messiah of God. (Luke 9:20)

The word Messiah is the same as Christ, and both mean the Anointed One. Kings are anointed when they enter into their position. The Messiah is God's Anointed One, the appointed one, who is King over all.

This was something that Peter said for himself, and no doubt for the disciples. Jesus is the Christ. Although it may be a small start, it is upon this that Jesus can build. At the moment they only know in part. They are hardly ready to accept that the Christ will suffer. But it is a start and on this beginning their faith will grow. It is when we make the affirmation of faith in Jesus, and seek a living relationship, that Jesus can build his Church in us and through us. It is no use just reciting what we have been told. Jesus wants to know what we think about him personally. For many of us the Gospel grows when we try to put it into our own words.

For the moment Jesus wants his disciples to tell no one. They do not yet quite fully understand and the people would also misunderstand. It was because of wrong ideas about the Messiah that Jesus had to keep out of Galilee. But the day would come after Easter and Pentecost when the disciples would go out into all the world.

Question time

Who do you say Jesus is? Can you affirm that he is the Christ, your Saviour?

Is there a danger of sending people out in mission before they personally know the Christ?

Illustration

Many people ask 'What do you believe in?' but for Christians it is not *what* but *whom*. We believe in the living Christ. We believe that Jesus is the Son of God and is our Saviour. We seek a living relationship with him.

Not what but whom

Not what, but whom, I do believe
that in my darkest hour of need
hath comfort that no mortal creed
to mortal man may give;
not what but whom!
For Christ is more than all the creeds
and his full life of gentle deeds
shall all the creeds outlive.
Not what I do believe but whom!
Who walks beside me in the gloom?
Who shares the burden wearisome?
Who all the dim way doth illume,
and bids me look beyond the tomb
the larger life to live?
Not what I do believe but whom!
Not what, but whom!

John Oxenham

Intercessions

Blessed are you, Lord our God,
for in your love you sent your Son Jesus Christ
to be our Saviour.
You deliver us from the darkness of sin and death
and open to us the way to eternal life.
Blessed are you, Father, Son and Holy Spirit.
To you be praise and glory for ever.

We give thanks for all who have witnessed
to your love and saving power.
We ask your blessing upon all preachers of the word
and ministers of the sacraments,
that they may keep us aware of your presence
and wonderful power.
We pray for all who are growing in the faith,
and remember before you
all who attend study groups and Bible class.
We pray especially today
for all who are struggling with their faith
and those who have fallen away.

Silence

Jesus, Saviour of the world,
we look to you to save and help us.

We give thanks for the wonders of creation
and the mystery of life.
We ask your blessing upon all who suffer
from injustice, war or violence.
We remember those caught up in natural disasters
and struggle due to famine or flood.
We pray for those who feel life has no purpose or meaning
and all who are tempted to despair.

Silence

Jesus, Saviour of the world,
we look to you to save and help us.

We give thanks for the love of our homes and dear ones,
for all the help and encouragement they have given us.
We ask your blessing on homes were life is restricted
and where there is little joy.
We remember all who are homeless,
all who are deeply in debt
and all who are uncertain of their future.

Silence

Jesus, Saviour of the world,
we look to you to save and help us.

We give thanks for all who share in your healing
and bringing of peace to peoples and nations.
We ask your blessing upon all who are struggling
against evil or with illness.
We remember especially
those for whom life brings little joy or hope.
We pray for friends and loved ones who are ill
and all who feel lonely or frightened at this time.

Silence

Jesus, Saviour of the world,
we look to you to save and help us.

We give thanks that through Christ
we are offered eternal life.
We ask your blessing upon all your saints
and our loved ones departed.
We commend them, this world and ourselves
to your unfailing love.

Silence

Merciful Father,
accept these prayers
for the sake of your Son,
our Saviour Jesus Christ.
Amen.

Memory verse

You are the Messiah, the Son of the living God.
Matthew 16:16

Suggested music

Praise, my soul, the King of heaven
And can it be
O Lord, my God

CANDLES

Aim

To see how much the children know about Jesus.

Activity

Who is this?

Describe what one of the children is wearing and see if the rest can guess who it is. Continue to describe a few children until they get the idea. You might like to describe a police officer or a firefighter or a fisherman for them to guess. Let this lead into the teaching.

Teaching

Can you tell me who was born in a stable? Do you know the name of his mother? Where was the stable? Who came to visit him at the stable?

What work did Joseph do in Nazareth? A carpenter is a person who works with wood and makes tables and chairs and mends things that are broken.

When Jesus grew up he asked 12 men to follow him. Do you know any of their names or what work they did?

Jesus did wonderful things. We call them miracles because they are very wonderful. Let us say, 'Miracles'. Can you tell me some of the miracles that Jesus did?

He fed 5000 people with five loaves and two small fish.

He spoke to the wind and waves and made the storm on the sea to stop.

He made people who were ill better. Can you tell me of one of the wonderful miracles Jesus did in making someone better?

One night when they were sitting around a campfire, Jesus asked the disciples if they knew who he was. Well, they were sure he was Jesus from Nazareth. They knew him because they had been working with him and living with him. Because of all the wonderful things they had seen Jesus do, they knew he was special. They believed God the Father had sent Jesus and chosen him to do wonderful work. So they not only called him Jesus; they said he had another name as well. Who knows what it is? They called him 'the Christ'. We now give Jesus these two names and call him Jesus Christ. Let us say this together: 'Jesus Christ'. Remember it means God's Chosen One.

Jesus Christ was very loving and kind but some people decided to kill him. Who knows how Jesus died? He died on a cross. (Look at a crucifix or a painting of the crucifixion.) Jesus died and was buried. Do you know in what sort of place Jesus Christ was buried? Yes, it was a cave and they rolled a big stone against its opening. But there was another miracle, another wonderful thing. Who knows what happened after three days? Jesus Christ rose again and is alive. Because he rose again he is able to be our friend and help us. Let us say a prayer to Jesus Christ.

Prayer

Jesus Christ, we thank you
for all the wonderful things you have done.
We know that you are alive
and want to be our friend
and to love us.
Jesus, we want to love you
because you are great.
Amen.

Song

Jesus' hands were kind hands

LAMPS

Aim

To declare that Jesus Christ is our Saviour.

Teaching

For a long time it was quite dangerous to be a Christian. The Roman Empire tried to make Christians worship other Gods. If they refused, they could be put to death. Christians had to be very brave and they often had to go into hiding. Christians refused to give up their love for Jesus. They continued to say their daily prayers and meet together for worship. Because the soldiers tried to kill them, the Christians often hid in caves underground, even in the city of Rome. Often in these tunnels they drew pictures of Jesus as a young man and wrote beside it the word 'Life'. They were proud that they knew Jesus and were able to speak to him in prayer. Many of them chose a secret sign to show they were Christians. It was the sign of the fish. (Sometimes today you can see this sign on a car to tell you a Christians owns that car.) It is a good sign when you think about it because at least four of the 12 disciples were fishermen. Jesus was often in a fishing boat. Jesus helped the fishermen to make a wonderful catch of fish. When he fed the 5000 he shared out two fish. After his resurrection he ate fish with his disciples. But it is also chosen because fish in Greek is ICHTHUS. (You can find the word used in Ichthyosaurus, which means fish lizard and is a dinosaur.) Each letter of ICHTHUS stood for something.

I is the same as J in Greek – it stood for 'Jesus'. Jesus is the same as Joshua and means deliverer. Jesus is the one who delivers us from evil.

CH is for 'Christ', God's 'Anointed One' or 'Appointed One' – the One chosen to be our Deliverer.

TH = God.

U is for son so **'thu'** is for 'God's Son'. Through Jesus we have special relationship with the Father.

S is for 'Saviour', the One who comes to help us and rescue us.

Now you know the Greek word for fish: ICHTHUS. You also know its secret meaning: JESUS CHRIST SON OF GOD SAVIOUR.

Activity

There is an opportunity on the worksheet to explore the lesson further and to make a secret sign to show that we are the ones who believe in Jesus.

Prayer

Jesus Christ, you are the Son of God,
our Saviour and our friend.
We come to give you our love,
for you gave your life for us
and you came to rescue us.
Thank you, Jesus.
Amen.

Song

Wide, wide as the ocean

TORCHES

Aim

To look at Jesus as 'the Christ'.

Teaching

People may ask you, 'What do you believe?' This is always a difficult question to answer. You can talk about how God made the world or tell the stories of Jesus. But in fact it is important to tell people we do not believe in creeds but in the living God. It is the fact that God is alive that is important and that we can have a relationship with him. God is always present and wants us to get to know him.

The disciples spent time with Jesus. Whenever possible he spent some time with them. They had seen miracles. They had asked, like others, 'Who is this that even the wind and waves obey him?' They were coming to the conclusion that Jesus is very special, that he is the Son of God. They were slowly beginning to see that Jesus is the Chosen One of God, the Anointed One (we would say the *appointed* one). In the Hebrew language the Anointed One is called 'the Messiah', and in Greek 'the Christ'. For a long time in their history the Jews looked forward to the time when God would send his Anointed One, when the Messiah, the Christ, would come to earth.

Now around a campfire, Jesus asks, 'Who do people say that the Son of Man is?' The disciples reply (read Matthew 16: 13, 14). This is quite impressive but Jesus wants to know if the disciples know him and truly recognise who he is (read Matthew 16:15, 16). Peter declares that Jesus is the Christ, the One who the people have longed for. This meant that Jesus was to be their deliverer and helper, to be their Saviour. The danger was that the disciples could only think in earthly terms and could not at this time understand what Jesus was about to do. But at least they recognised him as the One sent by God. It would only be after the crucifixion and the resurrection that they could see more clearly the deeper implication of calling Jesus the Christ.

It is important for each of us that we recognise the need for a Saviour and that Jesus is our Saviour. Like the disciples, we need to get to know him by spending time with him.

Activity

Encourage every member of the group to say why they call Jesus 'the Christ'.

Explore why we need a Saviour and what we need saving from. Try and avoid easy answers in single words. Remind the group you cannot talk about a person unless you really know them.

Prayer

Jesus, Son of God, Saviour,
we put our trust in you
and in your almighty power.
You are able to bring light to our darkness
and rescue us when we cannot help ourselves.
Jesus, help us to know you better
and to love you more.
Amen.

Song

What a wonderful Saviour is Jesus

Proper 17

Sunday between 28 August and 3 September inclusive

Aim

To show that we are to seek the will of God

Preparation

Have in the entrance a 'ONE WAY' sign and have along its arrow 'THE WILL OF GOD'. Have a crucifix and underneath the words, 'Jesus triumphed over evil by doing the will of God'. Put flowers around these words.

Opening activity

Four-way conversation:

1. I would come to church but I do not have time.
2. Is God not important to your life?
3. I meant to say my prayers but friends asked me out.
4. If you wanted, you could do both.
1. I am not good at doing what God wants me to do. I like to go my own way.
2. God's will and God's way leads to life eternal.
3. I fell out with God because he did not do what I asked him to do!
4. Do you think God is for you to control?
1. Why bother?
2. If you do not know, you should find out.

Opening prayer

Lord God, you have created us for your glory
in doing your will.
Help us to be the people that you want us to be
and to do what you want us to do.
Your will be done in us as in heaven.
Amen.

Opening song

Jesus is Lord!

Readings

Exodus 3:1-15 or Jeremiah 15:15-21
Psalm 105:1-6, 23-26, 45b or Psalm 26:1-8
Romans 12:9-21
Matthew 16:21-28

Thought for the day

The Gospel follows on from last week when Peter confessed that Jesus is the Christ. This is certainly seen as a high moment and turning point in the first three Gospels. It is also a turning point in every life when we discover for ourselves that Jesus is the Christ and our Saviour. It is a very exciting and important moment. It is for this reason we need to be sure we get it as right as possible.

Jesus is pleased with the answer of Peter. He can now build on this. On this awareness of him there is hope for the future. But there are dangers. There are so many false ideas of the Christ. Even now some wanted Jesus to become their king and drive out the Roman army. This danger would arise again when he entered Jerusalem. With all the joy of recognition, Jesus had to prepare the disciples for what lay ahead. Jesus told them how he must return to Jerusalem and the conflict. He warned them that he would be taken and killed. He even spoke of the resurrection.

The reaction of Peter must have been the same for all the disciples. They did not want this to happen. It would be better for them to stay where they were. Jesus being human must have been tempted: he did not look forward to conflict and death. But Jesus also knew it was for this he came. Only this way could he reveal the deep love of God. For a moment he sees Peter as the Tempter and says, 'Get behind me, Satan.' Peter's target is too low; it is not seeking the will of God but rather the saving of his skin. We can have great sympathy with Peter. He wanted to protect his friend from any troubles. Sadly, in the desire to protect us our friends sometimes prevent us doing what God asks of us.

Jesus then had to tell them clearly of what lay ahead and that this involved the denial of themselves and the taking up of the cross. They could escape this but it was those who laid down their lives for the sake of Christ who would enter into life. Jesus gave them something very hard to think about when he said, 'For what will it profit them if they gain the whole world but forfeit their life? Or what will they give in return for their life?' (Matthew 16:26) This is a question we should ask of ourselves!

Question time

Are we sure we have a God we seek to obey rather than one we want to do as we ask?

How much of our prayer is 'my will be done' and how much 'your will be done'?

Illustration

When the devil cannot get at us directly he will seek to lead us astray by our friends. It is sad how many people are led astray by friends and family. Sometimes our loved ones are only seeking to protect us but in so doing they stop us risking for God.

Columbanus was born in Ireland about 540 AD. He was of noble birth, strong and intelligent and destined to be a ruler of people. Columbanus heard the call of God and decided to dedicate his life to God in a monastery. His poor mother was heartbroken. He could have such a wonderful career and he was hardly ready to leave home. She tried to stop him, at first holding on to him and then lying down across the doorway sobbing. It was very difficult for Columbanus but he had set his sights on serving God. He stepped purposefully over his mother and set out for the monastery. If he had stayed at home, we would never have heard of him, but in time he became one of the greatest missionaries and teachers in Europe.

Intercessions

Blessed are you, Lord our God,
for in your Son you have come among us
and shared in our humanity,
that we may come to you
and share in your divinity.
You have given us a wonderful Saviour
and revealed the depth of your love.
Blessed are you, Father, Son and Holy Spirit.

Lord God, we seek to do your will,
that your Church may be the instrument
of your peace and salvation.
We ask your blessing upon all who go out in mission
and all who proclaim the Good News.
We remember especially
any who risk their lives or well being
for the sake of doing your will.
We pray for all who seek to dedicate their lives
to you and your glory.

Silence

Lord, your will be done
on earth as in heaven.

Lord God, may your will be done
on earth as it is in heaven.
We ask your blessing upon all
who strive to bring healing and wholeness
to peoples and nations.
We pray for peacekeeping forces
and all who endeavour to maintain law and order.
We pray for the United Nations
and for our queen and government.

Silence

Lord, your will be done
on earth as in heaven.

Lord God, may we reveal your will in our homes
by living together in love and peace.
We ask your blessing upon our loved ones and friends.
May we encourage one another to do your will.
We pray for all who suffer from bad housing
or live in areas of deprivation.
We ask your blessing
upon all who seek to relieve the needs of the poor.

Silence

Lord, your will be done
on earth as in heaven.

Lord God, we pray today for all who are suffering
from strained or broken relationships.
We remember all who are a bad influence
and lead others astray.
We pray for all caught up in drugs or vice.
May they be given the chance of new directions.
We pray for friends and loved ones who are ill
or in trouble.

Silence

Lord, your will be done
on earth as in heaven.

Lord God, we give thanks for our salvation
through Jesus Christ our Saviour.
Bless your saints and our loved ones departed
with the joy of your presence
and the fullness of life eternal.

Silence

Merciful Father,
**accept these prayers
for the sake of your Son,
our Saviour Jesus Christ.
Amen.**

Memory verse

Then Jesus told his disciples, 'If any want to become my followers, let them deny themselves and take up their cross and follow me.'
Matthew 16:24

Suggested music

Take up thy cross
The head that once was crowned with thorns
Thy way, not mine, O Lord

CANDLES

Aim

To show how we are to try and do what God wants us to do.

Teaching

Johnny was told not to play on the old bridge because it was too dangerous. But he did not listen. He went and played there. The bridge broke and he fell in the water. He was very lucky there was someone to rescue him. He had done wrong and suffered for it. He wished he had done what he was told.

Jenny had promised to do some jobs at home. A friend called and told her not to bother and they went out. The friend made Jenny break her promise. It would get Jenny into trouble when she got back home. She had not done what she promised.

God wants us to be kind and generous. He does not want us to be greedy or selfish. But we do not always do what God wants us to do. He wants us to be his friend and to pray to him – but sometimes we do not bother. God still loves us and wants us to be his friend.

Jesus was ready to do everything the Father God wanted him to do. He wanted to show how God loves everyone and wants us to love each other. He wanted us to see how God cares for anyone who is ill or suffering and would like us also to care. Jesus knew that some people were trying to kill him. If he went back to Jerusalem, they would capture him. Still, he wanted to go back there and tell of God's love. He wanted to do what God wanted him to do. Peter loved Jesus and did not want him to get caught or to suffer, so he told him not to go. But Jesus knew he had to. He had to show he would do all God wanted him to do.

Though wicked men tried to stop Jesus, because he did all that God wanted they could not. They killed Jesus (ask the children if they know how). But they could not stop Jesus doing what God wanted. Jesus rose again from the dead. He is alive and wants to help us to do what God wants us to do.

Activity

Play 'Simon/Susan says'. This is to get the children to listen and obey. They must not do things unless Simon/Susan says. Congratulate them every time they get it right.

Prayer

God, thank you for making us
and giving us this wonderful world.
Help us to look after the world
and do what you would like us to do.
Amen.

Song

Jesus' love is very wonderful

LAMPS

Aim

To show how Jesus seeks to do God's will.

Teaching

Roger was good with the ball but not a good footballer. He would not listen to the coach or the manager. He tended to keep the ball to himself and did not pass. He was dropped from the team.

In the army obedience is important because lives depend on it. If a command is given, it has to be obeyed immediately as the smooth running of the whole group will rely on it. It is for everyone's safety that they learn to obey. (Can the group suggest other times when obedience is important?)

Jesus came to do the Father's will and, through his obedience, win our salvation. Jesus is God's 'Chosen One', his appointed one. He came to triumph over evil by doing what God wanted him to do. Early in his work Jesus spent 40 days in the wilderness working out how to serve God and do his work.

Now there were people trying to stop Jesus. He left the Jerusalem area because some people wanted to kill him. Away from the danger, he spent time at Caesarea Philippi. He was preparing his disciples for what lay ahead. Peter had said the disciples believed that Jesus is the Chosen One, God's Anointed. Can you remember the word for the Chosen One? It is the Christ. Jesus praised and blessed Peter for being able to see this.

Now, almost straight after that, Jesus told the disciples that they must go back to Jerusalem. Jesus knew he would be taken prisoner there and killed. Peter, because he cared for Jesus, did not want this and told Jesus to avoid it. Now Jesus told Peter off. He saw that Peter was being used to tempt him to fail to do what God

wanted him to do. Sometimes our friends can tempt us to do things we know we should not do. Jesus came to do God's will and win people back to God. He would do this through what happened in Jerusalem. (At this stage let the group tell of the events of the crucifixion and resurrection.) Jesus did God's will and so triumphed over temptation and evil and won for us all a great victory. (Encourage the group to explore what that victory might be.)

Activity

Blindfold a person and ask someone else to guide them around a small group of obstacles by voice only. Show how clear directions have to be given and how the person who cannot see must obey. You can have imaginary pitfalls like shark-infested rivers and steep cliffs. Always be near to see the blindfolded person does not get into any real trouble.

Prayer

Lord God, help us to be faithful to you
and to do what you want us to do.
Help us to fight temptation
and to seek to do your will.
This will make us better disciples of Jesus
and help us to work for you.
Amen.

Song

What a wonderful Saviour is Jesus

TORCHES

Aim

To show that, like Jesus, we are called to resist temptation and seek to do the will of God.

Teaching

Disciples of Jesus learn from him and try to do what he wants them to do. Because Jesus came to do the will of God, this is what he wants the disciples to do. This is not easy and often disciples are tempted and led astray. All humans are tempted; even Jesus was tempted. Do you remember how he spent 40 days in the wilderness fighting against temptation? All this time he was seeking to do what God wanted him to do.

When people are strong and stand against evil there is always another way of tempting them and that is through friends. We all know this: friends can encourage us to do wrong things. This is the way many are led away and into trouble. A lot of people who get into deep trouble look back in sadness because it was a friend who led them down the wrong way.

Peter had spoken on behalf of the disciples when he said Jesus is the Christ, the Chosen One of God. But the disciples were only beginning to learn what it really meant. When Jesus told them that he was to go back to Jerusalem and to likely death, Peter objected. Could Jesus not avoid this by keeping out of Jerusalem? It was because Peter cared that he said this. He did not want Jesus to suffer or to be captured. Peter did not realise that Jesus had to go to Jerusalem if God's love for us all was to be fully revealed.

Jesus saw that his friend was tempting him to turn away from what God wanted him to do, and he spoke very strongly to Peter. It would be very easy to accept Peter's advice. But if Jesus did so, he would fail to do what God asked of him.

Read Matthew 16:21-23.

The disciples at this stage could not understand what Jesus was saying about his death and resurrection. They would only really know after the events themselves. It must have been very hard for them.

Jesus then warned them that their lives would not be easy. Surely if the leader was persecuted, people would also seek to persecute the disciples. Jesus was warning them but also asking them to remain faithful to him and to the Father. Being a Christian is not easy; there is always a battle against evil and temptation. But with the help of Jesus, even if we lose a few battles, the victory is ours. Read Matthew 16:24-28. Discuss the meaning of verse 26.

Activity

Ask the group to create or choose road signs about the dangers of temptation. If there is time, a good discussion could arise about why they created certain signs. If they need help with suggestions for signs they could look at these: ONE WAY ONLY, STOP, GIVE WAY TO THE RIGHT, DANGER AHEAD, KEEP WITHIN THE LIMITS, DEAD END, NO U-TURNS, NO ENTRANCE.

Prayer

Lord Jesus,
you gave your life in obedience to the Father
that we might live in the fullness of your kingdom.
Keep us faithful and true to you
and help us to resist all temptation.
Amen.

Song

Jesus is the name we worship

Proper 18

Aim

To look at forgiveness and the presence of Jesus.

Preparation

In the entrance have a crucifix surrounded by flowers and the words, 'Father, forgive them; for they do not know what they are doing'.

Opening activity

In the quiet of this church the Lord is here.
His Spirit is with us.
In our meeting together the Lord is here.
His Spirit is with us.
In the heart of each of us the Lord is here.
His Spirit is with us.
When it is dark the Lord is here.
His Spirit is with us.
When we are troubled the Lord is here.
His Spirit is with us.
When we feel afraid the Lord is here.
His Spirit is with us.
When we reach out in forgiveness the Lord is here.
His Spirit is with us.
When we celebrate with joy the Lord is here.
His Spirit is with us.

Opening prayer

Lord, you are always with us.
Though we are not worthy
you give us of yourself
and you forgive all who are penitent.
Teach us to forgive others
as you have forgiven us
and to be generous in all our dealings.
Amen.

Opening song

The King is among us

Readings

Exodus 12:1-14 or Ezekiel 33:7-11
Psalm 149 or Psalm 119:33-40
Romans 13:8-14
Matthew 18:15-20

Thought for the day

Today's Gospel is a difficult reading in that it does not sound like Jesus: it is more like statements from a committee! Jesus could not have said it in its present form because the Church did not as yet exist and the passage assumes an organised Church. It suggests that Gentiles and tax collectors are outcasts, but this was not the way of Jesus who was known as a friend of tax collectors and sinners. There is a danger: there are limits set on forgiveness. Next week's Gospel on forgiveness (Matthew 18:21-35) seems to be in contrast with the statement here. Much seems to have been lost in translation from the words of Jesus to these statements.

At its simplest, it is about the breakdown of relationships and their rebuilding. Here the advice is relatively simple.

Speak about your hurt or grievance rather than let the resentment or anger simmer until it boils over. Those who do not speak about anger often go around like unexploded bombs.

Meet up and talk it out. See if you can come to some sort of agreement.

If this fails, get help from friends.

If this still fails, try and deal with it within the community. There is a feeling that litigation and any legal proceedings only spell trouble. What underlies it all is that we are to seek to love and to forgive and that we are in the presence of God. Our God is always ready to help but we cannot ask God to heal broken relationships if we have made no effort ourselves. This is true of every request in prayer. God will work with us but not instead of us.

The passage ends with Jesus saying, 'Where two or three are gathered in my name, I am there among them' (Matthew 18:20). When we meet as the Church we need to spend time rejoicing in the presence and in the peace of our Lord. We do not come for sermons or hymns, good as they may be, but to rejoice that the Lord is here, that his Spirit is with us. Whenever we meet up and share with others we need to rejoice that the Lord is with us: he is in our homes, our schools and in all places. We can turn to the Lord whenever we want and he is there to help and protect us.

Question time

Do who show how we are forgiven by our attitude of forgiveness?

How do you rejoice in the presence of Jesus?

Illustration

In the story *Great Expectations* by Charles Dickens, Pip has dealt badly with Joe the blacksmith who cared for him in his early days. When Pip is ill and in debt, Joe comes to care for him. Joe stayed by him, gave him cooling drinks.

> At last, one day, I took courage, and said, 'Is it Joe?'
> And the dear old home-voice answered, 'Which it air, old chap.'
> 'Oh Joe, you break my heart! Look angry at me, Joe! Strike me, Joe! Tell me of my ingratitude. Don't be so good to me.'
> For Joe had actually laid his head down on the pillow at my side and put his arm around my neck, in his joy that I knew him.
> 'Which dear old Pip, old chap,' said Joe, 'you and me was ever friends. And when you are well enough to go out for a ride – what larks!'

After which Joe withdrew to the window and stood with his back towards me, wiping his eyes. And as my extreme weakness prevented me going to him, I lay there penitently whispering, 'O God bless him! God bless this gentle Christian man!'

Intercessions

Blessed are you, Lord our God,
for you accept us in our sin,
you forgive all who are penitent
and give us the opportunity of newness of life.
Blessed are you, Father, Son and Holy Spirit.

Loving and forgiving God,
we rejoice in your presence
and we remember before you
all who seek to build up your Church in love.
We ask your blessing upon all who are being prepared
for baptism or confirmation.
We pray for all who seek forgiveness
and want to start afresh.

Silence

Forgiving God,
hear us and help us.

Loving and forgiving God,
we remember in your presence
all who work for reconciliation
between peoples and nations.
We pray for all who seek to heal old hurts
and historical grievances.
Bless all peacemakers
and all who work to bring unity and understanding
within communities.
We pray for the work of the United Nations
and all who seek to bring justice and fair dealings
to our world.

Silence

Forgiving God,
hear us and help us.

Loving and forgiving God,
may our homes reflect your love.
Forgive our petty divisions and jealousies,
our quarrelling and our anger.
Lord, through our homes and loved ones
teach us forgiveness, tolerance and compassion.
May our homes and our community
be seen as caring and loving.

Silence

Forgiving God,
hear us and help us.

Loving and forgiving God,
we remember in your presence
all whose lives are spoiled by hatred
and the desire for revenge.
We pray for all who feel they cannot be forgiven
and who cannot forgive.
We ask your blessing
upon all who are troubled in mind or spirit
and all who are tempted to give up hope.

Silence

Forgiving God,
hear us and help us.

Loving and forgiving God, we give thanks
that we are ransomed, healed, forgiven.
We ask your blessing
upon our friends and loved ones departed,
that knowing your forgiveness
they may rejoice in your love.

Silence

Merciful Father,
**accept these prayers
for the sake of your Son,
our Saviour Jesus Christ.
Amen.**

Memory verse

Where two or three are gathered in my name, I am there among them.
Matthew 18:20

Suggested music

Lord, the light of your love (*Shine, Jesus, shine*)
Christ be with me
Jesus, where'er thy people meet

CANDLES

Aim

To tell the story of St Patrick and the presence of Jesus.

Teaching

Patrick wanted to tell the people of Ireland about the light of Christ. He knew that they needed to know all about Jesus. But he also knew that if the king of Tara was against him, then he would not be able to do much good. He would have to bring the light of Jesus to the king of Tara.

It was nearly Easter and Patrick decided to wait until it was dark and then light a big bonfire. He knew that at this time no one was allowed to light a fire except the king. But he would light one for Jesus who is alive and with us always. He lit a wonderfully big fire and you could see it for miles around.

The king was very angry and asked who was lighting a big fire. He was told it was Patrick and Patrick had done it because he believed in Jesus. Someone said to the king, 'If you do not stop it now, it will spread. Soon all the people will become followers of Jesus.' The king decided to send out an army to stop Patrick and to kill him. Soon an army of soldiers with swords and spears had surrounded where Patrick was. He could not hide because he had lit the big fire to say Jesus is alive. The soldiers were sure they would capture Patrick. But Patrick believed that Jesus Christ was with him in the dark and would help him. He said a prayer to Jesus Christ and asked him to protect him. He said:

Christ be with me: Christ within me,
Christ behind me, Christ before me,
Christ beside me, Christ to win me,
Christ to comfort and restore me;
Christ beneath me, Christ above me,
Christ in quiet, Christ in danger,
Christ is hearts of all that love me,
Christ in mouth of friend and stranger.

Patrick knew that Jesus Christ was with him and ready to help him. Now he went towards the king's palace and no one stopped him. In fact, they said that they did not see him. The king could not understand how he got to the palace but was so surprised that he asked Patrick to tell him about Jesus and to tell the people about Jesus. So Patrick helped the people of Ireland to know that Jesus loves them and is with them.

Activity

Let the children act this story out. Encourage them to say that Jesus is with them to protect them. Let them use the prayer that follows.

Prayer

Jesus is here.
Jesus is with me.
Jesus goes with me
Jesus is around me.
Jesus cares for me.
Jesus protects me.

Song

Sing the last verse of 'Away in a manger'

LAMPS

Aim

To show how Jesus Christ is always with us.

Teaching

More than 1600 years ago Ninian lived on the edge of the Roman Empire just beyond Hadrian's Wall. He is one of the first people we know of by name as a Christian in the British Isles. He had a church and a place of teaching built at Whithorn, which means the 'White House', and from there sent out people to tell others of Jesus.

In his travels Ninian used a special kind of prayer to remind him that Jesus was with him and that Jesus protected him. This sort of prayer was called a 'Caim', which means 'encircling'. Encircling prayers did not make Jesus come because he is already there, but they did *remind* Ninian that Jesus is always there. Sometimes Ninian would walk around where he was staying in a circle to remind him that God was all about him. At other times Ninian would raise his right hand as if pointing and then turn around slowly until he had made a circle. This would remind him that he was not alone

and that Jesus was with him. When it was dark or when there was trouble, Ninian would say an encircling prayer to remind him that he was not alone. He would get new courage by remembering that Jesus was with him.

We are going to learn to say encircling prayers to remind us that Jesus is with us.

Activity

Stand up and raise your right hand as if pointing. Say. 'Christ before me.'

Without moving your body, stretch your hand to the right side and say, 'Christ on my right.'

Now turn to face the opposite way, still pointing, and say, 'Christ behind me.'

Without moving your body, stretch your right hand and say, 'Christ on my left.'

Face the front again and bend down and touch the ground, saying, 'Christ beneath me.'

Now stretch up as high as you can and say, 'Christ above me.'

Then last of all point to your heart and say, 'Christ within me.'

Practise this prayer two or three times and then ask the group to say it each day with the actions. Remind the group it is affirming the presence of Jesus. The prayer does not make Jesus come to us; it reminds us that he is with us. We can say the same prayer to God the Father or to the Holy Spirit. During the day we can remind ourselves of this prayer and of the presence of God by simply saying, 'Circle me, O God.'

Prayer

Christ before me.
Christ on my right.
Christ behind me.
Christ on my left.
Christ beneath me.
Christ above me.
Christ in my heart.
Christ in all who love me.

Song

Christ be beside me

TORCHES

Aim

To rejoice in the presence of Jesus.

Teaching

In the play *The Trial of Jesus* by John Masefield, after the death of Jesus, the Centurion who had seen him die was asked, 'Where is he now?' and he replies, 'Let loose in the world, lady.' This is something that the disciples and then all Christians experience through their faith in him: Jesus is let loose in all the world. This is what makes believers different from those that talk about theories of God: we relate to a living and present Lord. Jesus is not just a figure of the past; he is present and with us now. This is how we can begin a service by saying, 'The Lord is here: his Spirit is with us.'

When going about in Galilee, Jesus, like any human, was restricted by time and space. No one can be in two places at once. If Jesus was in Jerusalem, he could not be in Nazareth; if he was in Galilee, he could not be in Bethany. Mary and Martha complained that Lazarus would not have died if Jesus had been there to help. They thought his coming was too late. There must have been many people who would have liked to have met Jesus or been helped by Jesus but he was not near to where they were.

After Jesus had risen from the dead, he appeared to the disciples in the garden, in a room, on the road, by the sea and on a mountain. Slowly they began to realise that Jesus was with them wherever they went. There is a sense in which the Ascension freed Jesus from space and time. He could now be with all who call upon him, all who seek him. Think on these words from today's Gospel: 'Where two or three are gathered in my name, I am there with them' (Matthew 18:20). We can rejoice in his presence and know he is with us to help us and guide us. We should learn to talk about Jesus in the present tense, not how he was but how he is now. (Get the group to discuss this and then get them to be still and quietly rejoice in the presence of Jesus.)

Activity

Create an affirmation prayer which tells us that Jesus is with us. Let everyone say a sentence and follow it with the words, 'The Lord is here', to which everyone replies, 'His Spirit is with us'. Here are a few examples:

When we meet with each other . . .
When darkness surrounds us . . .
When we feel alone and sad . . .
In our times of rejoicing . . .
When we need forgiving . . .
In our school and in our recreation . . .

Prayer

Lord Jesus, you are here,
your Spirit is with us.
Help us to know you as a friend and companion
throughout our life.
May we rejoice in your presence
and in your peace
this day and every day.
Amen.

Song

Christ be near at either hand

Proper 19

Sunday between 11 and 17 September inclusive

Aim

To show there are no limits to God's love and forgiveness.

Preparation

Have an open Bible with lots of IOUs around it. Have a red cross crossing out each of the IOUs. Also have a large heart set in flowers with the words, 'You must forgive from your heart (Matthew 18:35).'

Opening activity

Four voices:

1. I cannot go to the Sports Centre – I have fallen out with George.
2. Sin separates; forgiveness can unite.
3. I have banned Sylvia from our team.
2. Sin separates; forgiveness can unite.
4. I cannot forgive Bill for what he did. I do not want to see him.
2. Sin separates; forgiveness can unite. Lord, may we forgive from our heart as you have forgiven us.

Opening prayer

Lord, we owe our lives to you.
You have given us this world to enjoy
and all that is in it.
Help us to live in love and harmony with each other
and to forgive as you have forgiven us.
Amen.

Opening song

Praise, my soul, the King of heaven

Readings

Exodus 14:19-31 or Genesis 50:15-21
Psalm 114 or Exodus 15:1b-11, 21b
or Psalm 103:(1-7) 8-13
Romans 14:1-12
Matthew 18:21-35

Thought for the day

Peter was a practical sort of man and to go around with Jesus was not always easy. Peter felt there was a need for what we would now call damage limitation. He felt generosity was important, but surely forgiveness needs to have some limits. The Jewish teaching was quite simple: if someone sins, forgive them, once, twice, three times, but after that enough is enough; a sinner must be made to face consequences. That is sensible enough. Peter saw that Jesus was going beyond this and asked how often he should forgive. Seven times? Surely this was as far as anyone should go; it was more than reasonable. Jesus refused to put a limit on forgiveness and suggested 70 x 7 – in other words, without limit. There can be no limit to love and forgiveness.

Jesus then told a story about two debtors with whom the king wished to settle accounts. One was brought owing ten thousand talents. This is an extraordinary amount of money – it was greater than a king's ransom. It was more money than the revenue from all of Samaria and Galilee put together. It was an amount no one could pay. Yet the king forgave him this debt out of mercy, out of care for his wife and children.

This man, forgiven such an enormous debt, then attacked a fellow slave who owed him a hundred denarii – the sort of money that could be carried easily in a pocket. He was not merciful; he had the slave put into prison for his debt. He was a hard man. He demanded what was his by rights.

Fellow slaves were distressed by this and reported it to the king. The king was very angry and had the unforgiving slave put in prison until he could pay the debt, which he would never be able to do.

This tells us of the danger of an unforgiving heart. The unforgiving heart is damning. Hatred, vengeance, resentment can all poison our lives. God cannot forgive the unforgiving. It seems forgiveness cannot be poured in if forgiveness is not given out. As we receive, so we must give. Forgiveness, like love, grows only by our giving it out. We cannot claim forgiveness if we are unwilling to forgive others. We must all pray the Lord's Prayer with caution when we say, 'Forgive us . . . as we forgive'.

Question time

We cannot easily forget but we have been asked to forgive. Do we show this by the way we live?

Have you learnt of the love of God through the way you are accepted by him and forgiven?

Illustration

When John Wesley was sailing to America he witnessed the keel-hauling of a member of the crew for an offence on board ship. This was a particularly cruel form of punishment as it meant being tied to a rope, thrown overboard, drawn under the vessel and out the other side. There was always the chance you would drown or perish in some other way. The captain said to John Wesley as they watched, 'You see, Mr Wesley, I never forgive.' It was not for John Wesley to question the captain's power of command but he could and did question that statement. He replied, 'Then, sir, I hope that you never sin!'

Intercessions

Blessed are you, Lord our God,
for you have revealed your love and forgiveness
through your Son Jesus Christ.
Through him we are ransomed, healed and forgiven.
As we have freely received,
may we freely give.
Blessed are you, Father, Son and Holy Spirit.

God of mercy, we come to you
for forgiveness and renewal.
We ask you to bless
all who are seeking to change their lives
and live to serve others and to glorify you.
Though we are unworthy
we seek your acceptance of us.
May your Church reveal your love
in its care for all who come to it.
We pray today for prison chaplains and clergy
who work in areas of crime and vice.

Silence

Lord, forgive our sins
and heal our infirmities.

God of mercy, we ask your blessing
upon the poor, hungry and homeless of the world,
and all migrant and displaced peoples.
We remember nations that are in great debt
and the work of the world banks and governments
to relieve this debt.
We pray for all who are bankrupt
and all who have lost the little that they had.
We bring before you
all who are fearful for their future.

Silence

Lord, forgive our sins
and heal our infirmities.

God of mercy, you have given to us richly;
may we richly give.
Let us not hoard or squander
the good things you have given us.
Let us help those in need
and use our gifts to your glory.
We ask your blessing upon our homes
and upon all who have enriched our lives
by their goodness and love.

Silence

Lord, forgive our sins
and heal our infirmities.

God of mercy, we pray
for all who have become hard-hearted,
all who are unable to forgive and all who seek revenge.
Through your love
may they find a change of attitude and heart.
We ask your blessing upon all who are abused,
all who are used as cheap labour
and all who do not receive a fair wage.
We bring before you friends and loved ones who are ill.

Silence

Lord, forgive our sins
and heal our infirmities.

God of mercy, we give thanks
for all who have witnessed to your love and generosity.
We rejoice in the fellowship of the saints.
We commend our loved ones departed,
this world and ourselves
to your unfailing love and mercy.

Silence

Merciful Father,
**accept these prayers
for the sake of your Son,
our Saviour Jesus Christ.
Amen.**

Memory verse

Forgive us our debts as we also have forgiven our debtors.
Matthew 6:12

Suggested music

Bless the Lord, O my soul
Great is thy faithfulness
I have a friend

CANDLES

Aim

To show Joseph forgiving his brothers.

Teaching

A long time ago in the land of Egypt there was a very important man called Joseph (let us say his name together). He was nearly as powerful as the king. When he was a boy, his ten naughty brothers had sold him to men who would sell him as a slave. Joseph was sad because he would not see his father or mother again. He was separated from his family. Joseph was a strong boy and worked hard. At last he worked for the king of Egypt and became the second most important man in the country after the king. He looked after the food supplies and the harvests of the fields. In seven good years he saved a lot of grain for making bread – enough to feed the country for a long time. Then came a time of famine, when things did not grow and people had no food and were hungry. Joseph now carefully shared out the food to the hungry people.

One day, who came to buy corn but ten men from where he once lived! Who do you think they were? Yes, they were his brothers who, a long time ago, had hurt him and sold him. They did not recognise Joseph because he had grown and was now rich and important. But Joseph knew who they were and remembered how they had been unkind to him. Do you think Joseph sent them away? Or do you think Joseph refused to give them anything because they had been unkind?

Well, Joseph still loved his brothers. He gave them food to eat and food to take home. He gave them their money back. But there was someone Joseph wanted to see because he had a little brother called Benjamin. He asked the brothers to go home and when they came again to bring Benjamin with them.

The next time they came they brought Benjamin with them. They still did not know that Joseph was their brother. Joseph was very happy and held a big party for them in his own house. He asked them about their father and found out that after all this time his father was still alive. Joseph was so happy that tears of joy ran down his face. Then Joseph told them who he was. What a surprise it was! But now they were scared and they wondered what Joseph would do to them. Joseph might now punish them and put them in prison. But Joseph loved them and was happy to see them. He told them how God had looked after him and now he would look after his brothers. Just like God loves us all the time, Joseph loved his brothers, even though they had been unkind to him.

Joseph sent his brothers home to get his father and to bring him to Egypt. Though his brothers had been unkind and done horrible things Joseph still loved them and forgave them. In the same way, God loves us and forgives us when we are sorry for being naughty or doing wrong things.

Activity

This is a good story for the children to act out. On the activity sheet there are illustrations to show the sequence of the story.

Prayer

God, we thank you
because you love us always.
We thank you for our homes and families
and all who love us.
Amen.

Song

God loves you

LAMPS

Aim

To show how God forgives and wants us to forgive.

Teaching

Have you ever borrowed anything – a book, money, a pen? Did you remember to give it back? Sometimes people cannot pay back what they have borrowed and it becomes difficult.

Peter asked Jesus about forgiveness and wanted to know how many times he should forgive. The church people taught that we should forgive three times; Peter thought seven times would be a lot. Jesus said, no, not seven times but 70 x 7. Does anyone know how many times that is? 490! But Jesus did not really mean 490 times; he meant we are *always* to forgive from our hearts.

Jesus told a story about a king and two slaves. The first slave owed the king more than £10 million – probably more money than all our families put together could ever pay if they gave all their money. The slave could not possibly pay, so the king was ready to put him in prison along with his wife and children until he paid. But that would be for ever. The slave would never be out of the king's debt. But the king was a loving king and he felt sorry for the slave and his family, so he told him he would forgive him his debt. He did not have to

pay back the £10 million. It was amazing. The slave could not believe it: he had been forgiven and could go free.

When the slave went out he met a very poor slave who owed him a few pounds, quite a small amount of money. He took the slave by the throat and demanded his money. When the man could not pay, he had him cast into prison. He was not kind and loving like the king. He had a hard heart and took no notice of the slave's cries.

The fellow slaves were sad at this. Because the king had forgiven him, should he not have been kind to the other slave? He was forgiven a great big amount and now he demanded a small amount. The fellow slaves told the king and he was not happy. The slave had received so much from him; should he not also be kind? 'If that is the way you live, it is the way I will have to treat you,' the king told him. The king had the slave put in prison and he would not get back out until he paid what he owed, if he ever could.

Jesus reminds us that God wants us to be loving and forgiving. It is not easy, but this is what God would like us to do.

Activity

This is a good story to act out. It is important for them to realise forgiveness and love can only be poured in if we pour it out again. You can illustrate this by having a cup full to the brim and saying it needs some milk added. It is only possible if some is poured out. There is an opportunity on the activity sheet to make forgiving hearts.

Prayer

Father, we thank you for your love for us
and for giving us life.
We thank you for all who love us
and care for us
even when we do wrong.
Help us to be loving and caring
and to forgive from our hearts
those who have upset or hurt us.
Amen.

Song

O Lord, all the world belongs to you

TORCHES

Aim

To look at Jesus' teaching on forgiveness.

Teaching

In the Lord's Prayer, which Jesus gave us, what does Jesus ask us to pray concerning forgiveness? 'Forgive us . . . as we forgive.' Can you say such a prayer and then still think, 'just wait till I get out of here, I will get so-and-so for what she has done'?

Jesus practised what he preached. From the cross he looked down on his murderers and prayed, 'Father forgive them; for they do not know what they are doing' (Luke 23:34).

There are three ways in which we can deal with those who wrong us, and they all begin with the letter 'R': Revenge, Retaliation and Reconciliation.

Revenge is often given with interest – 'I will make her suffer for that.' Not only do we make them pay but we also make them pay dearly. In Corsica in the last century several villages were destroyed in a vendetta over a minor issue. Revenge sets out to be destructive. No one who seeks revenge can pray, 'Forgive us . . . as we forgive others'. Our vengeance can harm us in the same way a bee injures itself when it stings and leaves the sting.

Retaliation is more controlled: it is where we seek like for like and no more. It is what the Scriptures call 'an eye for an eye and a tooth for a tooth' (Exodus 21:24) and it was often taken quite literally. This is the way of justice and law courts and is represented by balance scales in the hand of statues of justice. This can be seen as the right way, the way of the righteous. But it is not the way of Jesus. How many dare ask God to treat us with justice? If we get what we deserve, it may prove to be not very good. But our God is a God of love. Jesus teaches us to forgive as we are forgiven.

Reconciliation is the way left to us. As sin divides, reconciliation seeks to bring us back together to be at one. This is the way of love and forgiveness. Surely there must be a limit to this. You cannot go on forgiving for ever. Peter was a sensible sort of person and asked Jesus about forgiveness. Read Matthew 18:21-35.

The Jewish teachers suggest forgiving someone three times. Peter suggested seven times was more than generous and further than many of us would like to go. Jesus in his reply – 70 x 7 – did not mean 490 times but rather that forgiveness should not have set limits.

Look at the parable. One slave owed the king more than the revenue of Galilee and Samaria put together. It was an impossible amount and could never be repaid. But the slave is forgiven. The same slave went out and found a fellow slave who owed him a few pounds and demanded the money. He would not let him off the debt, small as it was. He demanded his rights. Others were shocked at this and reported it to the king. The king was angry and had the man he had forgiven put into prison until he could pay. It would appear forgiveness is conditional: it is about our attitude and our ability to forgive. Look at the last verse and discuss how difficult it is (Matthew 18:35).

Activity

Get the group to sit in a circle and each have a heart-shaped piece of paper. Ask them to sit quietly for a minute and think of someone they have not forgiven. Let them think of that person and try to forgive them. As they do so, they place the heart in the centre of the circle.

Prayer

Lord God, help us not to be overcome with evil
but to overcome evil with good.
May we be known as loving and forgiving people,
people with a kind heart and a generous spirit.
Amen.

Song

Amazing grace

Proper 20

Sunday between 18 and 24 September inclusive

Aim

To show how caring and generous God is.

Preparation

Have posters in the church porch showing the hungry seeking food, unemployed people and refugees. Have the words, 'Just as you did not do it to one of the least of these, you did not do it to me'(Matthew 25:45).

Opening activity

Invite anyone from the congregation to come forward and say, 'Thank you, God, for . . .' and then mention one thing they want to give thanks for.

Opening prayer

Blessed are you, Lord God of all creation,
for all things come from you.
You give us life and love;
you give us the beauty and bounty of the earth.
May we respond in love to you
and in respect for your creation
this day and always.
Amen.

Opening song

Guide me, O thou great Redeemer

Readings

Exodus 16:2-15 or Jonah 3:10–4:11
Psalm 105:1-6, 37-45 or Psalm145:1-8
Philippians 1:21-30
Matthew 20:1-16

Thought for the day

The parable about the labourers in the vineyard is really more about the owner and employer than the labourers. It would be better to call it the parable of the generous employer. The Jews were used to such stories for they had many featuring a beloved father, *abba*, and a beloved son, *amon*, all relating to work in the vineyard. The vineyard is often used as a symbol of the people of God (see Isaiah 5:7).

Each time the owner goes out he finds workers idle in the market place – 'early', 'about nine o'clock', 'about noon', 'about three o'clock', and 'about five o'clock'. These are people thrown out of work by economic conditions. This is still a familiar sight – day-workers and immigrants waiting for someone to give them a day's employment. Usually they are paid below the 'going rate'.

At the end of the day all the labourers are given a normal day's wage. This is in keeping with the Torah, which said, 'You shall not keep for yourself the wages of a labourer until the morning'(Leviticus 19:13). Simply because they are so poor they need this money to survive.

That all are given the same rate would bring many a union worker forward to object. But no one is underpaid. The ones who worked the longest get a fair wage. The owner could have given the others less but he is generous towards all of them. This parable tells us about God's grace and generosity and how he gives bountifully to all. If we received from God what we deserved, most of us would be in a sorry state, but God is generous in giving himself and his love to us. Our relationship with God is not about rights and rewards but about grace and generosity on the part of God. There is a great lesson here to a society that is always chasing after its 'rights'. We need a fair and just society but rights alone are not enough; we need grace and generosity or life becomes tough and the survival of the fittest.

The parable expressed something about the care of Jesus for the marginalised and outcasts of society.

Question time

Does our church show a care for the marginalised in our society?

How do you respond to God for all that he has done for you and given you?

Illustration

Theo kept strange accounts. He gave equally and generously to all who worked for him. He did not count one worth more than another. All who were willing and able to work were given a whole day's pay whether they had been asked to work all day or only for an hour. It was the same with his relationships: he cared for all equally. Some thought that they clocked up a bigger balance for reward and expected to receive more. But Theo loved all equally. Some grumbled about this but in truth they were trying to buy his love and affection when it is freely given to all. There are always people who grumble. The only people Theo could not help were those who chose to turn away from him. Even these he gladly would give to if they allowed him to. Theo kept strange accounts.

Intercessions

Blessed are you, Lord our God,
for you have given us a good earth
and a wonderful life.
May we use the resources of the earth aright
to respect all of creation,
relieve the needs of the poor
and give you glory.
Blessed are you, Father, Son and Holy Spirit.

Creating and loving God,
we thank you for the beauty and balance of our world.
We give glory to you
for the mystery and wonders of creation.
May your Church help to witness
that the world belongs to you.

We pray for all who seek to proclaim the Good News in areas of deprivation or opposition.
We ask your blessing upon all who preach the word and all who do so by their example.

Silence

Gracious God, in your goodness,
hear us and help us.

Creating and loving God,
we ask you to bless with wisdom
all who are employers
and all who direct multinational companies.
May they not abuse or treat their workforce with injustice.
We pray for all who seek to bring about fair trade.
We remember also all who are unemployed
or do not have enough resources for healthy living.

Silence

Gracious God, in your goodness,
hear us and help us.

Creating and loving God,
we thank you for our homes and loved ones.
Help us to respect all who work
to supply us with our needs.
We pray for all who work
in the farming and retail industries.
May we always be aware that all good comes from you.
We ask your blessing upon all who are homeless
and all who feel they are not loved.

Silence

Gracious God, in your goodness,
hear us and help us.

Creating and loving God,
we remember all ill and suffering people.
We pray for those who are struggling to survive
and all who are oppressed
by war, violence and tyranny.
We ask your blessing upon all who have been injured
or who have suffered from acts of violence.

Silence

Gracious God, in your goodness,
hear us and help us.

Creating and loving God,
you give us all that we have
and you offer us life eternal.
We rejoice in the fellowship of all your saints
and we commend our loved ones departed,
the whole of your creation and ourselves
to your unfailing love.

Silence

Merciful Father,
accept these prayers
for the sake of your Son,
our Saviour Jesus Christ.
Amen.

Memory verse

Every day I will bless you and praise your name for ever and ever.
Psalm 145:2

Suggested music

God of life, God of love
Lord, today your voice is calling
Christ is the world's true light

CANDLES

Aim

To tell how Jonah obeyed God.

Activity

Let's play a game about listening. I want you to do what I tell you. (Give commands like 'stand up', 'sit down', etc.) You are very good at listening and doing what you are told. Now I want you to pretend you cannot hear me. Cover up your ears and do not do what I ask. (Give a few more commands and see if they understand what you mean.) Now I want you to pretend I am not here. Close your eyes so that you cannot see me. You cannot see me but I can see you because my eyes are open and I am looking. (We cannot see God but God can see us and knows where we are.)

Teaching

Today I want to tell you about a man who pretended he could not hear God. He is called Jonah. Let us say his name together.

God called to Jonah and said, 'Jonah, I want you to go to Nineveh, a very big city a long way away. I have a message for the people of Nineveh.' It was a long journey and Jonah did not like the people of Nineveh so he went the opposite way. He pretended he did not hear God. He did not want to listen to God or do what God wanted.

Jonah went on a ship to get away from God. He did not know that God was still there with him. God loved Jonah and cared for him, even when he ran away. God sent a great wind that rocked the ship and the sailors were afraid. They woke Jonah up and asked him to speak to God and help them. Jonah began to feel sorry that he had run away from God. He told the sailors it was his fault the sea was so stormy. He said to the sailors, 'Throw me into the sea and it will become calm.' The sailors really did not want to but they did what Jonah asked and the sea became still.

Jonah went down and down into the sea. But even in the sea God was there caring for him. God sent a great big fish and it swallowed Jonah. For three days and nights Jonah was in the dark in the fish's tummy. Jonah was now sorry he had not done what God wanted and he told God he was sorry. The big fish coughed Jonah up on to the seashore.

Now God called Jonah again. Once more he asked him to go to Nineveh. God showed Jonah how he loved the people of Nineveh and all the animals. God wanted the people to know he loved them and he wanted Jonah to tell them. This time Jonah went. And he did what God wanted him to do.

Prayer

For the world you have made
thank you, God.
For the sky, the earth and the sea
thank you, God.
For fish and birds and animals
thank you, God.
For people in every land
thank you, God.
For making us and loving us all
thank you, God.

Song

God who made the earth

LAMPS

Aim

To show how God is generous and gives to all.

Activity

Get the children to imagine they are in a vineyard. Tell them how warm it is, and how the vines are growing and the grapes are beginning to show. Sing this song to the tune of 'Here we go round the mulberry bush':

This is the way we grow the vines,
grow the vines, grow the vines.
This is the way we grow the vines
early in the morning.

This is the way we water the vines . . .

This is the way we pick the grapes . . .

This is the way we tread the grapes . . .

This is the way we make the wine . . .

Teaching

Jesus told a story about some workers in a vineyard. He wanted people to know how generous God is and how God cares for people.

The owner of a vineyard wanted his grapes harvested. This meant hiring people to pick the grapes. He went to the market place early in the morning at 6 o'clock and already there were men queuing for work. He took some men to help and promised to give them pay for a day's work. Then at 9 o'clock he went out and got some more men to join those who had already worked for three hours. At 12 o'clock he got some more men to help. Now some had already worked for six hours and some had worked for three. At 3 o'clock he went out and got more men to help those who had worked for nine, six and three hours. By 5 o'clock the owner decided

if they were to finish the work by 6 o'clock, he still needed more helpers. So he went and got some more men. They all worked until 6 o'clock. Who can tell me how long the last people worked and how long the first people worked? All the time the first people had been working the others were still waiting, hoping they might get work. They wanted to work but no one had asked them. It was not their fault that the last ones had only worked one hour while others had worked all day. They had wanted to work.

At the end of the day the owner came to pay the workmen. Those who had worked all day were happy because they would get a full day's money. The owner was a generous man and was happy that the work had been done. People had done what he had asked. Some had waited a long time until they were asked but they had come when asked. Then he gave the ones who worked one hour a whole day's pay: the same as those who worked three hours, six hours, nine hours and twelve hours. The ones who had worked the longest grumbled and complained to the owner. But he had given them what he had promised. He had not cheated them. With the others he had been generous and kind. Could they really complain because he had been generous? (Let the children talk about this. This is an issue about generosity but it does include acting fairly.)

God is generous in all that he gives us. He gives us life. He gives us this world. He gives us all that we have. Let us learn to say 'thank you' to him each day.

Prayer

For the world in which we live
thank you, God.
For all we are able to do
thank you, God.
For all who provide us with food
thank you, God.
For all who love us
thank you, God.
For your love and generosity
thank you, God.

Song

God, whose farm is all creation

TORCHES

Aim

To explore the generosity of God.

Teaching

Today's parable is told in reply to Peter who pointed out how much they had given up for Jesus and asked, 'What are we to get?' Jesus wants willing service given out of love and the joy of doing it. It is worth noting that all of our work – indeed, all of our life – is affected by the spirit in which we do everything.

Those who listened would understand this parable well: some would own vineyards, others would have worked in them; some were employers and some used to queuing for employment. It must be remembered that no employment equals no money and no way to look after your family. Unemployment is a hard thing to bear, especially if there are a few mouths to feed.

The listeners were aware that often the Church, or the people of Israel, are compared to a vine or a vineyard.

At 6 o'clock in the morning the queue for work is already long. Men are desperate to be used. Some are chosen and the owner of the vineyard agrees to give them a fair wage for harvesting the grapes. Others hang around, already anxious that they are missing out. They want to work. Three hours later the owner comes again, and again at noon. Still some are left who want work. He comes again at 3 o'clock. By late in the day the owner knows he needs more harvesters to get his crop in. The gathering of grapes at the right time is crucial. So he goes out at 5pm and asks others to come and work for the last hour. This way the harvest is gathered. The last men worked only one hour and some had worked all day for twelve whole hours. It was no fault of their own that the last had been idle: when asked, they came willingly. Now it was time for them to be paid. The ones who came last were given a whole day's pay, and they were so relieved and grateful. Because of this the ones who had worked all day thought they would receive more because they had worked a lot longer. But the owner gave them the same – exactly what he had agreed with them. They were paid fairly. But they grumbled and murmured about the owner. They thought they should have had more. They did not deserve more: they got what was fair. They were complaining about the generosity of the owner to the latecomers. They had no right to complain but they did.

Activity

Get the group to act out the parable.

Discuss what the parable tells us about the generosity and love of God. See if the group can also relate it to ideas of work for the love of doing it and working for reward only. In all this it is important to know that love and generosity cannot be bought.

Prayer

Lord God,
you are a generous and loving God,
giving us more than we deserve.
You are full of compassion,
slow to anger and of great kindness.
Help us to work for you
and to do your will out of love and joy.
Amen.

Song

God is love: his the care

Proper 21

Sunday between 25 September and 1 October inclusive

Aim

To look at making choices and practising what we profess.

Preparation

Have a crucifix with flowers around it in the porch. Underneath have the words, 'He became obedient to the point of death – even death on a cross.' You may like to add on a poster, 'Sin separates us from God; loving obedience brings us back'.

Opening activity

Pose these questions, asking for a show of hands:

> Who has promised to believe in God?
> Who has promised to do his will?
> Who has failed in their promise?
> Who has promised to pray every day?
> Who has not done this?

By disobedience, we separate ourselves from God, his grace and goodness. Through his loving obedience, Jesus seeks to bring us back.

Opening prayer

God our Father,
you have called us to know you,
to love you and to serve you.
Through the obedience of your Son,
you have opened to us the kingdom of heaven.
May we learn to obey you
whose service is perfect freedom.
Amen.

Opening song

God is here! As we his people

Readings

Exodus 17:1-7 or Ezekiel 18:1-4, 25-32
Psalm 78:1-4, 12-16 or Psalm 25:1-9
Philippians 2:1-13
Matthew 21:23-32

Thought for the day

At the beginning of Matthew 21, Jesus enters Jerusalem to a welcome of palm-waving by the people. He then proceeds to drive out the money changers from the temple. The chief priests and elders ask Jesus, 'By what authority are you doing these things, and who gave you the authority?' (21:23): this group will constitute the primary antagonists throughout the Passion narrative. They were the aristocracy and not like the many priests who came into Jerusalem to serve at the temple. The chief priests and elders are those who worked in collaboration with Rome and had vested interests in keeping the status quo. They are compromised leaders who will

not challenge the ruling authority. Jesus obviously disturbs them. They question Jesus but in turn he questions them and they dodge an answer. Out of this situation comes the parable of the two sons.

Remember that the vineyard is an image of the Israel of God, an image of the Church. The first son refused to work in the vineyard saying, 'I will not.' There seems little respect for the father here. But later he changes his mind and goes. The second answered the father with respect and said, 'I go, sir', but he did not go. Neither son is perfect. Neither seemed truly willing. One professes but does not practise; the other does not appear willing but in the end does what the father wants. If you had to choose, which of these two imperfect sons did the will of the father? The answer would have to be the son who did what the father wanted.

Jesus now takes this a stage further and says to the priests and elders, 'tax collectors and prostitutes will enter the kingdom of God ahead of you'. It may be worthwhile to note that tax collectors and prostitutes also served Rome. Jesus did not say, '*instead* of you', but '*ahead* of you'. As long as they live, each has the potential for change. If we profess something, we should show we believe it by the way we live. Words without deeds are of little worth.

This is all about promises and performance, words and deeds. It remains true, of course, that love, care, respect for the world and for each other can often be found in those who do not profess to serve God in any way.

Question time

Are you sure you practise what you profess?

How can we show that we are obedient out of love and that we are not forced to obey?

Illustration

In a community there was a group of people who were always ready to say, 'Yes, sir. Three bags full, sir.' They appeared to be willing to take on anything that was asked and always talked with respect. They appeared only too willing, ready and able. But when it came to the crunch they were too busy, too tired, couldn't be bothered, or had just forgotten what they had promised. When they were needed they did not turn up.

There was another group who always seemed reluctant. They did not particularly want to get involved. They had other things to do. Yet when they were aware of the need they had a change of heart and waded in. They would not profess to be part of any system, but out of love and care they got on and did what was needed.

It was hard to depend on either group but in the end the second group was more likely to get things done.

Intercessions

Blessed are you, God our Father,
for you have sent your Son to be our Saviour.
In him you have delivered us
from the dominion of darkness
and made us children of the day and of light.
Blessed are you, Father, Son and Holy Spirit.

Loving Father, we give you thanks
for the coming of our Lord Jesus Christ
for in him you have opened the gate to eternal life.
Bless all who seek to proclaim the Good News,
all who preach the word and go out in mission.
We remember all who witness in their daily life
and all who seek to serve you faithfully.

Silence

Holy God, holy and strong One,
hear us and help us.

Loving Father, we ask your blessing
upon all who have important decisions to make this week.
We pray for those who are rulers and politicians,
for scientists and research workers,
for judges and all who strive to bring peace.
We remember all who find it hard
to remain faithful and loyal
and pray that they may be given new strength
and courage.

Silence

Holy God, holy and strong One,
hear us and help us.

Loving Father, we give thanks
for our homes and our loved ones.
We pray for all who have influenced our lives
through their example and teaching.
We remember all families
where relationships are breaking down
or life has become hard.
We ask your blessing
upon those who have to make difficult decisions
about their homes, their relationships or their way of life.

Silence

Holy God, holy and strong One,
hear us and help us.

Loving Father, we remember all
who are confused by the many choices in life
and who find it hard to cope.
We pray for those who have lost their freedom
and all who suffer from tyranny.
We ask your blessing upon all who are ill
and those who have decided they need to go into care.

Silence

Holy God, holy and strong One,
hear us and help us.

Loving Father, we thank you
that Jesus came down to lift us up
into the fullness of your kingdom.
We rejoice in the fellowship of your saints in glory.

We remember before you
all our friends and loved ones departed.
We commit our lives and all of your creation
to your unfailing love.

Silence

Merciful Father,
**accept these prayers
for the sake of your Son,
our Saviour Jesus Christ.
Amen.**

Memory verse

At the name of Jesus every knee should bend, in heaven and on earth and under the earth, and every tongue should confess that Jesus Christ is Lord, to the glory of God the Father.
Philippians 2:10, 11

Suggested music

And can it be
Meekness and majesty
Jesus is Lord! Creation's voice proclaims it

CANDLES

Aim

To look at the ability to choose and to do what we are asked.

Teaching

Every day we have to use our minds to choose what things we are going to do. Maybe you start by choosing what you wear. What do you like to wear best of all? Then you may be able to choose what you have for your breakfast. What would you like most of all? It is interesting we are not all the same and we make different choices. We have favourite colours, favourite animals and things we like to do best of all.

Sometimes we are asked to do things by our parents. They may want us to go and tidy up our room or to help to dry the dishes. Hands up who helps to do things at home.

Jesus told a story about two sons and their father. They had a vineyard. Do you know what is grown in a vineyard? Grapes – not hundreds but thousands of grapes grow in a vineyard. When the grapes were ready to be picked the father needed all the help he could get. The father asked his sons to go and work in the vineyard. The first son said, 'I will not.' The father felt sad that his son would not help and would not do what he was asked to do. As the son walked away he felt sorry for what he had said. He knew his father needed help, and he had been naughty to say, 'No, I won't.' (I know some children who are like this at home.) The son changed his mind. He turned around and went into the vineyard and did what his father asked.

The other son was also asked to go and help his father and straightaway he said, 'Yes, I'll go, sir.' The father was so pleased that his son was ready to help. But the son did not do what he promised. He saw some friends and went off with them instead. The father waited for him to come and help but he never came.

Now, which son do you think did what the father asked? Was it the one who promised and said, 'Yes', or the one who began by saying, 'No'? It would have been better if they both had said, 'Yes', and both had gone to work – that would have really pleased their father.

Activity

Play any game that involves making choices, such as 'The farmer in the dell' or 'I wrote a letter to my love'. On the activity sheet there is a maze where the road to the vineyard has to be found by making choices.

Prayer

Lord God,
you have given us a wonderful world.
Help us to do what you want us to do
and to be kind and caring to all.
Amen.

Song

God, you can use me

LAMPS

Aim

To look at how choice affects our lives.

Teaching

Who likes playing computer games? In all of them we have to make choices and sometimes we make mistakes. Sometimes you can go back and put your mistake right but you still have to make a choice. There are times when we are enjoying playing a game and we are asked to do something else by our parents. Again we have to make a choice: will we do what we are asked or will we just promise to do it and then not bother? I am sure some of us upset our parents by not doing what we are asked. (Perhaps the group would volunteer examples.)

Jesus told a story about a man who had two sons. The father had a vineyard and he wanted help in it. His sons were old enough to be useful. He asked one son and he replied, 'I won't', and went off. How do you think the father would feel? He would certainly feel sad and he might feel angry. Maybe the son wanted to go and be with his friends or do something else. As he walked away he was suddenly sorry for what he had said. He thought how his father needed his help. He turned around and went into the vineyard and started to work. This made the father happy – it was good to have some help from his son.

The other son was asked to go to work in the vineyard and straightaway he said, 'Yes, I'll go, sir', and went out. The father was pleased. But this son did not do what he promised. Instead he went and did something

else. He had promised his father but did not turn up. You can imagine how very sad this made the father. The father did not force his sons to do things; he wanted them to do these things out of love.

Which of the two sons do you think made the father happy?

Explore how the children can make their parents happy and do what is asked. Then explore the idea of saying our prayers and coming to church as part of serving God.

Activity

Play a game of choice such as 'I spy' or a game of elimination due to wrong choice.

The simplest game is to have the corners of the room given the names of the points of the compass. The children run around to music, then go to a corner when the music stops. Someone who is not watching calls out a compass point. If it is 'north', then all those at north are out. Later change it so the only people in are the ones at the compass point called.

Prayer

God, you have chosen to make this wonderful world
and to give us life.
As you love us and give us so many things,
help us to show our love to you
by doing what you want us to do.
Amen.

Song

I can be what God wants me to be

TORCHES

Aim

To look at choice and the will of the Father.

Teaching

Let us look at the parable of the two sons. This is a story about freedom and the choices we make. Every day we make a multitude of choices, and not always the right ones. Sometimes we need to backtrack or turn around and make a better choice. We can spend our whole life in trivial pursuits and doing things just to fill up time, or we can choose to do something worthwhile and dedicate ourselves to it.

Read Matthew 21:28-32.

What was the first son's reaction when asked to go to work in the vineyard? He immediately said, 'I will not.' How often do you find yourself saying this at home when asked to help? Notice the father does not force his son to go, but it must have made him sad and perhaps angry. It is amazing how much is done for us in our homes and we sometimes begrudge taking part in the work.

When this son had time to think, he realised how he had done wrong. Perhaps he was aware of all his father had done, and the love of his parents. He turned around because he had a change of heart and went into the vineyard. His father would be glad to see him.

What did the second son say to the father when asked to help? He spoke in a tone of respect and made a promise: 'I go, sir.' But it was a promise he did not keep – it was words without actions. He sounded respectful but he went off and did something else. It is so easy to be sidetracked from what we say we will do. You can imagine the father waiting and hoping and being disappointed. How often have we caused our parents sorrow in this way?

Remember that the vineyard is a symbol for the people of God. Jesus is faced by the chief priests and elders who profess to do the work of God but are sidetracked by serving the state and their own safety before God. They speak of doing God's will but are in danger of serving the world first.

Because some notorious sinners had a change of heart and chose to follow John the Baptist or Jesus, because they chose to change their attitudes, they were nearer to doing what God wanted than those who openly professed that they sought God's will.

Spend some time talking about times when members of the group have had a change of heart and a turnaround from the direction they were going. Some things lead to a dead end and others to the road to life eternal. To seek to do the will of God is necessary for all Christians.

Activity

Get the group to suggest areas where people outside the Church are doing the sort of work God would want them to do. You could also look at choices and their consequences. Get the group to talk openly about wrong choices and their consequences, then good choices and their consequences.

Prayer

Lord God, we have promised to serve you
and be faithful to you.
Help us in all our choices
to seek to do what you want us to do
and to show our love for you and others.
Amen.

Song

I will offer up my life

Proper 22

Sunday between 2 and 8 October inclusive

Aim

To appreciate all that God has given us.

Preparation

Have a large bunch of grapes and a crucifix in the entrance. Add to these cuttings from newspapers of acts of vandalism, violence and misuse of the environment.

Opening activity

For five voices:

1. I did not know how good home was until I left it.
2. Six, seven, eight, whom do you appreciate?
3. I never realised how much I was loved until I walked out.
2. Six, seven, eight, whom do you appreciate?
4. I did not appreciate the love and sacrifice my parents made for me until I lived alone.
2. Six, seven, eight, whom do you appreciate?
5. I had not realised how good the Lord is.
2. Six, seven, eight, whom do you appreciate?

Opening prayer

Lord God, you give us life,
you give us love,
you give us yourself
and you give us a wonderful world
full of beauty and mystery.
Help us to use all these wonderful gifts
to your glory
and to the benefit of others.
Amen.

Opening song

O, how good is the Lord

Readings

Exodus 20:1-4, 7-9, 12-20 or Isaiah 5:1-7
Psalm 19 or Psalm 80:7-14
Philippians 3:4b-14
Matthew 21:33-46

Thought for the day

Once again Jesus talks about a vineyard and so the chief priests and scribes would be aware that Jesus was talking about the people of God (Isaiah 5:7, Psalm 80:8). There is a protective hedge around the vineyard, winepress and tower. This was a vineyard that was well provided for and protected. This is about privileged people.

The action of the owner was quite common in Palestine. The owner let the tenants have use of the vineyard and in return they paid him a portion of the harvest in kind or in money. Even the reaction of the vine growers was not unusual as there was much unrest and discontent in the land and tenants were feeling rebellious.

God gives us the world for our benefit, but God does want some response. It is still God's world. God gives his protection and provides for us. He then gives us the freedom to get on with our lives. God does not keep making demands. He trusts us and seeks a faithful relationship. In all his dealings God is patient, even when we ignore him and his messengers. God gives us chance after chance but this cannot go on for ever. If we ignore him, that has its own consequences. It is not that God turns away from us; we have turned away from God and not given him his due. We have misused our freedom and for this we are answerable to him. We are answerable to God for the way we use the world and how we live our lives. The privileges we have, come with responsibilities: privileges are meant to be used to the benefit of others and to the glory of God.

Through this parable it is easy to pass judgement on the House of Israel. This avoids the issue that we are often in the same position. Do we heed God's messengers? Do we give God his due? Are you certain you show respect for his world? Before we point at anyone else, we need to look at our own relationship with God and with his Son. It would seem that human attitudes are always repeating themselves. This is what makes the Scriptures so meaningful and relevant to us. By our actions do we exclude ourselves from the presence of God and the benefits of his kingdom?

Question time

Do you acknowledge that this is God's world and give him his due?

Do you seek to know Christ and the power of his resurrection?

Illustration

The group was given a new hall through the generosity of others and through national grants. But from the start they did not appreciate it. The walls were daubed with graffiti, the floor was covered with litter; inside the building they ran riot. Though people tried to care for them, they rejected any offers of oversight or help. In time the hall looked derelict and no one dared to go and look after it. Windows were broken and toilets were vandalised.

Sadly after all the efforts of some the hall was shut down. Those who were given it were causing too much trouble. It became a liability. The idea had been a good one but the group did not appreciate this. Finally it was dismantled and the land given to others.

Intercessions

Blessed are you, Lord our God,
for you are our Creator
and you have called us to know you
and proclaim your love.
Help us to be aware that you speak to us
through the Scriptures

and through those who tell
of your presence and power today.
Blessed are you, Father, Son and Holy Spirit.

Father Creator, raise up among us
prophets and preachers
who will tell of your mighty acts and your saving power.
To scientists and research workers
give vision of the wonder and mystery of your world.
Bless your Church with an awareness of
and living relationship with Christ,
that it may witness to the power of the resurrection.
We pray for all Christians who are suffering
from persecution or rejection.

Silence

Lord and Saviour of all,
hear us and help us.

Father Creator, we ask your blessing
upon leaders of peoples
and all who influence our lives by their decisions.
Give them wisdom and respect in all their dealings.
We pray for all who work in the field of genetics
and those who influence our world by their actions.
We remember all who seek to show us
how to care for the world.

Silence

Lord and Saviour of all,
hear us and help us.

Father Creator, we give thanks
for our homes and our loved ones.
We ask your blessing upon all homes
where there is tension and misunderstanding.
We pray for marriages that are struggling
and families that are in danger of falling apart.
We remember all who feel rejected or neglected.

Silence

Lord and Saviour of all,
hear us and help us.

Father Creator, we give thanks
for all you have given to us.
We pray for the world poor, the oppressed
and all who are suffering from violence.
We remember those
who have been driven off their own land
and all who are refugees.
We ask your blessing upon all who are ill
or who have been injured
and all who are fearful for their future.

Silence

Lord and Saviour of all,
hear us and help us.

Father Creator, we give thanks
for Jesus Christ the living Lord
and for the power of his resurrection.
We commit to your keeping our loved ones departed,
that they may rejoice in the fullness of your kingdom,
and we pray that we may share with them
in the knowledge of your love.

Silence

Merciful Father,
accept these prayers
for the sake of your Son,
our Saviour Jesus Christ.
Amen.

Memory verse

I want to know Christ and the power of his resurrection.
Philippians 3:10

Suggested music

Christ be with me
Come and celebrate
God of life, God of love

CANDLES

Aim

To encourage appreciation of each other and God's gifts
to us.

Teaching

Who looks after you at home? What do they do? Washing,
ironing, cleaning, cooking, bed-making, going to buy
food, taking you out, buying your clothes, giving you
gifts. (Ask the children to mime things that are done for
them at home.)

Do you remember to say 'thank you' – for your
breakfast, your clothes, your house? These things are
done for us because we are loved but do we remember
to say 'thank you' and that we love the people who do
all this for us? You could also show that you are thankful
by helping in the house. Who helps? What do you do? It
is always helpful to be tidy and to put our own things
away properly. We must remember that those who look
after us are not our servants; they do things for us
because they love us.

Who goes out to work in your house? (Ask the children
to mime what the worker does.) They might go out to
work because they like it. They also go out because they
work to get money so that you can eat and have the nice
things that you have. They do it because they love you
and care for you. Do you remember to say 'thank you'?
When we go home today we will take a 'thank you' gift,
but it would be nice if we also said 'thank you' and
remember to say it often.

God has made a wonderful world with all sorts of
creatures. Pretend to be your favourite animal and we
will try and guess what it is. God made the fish of the
sea, the birds of the air, and all the animals. God made
you – and me. Let us say, 'Thank you, God.' God made
the sun and the moon and the stars, all things that grow;
he made the seas, the rivers and the mountains. God
made everything and gave it to us to enjoy. Every day
when we wake up we should say, 'Thank you, God.'

Activity

Get the group to stand in a circle. Tell them they are to say 'thank you' to God for something in the world. When the first one has said, 'Thank you for . . .', we will all clap our hands and then the next one will say 'thank you'. We will go right round the circle in turns.

There is an opportunity on the activity sheet to make a 'thank you' card.

Prayer

God, thank you for the world
and all that is in it.
Thank you for our homes
and for all who love us.
Thank you for everything.
Amen.

Song

Thank you, Lord, for this new day

LAMPS

Aim

To look at the parable of the vineyard.

Teaching

A long time ago, before Jesus was born, there lived a man called Isaiah and he was a prophet. (Make sure the children understand the word 'prophet' as distinct from 'profit'.) Isaiah spent a lot of time talking to God and God showed him what the people should be doing. It made Isaiah sad because the people did not want to listen to him, to *any* of the prophets or to God. Isaiah said the people were like a vineyard. Do you know what a vineyard is? It is where vines are grown to produce grapes.

Because God cared for his people they were like a special vineyard in a very good place. The vineyard was on a hillside to catch the sunshine. It had a hedge around it to protect it from wild beasts. In the vineyard was a tower where the people could rest – they could keep a lookout from there and use it as a safe place if bandits came. Also in the vineyard was a special hole in the ground for the grapes to be pressed for making wine. It was all really, really good but the people did not care for it – they did not look after it. Soon it was going wild. The grapes were small and sour – they were not nice. Because of this Isaiah said the people would lose what God had given them. It would be taken away from them. But the people did not listen to him or to the other prophet who came to warn them.

Jesus knew this story and told it to the chief priests and people who were planning to capture him and kill him. Jesus knew they would not listen to him because they had not listened to the prophets – the messengers of God – who had come to warn them to look after God's world properly.

Have someone read Matthew 21:33-41.

Jesus changed the story a little bit – can you notice the changes? Jesus shows how the people killed the messengers and then they even killed the son. Who do you think this is meant to be? What happens to such people? What happens to the vineyard?

We are the people to whom God has given this world and the Church. He wants us to care for them and to use them properly and also to know they belong to him. In what ways can we show that we know this? (Look at conservation and respect. Also look at thanksgiving and prayer life.)

Activity

If possible look at a local conservation project, a beach or park tidy, and see why it is done. Involve the children in this if possible. You could have waste paper scattered around the room and get them to collect it. There is a vineyard and watchtower on the activity sheet.

Prayer

God, you made the world and all that is in it.
You sent your Son Jesus Christ
to show your love and to be our Saviour.
Help us to be careful and respectful
in how we use your world
and to give thanks and worship you.
Amen.

Song

Thank you for every new good morning

TORCHES

Aim

To compare the Isaiah parable and the Jesus parable.

Teaching

Isaiah was a prophet sent by God to the people of Israel to warn them that they must change their ways or they would bring about disaster. He spoke to the people in the way that some now talk about global warming and the dangers of overusing the resources of the world. Prophets are God's messengers. They have spent time in the presence of God and understand what God wants the people to do. Isaiah warned the people that they could not go on ignoring God and living in ways that were not right. He compared the people of Israel to a favoured vineyard.

Read Isaiah 5:1-7.

Note the favoured spot – 'a fertile hillside, cleared of stones. The vines are good ones. Around the vineyard there is a protecting hedge. Inside is a watchtower, where they can rest, keep a lookout and go to for safety. There is also a wine vat where they can press the grapes. All this is meant to be ideal. But the people do not care for it. The grapes are obviously not pruned properly and they go wild (like some people!). Such people do not deserve such a favoured vineyard and it is taken away from them. (Can the group find parallels in the world today?)

Read Psalm 80:7-14. It is the cry of those who have lost what should have been theirs.

Read Matthew 21:33-41. Though Jesus tells this parable it would have a lot more meaning after his death because by the time Matthew had completed this Gospel the temple at Jerusalem had been destroyed.

Compare this to the Isaiah parable. The vineyard belongs to a landowner (God). Slaves are sent (messengers) to ask the people to give the owner his dues. These messengers are abused, beaten and killed. Then the owner sent his son. (Who can this be?) He should have received better treatment but they kill the son too. They have no respect or fear at all. They may get away with this for a while but they will have to pay the consequences of their actions. The owner did not want this but they have brought it upon themselves.

If we are now the owners of the vineyard, how does this parable relate to us?

Activity

Look at the dangers of pollution, global warming and the overuse of resources.

Consider conservation projects, local efforts to tidy up public areas and to be rid of graffiti.

Think about lives ruined by drugs, vice or neglect.

Consider our relationship with God and giving him his due as well as respecting his world.

Prayer

God our Creator,
we thank you for our lives
and the wonders and mystery of your world.
Help us to use what you have given us
to your glory and the benefit of all.
We ask this through your Son,
Jesus Christ our Saviour.
Amen.

Song

God, whose farm is all creation

Proper 23

Sunday between 9 and 15 October inclusive

Aim

To encourage awareness that we are invited to share the joys of the kingdom in the presence of the King.

Preparation

Have a large printed invitation in the entrance.

> Today (and every day) you are invited
> to meet the King of kings,
> to share in his love and peace
> and to enjoy the benefits of his kingdom.
> RSVP

Opening activity

Nine readers:

1. Are you going to the match?
2. I can't be bothered.
3. Excuse yourself: exclude yourself.
4. Do you fancy going for a swim?
5. I am too busy.
3. Excuse yourself: exclude yourself.
6. Would you like to come to my party?
7. No, thank you.
3. Excuse yourself: exclude yourself.
8. Come and meet the king.
9. I've got too much to do.
3. Excuse yourself: exclude yourself.

Opening prayer

Lord God, you are ever present
and invite us to know you,
to love you and to enjoy you.
Grant that we may have the wisdom
to make ourselves aware of you
and the wonderful gifts you give us.
Amen.

Opening song

The King is among us

Readings

Exodus 32:1-14 or Isaiah 25:1-9
Psalm 106:1-6, 19-23 or Psalm 23
Philippians 4:1-9
Matthew 22:1-14

Thought for the day

The readings for today are full of joy. Isaiah and Jesus both talk about a feast. Isaiah says how God will wipe away all tears. In Psalm 23 the psalmist rejoices in the presence and protection of God who is compared to a shepherd. St Paul asks us 'to rejoice in the Lord always' and, to emphasise it, he repeats, 'again I say rejoice'. To be invited to come to God or to be a Christian is not a gloomy life-restricting event; it is life-extending and joyful. Jesus compares it to being invited to a wedding banquet. It is a joy to be invited into God's presence and we miss out on this if we refuse to come. Those who excuse themselves exclude themselves. God has given us an open invitation; if we do not come, the fault lies in ourselves.

It is interesting to look at the excuses because they are not bad things in themselves. People miss out by going about their daily work and doing that alone. Many of us allow the call of earthly things to deafen us to the heavenly. We spend a good deal of time on that which is passing away and ignore that which is eternal. Like Esau in the Old Testament, we trade our birthright for a bowl of food. We are in danger of seeing to our bodies and neglecting our souls. Because God does not force us, it is easy to have prayer and even God himself low on our agenda. But if so, it is we who miss out.

Jesus is not threatening us with punishment but rather telling us that we are in danger of missing out by the way we are living. It is very sad when we realise too late what we have missed. We often miss out by being unwilling to learn the disciplines so that we might then have the joy of playing an instrument, for example, or taking part in a sport.

In the parable, those from the highways and byways had no call on the king. You could not say they were worthy of an invitation. We see God's grace and goodness at work in the invitation he sends out to everyone. All are welcome, including you and me. We are called to enjoy God's presence and to feast on all that he offers us.

Matthew 22:6 sounds very like the parable from last week's Gospel and is a follow-on from it. There is a warning that all are invited, but if you reject the invitation, be it on your head. It is you who have made your choice. Verse 7 sees the fulfilment of that warning in the destruction of the Temple and Jerusalem by the Roman army in 70 AD. Many would say this was caused by the attitude of the Jews at the time.

Question time

Do you show your faith to be a great joy to you or just something you have to do?

Are you sure that you have answered God's call to you by giving him priority?

Illustration

Richard and Judy were invited to the palace to meet the king to enjoy sharing in the beauty of the surroundings and to take part in a banquet. It was a most generous invitation and they wondered what they had done to deserve it. In fact, it was sent out because of the love of the king. They showed lots of people the invitation with pride. They put it where it could be seen in their house. Most days they looked at it and said how wonderful it was. They had advance warning of the date and slowly it came near. One day Judy looked at her calendar and said, 'Oh, I am supposed to get my hair done today – what shall I do?' Richard replied, 'That's OK. Just go ahead. I fancy doing some gardening.' For all their talk and show, they counted the invitation of little value. By excusing themselves, they excluded themselves.

Intercessions

Blessed are you, Lord our God,
for you have called us
to know you and to love you.
You invite us to experience the joy
of coming into your presence
and to delight in your grace.
Lord, we come
depending on your grace and goodness.
Blessed are you, Father, Son and Holy Spirit.

Good and gracious God,
may our lives show the joy
of knowing you and your love.
Let preachers and teachers encourage all who hear them
to come to you in love.
Bless all who seek to extend our lives
by a vision of your grace and goodness.
We pray today for all religious writers and broadcasters.

Silence

Lord of life and love,
grant us the joy of your kingdom.

Good and gracious God,
as we go about our daily work
may we show our joy in your presence.
We ask your blessing upon all who encourage us
to relax, to be still and to be attentive.
We pray for artists and musicians,
for craftspeople and gardeners,
for all who beautify our world.
We remember all who live in deprived and derelict areas
and pray especially for the world poor.

Silence

Lord of life and love,
grant us the joy of your kingdom.

Good and gracious God,
we thank you for the love and attention
we have received through our homes and dear ones.
We ask your blessing upon our families and friends
and the communities in which we live and work.
We remember all who strive to improve our environment.
We pray for all who are homeless
and those who live on the streets
of our towns and cities.

Silence

Lord of life and love,
grant us the joy of your kingdom.

Good and gracious God,
we thank you for our well-being.
We ask your blessing upon all who are sad or depressed
and all whose lives are darkened with troubles.

We remember all who are ill
and their loved ones as they care for them.
We pray for those who work in hospitals
and all who care for people in trouble.

Silence

Lord of life and love,
grant us the joy of your kingdom.

Good and gracious God,
you invite us all into your presence,
and to life eternal.
May we not lose sight of the eternal
through the clamour and call of the world.
We ask your blessing upon our loved ones departed.
May they rejoice with the saints
in the fullness of eternal life.

Silence

Merciful Father,
**accept these prayers
for the sake of your Son,
our Saviour Jesus Christ.
Amen.**

Memory verse

Surely goodness and mercy shall follow me all the days of my life, and I shall dwell in the house of the Lord my whole life long.
Psalm 23:6

Suggested music

Jubilate, everybody
Joy to the world
We shall go out with hope of resurrection

CANDLES

Aim

To show how we are invited to know and love God and enjoy his presence.

Teaching

Have you ever been invited to a party? Sometimes you are sent an invitation and it tells you where the party is and at what time. Usually your invitation comes so that you and your parents can plan for you to get there. Sometimes it is a birthday party or a Christmas party, or it might be after a wedding or because it is a special day.

Who likes parties? What do you like best?

Sometimes we dress up for parties with special clothes, and sometimes we will be given a party hat. It is exciting to be asked to a party, and if we can help it, we would not like to miss it. Parties are such happy times.

Jesus told people about a party that a king was having. There would be lots of nice food and music. Everyone who came would have fun and enjoy themselves. But some did not bother; they were invited but they did not come. They just went about doing what they always did even though the king wanted to see them. The king would have liked them to enjoy themselves but they did not bother so they missed the party. It was really very sad.

Jesus wanted us to know that God is very like the king. God invites us to get to know him by speaking to him each day. What do you call speaking to God? Yes, it is called praying. God would like us to talk to him each day and to enjoy being with him. He would like us to learn about him. Where can we do that? Here at church and at school. But God especially wants us to love him because he loves us. He wants us to enjoy the world he has given to us and to remember that he made it all.

Activity

Learn the song for today with actions. There is an opportunity on the activity sheet to make a party hat and to say that they love God.

Prayer

God our King,
thank you for loving us
and inviting us to live in your world.
We thank you for all the nice things
you have given us.
Amen.

Song

Wide, wide as the ocean

LAMPS

Aim

To look at the story of the wedding feast and see how God wants us to enjoy him and his world.

Teaching

Let us all make sad faces. Do you think that is what God wants us to look like? God loves us and wants us to enjoy his world. Let us make smiley faces. Now that is more like how God wants us to be. God wants us to know him and his love and to enjoy being with him.

Do you like parties? Most people like a party even if it is a small one with just a few friends.

What do you like best about parties? What would you plan to have at a party?

Food, glorious food – lots of it and all sorts will be there if you are lucky. You might like special drinks, and it would be good to be with people you know. Sometimes it is good to get dressed up for a party. A very long time ago if you were invited to a rich man's party, he sent a new set of party clothes that you could wear.

Jesus was thinking about how God loves people and wants them to enjoy themselves. It made Jesus sad to think that people took no notice of God the Father and did not try to get to know him. He told the people a story about a king inviting people to a banquet he was having for his son. Who knows what a banquet is? It is a party with lots of food and nice things. The king sent his invitations out so that they would know they were

invited. Some took no notice at all – they just went on working and working and missed out on the party. Others said they were too busy. This made the king rather sad for he wanted people to meet his son and to enjoy the party. So he sent his servants out again. This time they went into the lanes and streets and invited everyone to come. He sent them all nice robes to wear so that it could be a splendid party and so that they could all enjoy meeting him and his son.

Now Jesus wanted us to know there are always two kinds of people. There are those who accept God's invitation to get to know him and there are those who do not bother. All are invited to enjoy the presence of God and his Son but some think they are too busy.

(Explore how we get to know God through prayer and thanksgiving, through the Church and the Bible. Show them how God wants us all to love him and enjoy him.)

Activity

Play 'I went to a party'. The first person says, for example, 'I went to a party and I wore a blue hat.' The next person has to say, 'I went to a party and wore a blue hat and a . . .', adding something else. Things are added as you go around the group until someone gets it wrong. They are out and you have to start again.

Prayer

Thank you, God, for inviting us
to know you and love you.
We seek to enjoy your presence
and the wonderful world you have given us.
Amen.

Song

Give me oil in my lamp

TORCHES

Aim

To show how we are invited to rejoice in God, in his love and in his world.

Teaching

Read the words from St Paul in Philippians 4:4-7. Paul repeats that we are to 'rejoice in the Lord'. We are to realise he is near and not to be anxious or worried but to take things to God in prayer. Through awareness of God and his love, God's peace will fill our hearts and minds. This is all offered to us for free. It sounds wonderful and many people prove it to be true but a lot of people never bother. The invitation is there but we often ignore it. We put off our prayers and ignore the call of God.

Sadly this has always been true about people. Jesus realised this and told the story about the guests invited by the king to a wedding banquet for his son.

Read Matthew 22:1-14.

Notice how people have been invited – there is a place set for them. Think how at some receptions there is a place just for you. Once it is all ready, the king sends for the people. But some decide to get on with their daily work. Why should the king's invitation interrupt them? Others treat his messengers badly and some even kill them. Can there be such opposition to a kind king? (See how this relates to last week's Gospel and to the life of Jesus.) Such reactions bring about the results that follow.

The king continues to be gracious. More are invited out of the streets and byways, both good and bad. In his love the king would welcome them and no doubt provide them all with a wedding robe. The king wanted them all to look splendid. This was a great honour for all who were invited.

Read Matthew 22:11-14. Here was someone who was disrespectful of the king and his gifts (by not wearing the wedding robe he was given) or someone who assumed he could gatecrash the wedding without the grace and welcome of the king. (Discuss what this means in relation to God and his invitation for us to enjoy his presence in the world.)

Can the group relate this story to how God calls his people and they often stall, including how we put off prayer and worship? There are some who violently oppose anything to do with God. Yet God continues to be gracious, even though we are unworthy. We should not abuse his graciousness by our disrespect or think it does not matter what we do.

There are many deep matters here for the group to look at together and discuss how they relate to them.

Activity

Explore how to put the words of Philippians 4:4-7 into practice. Spend some time encouraging stillness in the presence of God, simply reminding themselves by saying:

> You, Lord, are in this place,
> your presence fills it,
> your presence is peace.

(See *Celtic Hymn Book* number 217, which you may like to teach them.)

Prayer

Lord, you have called us
to enjoy your presence
and to feast at your table.
Forgive us when we have ignored you
or shown disrespect.
In your grace, help us to know we are loved
and that you come to us each day.
Amen.

Song

Rejoice in the Lord always

Proper 24

Sunday between 16 and 22 October inclusive

Aim

To show how we are meant to be concerned for the world as well as for God.

Preparation

Have cards in the entrance saying:

> **The government is taxing!**
> Income Tax
> Value Added Tax
> Community Charge
> Inheritance Tax
> Stamp Duty
> Petrol Duty
> Road Tax
> **Taxing indeed!**

You may like to add newspaper cuttings about taxes and their relief.

Opening activity

Three or more voices:

1. I read that I have to work for nearly three months a year for the government before I earn money for myself.
2. They have just improved the road down our street.
3. I had a spell in hospital and I was well looked after.
2. Our Jean is really doing well in her new school.
3. Our refuse collector does a good job. What would we do without him?
1. I am glad that some of our taxes are put to good use.
2. We pay taxes because we are forced to. Do you give God his dues?

Opening prayer

God, Creator of heaven and earth,
we give you thanks for your love revealed in creation
and for your grace and goodness towards us.
May we at all times reflect that love
in our caring for the world
and in giving ourselves to you.
Amen.

Opening song

To God be the glory

Readings

Exodus 33:12-23 or Isaiah 45:1-7
Psalm 99 or Psalm 96:1-9 (10-13)
1 Thessalonians 1:1-10
Matthew 22:15-22

Thought for the day

The Romans had tax systems that are not dissimilar to our own – and, as you would expect, they were not welcome. They had 'ground tax', which meant you had to pay 10 per cent on all grain and 20 per cent on oil and wine that you produced. This was paid in kind or in money. There was income tax at 1 per cent of your earnings. There was poll tax on every adult male from 14 to 65 and every female from 12 to 65. Obviously the women matured earlier! This tax was one denarius and was known as the 'tribute to Caesar'. The Roman coinage itself was offensive to the Jews for each coin not only depicted the head of Caesar but also gave him divine status. To carry such money was to accommodate oneself to imperial rule.

The Pharisees and Herodians were trying to lay a trap for Jesus by asking if it was right to pay tribute to Caesar or not. Matthew suggests they are doing this out of malice and describes them as hypocrites. They had presented Jesus with a real 'Catch 22' situation. Not to pay tribute would be a rebellion against the empire. For this Jesus would be reported for preaching sedition. If he said it was right to pay, Jesus would be discredited in the eyes of many of the ordinary people.

Jesus asks for a denarius and asks, 'Whose head is this and whose title?' When they answered, 'The Emperor's', Jesus replied, 'Give to the emperor the things that are the emperor's and to God the things that are God's.'

There is great wisdom in this answer – or you could say it is no answer at all. Who are we to give to? The answer is not either one or the other but both. It is a mistake to separate one from the other. The sacred and secular are not independent of each other; they are so intertwined that we cannot divide them, just as we cannot separate the human into body and soul. Both are woven together. God made the world, God loves the world and God is present in his world. The Christian who says that we must not get involved in politics does not realise what Christianity is about. We cannot hope for a new heaven and a new earth unless we work towards it happening. It is no use praying for peace if we do not help to bring it about. We give to the state – even if only by law – for our own benefit.

And we give to God – what? Does God get the priority he is due in our life? Do we respond to him in praise and thanksgiving? Do we seek to do his will? You must ask what do you render to God – and this is far bigger than talking about money.

Question time

Do we show in our lives how we are citizens of 'two kingdoms'?

You have to pay taxes. What dues do you give to God?

Illustration

One of the greatest witnesses to giving God his due was the early Christian martyrs. Catherine, who gives her name to the 'Catherine Wheel' firework, was born of a noble family and lived in the fourth century. The emperor was attracted to her and wanted to marry her. Catherine refused because she was already a 'bride of Christ'. She is said to have disputed with 50 philosophers whose job it was to convince her of her error and she defeated them. Because she refused to do as commanded by the emperor she was tortured by being fastened to a large wheel and driven around the arena – but the wheel broke. Finally she was beheaded.

Intercessions

Blessed are you, Lord our God.
All things come from you
and of your own do we give you.
From you come our life, this world
and all that we have and are.
Teach us to love and respect your creation
and give glory to you.
Blessed are you, Father, Son and Holy Spirit.

Lord God, Creator of all, we give thanks
for those who have taught us the faith.
We ask your blessing upon the mission of the Church,
which is your mission.
Guide and strengthen all who reach out to others
in faith and with the Good News.
We pray for all evangelists
and all who witness to your love.

Silence

Lord God, maker of heaven and earth,
in your love hear us.

Lord God, Creator of all, we give thanks
for all you have given us.
We ask your guidance on all who are led astray
by the glitter of gold
and the false promises of consumerism.
We pray for all who are impoverished in spirit.
We ask your blessing upon the governments of the world
and their striving for justice and fair dealing.

Silence

Lord God, maker of heaven and earth,
in your love hear us.

Lord God, Creator of all, we ask your blessing
upon our home and our loved ones.
We pray for all who provide us
with water, electricity and gas,
for those who collect our refuse and clean our streets.
We remember all who help to maintain law and order.

Silence

Lord God, maker of heaven and earth,
in your love hear us.

Lord God, Creator of all, we ask your blessing
upon all hospitals, care homes,
home visitors and the social services.
We remember before you
all suffering and impoverished peoples.
We pray for the world poor
and all who are without the basic needs of life.
We bring before you friends and loved ones who are ill.

Silence

Lord God, maker of heaven and earth,
in your love hear us.

Lord God, Creator of all, we come from you
and we return to you.
Bless our loved ones departed.
May they rejoice with your saints in glory.
We commit this world and ourselves
to you and your unfailing love.

Silence

Merciful Father,
**accept these prayers
for the sake of your Son,
our Saviour Jesus Christ.
Amen.**

Memory verse

Ascribe to the Lord glory and strength. Ascribe to the Lord the glory due to his name.
Psalm 96:7, 8

Suggested music

All my hope on God is founded
My God, I love thee
Take my life, and let it be

CANDLES

Aim

To show that the world and everything in it belongs to God.

Teaching

Look at coins from different parts of the world, noticing particularly the heads on the coins. Show the children how to make a rubbing of the coins. Show them a Roman coin – or a facsimile or picture of one – and ask if anyone knows who was in charge of the Romans and the countries they ruled. Tell them how he is called 'Caesar', which means 'king'. Who rules our country? Elizabeth our queen. The Americans do not have a king or queen – do you know who is in charge? Show a coin and explain that it is the president. There are lots of names for rulers and people in charge but I want you to remember the name of the Roman ruler. Let us say it together: 'Caesar'.

Who is on Roman coins? Caesar.

Some people tried to get Jesus into trouble by getting him to say that people didn't need to give money to help Caesar be in charge. If Jesus said people should not give any money to Caesar, they would tell the Romans who would come and put Jesus in prison. Jesus knew they were trying to set a trap to catch him. He asked to see a coin. (Show a Roman coin or a picture of one.) Jesus asked, 'Whose head is on the coin?' (Let the child who is holding the coin answer.) It is Caesar's head.

Then Jesus said, 'If it is Caesar's, give to him what is his.' Now they thought they had trapped Jesus but he did not stop speaking. He said, 'Give to Caesar what is his but give to God what belongs to God.'

Now they had to think – they knew what Caesar asked for, but what belonged to God? God made the whole world. God gives life to all the animals and plants. God gives us our lives and all that we have. What belongs to God? Everything and God wants us to say 'thank you' each day and to love him as he loves us.

Activity

Read a verse at a time of 'Who made the twinkling stars' (*Kidsource* 385), asking the children to say, 'Thank you, God, thank you, God' at the end of each verse. Then see if you can find four readers to do a verse each, repeating the process. Then sing the hymn.

Prayer

For the sun, the moon and stars
thank you, God, thank you, God.
For the world in which we live
thank you, God, thank you, God.
For the flowers, the fruit, the trees
thank you, God, thank you, God.
For all the animals, for fish and birds
thank you, God, thank you, God.
For my home and family
thank you, God, thank you, God.
For making me
thank you, God, thank you, God.

Song

Who made the twinkling stars

LAMPS

Aim

To show how we ought to give ourselves to God who gives us all that we have.

Teaching

Look at coins with different sovereigns' heads on the front. Look at various rulers and perhaps different currencies. You can tell when a ruler is in charge by the date on the coin. (If possible, have a Roman coin or a facsimile.) Tell them what was on Roman coins: one calls Caesar Augustus the 'son of god'; another says, 'Hail, lord of the earth'; a coin of Julius Caesar shows him rising to take his place with the gods. Do they think this is right? Many Jews did not like using Roman money because it suggested wrong things about God. They did not like paying taxes to the emperor's officials but knew they would have to.

The Pharisees were trying to trick Jesus into saying something wrong or something that would upset the people. They asked Jesus if they should pay tax to Caesar or not. Jesus asked them for a coin. They produced a Roman denarius, a coin that was about a day's wage, and on it was the head of Caesar. Jesus looked at it and asked, 'Whose head is on it?' They replied, 'The emperor's.' Jesus said, 'Give to the emperor the things that are the emperor's and to God the things that are God's.'

It was a clever answer showing that people had to think about what belonged to Caesar and what belonged to God. Because he was the ruler, the emperor, much belonged to Caesar. (Ask the children to say what did belong to Caesar. Tell them how Caesar also ruled in part of Britain. People had to pay taxes to help fund building work and also road-making. If people refused to give, there would be chaos or war.)

But those who believe in God have a greater ruler. The whole world belongs to God. God gives everything life and breath – even Caesar.

God gives us all that we have and gives us his love. What do you think God wants in return? He wants our love. He wants us to respect his world. He wants us to give our attention to him.

Caesar would force people to do what he wants. God wants us to do these things out of love and does not want to force us. We have to do what the government orders but how do we do what God wants?

(For the rest of the session explore how we give ourselves to God in prayer and through our actions.)

Activity

Spend some time doing rubbings of coins and ask the group if they can create a picture out of some of the rubbings. See if they can guess which country a coin belongs to, or if they look at the obverse side and the date, whose head it is on the front.

Prayer

Lord God, all power and strength belongs to you
for you have created the heavens and the earth
and all that is in them.
May we give our love to you each day
and care for the world that you have given us.
Amen.

Song

He's got the whole world in his hand

TORCHES

Aim

To explore how we should give to God who gives us all that we have.

Teaching

Who is the ruler of our country? Who helps her to govern? Do you know the name of the prime minister? America does not have a king or queen. Who is the head of the country? The president. Do you know his name? Nearly all Americans carry around an image of the president and we carry an image of our queen. How do we do this? Their head is on a coin. (Look at a few coins and see if the group can say which country they come from.)

When the Roman Empire was in control the same coins were used in this country as in all of the Mediterranean and wherever Rome ruled. What was the ruler called? 'Caesar' and his name was on the coins. On the other side of the coins Caesar was often depicted as a godlike figure. The Jewish people, like many others, did not like being under Roman rule, even though there were many benefits. They did not like to have to think of Caesar as a god because they only believed in the one true God. For this reason some did not even like to carry Roman coins and they refused to use Roman coinage in the Temple.

When the group of Pharisees and Herodians come and ask Jesus if they should pay to Caesar, they are obviously trying to trap him. Jesus knew if he said, 'Don't', he would be declared a rebel and an enemy of Rome. If he said, 'Do pay taxes to Rome', a lot of people would feel he had let them down because they were looking to him to set them free from Roman rule.

Jesus asks to see a denarius and then asks, 'Whose head is this and whose title?' When they answered, 'The emperor's', Jesus replied, 'Give to the emperor the things that are the emperor's and to God the things that are God's.'

Jesus was very wise in this and was saying to people: think about it and then do what you believe is right. If we are to have the benefits of a ruling body and what they provide, then we ought under normal circumstances to pay tax. Sometimes we may question a government when they use tax for things we do not approve of, but normally give the government their due – in a sense you are forced to because payment of taxes is demanded.

What about God who provides us with all things? God is our Creator. Not only does he give us life and love he also gives us this world to live in and all that is in it. God is gracious to each of us and reveals his love to us through Jesus. God does not send a demand like the tax man: he asks us to return his love out of our own free will. God wants us to recognise that everything belongs to him and to care for his world. God does not force us and so we are in danger of not giving God his due. A portion of money that is earned every day is given to tax; do we give in the same way each day to God?

Activity

Let the group say today's Psalm (96:1-11). Have different people read a verse and after each verse all say, 'Ascribe to the Lord glory and strength.' Then see if the group can write a similar song of praise to God the Creator by adding a verse each.

Prayer

Lord, the earth is yours and all that is in it.
All things come from you.
Help us to love the world
with the love that you have for the world
and to give glory to you
for all that we have each day.
Amen.

Song

O Lord, all the world belongs to you

Proper 25

Sunday between 23 and 29 October inclusive

Aim

To encourage us to love God with our whole being.

Preparation

Have Matthew 22:37-39 printed in large letters, replacing the following words with symbols: heart, mind, strength, neighbour. Use a heart shape, a brain, a muscle or a muscular person, and a large crowd of people. You could attach a mirror tile in the place of 'yourself'.

Opening activity

Teach everyone to do actions for Matthew 22:37-39 and Mark 12:28-34.

Love – make a heart shape over your head with your hand.

God – raise your arms upwards in praise.

Heart – touch where your heart is.

Soul – point to yourself.

Mind – touch the top of your head.

Strength – feel your muscles (in Mark, not Matthew).

Neighbour – hug or shake hands with the nearest person on each side of you.

Self – give yourself a hug.

(Do this activity two or three times.)

Opening prayer

God of the loving heart,
make mine loving too,
that I may become more like you
in all I say and do.
Let my love for you be shown
in all my relationships and actions.
Amen.

Opening song

Bind us together, Lord

Readings

Deuteronomy 34:1-12 or Leviticus 19:1-2, 15-18
Psalm 90:1-6, 13-17 or Psalm 1
1 Thessalonians 2:1-8
Matthew 22:34-46

Thought for the day

Every Jewish service starts with the same words: 'Hear, O Israel: The Lord is our God, the Lord is one. You shall love the Lord your God with all your heart, with all your soul, and with all your might.' The words continue by telling them to teach their children these words, to bind them to their hand, fix them on their forehead and write them on the door posts of their house. These words are called the 'Shema', which means 'Hear', and they ask people to listen and obey. Jews recite these words in the same way that Christians say the Creed. As commanded, these are the first words Jewish parents teach their children from the Scriptures. They put these words in little leather boxes, called phylacteries, and bind them on their wrists so that they may think of God in all their actions. They also fix them to their heads so that God may be known in their thinking. Then in a little cylinder, called a mezuzah, they fasten them to the doorpost of their houses and touch them as they go out and in, to remind them that God is with them in their going out and their coming in. All this is to encourage an awareness and deep love of God.

When Jesus was asked what the greatest commandment was, everyone would have agreed with him when he replied, 'Love God'. Love God with all your heart, and with all your soul, and with all your mind. Love God with your whole being. Every Jew would agree with that. Later St Augustine would say, 'Love God, and do what you like.' By this he meant if we love God, we will do nothing to hurt or go against him.

Jesus then added, 'And a second [commandment] is like it: "You shall love your neighbour as yourself." On these two commandments hang all the law and the prophets.' This can be found in the Old Testament in Leviticus 19:18. Jesus put the two together to make a Summary of the Law. Our love for God is to be reflected in our love for each other. Only when we love God are we able to love others as we ought, yet in a strange way we can only love God when we have learnt love from others. Through the love of our homes and our loved ones, God reveals his love to us. When we know love, we can love. We also learn to love ourselves and accept ourselves because we are counted worthy of the love of God and of others.

In the words of the song, 'All you need is love' – love God and love one another.

Question time

Do you take to heart this summary of the law and seek to live by love?

Illustration

'Christmas wouldn't be Christmas without any presents,' Jo had grumbled as she waited with her three sisters until their mother returned from church . . .

'Merry Christmas, Marmee! Many of them!'

'Merry Christmas, little daughters! But I want to say one word before we sit down. Not far away from here lies a poor woman with a little newborn baby. Six children are huddled into one bed to keep from freezing, for they have no fire. There is nothing to eat over there, and the oldest boy came to tell me they are suffering from hunger and cold. My girls, will you give them your breakfast as a Christmas present?'

They were all unusually hungry having waited nearly an hour, and for a minute no one spoke – only a minute, for Jo exclaimed impetuously, 'I am so glad you came before we began!'

'May I go and help to carry the things to the poor children?' asked Beth eagerly.

'I shall take the cream and the muffins,' added Amy, heroically giving up the articles she most liked.

Meg was already covering the buckwheats, and piling the bread into one big plate.

'I thought you would do it,' said Mrs March, smiling as if satisfied. 'You shall have bread and milk for breakfast and make up for it at dinner time.'

They were soon ready, and the procession set out.

Fortunately it was early and they went through the back streets, so few people saw them, and no one laughed at the queer party.

A poor bare miserable room it was with broken windows, no fire, ragged bedclothes, a sick mother, wailing baby and a group of pale, hungry children huddled under one old quilt to keep warm.

How the big eyes stared and the blue lips smiled as the girls went in!

'Ach mein Gott. It is good angels come to us!' said the poor woman crying for joy.

Louisa May Alcott, *Little Women* (1868)

Intercessions

Blessed are you, Lord our God,
for you love us with an everlasting love.
We rejoice that nothing can separate us
from your love in Christ Jesus.
Lord, help us to show your love to each other at all times.
Blessed are you, Father, Son and Holy Spirit.

Loving God, we give thanks
for the fellowship of the Church
and for all who have taught us the faith.
We pray for preachers and teachers,
for evangelists and Bible translators.
We ask your blessing upon all Sunday schools,
study groups and those who are learning to pray.
We remember all who are seeking to grow
in love of you and in faith.

Silence

God of love,
hear us and help us.

Loving God, we give thanks
for all who reveal your love and care
through dedicated lives.
We ask your blessing upon all those who work
among the deprived and under-privileged peoples
of the world.
We remember all who seek to bring peace and unity
to communities and nations.
We pray for all who are homeless and in need.

Silence

God of love,
hear us and help us.

Loving God, we give thanks
for all who have shown us love and care.
We ask your blessing upon our homes and loved ones.

We remember all who are separated from their loved ones
through illness or circumstance.
We pray especially for the lonely
and any who feel unloved.

Silence

God of love,
hear us and help us.

Loving God, we thank you
for all who reveal love
through working in the healing professions.
We pray for doctors and nurses
and remember our own doctors and hospitals.
We ask your blessing upon all who are ill or suffering,
especially those who have no one to care for them.

Silence

God of love,
hear us and help us.

Loving God, we give you thanks
for the gift of eternal life.
We rejoice in the fellowship of all your saints
and ask your blessing upon all our loved ones departed.
May we share with them
in the fullness and glory of your kingdom.

Silence

Merciful Father,
**accept these prayers
for the sake of your Son,
our Saviour Jesus Christ.
Amen.**

Memory verse

'You shall love the Lord your God with all your heart, and with all your soul, and with all your mind.' This is the greatest and first commandment. And a second is like it: 'You shall love your neighbour as yourself.' *Matthew 22:37-39*

Suggested music

Love is the only law
A new commandment
Love is his word

CANDLES

Aim

To show how God loves us and wants us to love one another.

Teaching

When God made the world, he did it because he wanted to love it and it to love him. God made a beautiful world and all sorts of wonderful creatures out of love and for us to love. Let each of you tell me something in the world that you love.

God made all the people in the world and wanted them to love each other and to love him. God does not want us to be unkind or cruel to any of his creatures because he loves them. God does not want us to spoil nice flowers or his beautiful earth because he cares for it and loves them.

Love – make a heart shape over your head with your hands

God – point upwards or raise both hands in praise

with all your heart – touch where your heart is

with all your soul – point to yourself

with all your mind – touch the top of your head

(Now get the children to stand in a circle and do the actions with you as you go over the words.)

But God wants us to love not only him but also the people he has made. Anyone who comes near to us – we call them neighbours – God wants us to love. Let us give the neighbour on each side of us a hug. God does not want anyone to be missed out because he loves us all – and that means God loves you. Now give yourself a hug to show that God loves you.

I will read to you what Jesus told the people who came to him. While I read it see if you can do the actions. When Jesus talks about commandments, he means things that we should all do.

Jesus said there were two commandments. The first is 'You shall love the Lord your God with all your heart, and with all your soul, and with all your mind'.

The second is 'You shall love your neighbour as yourself'.

Those are good rules to keep because we know God love us all.

Activity

There are loving hearts to colour in and then cut out and put in order. Encourage the children to get the order right.

Prayer

Thank you, God, for loving us.
Thank you for a wonderful world
and for our families and friends.
As we are loved, help us to love others.
Amen.

Song

One, two, three, Jesus loves me (verse 1 and chorus)

LAMPS

Aim

To learn the summary of the law.

Teaching

Who knows how many commandments Moses gave to the people? There were ten and everyone who came to

church had to learn them. One day some people came to Jesus and asked which he thought was the greatest commandment. Jesus did not choose any of the ten but chose one to include all of the ten. The one he chose did not surprise the Jewish people because everyone had to learn it as soon as they could. It said, 'You shall love the Lord your God with all your heart, and with all your soul, and with all your might' (Deuteronomy 6:5). That is a wonderful rule – God asks us to love him (notice how Jesus has included 'with all your mind').

They could not forget these words because every time they left their house they touched a little cylinder on their door and inside these words were written – even if they could not read, they knew these words. This reminded them that God was with them in their homes and when they went out, and at all times they were to give their love to God.

Some people had the words put in little leather boxes and they strapped them to their heads, to show they had to think of God and love him with their mind. Then some had them strapped to their wrist to remind them God was there with them in all that they did. God wanted them to show their love through their work and their actions.

This was to remind them to love God with their heart, their soul, their mind and their strength. No one was really surprised at this being the greatest commandment – but Jesus added another so that there were two commandments. Jesus knew the second one was also in the Bible (Leviticus 19:18). He said, 'The second is like it: "You shall love your neighbour as yourself."'

Activity

There are instructions for making a mezuzah from the work sheet, and they can learn the words inside it.

Prayer

Lord God, I am loved by you
and seek to love you.
You love all your creation –
help us to love it too.
Teach us to love each other
as we know we are loved.
And thank you for all who love us.
Amen.

Song

Can we love one another

TORCHES

Aim

To learn the summary of the law and see how it involves all of us.

Teaching

Once when people prepared for confirmation (explain) they had to learn the Lord's Prayer, the Creed and the

Ten Commandments. (Show all of these.) No doubt you know the Lord's Prayer and the Creed – but do any of you know the Ten Commandments? There is quite lot to remember and if you had to say which was the most important, what you would say?

This was a question the Pharisees asked Jesus: 'Which commandment in the law is the greatest?' Maybe they really wanted to know, or maybe they were trying to trap Jesus with a trick question.

The answer Jesus gave did not surprise them. (Read Matthew 22:37, 38.) They all knew these words. Every Jewish child had to learn them. Every service in the synagogue started with these words – it still does today. Every Jew had these words in a little box fixed to the doorpost of the house. They touched it as they went out to remind them that God was with them and seeking their love. When they returned home they touched it again to remind them that God was in their homes and sharing their love.

Those who came to Jesus and questioned him would be wearing these words in a little leather box strapped to their head, to remind them to love God with their mind and in their thinking. They would also have a little box containing these words strapped to their wrist. This was to remind them that God is present in all their actions and seeks their love. These were a people who were seeking to know and love God, so the first commandment would be very acceptable to them.

Jesus then added a second commandment. This one was not written on their doorposts or in the little boxes. Jesus said, 'And the second is like it: You shall love your neighbour as yourself.' This can also be found in the Old Testament in Leviticus 19:18. Jesus was not giving new rules but reminding them of how they should be living as believers. (Explore what is meant by 'neighbour' and how we need also to 'love ourself'.)

Activity

Encourage the group to learn these words off by heart. Tell them they should not only know them but live by them. They may like to make a mezuzah to hold the words and act as an aid to learning.

Prayer

Lord God, you give us your love
and count us as your children.
Help us to give our love to you
and to reveal your love for others
through our actions and words.
Amen.

Song

Brother, sister, let me serve you

All Saints' Day

1 November
or Sunday between 30 October and 5 November inclusive

Aim

To show how the blessed share in the eternal.

Preparation

This is a good day to have a procession around the church. Stop at any images of saints in stained glass or pictures, and give thanks for those saints. Provide candles for all who would like to light a candle in thanksgiving for a holy person. Give thanks for the patron saint of your church.

Opening activity

Two voices:

1. Mr X had a string of shops, a good business and lots of people worked for him.
2. What did he leave?
1. All of it.
2. Ms A was a very popular actress. She had some wonderful clothes and a big limo – she was worth a fortune. She died last week.
1. What did she leave?
2. All of it.
1. Mrs B was always caring for others. She was a kind soul and tried to serve God. We were sorry when she died.
2. I suppose she left everything?
1. No, she took what was precious with her into eternal life.

Opening prayer

Blessed are you, Lord our God,
for you have given us life eternal.
As we rejoice in your saints
may we seek to do your will
and reveal your glory in the world.
We ask this in the name of our Saviour Jesus Christ.
Amen.

Opening song

Rejoice in God's saints

Readings

Revelation 7:9-17
Psalm 34:1-10
1 John 3:1-3
Matthew 5:1-12

Thought for the day

Today's Gospel is known as the Beatitudes: the word 'Blessed' is used nine times in three groups of three. Blessed means happy but much more besides because it also means not being subject to fate or circumstance. To be blessed means to have an imperishable quality. For this reason many Jewish prayers begin with the words 'Blessed are you, Lord our God'. For God is imperishable, God is eternal – our blessedness can only come from God. We show our blessedness by living the way God wants us to live.

The first three 'Blesseds' are about our attitude to the world around us. The poor in spirit are those who are not grabbing and seeking to get all the time. They are able to let go and live simply. Those who mourn are people with feelings: they have passions and have not become hard-hearted; they feel for others. When you say, 'good grief', you mean such people. The meek are those who do not force others but are gentle in their dealings.

The next three are about relationships. To hunger and thirst for righteousness is to seek to live in right relationships with people and to strive for justice. The merciful do not demand their rights but are forgiving and kind towards others. The pure in heart are the single-minded who seek to live God's way.

The third group concerns our position in a difficult world. Those who seek peace are those who seek to bring harmony and balance to the world and they are seen to be children of God as his image is seen in them. Those who endure persecution for righteousness show themselves to be followers of Jesus who died for us and they shall inherit the kingdom. Then there are those who do not let persecution get the better of them but stand firm in the faith. Those who remain loyal will not lose out. Even if they lose their life, they will have life eternal.

These are the qualities that make a saint: they show the people who are striving to serve God. The saints were not perfect but they sought to live the life of the blessed and they have given us an example to follow.

Question time

What do you understand by the word 'Blessed'?

Why do you think that the day they died is celebrated as the saint's day?

Illustration

The word 'blessed' comes from the Greek word 'makarios' and is used to describe the gods. Jesus uses it to describe those who do God's will. The Greeks called Cyprus the 'blessed island' or the 'happy island' because it was such a rich and fertile land with a good climate, rich in minerals and natural resources. Fruit and grain and flowers could grow in abundance. It was a place where people should be perfectly happy. It should be a place of peace and harmony. In the same way, those who lived the beatitudes would find peace and harmony in God's presence and God's love.

Intercessions

Blessed are you, Lord our God,
for you have called us to share
in the blessedness of your saints.
Grant that in the darkness that is around us

we may be guided by their example
and so serve you in love and peace.
Blessed are you, Father, Son and Holy Spirit.

Rejoicing in the fellowship of all the saints
we pray to the Lord:

Lord, make us to be numbered with your saints
in your eternal glory.

Blessed God, we remember before you
all who have witnessed to your love and mercy.
We ask your blessing
upon all who seek to bring reconciliation
and forgiveness
to peoples and communities.
We pray for all who are involved in pastoral work
and the ministry of healing.

Silence

Lord, make us to be numbered with your saints
in your eternal glory.

Blessed God, we remember before you
all who have witnessed to your peace.
We ask your blessing
upon the work of the United Nations
and all peace-keeping forces.
We pray for all who are not at peace
with themselves or with the world around them
and all who suffer through war.

Silence

Lord, make us to be numbered with your saints
in your eternal glory.

Blessed God, we remember before you
all who have set us an example
by their grace and goodness.
We ask your blessing upon our homes and families.
We pray for all who are suffering
from broken relationships
and all who feel lonely.

Silence

Lord, make us to be numbered with your saints
in your eternal glory.

Blessed God, we remember before you
all who have suffered persecution for their faith.
We ask you to bless
those who strive against injustice and evil.
We pray for all who suffer from tyranny or oppression.
We remember also all who are ill at home
or in hospital,
those injured in accidents and all victims of violence.

Silence

Lord, make us to be numbered with your saints
in your eternal glory.

Blessed God, we remember before you
all the faithful departed.
We pray that our loved ones who are gone from us
may rejoice in the fellowship of all your saints in glory.

Silence

Merciful Father,
**accept these prayers
for the sake of your Son,
our Saviour Jesus Christ.
Amen.**

Memory verse

O taste and see that the Lord is good; happy are those
who take refuge in him.
Psalm 34:8

Suggested music

For all the saints
Who are these like stars appearing
Glory to thee, O God

CANDLES

Aim

To tell the story of St Boniface.

Teaching

A long time ago there was a man who lived at Crediton
in Devon. He decided he wanted to learn more about
God and to give his whole life to God. He was very
clever and joined a monastery in a city called Exeter. A
monastery is a place where people pray to God and
learn about God. He was good at reading and writing.
He also wrote poetry and he said his prayers lots of
times every day. This man was called Boniface. Let us
say his name together: Boniface.

Boniface became a priest because he wanted to go
and tell others about Jesus and his love. He could have
stayed in England but he wanted to tell people who had
never heard of Jesus all about him. Boniface would tell
people how Jesus showed the love of God and how
Jesus died on the cross and rose again. Sometimes he
risked his life to tell other people about Jesus. Boniface
got into a boat and went over the sea to a forest area
where people did not know about Jesus.

In one place it was hard to tell anyone about Jesus
because they said their prayers to a god who had a
special tree. It was a great big oak tree. People told him
if he harmed the oak tree, their god would harm him.
They were afraid of the tree but Boniface was not afraid.
He knew there is only one God and he is a God of love.
Boniface told them that his God was stronger than the
god they believed in and his God would protect him
from any trouble.

Boniface got a sharp axe and chopped the great big
tree down. (Act out the chopping.) Every time he hit the
tree the people thought something awful would happen
to him. But it did not. Soon the tree fell with a great big
crack and a bang and it lay on the ground. Boniface was
still safe; nothing had harmed him. In this way Boniface
showed the people about the God he believed in and
then told them how God is a loving God.

People saw that the God of Boniface made him brave
and protected him. They saw that because of God's love

Boniface was a good person and they asked him to tell them about God and Jesus.

Because Boniface loved God and spent his life telling people about God, he is called a 'saint'. If someone is called a saint, it means they love God and show his love to others.

Activity

On the activity sheet there is a picture of Boniface to colour in. The children could act out the chopping down of the tree and say 'thank you' to God for caring for them.

Prayer

God, thank you for St Boniface
for he was brave and loved you.
Help us to be brave
and to tell others of your love.
Let us remember
to say our prayers to you every day.
Thank you, God, for loving us.
Amen.

Song

Come on and shine

LAMPS

Aim

To show we are called by God to share in the work of the saints.

Teaching

Jesus wants us all to know that we are children of God. If we know God loves us and helps us, it should make us very happy. When we were tiny most of us were offered to God by our parents. Do you know how it was done? (Tell the children about baptism and see how much they know.) This tells us we come from God – who made us all – and we belong to God. We are God's people.

Those who have shown by their lives that they belong to God are called saints. These are people who have tried to do what God wants them to do, even when other people tried to stop them. Many ordinary people are known as saints.

St Peter was a . . . ? (Fisherman)
St Matthew was a . . . ? (Tax collector)
St George was a . . . ? (Soldier)
St Nicholas was a . . . ? (Bishop)
St Cuthbert was a . . . ? (Shepherd)

They are saints because they tried to show the light and love of God to the world. Just as a stained-glass window lets in light, they let the light of God shine in their lives.

God wants us all to be saints. He wants us to love him and show others that we love him. The saints are like those who have been chosen for their skill in showing

us about God and his love – like someone is chosen for a team. But we are all called to be part of that team. This means we need to practise every day. We need to make sure we do not miss our prayers or opportunities to help others, or any chance of telling others of Jesus.

Activity

If your church has stained-glass windows, it would be good to look at them and talk about the saints depicted there. Do the children know the dedication of your church if it is dedicated to a saint? There is an opportunity on the sheet to make a stained-glass window.

Prayer

God, we thank you for your saints,
for all the men and women
who spoke of your love
and gave their lives to you.
As they needed your help to be saints,
help us to give our love to you.
Amen.

Song

O when the saints

TORCHES

Aim

To know we are called to be saints, to be God's dedicated people.

Teaching

Today we celebrate All Saints, all the men and women who dedicated their lives in the service of God. They come from every nation and from all walks of life.

What are saints? Can you name any saints?

'Saint' comes from the same word for holy, 'sanctus'. A saint means a holy person. But it does not mean they are perfect; it does not mean they never sin or do wrong. Rather it means they belong to God. Just as the Holy Bible is God's book, and the Holy Church is God's Church. Saints are God's people. But wait a minute – are you not God's people? Of course you are! When St Paul wrote to different churches he wrote to those called to be saints (Romans 1:7; 1 Corinthians 1:2; 2 Corinthians 1:1; Ephesians 1:1; Philippians 1:1; Colossians 1:2). If he was writing to our church, he would write to the saints in (*your town*).

That means everyone of us: so you are St (*mention a few names*). Now that must come as a surprise but it should not. It does not mean you are ever so good, though you should try to be. Rather it means you know you belong to God and that you are trying to dedicate your life to God. Sometimes instead of saints the word is translated as 'dedicated people' or even 'the Church'. In our baptism we are dedicated to God, Father, Son and Holy Spirit. We are meant to show that dedication by the way we live, by our love for God and our care of others. God's dedicated people are meant to reveal God to others by the way they live. A child once described saints as 'people who let light in' – thinking of a stained-glass window. That is exactly what they are: people who reveal the light and love of God. You are called to be saints – live up to your calling.

Activity

There is a wordsearch on saints' names and days on the activity sheet. If you have time, get the group to read and discuss 1 Corinthians 1:26-31.

For the quiz it would be helpful to have a calendar of saints' days.

Prayer

Lord God, you have called us
to be your people,
to give our lives to you
and in the service of others.
As you have called us,
strengthen us
and make us worthy of our calling.
Amen.

Song

Be holy, be holy

Fourth Sunday before Advent

Sunday between 30 October and 5 November inclusive
For use if the Feast of All Saints was celebrated on 1 November and alternative propers are needed

Aim

To show that our God cares for us in all our troubles.

Preparation

In the entrance show a picture of the earth from space. Beside it have some words of Julian of Norwich:

It lasts because
God made it,
God loves it,
God keeps it.

Opening activity

Good News, Bad News

1. Good News – Free drinks tomorrow.
2. Bad News – Tomorrow never comes.

1. Good News – You can have a day off tomorrow.
2. Bad News – You're sacked.

1. Bad News – The world is hurtling to destruction.
2. Good News – It will take another few billion years.

1. Bad News – There are troubles ahead.
2. Good News – God is with us and give us eternal life.

Opening prayer

Praise and glory to you, Lord God,
for you have made us.
You are our Creator and Redeemer;
you are our Guide and our Strength.
To you be glory, Father, Son and Holy Spirit.
Amen.

Opening song

All my hope on God is founded

Readings

Micah 3:5-12
Psalm 43
1 Thessalonians 2:9-13
Matthew 24:1-14

Thought for the day

Today the Church's yearly cycle takes on a new dimension: we begin to look towards the preparation for Advent and Christmas. This period is kept as the 'Kingdom Season': we look at the kingdoms of the world and the kingdom of Christ.

Jesus grieves for Jerusalem and the Temple. It could be that some of the followers of Jesus had never seen another building like the Temple. The white marble of the Temple and the gold-leaf made it look radiant. At the corners of the Temple were stones that were 20 to 40 feet in length and weighed up to 100 tons. You would imagine they were unmovable. It was a very spectacular building when most people lived in small houses made of mud bricks. It looked as if it would last for ever – and because it was God's house they thought it would.

Jesus realises that the prophecy of Micah is about to come to pass. God is not condemning Jerusalem. The people are bringing the trouble upon themselves. The disciples are horrified when Jesus says that the Temple will be destroyed.

It is only when they are alone on the Mount of Olives that they question Jesus and ask to know more. Jesus then talks of the unrest not only of people but the earth itself. People will be led astray by false-Christs, there will be wars and rumours of war, with nation rising against nation. Along with this there will be famine and earthquakes. It sounds a real picture of doom and yet it is something that is always happening to the world and temporal powers. Many kingdoms have come and gone. It is easy to despair. But Jesus does not want us to concentrate on the troubles, only to be aware that they come.

Jesus does not want us to be led astray by false claims. He wants us to stay loyal to him because all the troubles are like birth pangs. A new kingdom is coming in with Christ as King. God has not abandoned his world. For all its troubles, God still loves the world. God still cares for his creation. God seeks to redeem the world and to free it from captivity.

Jesus was well aware of the mounting opposition to him and therefore to his disciples. Jesus does not promise a good time. In this world there will be all sorts of persecution. People will lose faith and fall away. False prophets will mislead many, and lawlessness will increase. In all this love will appear to die because people will harden their hearts. Can we not see much of this going on in our society today?

That is the bad news. The Good News is that these are signs of the coming of Christ. His kingdom is near. Christ the King will bring in the age of peace. We are not left on our own in all this trouble. For us the end is not the end because Christ is our Saviour and he brings us into his kingdom. All our troubles are to be looked upon as birth pangs and the bringing in of the new age, where the kingdoms of the world are the kingdoms of Christ and of God. We are not promised a journey without storms but are promised we will not be alone and at the end of the journey we will arrive into the fullness of his kingdom.

Question time

In times of trouble do you find strength from the Good News of the love of God?

Do you see that Jesus does not threaten us with a bleak future but does warn us of the danger of some of our actions?

Illustration

When we have dark or bad days we need to remind ourselves that God is with us and cares for us. Here is a prayer from the Hebrides which you may find helpful:

Though the dawn breaks cheerless on this Isle today,
my spirit walks in a path of light.
For I know my greatness.
Thou has built me a throne within thy heart.
I dwell safely within the circle of thy care.
I cannot for a moment fall out of the everlasting arms.
I am on my way to thy glory.

Alistair Maclean, *Hebridean Altars* (1937)

Now that is Good News, whatever the day!

Intercessions

Blessed are you, Lord our God,
for amidst the trials and troubles of the world
you are present and ready to help us.
You sent your Son
so that we should not perish
but have eternal life.
Blessed are you, Father, Son and Holy Spirit.

We give thanks to you, O Lord,
for the Church
and the hope that it brings to troubled lives.
We ask your blessing upon Christians
who are being persecuted for their faith
or who risk their lives in the care of others.
We remember all relief agencies
and those who work in war-torn areas,
in areas of earthquake or famine.

Silence

Lord, we put our trust in you:
hear us and help us.

We give thanks, O Lord,
for all who seek to bring peace and harmony
to our world.
We ask your blessing upon leaders of nations
and all peace-keeping forces.
We pray especially
for those whose lives are endangered at this time.

Silence

Lord, we put our trust in you:
hear us and help us.

We give thanks, O Lord,
for our homes and our loved ones.
We ask your blessing
upon all who have been driven out of their homes
through acts of violence, natural disaster or debt.
We pray for those who find they can no longer cope
in their own home.

Silence

Lord, we put our trust in you:
hear us and help us.

We give thanks, O Lord,
for the healing services.

We pray for all doctors and nurses,
for paramedics and those who work in ambulances
or rescue vehicles.
We ask your blessing
upon all whose world has fallen apart
through sickness or loss of a loved one.

Silence

Lord, we put our trust in you:
hear us and help us.

We give thanks, O Lord,
for the gift of eternal life.
We rejoice in the fellowship of all your saints
and ask your blessing upon our loved ones departed.
May we all share with you
in the fullness of your kingdom.

Silence

Merciful Father,
**accept these prayers
for the sake of your Son,
our Saviour Jesus Christ.
Amen.**

Memory verse

Hope in God; for I shall again praise him, my help and my God.
Psalm 43:5b

Suggested music

We have a Gospel
I give myself to you
O Jesus, I have promised

CANDLES

Aim

To know that God is with us and loves us all the time.

Teaching

At home when it is dark, what does your mother or father do to make you all see better? They put some lights on in the house. Sometimes when you are left alone in your bedroom and it is dark, what does your mother or father do to help you not be afraid? They put a light on. If you are very afraid or if you are where there is something dangerous, your mother or father will stay with you to look after you and protect you. Sometimes they will hold your hand to make sure you do not get hurt or lost. Why do you think they do this?

Yes, it is because they love us and do not want anything to hurt us. Our parents love us and protect us and when we need help they are ready to help us.

We call God 'our Father' because he made the whole world and us. He loves the world he has made. He wants us to enjoy it. Yet sometimes terrible things can happen in our world – things that God does not really want to happen. But whatever happens, God loves us and wants to look after us. It is good to talk to God when we are afraid or when something bothers us. It is good to know that God is with us always; even when sad or bad things happen, he still loves us.

(Get the children to say, 'God is there' and to clap each time they say it.)

When it is bright and sunny
God is there.
When it is dark and nasty
God is there.
When we are happy and joyful
God is there.
When we are sad and upset
God is there.
When we are with our friends
God is there.
When we are alone and it is dark.
God is there.
God is always there.

Activity

Play a tag game of 'Rescue'. If you are touched, you have to sit on the floor and cover your eyes. If someone who has not been caught touches you, you can get up and run around again. If too many are being rescued, then have more people tagging.

Prayer

God, we thank you
that you are with us always
and that you love us.
We ask you to look after us
and keep us safe and in your love.
Amen.

Song

God who made the earth

LAMPS

Aim

To show that God is our maker, keeper and friend, and that we are in the hand of God.

Teaching

Once there was a woman called Julian who lived in Norwich. As far as we know, she was the first woman in England to write a book. Julian wrote about how God loves us and cares for us. Once she had been very ill and nearly died but she knew that God loved her. At the time she lived lots of people were dying because of a terrible sickness called the Black Death; other people were dying because of a war. England was fighting. There were lots of people suffering but Julian knew that God was still with every one of them and cared for them.

One day she held in her hand a little hazelnut. (If possible show a tiny hazelnut in the palm of your hand.) It was quite small in her hand and very small compared with the size of the world. Julian wondered how it could survive, how it could last. Then she realised that . . .

God made it,
God loves it
and God cares for it.

God loves all that he has made, even the tiniest of nuts – the whole big world, even the universe. They last because God loves them and God looks after them. She learnt all this by looking at and thinking about a hazelnut.

Julian of Norwich realised this was true not only of the hazelnut but also of the world and of herself. Everything was in the hand of God. She knew that God made her, God loved her and God looked after her. This is also true for every one of us. Say after me:

God made me.
God loves me.
God cares for me.
I am in the hand of God

Activity

Have an obstacle course and one member of the team blindfolded. The team have to help their blindfolded member to get around the course and then remove the blindfold. If anyone bumps into anything the whole team must start again. This can be repeated two or three times.

Prayer

Lord God, we thank you for giving us life,
for loving us and all that you have made.
Help us to know that you are with us
and care for us always.
Amen.

Song

He's got the whole world in his hand

TORCHES

Aim

To know that, among all the troubles of the world, God is with us and cares for us.

Teaching

The Temple at Jerusalem was a most wonderful building – one of the greatest buildings in the world – and it was built to last. Some of its cornerstones were over 12 metres long and weighed more than a 100 tons. They looked as if they would never move. Building of the Temple started 19 years before Jesus was born and parts of it were still being built when Jesus was visiting it, though most of it was finished nine years before he was born. The white marble of the temple and the gold leaf made it stand out and shine. It was a very spectacular building when most people lived in small houses made

FOURTH SUNDAY BEFORE ADVENT

of mud bricks. It looked as if it would last for ever – and because it was God's house they thought it would. Imagine the shock, horror when Jesus said it would not last. He told them it would all be pulled down.

Soon after this he told the disciples about the terrible things that were going to happen. There would be wars, famines and earthquakes. He told the disciples that they would be hated and tortured. There would be lawlessness and people betraying one another – not good news, is it? Where is the Good News in today's Gospel?

Jesus was showing the way the world was going and the troubles people were bringing on themselves or that evil people bring upon them. He showed that nothing in the world is safe. Not really good news, but honest. Jesus did not pretend. In this world we will not escape trouble.

The Good News is that God cares for us in all of this and God is with us in all these troubles (as the crucifixion witnesses).

More Good News: Jesus is our Saviour and not even death shall separate us from the love of God in Christ Jesus. The Good News for us is that we have a God who not only loves us but also gives us eternal life. When the days are dark and troubles come, we need to remember that our God is with us and gives us the victory. We may feel we lose round after round in the battles we face but in Jesus we are assured the victory. Learn John 3:16 and take it to heart.

Activity

There is an opportunity on the sheet to look at the prophecies of Micah and what Jesus has been saying about the Temple. They can also look at the warnings we are given today.

Prayer

Lord God,
you know we are often in the midst of troubles
and there are dangers all around.
Keep us in the protection of your love
and in the life which is eternal.
Amen.

Song

We are marching in the light of God

Third Sunday before Advent

Sunday between 6 and 12 November inclusive

Aim

To show how we need to keep ourselves aware that Jesus comes to us.

Preparation

Have a variety of lamps and torches to switch on and, if possible, a wind-up torch and a photograph of someone asleep in a public place.

Opening activity

Three voices:

1. I was going to ring for help but I forgot to recharge my phone.
2. I was going along this road when my lights failed me.
3. One of our lights went pop and it fused the whole lot.
1. I am a Scout and I keep our motto, 'Be prepared'.
2. I have an emergency light that I can use when all other power fails.
3. When I feel the darkness of the world closing in, I turn to Jesus who is the Light of the World.

Opening prayer

Lord God, may we be ready
for your coming to us this day
and so invite you into our lives and homes.
May we know that you invite us
to share in your love
and to welcome you.
Amen.

Opening song

Wake, O wake

Readings

Amos 5:18-24 or Wisdom of Solomon 6:12-16
Psalm 70 or Wisdom of Solomon 6:17-20
1 Thessalonians 4:13-18
Matthew 25:1-13

Thought for the day

It is amazing how many people are willing to pray 'your kingdom come; your will be done', but then put it all off to another day. Jesus wanted us to know the kingdom of heaven is at hand (Mark 1:15) and we should be entering into it. In this 'Kingdom Season' we look at another parable of the kingdom. The parable of the ten bridesmaids is full of warnings. There is no doubt they are all invited; they are all given the opportunity to share in the joy of the wedding. They are all excited about it. There is no suggestion that the foolish ones were wicked or evil, only that they had neglected certain things that were required of them. It was a small matter to make sure they had oil and light – they could have

done it but they never bothered. How often have we made excuses for not saying our prayers and welcoming God into our homes? There comes a time when it is too late. The night comes and the time for getting oil is past. The time for meeting the king passed; the time for entering the banquet passed – and all for the want of a little oil, a little thought and preparation. The artist Pablo Picasso said, 'Never put off today anything you do not want to leave undone for ever.'

To live our lives without due care and proper attention courts disaster. We ignore the things of God at our peril.

The words of the bridegroom to those clamouring to come in are a terrible statement: 'I never knew you.' Often we ask, 'Do you two know each other?' Have we taken the time and made the effort to know Jesus, to be friends with him, or have we been too preoccupied? Can Jesus say to us, 'I never knew you'? God does not exclude us from his kingdom. He has given us an open invitation. Only we can exclude ourselves by excusing ourselves.

Question time

Are you in danger of putting off your prayers and your relationship with God to another day?

Do you understand that the judgement is not to be there when the Lord comes to you?

Illustration

John could have learnt much more at school but he was always fooling around or thinking about what he was going to do after school. He never listened. He was there in body but not in mind or spirit.

Jean knew it was no use talking to her father while he was watching a football match on the television. He was in the same room but he was not really where she was and he would not hear.

There is a danger that we are never really aware of our Lord's coming and we miss the wonderful relationship that is offered to us: we miss the moment even though it is offered to us more than once. Too often Jesus finds we are 'not there' when he comes. He seeks us out but we do not give him any attention. Think of Jesus saying:

I called your name but you were out or preoccupied.
I came to you in the night but you did not notice.
I knocked on your door and your heart but they remained closed.
I asked for your help but you were too busy.
I wanted to know you, to give my love to you, but you were otherwise engaged.

Intercessions

Blessed are you, Lord our God,
for you come to us and abide with us always.
Your light scatters the darkness from before us
and you invite us to let this shine through us
and reveal you to the world.

THIRD SUNDAY BEFORE ADVENT

In your love help us to be children of light.
Blessed are you, Father, Son and Holy Spirit.

Lord of light and love,
we ask your blessing upon the Church
throughout the world.
We pray especially for areas
where the faith has grown dim
and vision has been lost.
We remember all who are struggling
against dark and evil forces.
We pray for all who seek
to bring the light of Christ to others.

Silence

Lord of light,
awaken us to your presence.

Lord of light and love,
strengthen all who are on their guard against evil
and seek to bring peace and harmony to our world.
We remember before you
all who are suffering through oppression or violence,
all who are used as cheap labour
and all who are without proper homes or enough food.
Bless all who work tirelessly for their relief.

Silence

Lord of light,
awaken us to your presence.

Lord of light and love,
make us alert to your presence with us
and in our homes.
Bless and protect our families and our friends.
Make us alert to the needs of our community,
where we can help and be of use.
Let us not miss opportunities of showing your love.

Silence

Lord of light,
awaken us to your presence.

Lord of light and love,
bless all whose lives are darkened
by illness or tragedy.
We remember all who feel afraid
and those who regret work undone
or doing what they should not have done.
We pray for all who are terminally ill
and all who can no longer look after themselves.

Silence

Lord of light,
awaken us to your presence.

Lord of light and love,
we ask your blessing
upon all our friends and loved ones
who are departed from us.
May they rejoice in your light and love
in your kingdom.
We pray for all your saints
and all who have reflected your light in the world.

Silence

Merciful Father,
accept these prayers
for the sake of your Son,
our Saviour Jesus Christ.
Amen.

Memory verse

Keep awake therefore, for you know neither the day nor the hour.
Matthew 25:13

Suggested music

Give me oil in my lamp
Peace is flowing like a river
Will you come and follow me

CANDLES

Aim

To show that we need to be ready to make friends with Jesus.

Teaching

Has anyone been to a wedding? It is lovely to welcome the bride into church. Has anyone been a bridesmaid or a pageboy? Did you have to wear anything special or carry anything special? Sometimes things make a wedding late because the bride is not ready or the photographer holds them up.

Jesus told a story about a wedding. There were ten young women with lamps. They were not really bridesmaids because they were waiting on the man rather than the woman. They were waiting to welcome him home. Each of these young women had a lamp. It did not have batteries but it had a light like you get from a candle. It was a little container filled with oil and a wick, which is like a piece of string. When this was lit it gave some light. (At this stage light ten tea lights or candles – close to the children but taking the necessary safety precautions.)

All of the ten had oil lamps and when they started the lamps were full of oil. But because the bridegroom was late the oil began to run out. First one lamp went out, then two, then three, then four and then five. (Allow five children to blow out the lights one after another.) The other five had each brought a container of oil to keep their lamps burning. When those whose lamps had gone out saw this they asked for some oil. But the five could not give them any in case they needed still more before the bridegroom came. The five with no lights on had to go and get some more from another place. While the five had gone away, the bridegroom came to the house and was welcomed by five lamps burning. They all went into the house to have a party. They were all happy to be with the bridegroom. When the others came back they found the doors were locked and they could not get into the house. They were very sad and went away wishing they had been wise and got ready for the coming of the bridegroom.

Jesus wants us to be his friends. He wants us to get to know him by talking to him, by saying our prayers each day and giving him our love. Every day Jesus is with us. He wants us to know that and for us to help other people to know him.

Activity

There are ten lamps on the activity sheet to match up to ten faces.

Light ten tea lights and get ten children to stand behind them smiling. All the lights are then blown out and all the children have to show sad faces. Now relight five of the tea lights – the five children behind these have to smile and the others have to pretend to be sad as they go back to their seats.

Prayer

Jesus,
help us to shine as lights in your world.
Let us show that we love you
and help others to know of your love.
Amen.

Song

Jesus bids us shine

LAMPS

Aim

To look at the parable of the ten bridesmaids and its meaning.

Teaching

Has anyone gone somewhere and arrived too late and been locked out? Sometimes you may want to go shopping but if you leave it late you will find the shop closed. (Share experiences of being locked out.)

Jesus told a story of ten young women who were invited to a wedding party. They were not really bridesmaids because they were waiting on the groom. They did not carry flowers but all of them carried an oil lamp. This was in the days before electricity and the only way of getting light was through oil lamps, burning torches or a fire. If your lamp went out, you would not have any matches so you would have to get a light from a friend or a fire.

The women waited for the groom to come but something held him up. He was late. While they waited, the oil in their lamps burnt low. Soon the lamps started to go out. Some had prepared for this: they had little leather bottles with oil in and they poured more into their lamps. Five of them had brought oil and five did not bother. Five wanted to borrow oil – but the other five were afraid they might run out of oil and then it would be dark when the groom came. The ones whose

lamps went out had to go away and see if they could find a place where they could buy some oil.

By the time they came back, the bride and groom had been met by the others and gone into the house for a party. The door was locked so that people could not just walk in. They were locked out and when they shouted they were told to go away because the groom did not recognise them.

It is all very sad. Jesus wants people to be ready for when he comes to them. He comes every day and we get a chance to know him through speaking to him in our prayers. He wants to know us. It would be terrible if he could say, 'I don't know you.' Let us remember to give our love to Jesus every day.

Activity

Act this parable out with tea lights in jars. Let someone pretend to be darkness and after a while start blowing all the candles out. Then five relight their candles and five go off and search for oil. Have a bride and groom welcomed by the five lights and once all are inside get them to clap and cheer. The other five knock and try and get in and then go way looking sad.

Prayer

Jesus, we love you
and want to shine as lights in your world.
Help us to show we love you
by saying our prayers
and by telling others about you.
Amen.

Song

This little light of mine

TORCHES

Aim

To look at the parable of the ten bridesmaids and explore its meaning for us.

Teaching

Providing light is important for safety and for welcoming people when it is dark. This is a story of ten young women who were invited to a wedding. Their job was to provide a welcome for the groom and his bride. They would show joy by filling the way with light. Each would have an oil lamp or a blazing torch. These lights would need to be topped up with oil every so often or they would go out.

What is the motto of the Scouts? 'Be Prepared'. Well, half the young women were prepared. They brought extra oil in case there was a hold-up – there often is at weddings. The other five only had what was in their lamps or on the torches and soon lamps began to go out. The ones who had no extra oil wanted to borrow some but the others would not let them have any because then the oil might run out in all the lamps. Some needed to be ready with their lamps shining brightly when the bride and groom came.

Five had to go away into the dark to see if they could find somewhere to buy oil. While they were away the groom and his bride came. Those with lighted lamps entered the house and the celebrations – the rest were locked out. It is all rather sad. The groom had some terrible words to say. See if you can notice these words while someone reads Matthew 25:1-13.

'I never knew you.' Can Jesus say that to us? Do we say our prayers or are we not bothered? Do we welcome Jesus into our homes and our lives by speaking to him? He is the Lord of Light: to turn away from him is to enter the darkness. Let us make sure that we keep our faith alive by our daily relationship with Jesus who comes to us each day.

Activity

There is an opportunity on the activity sheet to see the importance of light and how it was used at a wedding.

Prayer

Jesus, help us to shine with love for you
and by our lives show that we know you
and love you.
May we share with others
the love that you give to us.
Amen.

Song

We are marching in the light of God

Second Sunday before Advent

Sunday between 13 and 19 November inclusive

Aim

To encourage the awareness that we all have talents to share and develop.

Preparation

Have photographs of various talented people – playing music, producing artwork, gardeners, etc. Include local people helping at odd jobs in the community. Beside them have the words, 'Well done, you good and faithful servant'. You may also like to show local shops and services due for closure and have beside them the words, 'Use them or lose them'.

Opening activity

Have some of the youngest show their talents in artwork, singing or playing musical instruments. Use young readers for at least one if not more of the readings. Encourage a group to do the intercessions.

Opening prayer

God, you have given life and talent to each of us
for our own good
and for the benefit of others.
Help us to use and to share the gifts you have given us
that we may live to your glory.
Amen.

Opening song

O God, our help in ages past

Readings

Zephaniah 1:7, 12-18
Psalm 90:1-8 (9-11) 12
1 Thessalonians 5:1-11
Matthew 25:14-30

Thought for the day

Today's parable for the Kingdom Season tells how we are trusted by the king to do something with our lives and not just waste them. Each of us is expected to work according to our ability and talents.

We are told of a man leaving his property in the trust of his slaves. He gives them varying quantities of resources. To one he gives five talents, to another two and to another one. They are not all the same; each has different gifts. They are not equal in talent but they all need to make an effort with what they have. It is not how many talents you have that counts but how you use them.

The talent Jesus talks about was not money but rather an ingot of gold, silver or copper. The most common was silver and in today's value would be well over £2000, when a working man was only getting a penny a day!

There is no doubt all could do something with such talent.

Two of the slaves show a profit. It is not about money but about not wasting or failing to use what you are given. If we do not use our God-given talents, we are in danger of losing them. This is what happens to the third slave. He was afraid to risk or be adventurous: he did not invest the talents. In fact, he did nothing at all: he hid the talent. This angered the master because he wanted the talents to be used. The talent was taken from this man and given to another.

Because we are all unique human beings, we all have something to offer that no one else can offer – even if that offering is only of our self and our time. No one is without something to offer. Yet we all know that if talent is not used, it atrophies and dies. For talent to grow and develop we need to use it. We need to use our lives for the benefit of the King and the kingdom.

Question time

How can you use your talents to the benefit of God and of others?

Can you see ways of encouraging others to use their talents and not waste them?

Illustration

Millie was now quite old but she always had a strange attitude to gifts. If she was given a present, she would thank the person profusely and say how kind it was of them to give her a gift. She said she would treasure it. Then without unwrapping it she put it away in a drawer for another day. When a niece came to help her to move she discovered many unused gifts, still wrapped. There were biscuits and cakes that had moulded away; there was jars of things that had long passed their sell-by date; there were clothes that now would no longer fit Millie. Drawer after drawer of gifts were put out in the bin. Because she did no use them she lost them; she never had the benefit of them.

In the same way we will lose our local small shops unless we use them. We will lose bus services unless we use them. We will lose our God-given gifts and talents unless we use them. The thing we need understand is 'Use it or lose it'.

Intercessions

Blessed are you, Lord our God,
for you have given us all talents and abilities.
You have created each of us in a unique way,
that we may give our own unique service
and talents to you.
Blessed are you, Father, Son and Holy Spirit.

Lord, giver of all good gifts,
we give you thanks for all you have given us.
May we share our talents and use them
to the benefit of others and for your glory.

We pray today for all who tell others of your love
and proclaim the Gospel.
We ask your blessing upon all who minister to others.

Silence

Giver of all good gifts,
hear us and help us to live to your glory.

Lord, giver of all good gifts,
we ask your blessing
upon all artists, musicians, craftspeople,
gardeners, architects, politicians
and all who use their gifts to improve our world.
We remember all who are unable
to use their talents to the full
through oppression or other circumstance.

Silence

Giver of all good gifts,
hear us and help us to live to your glory.

Lord, giver of all good gifts,
bless us and our loved ones.
We pray that our homes may be places
where talent is fostered
and given the chance to grow.
We ask your blessing upon all schools
and places of learning
and all who help others to develop skills.

Silence

Giver of all good gifts,
hear us and help us to live to your glory.

Lord, giver of all good gifts,
bless all who are thwarted in their ability
through illness, oppression or the lack of opportunity.
We pray for all who are struggling
due to poverty and hunger.
We remember before you
loved ones and friends who are ill.

Silence

Giver of all good gifts,
hear us and help us to live to your glory.

Lord, giver of all good gifts,
we thank you for the gift of life eternal.
We rejoice in the fellowship of all your saints
and ask your blessing on our loved ones departed,
that they may be at home with you
in your kingdom of love.

Silence

Merciful Father,
**accept these prayers
for the sake of your Son,
our Saviour Jesus Christ.
Amen.**

Memory verse
Be silent before the Lord God! For the day of the Lord is
at hand.
Zephaniah 1:7

Suggested music
Take my life, and let it be
Light a candle for thanksgiving
Take my hands, Lord

CANDLES

Aim
To know that God has made each of us special and
wants us to do special things for him.

Activity
Have a guessing game where you describe one of the
children and they have to guess who you are talking
about. Describe the colours they are wearing and their
clothes, the colour of their hair and where they live.

Teaching
Start with the Activity.

Now supposing two of you exchanged all your clothes,
would we think that John became Peter or Peter became
John? Do you think if Abigail wore Amy's clothes,
Abigail would become Amy? Of course not, that is
silly. Supposing I started to call Amy 'Abigail', would
she turn into Abigail? No, she would still be herself. We
are all special; no two of us are exactly the same – even
twins are different and they have different names.

When we come to church and are baptised, what are
we given? We are given our name. It would not be nice
if we were just given a number, would it? We are given
a name because we are special and no other child in
your house would be given the same name. People who
know us call us by our name. God also knows our name
and seeks to give his love to us.

No one else is quite like you. Some of us can read
easily, some can draw clever pictures, others can sing
nicely, and others can be very good at helping. All of us
are different and we can help each other to learn and do
new things. Each one of us is special and has something
we alone can share with others. No one else can love
God instead of us – or be helpful at home instead of us.
God wants you, especially you, to love him and to
speak to him each day. If you do not speak to him, he
will miss you. Do not forget to give your love to him
each day.

Prayer
Thank you, God,
for making each of us so special.
You know and love every one of us.
Help us to give our special love to you.
Amen.

Song
There are hundreds of sparrows

LAMPS

Aim

To look at the parable of the talents and see how God wants us to use our gifts.

Teaching

Jesus told a story about a very kind man who gave gifts to three of his servants. The man was going away for a while and he wanted his servants to be able to do things on their own and for him. He gave the servants different amounts of talents. Talents were either silver, gold or copper bars and this showed that the master trusted his servants. To one he gave five talents, to another two and to the third he gave one. They did not all receive the same and were not all expected to do the same thing. But they were all given the talents to use.

The one with five talents sold them and traded with the money. He bought things and sold things. He had to take some risks but he worked hard. When the master returned he had doubled what he was given. (What is 2 x 5?) He gave the master ten talents when he returned. The master was very pleased because the servant had done well, and so he gave him even more to work with. He invited him to enjoy all that the master had.

The one with two talents had also exchanged them and used the money to do all sorts of wonderful things. When the master returned he had doubled his two talents. (What is 2 x 2?) He gave the master four talents when he returned. The master was very pleased because the servant had done well and he gave him even more to work with. The master invited him to enjoy all that he had.

The servant with one talent did nothing with it. He did very little while the master was away. He took it easy. He buried the talent in the ground. He did not use it but hid it until the master came back. It was such a waste. He returned the talent exactly as he had received it. It had not grown: it had not been used. The master was not happy because he might as well not have given the servant the talent. As he did not use it, the master took it from him and gave it to others. Isn't that sad?

Activity

Get the children to talk about how we all have different God-given gifts – art, music, kindness, etc. – and how we have to use them or they will not grow. See if they can give examples such as playing a musical instrument, going to dancing lessons or practising a sport. Help them to see how it is necessary to use their talents or they may lose the ability to use them.

Prayer

Lord God, you give us life
and the ability to do things.
May we use our talents and gifts
to your praise and to the benefit of all.
Amen.

Song

I can be what God wants me to be

TORCHES

Aim

To show how it is important to use our talents and to recognise the tragedy of unused gifts.

Teaching

Have four people use the script below and a fifth to read the parable of the talents.

Narrator   Here is a man who used his God-given gifts.

Man   I was given the chance to be a farmer. With the money I was given I bought land and seed. I ploughed the land and sowed the seed. It was hard work but it helped me to grow strong. For a while I had nothing to show – no money left, only a bit of brown land. But then the seed appeared and it grew. The harvest was hard work but it made me happy. I could then sell grain, buy more land and grow more seed. What was most important in all this was that I also grew and used the gifts I was given.

Narrator   In developing the farm he developed himself and used his talents fully.

Here is a woman who used her God-given gifts.

Woman   I was given the chance to be a sculptor. With the money I bought rock – big pieces of rock – and tools to work with. At first I did not do very well. I got tired with using hammers and chisels. But as the rock took shape, so did I. I grew stronger and my hands became more able to do the work. Soon I was selling statues and carvings. I had become more interesting as my interest in carving grew. I not only made many statues, I made many friends. As my work developed, so did I. I thank God for all I am able to do.

Narrator   In creating lovely things she became more lovely and shaped herself in shaping stone. She used her talent well.

Here is a mouse – sorry, I mean a man – who did not use his God-given gifts.

Mouse/man   Squeak! Squeak! I could have been a pianist. My teacher said so. But I could not be bothered to sit at a piano each day.

My art teacher said I could make a living at art. I had a good eye and a steady hand. But I preferred to watch the TV and play video games.

I had a good job for a while but they said I did not give myself to it and they sacked me.

Now I have no job and no money. Poor me, I feel useless.

Narrator   Here is wasted talent and a wasted life. Here is a person who failed to do what God created him for.

Reader   (Reads Matthew 25:14-30)

Activity

Discuss the mini-drama and the Parable and how it relates to each of us. Ask them to find something that is being lost through not being used – local shops and buses, for example.

Prayer

God, we thank you for giving us life
and making each one of us special.
May we use the talents you have given us
to your glory and to the benefit of others.
Amen.

Song

Make me a channel of your peace

Christic the King

Sunday between 20 and 26 November inclusive

Aim

To make people aware that Christ comes to us in our encounter with others and in the needs of the poor.

Preparation

Have a display in the entrance of some of the world's poorest people. Use posters from one of the relief agencies.

Have the words, 'Just as you did it to one of the least of these who are members of my family, you did it to me' and 'Just as you did not do it to one of the least of these, you did not do it to me'.

Opening activity

For five voices:

1. Ignore the poor and they will go away – go away and die.
2. Just as you did not do it to one of the least of these; you did not do it to me.
3. Why should I bother? Let them look after themselves.
2. Just as you did not do it to one of the least of these; you did not do it to me.
4. Give a man a fish and he will hunger again. Teach him to fish and you feed him for life.
2. Just as you did it to one of the least of these who are members of my family, you did it to me.
5. He who has bread is responsible for him who has none.
2. Just as you did it to one of the least of these who are members of my family, you did it to me.

Opening prayer

Lord Jesus. you are the King of kings,
the King of Love and the Servant King.
May we show your love
in the way we serve each other,
that your kingdom may come on earth
as it is in heaven.
Amen.

Opening song

When I needed a neighbour

Readings

Ezekiel 34:11-16, 20-24
Psalm 95:1-7a
Ephesians 1:15-23
Matthew 25:31-46

Thought for the day

For the last Sunday in the Kingdom Season we have a vivid parable that tells us what will happen when the Son of Man comes in glory. Christ the King will separate the sheep from the goats. He will welcome the sheep on his right hand and offer them the kingdom that has been prepared for them since the creation of the world.

This in itself is a wonderful thought: there is a place that has been reserved for you from the beginning. There is a place that is just yours, it has your name on it and no one else can take it. We need to be aware, however, that there is a judgement and it is about love. If we have expressed love, we need have no fear.

Listen to what the King says:

I was hungry and you gave me food.
I was thirsty and you gave me something to drink.
I was a stranger and you welcomed me.
I was naked and you gave me clothing.
I was sick and you took care of me.
I was in prison and you visited me.

When the people ask when was this the reply is:

Just as you did it to the least of these who are members of my family, you did it to me.

Time and again we will learn that the way we deal with others is the way we deal with God. If we do not listen to others, we are not likely to listen to God. If we are mean towards others, we have a mean relationship with God. If we only like people who will obey us, we will seek a puppet God. Our faith is not one that is out of this world; our faith is reflected in our relationships with each other as well as with God.

As God is in each person, though sometimes so hidden that he is hard to find, we have to treat everyone with reverence and respect. There is no one single person who does not have God hidden within, even though they may live in total disobedience to God. The tramp and the criminal have no less of God than the archbishop or saint.

Question time

Are you aware that we have the opportunity to meet the Christ in others?

Is it enough that we have not harmed anyone when there are so many people in need in our world? Remember, 'those who have bread are responsible for those who have none'.

Illustration

Christopher wanted to serve the king. He wanted to go to the palace and give himself to serve the king. But he was held up. First he had to look after aging parents. When he set off he had a gift for the king but he met a poor family who had been robbed of their belongings and he gave the gift to them. Later on he met a family whose cart had stuck deep in the mud. He stayed to help them and got sprayed with mud. Now he had no gift and his fine clothes were filthy. He felt he could not journey on but something encouraged him – words he had heard long ago. When he finally reached the palace, he received a royal welcome. He was about to apologise for the state he was in but the king said, 'You have been a great help to me over the years, in the way you cared for your parents, in the way you gave to the poor and when you helped those in need. I was there and it was me you gave your help and love to. Welcome to the fullness of the kingdom which you have served for a long time.'

Intercessions

Blessed are you, Lord our King and our God,
for you have made us and we belong to you.
You have revealed your love for us
in the coming of Christ our Lord
and in the sending of the Holy Spirit.
Blessed are you, Father, Son and Holy Spirit.

Loving Lord, we ask your blessing
upon all who seek to care for your people.
We pray for all bishops, priests and deacons,
all who preach the word,
administer the sacraments
and show pastoral care.
May we all share in your outreach
and mission of love.
We remember especially those who are reaching out
to the confused and the lost.

Silence

King of Love,
Good Shepherd, hear us.

Loving Lord, we ask your blessing
upon this world, which is your creation.
We remember today all who are struggling
against evil, war or poverty.
We pray for all who share in your redeeming work
through their caring for others
and seeking to bring them freedom.
We pray for all relief agencies
and all who reach out to those in need.

Silence

King of Love,
Good Shepherd, hear us.

Loving Lord, we ask your blessing
upon our homes and our loved ones.
We remember today all who live alone
and those who are homeless.
We pray especially for young people
living on the streets of our towns and cities
and all whose lives were diminished
by circumstances they could not avoid.

Silence

King of Love,
Good Shepherd, hear us.

Loving Lord, we ask your blessing
upon all who are ill at home or in hospital.
We remember also loved ones
who are caring for them
and are anxious and fearful.
We pray for all who cannot cope on their own.
We ask your blessing upon all carers
and those involved in medical care
and the rescue services.

Silence

King of Love,
Good Shepherd, hear us.

Loving Lord, we ask your blessing
upon our friends and loved ones
who have departed from us.
May they share with your saints in glory.
To you and your loving presence
we commit this world and ourselves
and ask that we may know you
as the King of Love, our Saviour
and our Friend.

Silence

Merciful Father,
accept these prayers
for the sake of your Son,
our Saviour Jesus Christ.
Amen.

Memory verse

Just as you did it to the least of these who are members of my family, you did it to me.
Matthew 25:40

Suggested music

Rejoice, the Lord is King
Hail the coming Prince of Peace
O worship the King

CANDLES

Aim

To know that Jesus our King comes to us.

Teaching

Who knows who is the ruler of our country and lives at Buckingham Palace in London? Yes, it is Queen Elizabeth. If a man was the ruler, what would he be called? He would be the king.

Now who is the King of the whole world? Yes, God/Jesus. That means that God/Jesus is the ruler of the whole world. Some kings force the people to do what they want and make them obey. Jesus is not like that because he loves each of us and wants us to do things not because he is powerful but because we love him. Once, to show that he was not a king who wanted to force people, he rode into Jerusalem on a . . . ? Yes, he rode on a donkey. He wanted people to know that he comes not to make them do things but to give them his love and his peace. He wants his people to be peaceful and loving like him. Sometimes we call Jesus the King of Love. Let us say together: 'Jesus is the King of Love.'

Kings usually have servants to look after them but Jesus came to look after other people. He came to help people and to give himself for people. Once he washed the disciples' feet. Sometimes Jesus is known as the

245

Servant King because he looks after us all. Let us say together: 'Jesus is the Servant King.'

Jesus our King comes to us and we can speak to him when we pray. He wants us to love others as he loves them and to be kind to others as he is kind to us all.

Activity

Make a crown of gold card. Play 'pass the crown'. The children make a circle and then all turn to face the back of the person on their right. While the music plays they pass the crown from head to head. When the music stops, whoever is wearing the crown says, 'Jesus is our King'. Everyone claps their hands and says, 'Hurrah! Alleluia.' The music starts again and they continue.

Prayer

Jesus, you are the King of Love.
We love you
and thank you for caring for us.
We will serve you
by loving and caring for each other.
Amen.

Song

We have a king who rides a donkey

LAMPS

Aim

To know Jesus as King and to revise what the children know about him.

Teaching

Use today as a time to revise all that the children know about Jesus.

Jesus is our King and our God. Kings are born in palaces. Where was Jesus born? What do you call the day when we celebrate the birth of Jesus?

Kings live in rich houses. Where did Jesus live as a boy? What was the name of his mother? What sort of work did Joseph do?

When kings go travelling they go with lots of servants, who have to do what they are told. Jesus left home and sought help from twelve men. They are called the twelve . . .?

Kings make people do things. Jesus came to serve people and give himself to them. Ask for examples of Jesus caring for others.

Jesus is sometime known as the King of Love by the way he cares for everyone. Sometime he is known as the Servant King because he gives himself for others.

Kings usually rode on powerful war-horses to show they were in charge. What did Jesus ride when he went into Jerusalem? What is that day called? Why?

Kings expect people to be willing to die for them. But Jesus was willing to give his life for us. How did Jesus die? Do you know what we call that day?

Jesus did not stay in the tomb. What happened on the third day? Jesus rose again and was seen for forty days.

After this Jesus went to a mountain with his disciples. What happened? He went back to his Father in heaven and is now King of heaven and earth.

Jesus is our King who gives himself in love to everyone. He cares for them and wants to help them. This is why we call him the King of Love and the Servant King. He wants us to love him and serve him by caring for each other as he cares for us.

Activity

On the activity sheet there is a further opportunity to revise the life of Christ the King.

Prayer

Jesus, you are the King of kings.
You are the ruler of the whole world.
Yet in love you come to serve us and help us.
You gave your life for us.
Help us to give ourselves to you
and to serve you in caring for others.
Amen.

Song

We're the kids of the King

TORCHES

Aim

To show how Christ meets us in others and how his work is done when we care for others.

Teaching

In the ancient world, if you hurt a member of a family or insulted them, it was assumed that you hurt and insulted the whole family. Usually the head of the family would seek revenge. If you harmed a member of the royal family, even a servant, it was counted as harming the king himself, and the king would take up his servant's cause.

In many ways this is still true today. If one nation attacks a ship or aeroplane of another nation, it is counted as an attack on that nation and the leaders then have to take action. If someone is taken hostage, then their country's leaders have to speak out for them.

This should help us to understand the parable of the sheep and the goats (Matthew 25:31-46).

It begins with all the nations gathered before the Son of Man. Jesus wants to show that not only Jews but all people are God's people. Sometimes we need to learn that not only Christians but all people are God's people. God loves everyone. There are no privileges: God loves us all equally. Jesus is talking about how our lives will be judged, and it is not by what we *say* we believe, but how we act. We are judged by our deeds. Jesus talks of the Son of Man coming in glory – there is no doubt this is meant to be Jesus.

Some people believe they are privileged – well, if they are, that makes them responsible for those who are not. Sometimes wealth is gained at a cost to others. If we have lots of food and others have none, then we are responsible for their hunger.

Now let us read the parable from Matthew 25 using different readers as follows:

Narrator – verses 31- 34a
Jesus – 34b-36
Narrator – 37a
Reader 3 – 37b-39
Narrator – 40a
Jesus – 40b
Narrator – 41a
Jesus – 41b-43
Narrator – 44a
Reader 4 – 44b
Narrator – 45a
Jesus – 45b
Narrator – 46

Jesus is concerned how we deal with each other, no matter how unimportant or unworthy a person seems.

Activity

Explore ways in which the Church is involved in caring for others. Can the group take on a project from one of the relief agencies? Make sure they understand it is their own relationships with people that Jesus is talking about.

Prayer

Lord Jesus, teach us to love the world
with the love that you have for the world.
May we learn to care for each other
and help any who are in need,
for as much as we do it to the least
we do it to you.
Amen.

Song

Brother, sister, let me serve you